Russell

Bertrand Russell (1872–1970) was one of the founding figures of analytic philosophy and renowned for his lasting contributions to the study of logic, philosophy of language, philosophy of mathematics and epistemology. He was also famous for his popular works, where his humanism, ethics and antipathy towards religion came through in books such as *The Problems of Philosophy*, *Why I am Not A Christian*, and *The Conquest of Happiness*.

Beginning with an overview of Russell's life and work, Gregory Landini carefully explains Russell's philosophy, to show why he ranks as one of the giants of British and Twentieth century philosophy. He discusses Russell's major early works in philosophy of mathematics, including *The Principles of Mathematics*, wherein Russell illuminated and developed the ideas of Gottlob Frege; and the monumental three-volume work written with Alfred North Whitehead, *Principia Mathematica*, where the authors attempted to show that all mathematical theory is part of logic understood as a science of structure.

Landini discusses the second edition of *Principia Mathematica*, to show Russell's intellectual relationship with Wittgenstein and Ramsey. He discusses Russell's epistemology and neutral monism before concluding with a discussion on Russell's ethics, and the relationship between science and religion.

Featuring a chronology and a glossary of terms, as well as suggestions for further reading at the end of each chapter, *Russell* is essential reading for anyone studying philosophy, and is an ideal guidebook for those coming to Russell for the first time.

Gregory Landini is Professor of Philosophy at the University of Iowa. He is the author of *Wittgenstein's Apprenticeship With Russell* (2007), and *Russell's Hidden Substitutional Theory* (1998).

Routledge Philosophers

Edited by Brian Leiter
University of Chicago

Routledge Philosophers is a major series of introductions to the great Western philosophers. Each book places a major philosopher or thinker in historical context, explains and assesses their key arguments, and considers their legacy. Additional features include a chronology of major dates and events, chapter summaries, annotated suggestions for further reading, and a glossary of technical terms.

An ideal starting point for those new to philosophy, they are also essential reading for those interested in the subject at any level.

Hobbes	A. P. Martinich
Leibniz	Nicholas Jolley
Locke	E. J. Lowe
Hegel	Frederick Beiser
Rousseau	Nicholas Dent
Schopenhauer	Julian Young
Freud	Jonathan Lear
Kant	Paul Guyer
Husserl	David Woodruff Smith
Darwin	Tim Lewens
Aristotle	Christopher Shields
Rawls	Samuel Freeman
Spinoza	Michael Della Rocca
Merleau-Ponty	Taylor Carman

Forthcoming:

Adorno	Brian O'Connor
Habermas	Kenneth Baynes
Heidegger	John Richardson
Hume	Don Garrett
Wittgenstein	William Child

Gregory Landini

Russell

LONDON AND NEW YORK

This edition published 2011
by Routledge
2 Park Square, Milton Park, Abingdon, Oxon OX14 4RN

Simultaneously published in the USA and Canada
by Routledge
711 Third Avenue, New York, NY 10017

Routledge is an imprint of the Taylor & Francis Group, an informa business

© 2011 Gregory Landini

The right of Gregory Landini to be identified as author of this work has been asserted by him in accordance with sections 77 and 78 of the Copyright, Designs and Patents Act 1988.

Typeset in Joanna MT and Din by
RefineCatch Ltd, Bungay, Suffolk

All rights reserved. No part of this book may be reprinted or reproduced or utilised in any form or by any electronic, mechanical, or other means, now known or hereafter invented, including photocopying and recording, or in any information storage or retrieval system, without permission in writing from the publishers.

British Library Cataloguing in Publication Data
A catalogue record for this book is available from the British Library

Library of Congress Cataloging in Publication Data
Landini, Gregory.
　Russell / by Gregory Landini.
　　p. cm.—(Routledge philosophers)
　Includes bibliographical references and index.
　1. Russell, Bertrand, 1872–1970.　I. Title.
　B1649.R94L35 2010
　192—dc22　　　　　　　　　2010008766

ISBN 13: 978-0-415-39626-4 (hbk)
ISBN 13: 978-0-415-39627-1 (pbk)
ISBN 13: 978-0-203-84649-0 (ebk)

For Austin and Ansel

Acknowledgments		x
Abbreviations		xi
Chronology		xiii

Life and Work One 1

Further Reading 42

Mathematics and the Metaphysicians Two 43

Number Devils 46
Honest Toil Over Theft 55
Taming the Infinite 67
Logicism 78
Natural Numbers as Objects 90
The Number of Numbers 95
Further Reading 104

Principia Mathematica Three 105

$Principia^L$ 107
$Principia^C$ 112
The No-Classes Theory 115
Principia's Nominalistic Semantics 124
From *Principles* to *Principia* 135
Further Reading 161

The Philosophy of Logical Atomism Four 162

Ways of Paradox 168
Russell's Paradigm: Definite Descriptions 184
The Logical Mirage 206
Further Reading 217

Scientific Epistemology — Five — 218

The Problems of Philosophy 221
Our Knowledge of the External World 244
Russell's Lost Book: *Theory of Knowledge* 251
Acquaintance and Logic 273
Further Reading 279

Mind and Matter — Six — 280

Matter: The Problem Stated 284
Neutral Stuff: Is It Really Neutral? 289
The Problem of Indexicals 306
Images and Sensations Constitute Minds 312
Neutral Monism and Truth 317
Structural Realism 330
Further Reading 339

Principia's Second Edition — Seven — 341

Russell's Apprentice 344
Russell and Ramsey on the Oracle 360
Further Reading 368

Probable Knowledge — Eight — 369

Logic is Not Part of Philosophy? 370
Probability and Induction 375
On the Notion of Cause 393
Further Reading 397

Icarus **Nine** 398

A Liberal Decalogue 398
Sub Specie Aeternitatis 407
A Science of Ethics 411
Further Reading 416

Glossary 417
Notes 425
Bibliography 446
Index 455

Acknowledgments

Thanks to Brian Leiter and Tony Bruce for the opportunity to write what will undoubtedly be considered a controversial introduction to Russell's philosophy. Special thanks is due to Richard Fumerton, Nicholas Griffin, and Francesco Orilia for many helpful suggestions and especially criticisms. Frann Ostroff helped me to use fewer logical symbols than English. Nino Cocchiarella provided the foundation for most everything I know about Russell's philosophy.

Gregory Landini

The publisher and the author wish to thank the following for permission to reprint material under copyright:

'Russell's dedication to Edith', taken from *Autobiography*, by Bertrand Russell. © 2009 The Bertrand Russell Peace Foundation Ltd. Reprinted by kind permission of Taylor & Francis Group.

'Hand-written excerpt', taken from **Theory of Knowledge**, by Bertrand Russell. © 1992 The Bertrand Russell Peace Foundation Ltd. Reprinted by kind permission of Taylor & Francis Group.

'1907 letter to Hawtrey', reproduced by kind permission of The Bertrand Russell Archives and Research Center, McMaster University. © The Bertrand Russell Peace Foundation.

Abbreviations

A	*The Autobiography of Bertrand Russell*
ABC	*The ABC of Relativity*
AMa	*The Analysis of Matter*
AMi	*The Analysis of Mind*
AofP	*The Art of Philosophizing And Other Essays*
B	*What I Believe*
CH	*The Conquest of Happiness*
FT	*Free Thought and Official Propaganda*
GG	*Dear Russell—Dear Jourdain*
HK	*Human Knowledge: Its Scope and Limits*
HWP	*A History of Western Philosophy*
I	*Icarus or The Future of Science*
IPI	"In Praise of Idleness"
IMP	*Introduction to Mathematical Philosophy*
IMT	*An Inquiry into Meaning and Truth*
InS	"On 'Insolubila' and Their Solution By Symbolic Logic"
LA	"Logical Atomism"
Letters	*The Selected Letters of Bertrand Russell vol. 1 The Private Years 1884–1914*
LK	*Logic and Knowledge: Essays 1901–1950*
MaM	*Marriage and Morals*
ML	"Mathematical Logic as Based on the Theory of Types"
MM	"Mathematics and the Metaphysicians"
MMD	"My Mental Development"

MPD	My Philosophical Development
MyL	Mysticism and Logic and Other Essays
NEP	Nightmares of Eminent Persons and Other Stories
OD	"On Denoting"
OIR	An Outline of Intellectual Rubbish
OKEW	Our Knowledge of the External World as a Field for Scientific Method in Philosophy
OP	Outline of Philosophy
ORSP	"On the Relation of Sense-Data to Physics"
OT	"On the theory of Transfinite Numbers and Order Types"
P	The Problems of Philosophy
PfM	Portraits From Memory
PIC	The Prospects of Industrial Civilization
PLA	"The Philosophy of Logical Atomism"
PM	Principia Mathematica
PM to *56	Principia Mathematica to *56
PoM	The Principles of Mathematics
Pr	Power: A New Social Analysis
PSR	Principles of Social Reconstruction
PTB	The Practice and Theory of Bolshevism
RaS	Religion and Science
STCR	"On the Substitutional Theory of Classes and Relations"
TK	Theory of Knowledge: The 1913 Manuscript
TLP	Tractatus Logico-Philosophicus
TN	"On Some Difficulties in the Theory of Transfinite Numbers and Order Types"

Chronology
Russell's Ontological Development (1903–1913)

1903: *THE PRINCIPLES OF MATHEMATICS*

- Language for logic is type-free and has only individual variables
- Logic is the general theory of the structure of propositions
  - Propositions elementary and general as states of affairs (obtaining vs. non-obtaining)
  - Logical connectives are relation signs
  - Categorical propositions and others containing denoting concepts
  - Theory of denoting concepts as a bridge from categorical logic to the new quantification theory (Variables of the new quantification theory explained via denoting concepts)
- Universals (type-free with both a predicable and individual nature)
- Comprehension axioms for classes (tentatively)
- No comprehension axioms for attributes (propositional functions) in intension
- Non-existent objects since genuine names denote, but no round-squares

1905: "ON DENOTING"

- Language for logic is type-free and has only individual variables
- Logic is the general theory of the structure of propositions
  - Propositions elementary and general as states of affairs (obtaining vs. non-obtaining)

- Logical connectives are relation signs
  - No denoting concepts
  - No bridge between categorical logic and the new quantification theory
- Universals (type-free with both a predicable an individual nature)
- Variables of the new quantification theory taken as primitive
- No-denoting concepts
- No-comprehension axioms for classes
- No-comprehension axioms for attributes in intension
- Substitutional theory of propositions emulating simple types of attributes/classes
- No non-existent objects since truth-conditions for names can be given by descriptions
- Acquaintance with universals, particulars, propositions, and self

1906: "ON 'INSOLUBILIA' AND THEIR SOLUTION BY SYMBOLIC LOGIC"

- Language for logic is type-free and has only individual variables
  - Logic is the general theory of the structure of propositions
  - Propositions as states of affairs (obtaining vs. non-obtaining)
  - No general propositions
  - Logical connectives are relation signs
- Universals (type-free with both a predicable an individual nature)
- Variables of the new quantification theory taken as primitive
- No-denoting concepts
- No-comprehension axioms for classes
- No-comprehension axioms for attributes in intension
- Substitutional theory of propositions emulating simple types of attributes/classes
- Semantic paradoxes distinct from logical paradoxes

- No non-existent objects since truth-conditions for names can be given by descriptions
- Acquaintance with universals, particulars, propositions, and self

1908: "MATHEMATICAL LOGIC AS BASED ON THE THEORY OF TYPES"

- Language for logic is type-free and has only individual variables
- Logic is the general theory of the structure of propositions
  - Propositions (elementary and general) as states of affairs (obtaining vs. non-obtaining)
  - Logical connectives are relation signs
  - Hierarchy of orders of general propositions
- Universals (type-free with both a predicable an individual nature)
- Variables of the new quantification theory taken as primitive
- No-denoting concepts
- No-comprehension axioms for classes
- No-comprehension axioms for attributes in intension
- Substitutional theory of propositions emulating simple types of attributes/classes
- Semantic paradoxes distinct from logical paradoxes
- Axiom of Reducibility of orders of propositions
- No non-existent objects since truth-conditions for names can be given by descriptions
- Acquaintance with universals, particulars, propositions, and self

1910–1913: *PRINCIPIA MATHEMATICA*

- Language for logic has predicate variables with order\type indices and individual variables
- No Propositions (elementary or general) as states of affairs (obtaining vs. non-obtaining)
- Logic is the general theory of structure
- Logical connectives are not relation signs

- Universals (type-free with both a predicable an individual nature)
- Facts (complexes united by their relating relation)
- Variables of the new quantification theory taken as primitive
- No denoting concepts
- No comprehension axioms for classes
- No comprehension axioms for attributes in intension
- No substitutional theory of propositions emulating simple types of attributes/classes
- Semantic paradoxes distinct from logical paradoxes
- Comprehension "axiom of reducibility" given a nominalistic semantics
- Recursive definition of "truth" and "falsehood" justifying order component of the order\type indices on predicate variables
- No non-existent objects since truth-conditions for names can be given by descriptions
- Acquaintance with universals, sense-data, and the subject

One

Life and Work

The good life is one inspired by love and guided by knowledge.
What I Believe

Bertrand Russell was born into aristocracy in Ravenscroft, Wales during the Victorian age in England on 18 May 1872. His family was famous, a cadet branch of the Dukes of Bedford. His father, Viscount Amberly, was an avowed atheist whose political career in Parliament was destroyed by views then still shocking to public sentiment, such as support of women's suffrage and birth control. His mother's intellectual freedom from the subjugations of the age was a product of her friendship with John Stuart Mill, who was appointed as little Bertie's honorific godfather. Tragically, his mother and sister died of diphtheria when he was two and his father died some eighteen months later. Amberly's will left instructions for his sons to be raised by agnostics, one of whom was scientist D. A. Spalding, who was originally employed as a tutor to Bertie's older brother Frank. But the grandparents won the ensuing court battle. Frank found life in the house of his grandfather John Russell unhappy and his rebellions eventuated in his being sent away to boarding school. His grandfather died shortly thereafter, and Bertie was left at the mercy of his puritanical Scottish Presbyterian grandmother, practicing the virtues of Victorian middle-class morality.

They lived in Pembroke Lodge, where Bertie's German and Swiss governesses made him fluent in German from an early age. Isolated by class from a usual childhood and adolescent socializing, he

2 Life and Work

found refuge in his succession of tutors and his rebellions were directed at the "proofs" found in Euclid's geometry. Tutored at age eleven by his brother Frank, Russell developed a love of geometry—a love soon lost when geometry failed to deliver his independence from his prison. All the same, this "dazzling first love" eventually brought him to win a scholarship in 1890 to study mathematics at Trinity College, Cambridge. Alfred North Whitehead, a mathematician there, had favorably read his scholarship examination, and took an interest in him. Their interest in foundational studies would mature into a lifetime friendship.

At Cambridge, the teaching of mathematics was poor. Russell soon became jaded and turned his mind to the study of philosophy. He explains:

> My teachers offered me proofs which I felt to be fallacious and which, as I learnt later, had been recognized as fallacious. I did not know then, or for some time after I had left Cambridge, that better proofs had been found by German mathematicians . . .
>
> (*PfM*, p. 15)

The dominance of applied mathematics at Cambridge was a product of the examinations (the Tripos system). It effectively held the teaching of abstract mathematics hostage to boring exercises. The happy consequence for philosophy was that it brought Russell to the field. Grandmother was not pleased, as this is a study not suitable for a "future prime minister." He had a brief bout with faith based on reason, not yet free of the dogmatisms of his childhood. "For two or three years," he writes,

> I was a Hegelian. I remember the exact moment during my fourth year [in 1894] when I became one. I had gone out to buy a tin of tobacco, and was going back with it along Trinity Lane, when I suddenly threw it up in the air and exclaimed: "Great God in Boots!—the ontological argument is sound!"
>
> (*A*, vol. I, p. 84)

Russell would soon have a change of heart, both about God and Hegel. In 1895 he completed his dissertation on the philosophy of geometry—grappling to save Kantianism in the face of non-Euclidean spaces. On the basis of this dissertation, Russell won a prize fellowship at Cambridge as a six-year, non-teaching Research Fellow.

Russell's years as a student at Cambridge came to seem to him as years of liberation from the influence of his grandmother and the oppressive, highly bourgeois atmosphere at Pembroke Lodge. Indeed, in zealous liberation he had all too fast fallen in love with a rich American Quaker, Alys Pearsall Smith, someone of whom his grandmother would naturally disapprove. At age twenty-one and with an inheritance from his father, Bertie was happy to have found a road to independence. They married and spent most of the time of the Cambridge Fellowship in Germany on honeymoon, with Bertie working on the philosophy of mathematics and rekindling his common interests with Alys in economics and the German Social Democratic movement. The immediate outcome was a series of lectures in 1896, published as *German Social Democracy*. In the following year his dissertation, *An Essay on the Foundations of Geometry*, was published. In the years from 1896 through 1900, living happily with Alys, Russell transformed himself from a Cambridge student into a philosopher of no small importance.

While the eminent Hegelian scholar John McTaggart was on leave from Cambridge, visiting family in New Zealand, Russell was assigned to teach his course on Leibniz. This resulted in the book *The Philosophy of Leibniz* (1900). The pace of Russell's transformation was staggering. Having read Hegel's *Greater Logic*, Russell reports that he came to believe that ". . . all he says about mathematics is muddle headed nonsense . . ." He rejected Hegel's conception of history as dialectic and he rejected Bradley's idealist doctrine that relations determine the natures of the objects related. In a rebellion inspired by his friend G. E. Moore, he allowed himself to think,

> with a sense of escaping from prison, ... that grass is green, that the sun and stars would exist if no one was aware of them, and also that there is a pluralistic timeless realm of Platonic ideas. ... Mathematics could be *quite* true, and not merely a stage in dialectic.¹

Recovering from the weak mathematics taught at Trinity, he started out with an ambitious Kantian effort at an encyclopedia of the sciences, but he soon dropped his Kantian ideas on geometry and freed himself of the influence of McTaggart's neo-Hegelianism. For some time he had been working on a book on the nature of mathematics, with many false starts and changes of mind. He attended for the first time the International Congress of Philosophy in Paris and mastered the new techniques of Peano's Italian school of mathematicians together with Cantor's set theory. He would later write that 1900 was "the most important year of my intellectual life." Benighted by Trinity, Russell's discovery of Peano now brought his study of mathematics up to date. Together with Whitehead, he worked out definitions of "cardinal," "series," *and* "ordinals" and sketched the relationship between arithmetic and logic. Through Peano and the Italians, he was brought to a study of Weierstrass, Dedekind, Cantor, Pieri, and Hilbert.

Abandoning the view that mathematics is founded on the notion of quantity, Russell came to think that it is founded upon the notion of order and so consists of the logic of relations. On the heels of the Paris conference, he wrote a paper in 1900 called "On the Logic of Relations," translated it into French and published it in Peano's journal *Revista di Mathematica* (1901). The paper proves a "principle of abstraction" in its effort to show that definition by abstraction is illicit. Peano had imagined definition by "abstraction," which employs a function that assigns a unique representative to each distinct equivalence grouping under a given equivalence relation. Russell argued that this is not a proper "definition" since quite different functions can be used to assign representatives for each equivalence grouping. For example, during tax season in the USA, our adjusted income places us in an equivalence group (i.e. a tax bracket). The government determines a function (i.e. tax table for the year) that assigns to each such group an amount of taxes owed. We know perfectly well that some other function could have worked as well. Abstraction from this equivalence relation does not define the notion of "the tax I owe for this year." It defines "the tax I owe for this year relative to IRS table m." Similarly, Hume observed that if we pair As with Bs without any Bs left over, we can speak that As and Bs have the same cardinal number. But Russell thought it illicit to define "the cardinal number of As" by a function f which assigns a unique representative to each equivalence group formed from the relation "pairing off without any left over." As in the case of the tax table, we do not get a definition of "the cardinal number of As" but only "the cardinal number of As relative to function f." Instead, Russell offered a new and proper definition of "the cardinal number of As." The innovative paper on relations would eventually be the basis for Russell's election to the Royal Society at the unusually young age of thirty-five.

Russell's definition of cardinal number was anticipated by Gottlob Frege by some eighteen years. He had a copy of the first volume of Frege's magnum opus, *Grundgesetze der Arithmetik* (1893). But its seemingly forbidding two-dimensional notation seemed at first impenetrable. He caught up to Frege only in 1902. Russell's book *The Principles of Mathematics* (1903) included an appendix on Frege that was added late in the production of the book. The book is a remarkable achievement and is still widely read today. It remains Russell's best understood work on the foundations of mathematics and geometry. It contains analyses and logical constructions of natural numbers, integers (positive and negative numbers), rationals, irrationals, cardinals, ordinals, complex numbers (e.g. the square root of -1), the foundations of analysis (limits and continuity in Weierstass and Cantor), and a discussion of non-Euclidean geometry. It argues that the only necessity is logical necessity, and thus it contains an extensive criticism of Kant's thesis that there are uniquely arithmetic and uniquely geometric (spatial) necessities. He accepts a new definition of "congruence" (later repeated by Wittgenstein[2]), which avoids spatial intuitions of motion and superposition in space. In this way, it rejects Kant's famous thesis that it is a uniquely spatial necessity that right-hand and left-hand figures are incongruent. It takes up Zeno's paradoxes of motion and discusses logical reconstructions of notions of "matter" such as Hertz's analytic efforts to avoid Newton's "forces acting at a distance."[3]

Also of central focus in *Principles* was Russell's discovery of a new paradox—an interruption of his dream that the new rigor in the foundations of mathematics had at last shown the way to genuine progress on the many great problems of philosophy. The discovery of the paradox came in 1901 when Russell was investigating Cantor's methods for taming the infinite. The paradox made him world famous in mathematics and philosophy.

Cantor had shown that for any subclass y of a class u, there is no function correlating each member of y with a unique subclass of u in such a way that leaves no subclass of u out. It follows from Cantor's definition of "more" as applied to the infinite, that for any subclass y of u, $y < \wp u$. There are "more" subclasses of u in the class $\wp u$ of all subclasses of u than there are members of y. Suppose, for example, that u is the class $\{a, b\}$ and $y = u$. Then the members of $\wp u$ are the subclasses ø, $\{a\}$, $\{b\}$, $\{a, b\}$. We see that Cantor's result is obvious where u is finite. But it is a remarkable discovery when u is infinite. Cantor shows that no matter what function one tries, he has a technique for finding a subclass of u left out of the correlation. Russell was worried. There is a fly in the ointment:

> There is a greatest of all infinite numbers, which is the number of things altogether, of every sort and kind. It is obvious that there cannot be a greater number than this, because, if everything has been taken, there is nothing left to add. Cantor has a proof that

there is no greatest number, and if this proof is valid, the contradictions of infinity would reappear in a sublimated form. But in this one point, the master has been guilty of a very subtle fallacy, which I hope to explain in some future work.

(MM, p. 69)

Russell applied Cantor's result to the case where u is the universal class V (whose members include everything whatsoever, including classes, trees, rocks, people, etc.). Surely the number of this class has to be largest. There cannot be more subclasses of the universal class than there are members of the universal class since every such subclass is itself a member of the universals class! Something has gone wrong in Cantor's argument. Let y be $\wp V$ (i.e. the class of all subclasses of V). Then Cantor's result says that $\wp V < \wp V$.

In investigating what went wrong with the universal class, Russell follows Cantor's technique to find the class left out of the correlation and it is the paradoxical class r of all classes not members of themselves. To avoid the paradox, it is not enough to reject Cantor's technique. Russell's paradoxical class jeopardizes the very notion of a class itself and thus all mathematics which makes use of it. Naively, it seems that every condition determines a class of all and only those entities that satisfy the condition. Some classes are members of themselves and others are not. For instance, the class of all people is not a person. Hence it is not a member of itself. The class of all classes, however, is a class and thus a member of itself. Russell then considers the class of all classes not members of themselves. It is a member of itself if and only if it is not a member of itself. We have a contradiction—a paradox of classes. "Never glad confident morning again," were Whitehead's reported words (MPD, p. 58).

Russell sent the paradox in a letter to Frege in 1902. Frege immediately recognized the gravity of the situation, not only for his own philosophy of arithmetic, but also for all possible foundations of arithmetic. He graciously wrote to Russell:

8 Life and Work

> Your discovery of the contradiction has surprised me beyond words and, I should almost like to say, left me thunderstruck, because it has rocked the ground on which I meant to build arithmetic. . . . It is all the more serious as the collapse of my law V seems to undermine not only the foundations of my arithmetic but the only possible foundations of arithmetic as such. . . . Your discovery is at any rate a very remarkable one, and it may perhaps lead to a great advance in logic, undesirable as it may seem at first sight.
>
> . . . The second volume of my Basic Laws is to appear shortly. I shall have to give it an appendix, where I will do justice to your discovery. If only I could find the right way of looking at it![4]

Frege's second volume discussed the contradiction and suggested a way out. Russell soon came to see that Frege's suggestion did not work. The paradox he discovered was only one of infinitely many unruly paradoxes plaguing the notion of a class. If arithmetic is tied to the notion of a class then arithmetic totters.[5]

Russell remarks that in 1903 and 1904 his efforts to find a genuine solution to the paradoxes within logic were preoccupied with chasing will-o'-the-wisps. But he did have many a glad new confident morning. A notable one, long shrouded in mystery, occurred on 23 May 1903. Russell wrote in his journal: "Four days ago I solved the Contradiction—the relief of this is unspeakable" (*Collected Papers* 12, p. 24). The "solution" was communicated to Whitehead, who responded by telegram: "Heartiest congratulations. *Aristoteles secundus*. I am delighted.[6] On 24 May Russell wrote to Frege:

> I received your letter this morning, and I am replying to it at once, for I believe I have discovered that classes are entirely superfluous. Your designation $\acute{z}(\varphi z)$ can be used for φ itself, and $x \in \acute{z}(\varphi z)$ for φx
> . . . This seems to me to avoid the contradiction.[7]

Frege was less than enthusiastic. And in fact, even before Russell had received Frege's letter of reply, he had already come to reject the proposal. On Whitehead's telegram he wrote: "*A propos* of solving the Contradiction. (But the solution was wrong.)"

Why was the solution wrong? What did Russell have in mind? He surely did not have in mind that there was a paradox of properties analogous to his paradox of classes. When he sent his original letter of 1901 to Frege explaining his paradox of classes, Russell was well aware that the paradox has an analog for properties. Instead of the class of all and only entities not members of themselves, consider the property R of all and only those entities that do not have themselves. The property *wisdom* has R since *wisdom* is not wise. The property *abstractness*, on the other hand, is abstract. So it has R. But R has itself if and only if R lacks itself. We have Russell's contradiction of properties (attributes, propositional functions). Later Russell expressed the dark lesson as follows: "It must be understood that the postulate of the existence of classes . . . is exposed to the same arguments, pro and con, as the existence of propositional functions as separable entities distinct from all their values" (TN, p. 154, ft. 1). Russell's doctrine that classes are "superfluous" could not have been so simply undermined by a paradox of properties.[8] This is but one of the many wonderful topics for research that one encounters in reading the letters of correspondence and volumes of work notes Russell left to posterity.

In 1905 Russell had yet another confident new morning: his theory of definite descriptions. It was published in the October issue of *Mind* as "On Denoting." The paper came to be regarded as a "paradigm of philosophy."[9] Russell courageously defended his view in spite of Stout's assessment, as editor of the journal *Mind*, that the paper was "preposterous" (*MPD*, p. 83). Armed with the theory of definite descriptions, Russell finally had the solution of the paradoxes he was looking for. He set out the theory in December of 1905 and developed it fully in 1906. It is a theory of propositional structure that Russell came to describe as his "substitutional theory of classes" and his "no-classes" theory. The *Principles of Mathematics* was originally to have a sequel, co-authored by Whitehead, which dissolved the paradoxes and formally expressed the foundations of mathematics of the first volume. This new volume was to contain Russell's substitutional theory as the solution of the paradoxes plaguing the foundations of mathematics.

Russell knew that a doctrine of types of classes avoids the paradoxes of classes. Begin with classes of *individuals* (non-classes). Next there are classes of classes of individuals, classes of classes of classes of individuals, and so on. The theory of types of classes demands that no class can be a member of itself or a member of a member of itself, etc. A theory of types of classes, however, does not solve (or dissolve) the paradox of classes. If there are classes, surely it is meaningful for a class to be a member of itself, even if it were to always turn out to be false. Russell's new idea is that the existence of classes is not needed for the foundations of mathematics. The paradoxes are to be dissolved by explaining away statements about types of classes. In this way, mathematical constructions that employed an ontology of classes can be emulated in a no-classes theory of propositional structure. The new theory of definite descriptions was the linchpin. Russell explains:

> What was of importance in this theory was the discovery that, in analyzing a significant sentence, one must not assume that each separate word or phrase has significance on its own account . . . It soon appeared that class-symbols could be treated like descriptions, i.e., as non-significant parts of significant sentences. This made it possible to see, in a general way, how a solution to the contradictions might be possible.
>
> (*MMD*, p. 106)

Unfortunately, Russell called this new dissolution of the paradoxes "the theory of types." This is misleading since it gives the incorrect impression of a theory of types of entities. Russell's idea is that there are no types of entities. His plan is to emulate the structure of a theory of types of classes within a type-free theory of the structure of propositions. A proposition is part of the world. It is not something mental or linguistic. Some propositions obtain (i.e. are true), and some do not obtain (i.e. are false). The substitutional theory rejects an ontology of classes, but it recovers everything mathematicians would want to do with types of classes. Russell explains:

> *Technically*, the theory of types . . . differs little from the no-classes theory. The only thing that induced me at that time [in *The Principles of Mathematics*] to retain classes was the technical difficulty of stating the propositions of elementary arithmetic without them—a difficulty which then seemed to me to be insuperable.
>
> (*InS*, p. 193)

The theory is type-free. There are no types of classes since there are no classes. And there are no types of propositions. It adheres, as Russell colorfully put it, ". . . with drastic pedantry to the old maxim that, 'whatever is, is one' " (*STCR*, p. 189).

This time of remarkable inspiration is cobbled to a time that is perhaps among Russell's most emotionally trying. He confesses that in 1902 "I went out bicycling one afternoon, and suddenly, as I was riding along a country road, I realized that I no longer loved Alys" (*A*, vol. I, p. 222). They had cherished honesty in relationships and it was not long before Russell could no longer hide his failure to desire her. It is not fully clear why. Perhaps it was because Alys was incapable of having children. Perhaps Russell's relentless need for others' affections blocked feelings of being in love with Alys. Though he had freed his mind of the tyranny of Victorian social morals and he reports that Alys had advocated free love,[10] something that produced a scandal when lecturing at Bryn Mawr, the torment of not feeling in love with Alys plagued him. Alys loved him dearly, and the devastation of his new coldness to her nearly brought about her suicide. Their subsequent years together collapsed into a long depression for both. They did not finalize their divorce until 1921.

Alys had agreed to live in Oxford and they built a house in Bagley

12 Life and Work

Wood. Shortly after moving in, and poured into mathematics by emotional tumult, Russell did some of his most remarkable work. The sequel to *Principles* was never written. Instead, Whitehead and Russell made a new start. The wonderful, long, and tangled intellectual journey from here to the completion of *Principia* is contracted by Russell for purposes of drama in the following account:

> We went to live there in the spring of 1905, and very shortly after we had moved in I discovered my Theory of Definite Descriptions, which was the first step in solving the difficulties which had baffled me for so long. . . . In 1906 I discovered the Theory of Types. After this it only remained to write the book out. Whitehead's teaching work left him not enough leisure for this mechanical job. I worked at it from ten to twelve hours a day for about eight months in the year, from 1907 to 1910. The manuscript became more and more vast, and every time that I went out for a walk I used to be afraid that the house would catch fire and the manuscript get burned up. It was not, of course, the sort of manuscript that could be typed, or even copied. When we finally took it to the University Press, it was so large that we had to hire an old four-wheeler for the purpose. Even then our difficulties were not at an end. The University Press estimated that there would be a loss of £600 on the book, and while the syndics were willing to bear a loss of £300, they did not feel that they could go above this figure. The Royals Society very generously contributed £200, and the remaining £100 we had to find ourselves. We thus earned minus £50 each by ten years' work. This beats the record of *Paradise Lost*.
>
> (A, vol. I, p. 229)

Considerably more happened than "writing the book out."

In 1910 the first volume of *Principia Mathematica* appeared. Co-authored by Whitehead, the second volume was published in 1911, and the third volume appeared in 1913. The fourth volume, on the logical foundations of geometry, was to have been Whitehead's work alone. This period of intense collaboration over

Principia also brought Russell close to Evelyn Whitehead. She was a complex and theatrical woman who was jaded and deeply lonely because of Alfred's neglect of her in favor his academic work. They had three children, but Russell reports that he had become especially close to their young son Eric. He comforted him during his distress over his mother's constant depressions and fear of a heart condition (perhaps due to a hiatal hernia and severe acid reflux). He secretly gave money to Evelyn when Alfred's financial incompetence threatened crisis. However, the popular claim that they hid an affair from him is myth.[11] Whitehead became transfixed by Einstein's relativity theory and the many new issues that wanted detailed attention because of the implications curvature of spacetime might have for the nature of geometry. Unfortunately, shortly after 1918 brought the death of his son Eric in the First World War—with Russell taking a pacifistic stand against the economic greed that generated it—Whitehead gave up work on geometry. Evelyn dutifully honored his request to burn his work notes after his death in 1947. It is a substantial loss, although one can imagine a logicist treatment of geometry, Euclidean and non-Euclidean, from the constructions of modern analytic geometry.

During this period of great intellectual achievement, Russell kept up a lively interest in politics. He stood as a parliamentary candidate, campaigning for woman's suffrage at the Wimbledon byelection of 1907. Russell tells of his surprise that a great deal of the acrimony came from women, who were themselves wedded to the dogmatisms of the day. In his *Autobiography*, Russell recalls a particularly memorable incident: "At my first meeting rats were let loose to frighten the ladies, and the ladies who were in the plot screamed in pretended terror with a view to disgracing their sex" (*A*, vol. 1, p. 154). Women's suffrage was then an intensely unpopular cause, provoking anger and underhanded tactics from the opposition. (See news article below.) Similar tactics abound today. They exploit the fear that our cherished dogmatisms might be false. Russell put it jocularly in another context:

We all have a tendency to think that the world must conform to our prejudices. The opposite view involves some effort of thought, and most people would die sooner than think—in fact, they do so. . . . There is no law of nature to the effect that what is taught at school must be true.[12]

RATS AS POLITICAL AGENTS.

Used Successfully to Break Up Woman Suffrage Candidate's Meeting.

Special Cablegram.

Copyright, 1907, by THE NEW YORK TIMES CO.

LONDON, May 11.—A new use has been found for rats. They have been drafted into politics, and have shown themselves marvelously efficient in the line of work to which they have been assigned. Out at Wimbledon the Hon. Bertrand Russell, woman suffrage and Liberal candidate for Parliament, decided to open his campaign with a public meeting. The hall was crowded, mostly with women. The meeting had no sooner opened than a plain, organized attempt was made to break it up.

"We are met here to-night to pledge our support to a worthy candidate," said the Chairman in opening the meeting.

"Really," exclaimed a man in the back of the hall, and then there were guffaws, shouts, shrieks, catcalls, and toots on motor car horns.

"I trust we shall have order in this meeting," pleaded the Chairman.

"Will you please sit down?" demanded a man with a megaphone, and then came a great uproar, which lasted five minutes. So the meeting progressed until Candidate Russell rose to speak. He had said about three words, when the man with the megaphone shouted:

"Let 'em loose."

That was the signal for the rats to make their début in British politics. An instant later forty whopping big fellows were scampering over the floor, terrorizing the audience, and especially the women. To say that the meeting adjourned in great disorder is an extremely conservative statement. At subsequent meetings in Mr. Russells's interest it was notable that a small number of women were present.

The more harmful the practices of a dogmatism, the greater the resistance will be to its rational evaluation.

The publication of *Principia Mathematica* swept away most all attention to Russell's earlier writings on the logical foundations of mathematics. In *Principia*, we find a no-propositions theory. Not two years earlier, in the 1907/1908 paper "Mathematical Logic as Based on the Theory of Types," propositions were still at center stage and the structure of a simple type-theory of classes is to be emulated by adopting propositional substitutions. The seemingly sudden alterations have befuddled historians ever since. The evolution of *Principia* is one of the most engaging episodes in the history of ideas.

It is not well known that Russell solved the paradoxes of classes and the paradox of attributes by his substitutional no-classes theory of propositional structure. This fact, buried in his work notes, has only recently been discovered. What he failed to solve was a paradox of propositions unique to the substitutional theory.[13] This was an annoying paradox, another fly in the ointment. It was technical and unique to the substitutional theory of propositional structure. Russell shared it with some friends, perhaps including the mathematician Louis Couturat.[14] One can take heart in being in the good company of those bewildered by it.[15] All the same, its role in Russell's thought is the key to understanding the nature and evolution of the logic of *Principia*. We need not worry about the details at present. Russell discovered it in April of 1906. Late in the year he thought he had found a solution: Abandon general propositions! He published a paper on it only in French with the title "Les Paradoxes de la Logique" to contravene the points made by the famous mathematician and scientist Henri Poincaré in a paper "Les mathématique et la loqique." But Russell's English title is bold and inspirational: "On 'Insolubilia' and Their Solution by Symbolic Logic" (InS). In the paper, he abandons general propositions. This solves the paradox of propositions. But he has to introduce a new mitigating axiom for propositions to succeed in emulating types of classes. To his dismay, the mitigating axiom was too strong.

It revived a new form of the paradox. Chagrined, but undaunted, Russell wrote "Mathematical Logic as Based on the Theory of Types." It was completed in 1907, but it was not published until 1908. It adheres to the substitutional theory and returns to the assumption of general propositions. But it now retrofits the substitutional theory by adding a ramified theory: a hierarchy of orders of propositions based on the sort of generality they contain. The quantifier "all propositions" is no longer allowed. One must have "all order n propositions." It is often joked that "There are no absolutes" is self-refuting since it denies what it intends to say. In Russell's view, the joke has become serious.

The ramification of propositions into orders is not a type theory of entities such as classes. It is a substitutional no-classes theory of propositions that emulates a type theory of classes. It embraces a hierarchy of orders of propositions. A new mitigating axiom for propositions is introduced—a Reducibility axiom for propositions—which mitigates the impact that orders of propositions has on the development of mathematics within the system. Unfortunately, the new Reducibility axiom for propositions is not easy to justify.[16] Unlike the earlier mitigating axiom for propositions which were justified by the abandonment of general propositions, Russell was only too aware that orders of propositions are a disaster to justify from a philosophical standpoint.

"Mathematical Logic" was a work in transition. Its new Reducibility axiom for orders of propositions found no philosophical justification. *Principia* rectified this. It is a remarkable philosophical and technical achievement. In *Principia* there is no type-theory of entities, and there is no ramified hierarchy either. It is a no-classes theory as well as a no-propositions theory. Its formal expressions make it appear to be a ramified type theory of attributes. But in truth, it endeavors to show how logic can reach mathematics without making any general assumptions about what attributes there are! It emulates a simple type-theory of classes in a new no-classes theory that is even more austere than the substitutional theory that was its predecessor. It is to the theory of classes what Einstein's relativity theory is to the aether (and the wave theory of light). Just as Einstein's "no-aether" theory preserves the physicist's use of Maxwell's equations for the propagation of light, Russell's no-classes theory preserves the mathematician's uses of classes. *Principia* is a strikingly simple and austere theory—a pillar of strength holding up a Mount Everest of mathematical results.

Unfortunately, *Principia* did not become the system of choice for working mathematicians. Russell himself expressed disappointment. He wrote:

> People were interested in what was said about the contradictions and in the question whether ordinary mathematics had been validly deduced from purely logical premises, but they were not interested in the mathematical techniques developed in the course of the work. I used to know of only six people who had read the later parts of the book. Three of these were Poles, subsequently (I believe) liquidated by Hitler. The others were Texans, subsequently successfully assimilated. Even those who were working on exactly the same subjects did not think it worthwhile to find out what *Principia Mathematica* had to say on them.
>
> (*MPD*, p. 86)

The cause of this was the practical preference mathematicians developed for couching constructions within Zermelo-Frankel (ZF) set theory instead of *Principia*'s type-theory. Type-theory is a no-classes theory. Unfortunately, few readers understood this. Many philosophers regarded it as an artificial type-theory of classes. Mathematicians followed suit, and, although there are rival set theories, Zermelo's set theory caught hold. Indeed, the study of set theory became a new discipline within mathematics departments as if it was itself a branch of mathematics! Advocates of sets felt emboldened to deplore types once there was a rival approach which avoided Russell's paradoxes of non-self-membership. They were looking for intuitions about sets, not dissolutions of the paradoxes. Zermelo provided such intuitions in 1908, with some encouragement from private correspondences with Russell. A founding idea was to introduce axioms for sets in an unabashedly piecemeal and intuitive way—characteristic of the historical development of mathematical ideas generally. Allow, for example, an empty set. Allow the intersection and union of any two sets. Allow a pair set whose members are just any two entities. Allow a set consisting of all the subsets of any set. Moreover, if we are given a set, then there is a subset which meets any conditions whatsoever, including non-self membership. This is Zermelo's Aussonderungs axiom (axiom of separation) of 1908. Of course, the viability of the axiom requires that one had better not countenance a universal set, else Russell's paradox returns. And the complement of a set must go as well.[17] These piecemeal (and seemingly uniquely mathematical) intuitions about the necessary existence of sets contrast starkly with the natural conception of a class as an object whose members are all and only those entities meeting a given condition. Russell's no-classes theory captures this natural conception of a class as modified by types. There is a universal class $V^{(o)}$ of individuals which are not classes, a universal class $V^{((o))}$ of classes of such individuals, and so on. Constructions of numbers as types of classes, therefore, split. We have $0^{(o)}$ as the class of non-self-identical individuals, $0^{((o))}$ as the class of all non-self-identical classes of classes of individuals, and so on. Type-theory prevents the emulation of a class which contains as members an entity and a class. Zermelo set theory does not, and in this it seemed to many mathematicians more beautiful.

Pulchritudo in oculis aspicientis est.[18] What is more jarring to intuition, that there is no universal set and no complement (as ZF demands) or that one should work with a no-classes theory which emulates a theory of types of classes? It has been said that in type-theory, arithmetic repeats in each type. But this objection conflates arithmetic which is fundamentally part of the logic of relations and requires only the existence of functions, with emulations of arithmetic objects such as numbers in a theory of sets (or classes). To attempt to explain arithmetic in terms of a theory of the existence of sets (or classes) is at best a case of *obscurum per obscurius*.[19] This is not because arithmetic objects such as numbers are less obscure than sets (or classes), but because *Principia* showed that arithmetic has no need whatever for the existence of objects that are numbers!

Principia provides a logical foundation for mathematics without appeal to axioms for the existence of classes and numbers, or axioms for the existence of attributes, and without axioms for the existence of propositions. Arithmetic is part of the logic of relations. It is foundational in *Principia*'s no-classes theory. We shall have much to say of its philosophical austerity in subsequent chapters, and we shall find *Principia*'s "no-Xs" lessons are of utmost importance for understanding Russell's philosophy of Logical Atomism and for understanding his ideas for solving (and dissolving) the many problems of philosophy. These included papers addressing themselves to the problems of the nature of causation in physics, and the relationship between the data available to the senses and the empirical evidence for the shocking scientific theories of the day. (Special relativity appeared in 1905 and heralded the frame dependence of time. In 1915 general relativity offered the elimination of the force of gravitation in favor of non-Euclidean conception of space-time.) Russell was scheduled for lectures at Harvard University on the new physical challenges to the traditional materialist conception of matter. He wrote lectures that would be the first of many emendations to his book *Our Knowledge of the External World* (1914).

Russell was quick to draw lessons from *Principia* for a new scientific conception of philosophy, but not before falling in love in 1910 with the flamboyant thirty-seven-year-old wife of Phillip Morrell. The Morrells had an open marriage in spite of Phillip being a Member of Parliament. Lady Ottoline Morrell frequently met Russell at her home at Garsington, the Morrell's country home at Oxfordshire. Ottoline fancied herself a patron of poets, intellectuals, and artists and frequently entertained, befriending, among others, Aldous Huxley, Siegfried Sassoon, T. S. Eliot, D. H. Lawrence, and Virginia Woolf. On weekends she hosted the Bloomsbury Group, a collective of friends and lovers living near London. Many of them were fellow graduates at Cambridge, including Virginia Woolf, economist John Maynard Keynes, E. M. Forster, and Lytton Strachey.

Her affair with Russell was traumatic for both, but its halcyon days gave expression to Russell's hope that emotional peace can flow from a love of knowledge. The spiritual life of atheism was often their topic. And with Ottoline's encouragement, Russell set himself to explaining how feelings of wonder are evoked by our splendidly complicated universe when contemplated, as Spinoza had taught, *sub specie aeternitatis*. "It is this happy contemplation of what is eternal," Russell would later write, "that Spinoza calls the intellectual love of God. To those who have once known it, it is the key of wisdom" (PSR, p. 269). This scientific spirituality frees the mind from the imprisonment produced by ambitions for wealth and power. Russell's Spinozism blossomed at this time and Leopardi's poetry comforted them. He wrote a flowery piece as a follow-up to his "A Free Man's Worship" (1903) and called it "The Essence of Religion" (1911). They outlined a book together called "Prisons," and some of its ideas made their way into Russell's "shilling shocker," *The Problems of Philosophy* (1912). But Ottoline had a daughter with Morrell and in spite of Russell's increasingly desperate hope of running away with her, she made it clear to him that she had no intention of leaving her marriage. The rejection sank Russell into a serious depression and his many letters are punctuated with it. It speaks well of both that they remained lifelong friends. Ottoline died in 1938 from heart failure due to an overdose of the antibiotic Prontosil prescribed by the clinic of H. C. Cameron.

In his desperation for children, he married Dora Black, an ardent feminist whose conception of open marriage and ideas for restructuring education and the family at first seemed a perfect fit for Russell. He met Dora in 1916. Soon after, he proposed marriage for the purpose of having a child. Dora detested marriage as an institution designed for the subjugation of women (and so it then was). But they seemed to find much in common intellectually and continued their friendship over the years. In the First World War, Dora joined Russell's campaign against military conscription. In the frenzy of pro-war rhetoric, his activities provoked consternation from the governing council at Trinity. In a series of odd circumstances in 1916, Russell came to take responsibility for the anti-conscription leaflet, "Two Years of Hard Labour for not Disobeying the Dictates of Conscious." The leaflet expressed outrage at the severe prison sentence of conscious objector Ernest Everett. Russell wrote a short piece "*Adsum qui feci*" and sent it to *The Times*, claiming authorship and daring the authorities to go after its author. The embarrassment proved too much for them. Russell's tactic worked. It won him a fine of £100, which he refused to pay. In retaliation, his personal belongings were seized for auction. (Personal friends came to his defense and his belongings were returned.) The governing council at Trinity was embarrassed, too. They dismissed Russell from his lectureship in spite of the vehement protests of the junior fellows, including the mathematician G. H. Hardy. Even more oddly, Russell resigned from the No-conscription Fellowship (NCF) in 1917, yet it was an article of 1918 for the NCF journal *Tribunal* that landed him six months in the Brixton Prison. The charge was for insulting an ally (the United States) by insinuating that a prolonged American troop presence in France and Britain should be avoided as it would be likely to be used to reinforce unfair labor practices.

The solitude in the Brixton prison was useful. Russell wrote a wonderful and very accessible short introduction to *Principia Mathematica*. He called it *Introduction to Mathematical Philosophy* (1919). In it he colorfully explains logicism as the thesis that mathematical necessity is logical necessity: "Pure logic, and pure mathematics (which is the same thing), aims at being true, in Leibnizian phraseology, in all possible worlds, not only this higgledy-piggledy job-lot of a world in which chance imprisons us" (IMP, p. 192). He also began to devise a dissolution of the mind-body problem by a unique new form of neutral monism. This yielded The Analysis of Mind (1921). In 1920 Russell visited Russia (shortly after the revolution) and met Lenin. He insisted on not going with Dora, but while he was gone she arranged her own trip. During this period, Russell wrote The Practice and Theory of Bolshevism (1920). "I cannot share the hopes of the Bolsheviks," he wrote, "any more that those of the Egyptian anchorites: I regard both as tragic delusions, destined to bring upon the world centuries of darkness and futile violence" (PTB, pp. 13–14).

> I am compelled to reject Bolshevism for two reasons: First because the price mankind must pay to achieve Communism by Bolshevik method is too terrible; and secondly because, even after paying the price, I do not believe the result would be what the Bolsheviks profess to desire.
>
> (*PTB*, p. 160)

Unlike Dora, he was not at all caught up by the widespread enthusiasm of "the new world order" it promised.

Trinity would eventually reinstate Russell's lectureship. But Russell would decline in an effort to protect it from the predictable scandal of his relation to Dora with his divorce from Alys still intractable. Dora finally married Bertie in 1921. They enjoyed China together when Russell was invited as a visiting professor in Peking. He wrote a book, The Problem of China (1921), setting out a very positive appreciation and respect for China and its bright future. In China, Russell fell seriously ill with pneumonia. With Japanese journalists anticipating this death, he read his own obituary notices, including a one-liner that read "Missionaries may be pardoned for breathing a sign of relief at the news of Mr. Russell's death." While recuperating, Russell began to joke about the misunderstanding to Lady Ottoline Morrell:

> I have missed much by not dying here, as the Chinese were going to have given me a terrific funeral in Central Park, and then buried me in an island in the Western Lake, where the greatest poets and emperors lived, died, and were buried. Probably I should have become a god. What an opportunity missed![20]

Russell later wrote a lighthearted letter to the editor of the *Manchester Guardian* on 17 February 1955 concerning the reports of his death that had surfaced in the British press:

> Sir, in your issue of February 15 you say, "Fellows of the Royal Society must have one deep regret: they cannot read their own obituary notices." You do yourself an injustice. I had the pleasure of reading my own obituary notice in your forward-looking journal thirty-four years ago.—Yours etc., Bertrand Russell.

It actually happened twice. The second time was when *The Times* of London got a report of his death in 1954 after an interview with Japanese journalists was canceled because he was seriously ill with bronchitis. As it happens, in 1937 Russell wrote a mock obituary of himself for amusement. A part of it was eventually quoted in his real obituary for the *Times*.

Dora and Bertie had two children, John and Kate. In 1927, Dora opened an alternative school for children at Beacon Hill. The education was non-traditional and visionary, similar in important ways to Montessori. It proved to be a financial disaster. But it was a wonderful experiment, and sad when it came to a close at the Second World War. Meanwhile, Dora was causing a quiet scandal with her books *The Prospects of Industrial Civilization* (1923), *Hypatia: Women and Knowledge* (1925), and *The Right to Be Happy* (1927). Russell wrote introductions to the new physics sweeping the world. His book *The ABC of Relativity* (1925) remains today one of the best introductions to relativity theory. He was not unaware of the radically new revolutions occurring in quantum mechanics as well, and these ideas appeared in *The ABC of Atoms* (1923). But Russell's most striking and important analytic work of the period is *Outline of Philosophy* (1927). This is not a simple introduction to the problems of philosophy. It sets out the dramatic consequences that Russell's research program of Logical Atomism has for dissolving traditional problems of philosophy. It should be read in conjunction with Russell's paper "Logical Atomism," published in 1924. Russell rejects solipsism as a starting point for empirical knowledge. While rejecting the behaviorism which was then in vogue, Russell embraced the naturalization of epistemology—something Quine endorsed as late as 1968. In the work, Russell advocates a form of neutral monism different from any in the history of philosophy. The "neutral stuff" is physical space-time events, minds (continuing streams of consciousness), and physical objects (continuing through time) are orderings of events. "The gap between mind and matter has been filled in," he observes, "partly by new views of mind, but much more by the realization that physics tells us nothing as to the intrinsic character of matter" (OP, p. 148). Moreover, he advocates a form of structural realism. "Physical is mathematical," he writes, "not because we know so much about the physical world, but because we know so little; it is only its mathematical properties that we can discover" (OP, p. 157). The implications for philosophy are dramatic. Written concurrently with *The Analysis of Matter* (1927), it is a very important work, and more important than any subsequent work Russell would produce in technical philosophy. It also contains perhaps one of Russell's most famous phrases: "The good life is one inspired by love and guided by knowledge"(OP, p. 235).[21]

In his efforts to keep financially sound, Russell wrote nontechnical books such *Icarus* or *The Future of Science* (1924) and *What I Believe* (1925) and with Dora he made efforts to reform practices of education in his book *On Education*. In *Free Thought and Official Propaganda*, we have an example of Russell's wit: "We are faced with the paradoxical fact that education has become one of the chief obstacles to intelligence and freedom of thought" (FT, p. 35). He also managed to dash off *The Conquest of Happiness* (1930), which has some really wonderful lines:

> For my own part, speaking personally, I have found the happiness of parenthood greater than any other that I have experienced. I believe that when the circumstances led men or women to forgo this happiness, a very deep need remains ungratified, and that this produces a dissatisfaction and listlessness of which the cause may remain quite unknown. To be happy in this world, especially when youth is past, it is necessary to feel oneself not merely an isolated individual whose day will be over, but part of the stream of life flowing on from the first germ to the remote and unknown future.
>
> (*CH*, p. 197)

Of course, *On Marriage and Morals* (1929) is the best of his popular works of the time. Not a little influenced by Dora, it was no less scandalous with its advocacy of equality for women, sex education, birth control, toleration of affairs within marriage, the legalization of prostitution, and easy divorce for childless marriages. Perhaps these last lines of the book best capture the idealistic spirit, if not the practice, of their own relationship. Russell wrote:

> The essence of a good marriage is respect for each other's personality combined with that deep intimacy, physical, mental and spiritual, which makes a serious love between a man and a woman the most fructifying of all human experiences. Such love, like everything that is great and precious, demands its own morality, and frequently entails a sacrifice of the less to the greater; but such sacrifice must be voluntary, for, where it is not, it will destroy the very basis of the love for the sake of which it is made.
>
> (*MaM*, p. 320)

Dora and Bertie seemed at first well matched, but quarreling was not infrequent. In the end, Dora's radical ideas for restructuring the concept of the family bested Russell's own. She believed not only in the naturalness of open marriage, but also in the naturalness of having children with her lovers! Dora had a child with the young American journalist Griffin Barry, expecting a communal family with Bertie accepting the child as if his own. With natural emotions strained to their limit, Russell brought his logical mind to entertain the impractical—for a while. When she did it again in 1937, he could no longer withstand the pain. In 1935, in an act that was not a little reactionary, Russell had begun a relationship with his own young lover and student, Patricia Spence. They had a child, Conrad, in 1937, when Russell was sixty-five.

In 1931, Russell's brother Frank suddenly died. Russell inherited the earldom together with his brother's debts and obligations of alimony! The financial burden set him to dashing off books for popular audiences. This soon grew into an imperative. In 1934 he published *Freedom and Organization 1814–1914*. It did not do well at first. In 1935 he wrote *Religion and Science*, and in 1936 *In Praise of Idleness* and *Which Way to Peace?*, which revealed his commitment to pacifism—something soon to change. In 1937, he published *The Amberley Papers* on the life of his parents. Russell managed to write the technical article "On Order in Time" (1935) and deliver it to the Cambridge Philosophical Society. It is closely related to another essay, "Determinism and Physics." But the imperative to stay financially afloat left no time for technical philosophical works and small readerships. In the aftermath of separation from Dora and with the burden of significant new debts and little Conrad, Russell was ever more pushed to write popular essays and books. In his 1932 essay "In praise of Idleness" we find:

> The more we know the more harm we can do to each other. If human beings, in their rage against each other, invoke the aid of insects and microorganisms, as they certainly will do if there is another big war, it is by no means unlikely that the insects will remain the sole ultimate victors. Perhaps from a cosmic point of view, this is not to be regretted; but as a human being I cannot help heaving a sigh over my own species.
>
> (*IPI*, p. 234)

Popular, they are, but they are not superficial. In some of his books, we are reminded of Russell's halcyon days with Ottoline,

> These lands that now are strewn
> With sterilizing cinders, and embossed
> With lava frozen to the stone,
> That echoes to the lonely pilgrims foot,
> Where nestling in the sun the snake lies coiled,
> And where in some cleft
> In cavernous rocks the rabbit hurries home ---
> And tilth, and yelling harvests, and the sound
> Of loving herds, here too
> Gardens and places
> Retreats clear to the leisure
> Of powerful lords, and here were famous towns,
> Which the implacable mountain thundering forth
> Molten streams from its fiery mouth, destroyed
> With all their habitants, Now all around
> Lies crushed 'neath one vast ruin'.

together reading aloud verses of the poet Leopardi and marveling at the inconceivably vast and marvelous universe and the insignificant position mankind has in it. One of Russell's favorites was Leopardi's *La Ginestra*, which describes the devastation of Pompeii and Herculaneum by the eruption of Mount Vesuvius (see excerpt above). It is now believed that a pyroclastic flow poured down the mountainside at perhaps four hundred miles per hour, completely burying the towns, their people, and high culture in searing ash. The contorted bodies preserve the horror of lungs cremated and the area is a testament to both the folly and the achievements of man in a world that cares nothing of them. After the First World War, this emotional detachment seemed no longer possible for Russell. Leopardi's description of Vesuvius made its way into *Power: A New Social Analysis* (1938). But Russell uses it as a warning of the imminent and senseless self-destruction of our species by human forces as devastating as Vesuvius. Here is a poignant passage:

> Power over men, not power over matter, is my theme in this book . . .
>
> Leopardi describes what volcanic action has achieved on the slopes of Vesuvius . . .
>
> These results can now be achieved by man. They have been achieved at Guernica; perhaps before long they will be achieved where as yet London stands. What good is to be expected of an oligarchy which will have climbed to dominion through such destruction? And if it were Berlin and Rome, not London and Paris, that were destroyed by the thunderbolts of the new gods, could any humanity survive in the destroyers after such a deed? . . . In former days, men sold themselves to the Devil to acquire magical powers. Nowadays they acquire these powers from science, and find themselves compelled to become devils. There is no hope for the world unless power can be tamed, and brought into the service, not of this or that group or fanatical tyrant, but of the whole human race, white and yellow and black, Fascist and Communist and Democrat; for science has made it inevitable that all must live or all must die.
>
> (*Pr*, p. 32)

Russell's thoughts proved to be portentous. Here we see the beginning of Russell's departure from the romantic innocence of a Spinozistic intellectual love of God.

Russell settled for a time with Patricia in Oxford. He composed lectures yielding both an influence on the young A. J. Ayer and a book, *Words and Facts*. The work returned Russell to analytic philosophy. It was later published as *An Inquiry into Meaning and Truth* (1940). In 1938 the young, new Russell family were then off to the University of Chicago, where Russell had accepted a visiting professorship. Russell met Carnap there, but he disliked the department at Chicago and so left for the University of California, Los Angeles (UCLA) the next year. He wrote a rather critical review of John Dewey's book *Logic: The Theory of Inquiry*, which had appeared in 1938. The review, together with Dewey's reply, was composed for the 1939 volume of the *Library of Living Philosophers* devoted to Dewey.²² A debate that upset Dewey broke out, with Russell lampooning pragmatism's replacement of the notion of truth with warranted assertibility. Russell wrote a follow-up called "Warranted Assertibility," which became a chapter of his book *Inquiry into Meaning and Truth*. Dewey replied in 1941, and Russell continued the discussion in a chapter on Dewey in *A History of Western Philosophy*. The debate was cordial, but Russell's wit carried the day. Dewey was a naturalist and his orientation to human cognition was biological and evolutionary. He held that meaning is a property of behavior and he rejected the role that private experiences have in traditional epistemology. This had led him to abandon notions of representation and truth in favor of an emphasis on states of equilibrium (or harmony) between an organism and its environment. Pragmatic notions of workability (or warranted assertibility) are to supplant truth. Russell was sympathetic to naturalism in epistemology, but he endeavored to preserve traditional notions of truth and representation in a way that logic (and mathematics) is not given over to empirical psychology.

While in California in 1939, Russell's children John and Kate visited. The outbreak of the war made it impossible for them to return home, so they became students at UCLA. But Russell was again unhappy, and planned the next year to accept a professorship to teach mathematical logic at City College of New York. An Episcopalian Bishop of New York, who for some time had been had vociferously criticizing Russell's liberal values, embarrassed the city government running the College. Church groups, teachers, priests, and outraged parents inundated the papers with attacks on Russell's character. Somehow an organized effort was formed against Russell, and the mother of a prospective student was encouraged to bring a law suit against the Municipality of New York on grounds that the appointment would encourage the "lecherous" and "erotomaniac" views that characterized Russell's life and books on marriage and family. Russell was not allowed to defend himself in court since he was not indicted in the case. He was advised by his lawyer to remain silent. Caught up by the vitriol, the Board of Higher Education in New York, a collection of venerable attorneys, accountants, doctors, and professors met and voted sixteen to five to block the appointment. The case became a cause célèbre for academic freedom and many of the most prominent intellectuals of the day rose up in support of Russell. These included Alfred Whitehead, Albert Einstein, and John Dewey. The American Civil Liberties Union, with the help of Dewey, challenged the legal proceedings. The hysteria quickly spread to UCLA, where a movement was organized toward a similar cause. Russell was worried about Kate and John studying there. Three judges threw out the suit, but the point was moot since Russell had no intention of returning to California.

Dr. Pretorius, a character of director James Whale's intermittently highbrow sequel to *Frankenstein*, dares to scientifically investigate the source of life and apply reason in ethics, impiously challenging God's authority over life and death. I have often thought this Dr. Pretorius to be a caricature of Russell. In the 1935 film, Pretorius reports that he was thrown out of the university for "knowing too much."

Now out of work and with no access to England because of the war, he was in a desperate situation. Harvard University came to his immediate rescue, offering him a lectureship for 1940. But the longer-term solution was provided with the aid of Dewey by the Philadelphia millionaire and art collector Albert C. Barnes, who established a foundation in 1922 to "promote the advancement of education and the appreciation of the fine arts." Barnes was eager to promote the study of the history of art. Barnes liked the idea of offering sanctuary for the iconoclastic Russell. He knew it would bring attention to the foundation. Russell was given a five-year appointment to lecture on the history of Western philosophy at the foundation. Russell accepted and found it amusing, after the illiberalism of New York and California, that he lectured in a hall ordained with some of the most controversial art of the day, including paintings of French nudes. The lectures produced about two-thirds of what would become one of his most popular and successful books, *The History of Western Philosophy* (1945).

The relationship with Barnes was uneasy partly because the millionaire incessantly trying to coerce the respect and admiration of others. Beholden to no one, Russell found Barnes boorish and became increasingly irritated by his self-congratulatory behavior and dinner parties, the attendance of which was mandatory. Sensing the rebuff, Barnes fought back by belittling Patricia's knitting while attending Russell's lectures. Patricia insisted and Russell came to defend her. The cycles of insult and rebuff persisted until Barnes's embarrassment caused him to dismiss Russell from his lectureship. Russell filed suit for breach of contract and, presenting the judge his book manuscript, won the case against Barnes's obviously contrived charge that the lectures were disorganized. But the settlement was slow in producing a pay-out and the situation left Russell once again without financial security. The situation had become acute and Patricia's bouts with depression and alienation deepened. Meanwhile, Russell began longing to return home. Some of his long-time companions and friends had died, including Ottoline Morrell and Beatrice Webb. Trinity College, Cambridge had offered him a Fellowship and an advance for *History*. While he waited for the British embassy to arrange the Atlantic crossing to England, which was still treacherous due to German submarines, Paul Weiss arranged for him to continue working on *History* at Bryn Mawr College. He also spent a brief period at Princeton, where he engaged with Wolfgang Pauli, Albert Einstein, and Kurt Gödel.

The next years at Trinity produced *Human Knowledge: Its Scope and Limits* (1948), a work devoted to probability and induction ("nondemonstrative inference"). The book contains some gems, including a challenge to the conception of knowledge as justified true belief (later extended by Gettier) and a causal (externalist) theory of indexicals ("egocentric particulars").

Illustrating the psychological implausibility of solipsism, one finds Russell's sardonic comment: "I once received a letter from the eminent logician Mrs. Christine Ladd Franklin, saying that she was a solipsist, and was surprised that there were no others. Coming from a logician, this surprised me" (HK, p. 180). In the book, Russell explains in detail the nature of our knowledge of the new physics. The often-quoted passage from Inquiry "Naïve realism leads to physics, and physics, if true, shows that naïve realism is false," is explored in detail. Russell remarks wryly that,

> Historically, physicists started from naïve realism, that is to say, from the belief that external objects are exactly as they seem. On the basis of this assumption, they developed a theory which made matter something quite unlike what we perceive. Thus their conclusion contradicted their premise, though no one except a few philosophers noticed this.
>
> (*HK*, p. 197)

The task of the book is to explain how naïve realism can be modified so that the new physics, if true, is knowable on its basis.

Russell was disappointed at its reception, especially among the Oxford philosophers. Russell found that a dismissive attitude toward analytic philosophy and epistemology was in vogue. It was little more than a fad of dismissing philosophical problems as if they all rely on confusions produced by demented philosophers who are obsessed with puzzles and misunderstand the ordinary uses of language. A cure for philosophical dementia was being sought, not Russell's quest for solutions (and dissolutions) of philosophical problems. Even as late as 1959, Russell still reflected despairingly of trends in philosophy. He wrote:

> It is not an altogether pleasant experience to find oneself regarded as antiquated after having been, for a time, in the fashion. It is difficult to accept this experience gracefully. When Leibniz, in old age, heard the praises of Berkeley, he remarked: "The young man in Ireland who disputes the reality of bodies seems neither to explain himself sufficiently nor to produce adequate

arguments. I suspect him of wishing to be known for his paradoxes." I could not say quite the same of Wittgenstein, by whom I was superseded in the opinion of many British philosophers. It was not by paradoxes that *he* wished to be known, but by a suave evasion of paradoxes. . . .

There are two great men in history whom he somewhat resembles. One was Pascal, the other was Tolstoy. Pascal was a mathematician of genius, but abandoned mathematics for piety. Tolstoy sacrificed his genius as a writer to a kind of bogus humility which made him prefer peasants to educated men and *Uncle Tom's Cabin* to all other works of fiction. Wittgenstein, who could play metaphysical intricacies as cleverly as Pascal with hexagons or Tolstoy with emperors, threw away his talent and debased himself before common sense as Tolstoy debased himself before peasants—in each case from an impulse of pride. I admired Wittgenstein's *Tractatus* but not his later work, which seemed to me to involve an abrogation of his own best talent very similar to those of Pascal and Tolstoy.

(*MPD*, p. 218)

In Russell's view, Wittgenstein had successfully promoted the idea that ordinary practice, together with therapy for those who appreciate philosophical problems, obviates philosophical analysis. Once a student of Russell at Cambridge in 1912, Wittgenstein was an eccentric who wrote a cryptic book of his aphorisms and thoughts under Russell's tutelage. It was originally called "*Logisch-Philosophische Abhandlung.*" With Russell's help, the book found its way to publication in 1921 with the title *Tractatus Logico-Philosophicus*. It had been inspired by Russell's new scientific approach to philosophy. Metaphysicians, captivated by what they thought were non-logical necessities in mathematics and geometry, introduced muddles into philosophy. Russell's work endeavored to solve (and dissolve) many traditional philosophical problems by offering reconstructions of the sciences, showing that the only necessity is logical necessity.

Wittgenstein had been Russell's protégé and ally. Russell saw to it that the unorthodox book counted as his Ph.D. dissertation. Later, in 1930, he was instrumental in assuring the continuation of Wittgenstein's fellowships at Cambridge, in spite of his having produced a mountain of disorganized remarks. But Wittgenstein's later work did not impress Russell. It seemed to dismiss philosophical problems as mere misuses of language and reduce logic to social conventions on the use of ordinary words. As Russell put it, "Adherents of WII [Wittgenstein's later remarks] are fond of pointing out, as if it were a discovery, that sentences may be interrogative, imperative or optative as well as indicative" (MPD, p. 217).

The fad of dismissing philosophical analysis was not due to Wittgenstein. It was due to some of his followers. In a scathing criticism of this fad of philosophy by dismissal, Russell wrote:

> The earlier Wittgenstein whom I knew intimately, was a man addicted to passionately intense thinking, profoundly aware of the difficulties of which I, like him, felt the importance, and possesses (or at least so I thought) of true philosophical genius. The later Wittgenstein, on the contrary, seems to have grown tired of serious thinking and to have invented a doctrine which would make such an activity unnecessary. I do not for one moment believe that the doctrine which has these lazy consequences is true. I realize, however, that I have an overpoweringly strong bias against it, for, if it is true, philosophy is, at best, a slight help to lexicographers, and at worst, an idle tea-table amusement.
>
> (MPD, p. 217)

Russell lived to see his vindication when the fad eventually ran its course. But in a television interview by Lawrence Spivak on Meet the Press (28 October 1951), he was asked what book of his he would like to "survive" in one hundred years and what book he would expect it to be. He replied: "I should like it to be Principia Mathematica, of which I only wrote half.... I think in a hundred years the world will be so different they won't read the books of our time." "They won't read any of your books?" asked Lawrence Spivak. "No," said Russell.

It is a trifling question to ask "Who will be the Descartes or Kant of the twenty-first or even the twenty-second century?" But since it has been asked by some philosophers[23] writing a slanted history to favor Wittgenstein, it is worth a response. Only Russell is a plausible candidate for that status. He influenced most everyone in analytic philosophy throughout the twentieth century and his work is at the foundation of every important new school of thought. His philosophical work generated a revolution from which nearly all modern schools of philosophy developed. He is without question the most important philosopher of the twentieth century.

Russell's great contributions were renowned by the year 1949—a year which Russell came to describe as the "apogee of his respectability." Trinity offered him a Fellowship for life without teaching duties. He was elected to an Honorary Fellowship of the British Academy and the BBC invited him to give talks as part of its *Brains Trust* program, where various experts answered questions sent in by the public. Within the BBC, Russell was soon seen as the authentic voice of the liberal world. He spoke out against racial prejudice, urged the public to tolerate marriage of Jews and Gentiles, called hunting "a disgrace to the country," and rejected ghosts as "absolute nonsense and that is all I've got to say."[24] He joined Father Frederick Copleston, who had justifiably achieved acclaim for the outstanding volumes of his history of philosophy, for a BBC debate on the existence of God. The debate is a captivating window into the use of analytic methods to dissolve metaphysical issues surrounding the origins of the universe, existence, necessity, and the notion of explanation in science. Later that year, Russell was invited to give the first series of BBC lectures to honor its director, Lord Reith. These lectures led to Russell's very popular book *Authority and the Individual*.

Now respectable, the British Government asked him to lecture to the forces and even to persuade Berliners to resist the Russian attempt to drive the Allies out of Berlin during the Berlin Airlift. On a journey to Norway in 1948 to help the British Government sway public opinion against the Russians, Russell's seaplane, called the *Bukken Bruse*, made a landing in rough weather into Trondheim harbor and began to sink, killing nineteen in the front section. Proclaiming "If I cannot smoke, I shall die," Russell had fortuitously requested a seat in the smoking section at the rear of plane, where it so happened that the emergency exit was located.

In 1949 King George VI gave him Britain's most prestigious civilian award, the Order of Merit. The King reportedly took him aside to say: "You have sometimes behaved in a way which would not do if generally adopted." Russell tells us that he replied,

> How a man should behave depends on his profession. A postman, for instance, should knock on all the doors in a street at which he has letters to deliver, but if anybody else knocked on all the doors, he would be considered a public nuisance.
>
> (*A*, vol. III, p. 516)

Then while at Princeton on yet another visit to America, he got the news that he was awarded the Nobel Prize in Literature for his lifetime of achievements.

Russell had become respectable, but his days of being a nuisance were far from over. Russell maintained that the destruction of Berlin during the war was "monstrous" and the bombing of Dresden was "sickening," warning that such acts set the stage of a third world war. A month after the atomic bomb fell on Hiroshima, Russell felt the world racing headlong toward its annihilation—with nuclear weapons. His mistrust of the Soviet Union was at an apex and he felt it imperative that it not acquire the bomb. Speaking before the House of Lords, he argued that the United Nations must set up an international atomic development agency to prevent nuclear proliferation. Speaking before an audience of boys at Westminster School in 1949, he suggested that if necessary there be a preemptive strike against the Soviet Union to prevent them from getting nuclear weapons and thereby securing the intractability of their persecution of its people and the people of Eastern Europe. The Soviets stole important technical information for the atomic bomb in 1949, and Russell's warning of the ensuing persecutions proved well-founded. Russell came to mistrust American power as well and its growingly illiberal arguments that freedom must be sacrificed for protection from the "enemy from within" (i.e. Communism). Adlai Stevenson, an opponent of the growing McCarthyist attack on civil liberties in America, lost the presidential election of 1952.

Russell's outlook for the future was gloomy. His personal life was also a shambles. His marriage with Patricia Spence had finally collapsed. Later she felt that they had never been happy together. She was bitter and did her best to poison Conrad's mind against his father. She isolated the two of them in Cornwall in a remote and undeveloped place where homes had no electricity. Conrad never received Russell's letters to him. Long unhappy with Patricia, Russell courted a dear friend, Edith Finch, with many overtures of love. With his profound ardor flowing like never before, she agreed to marry him in 1952. She was fifty-one and he was eighty. The dedication to Edith in Russell's *Autobiography* speaks volumes (see below). The new marriage breathed new life and new motivations. The two were very happy together. It was not the kind of happiness he had glimpsed with Ottoline, but it was a happiness every bit as inspiring to him. Russell tried his hand at stories, intended, as he put it "to merely amuse." The published collection *Satan in the Suburbs* (1953) was followed with a sequel, *Nightmares of Eminent Persons*. The stories were not much appreciated. But there is no doubt that they are very amusing. Stories of mathematicians with nightmares that no objects are numbers reflect not a little on Russell's own rejection of the Pythagorean number heaven. Russell

> *To Edith*
>
> Through the long years
>   I sought peace.
> I found ecstasy, I found anguish,
>   I found madness,
>   I found loneliness.
> I found the solitary pain
>   that gnaws the heart,
> But peace I did not find.
>
> Now, old & near my end,
>   I have known you,
> And, knowing you,
> I have found both ecstasy & peace,
> I know rest.
> After so many lonely years,
> I know what life & love may be.
> Now, if I sleep,
> I shall sleep fulfilled.

then wrote Portraits from Memory, a collection of reminiscences of his many friends and acquaintances. The book is a further chronicle of Russell's retreat from Pythagoras.

Meanwhile, scientists corroborated Russell's fear that use of the new hydrogen bombs in war would result in total annihilation, with a quick death for some and a slow torture of radiation disease and anarchy for most. In 1954 Russell gave what would be his most dramatic talk on the BBC:

> There lies before us if we choose continual progress in happiness, knowledge and wisdom. Shall we, instead, choose death, because

we cannot forget our quarrels? I appeal, as a human being to
human beings; remember your humanity, and forget the rest . . .²⁵

Einstein, whose theories on the relationship between energy and matter played a role in creating the bomb, was a kindred spirit, profoundly concerned with nuclear proliferation and the dangers of misuse of such power in the hands of one government. Russell wrote to Einstein in 1955. Einstein then agreed that prominent scientists would sign a manifesto, drawing the attention of world leaders to the impending destruction of the human race. Russell drafted the manifesto. After discussions with various concerned but not yet agreed scientists, he sent a draft to Einstein. Suddenly Einstein died, just days after sending a letter endorsing the manifesto to Russell. The Einstein–Russell manifesto received enormous attention throughout the world, from scientists and politicians alike.

In 1957, despite outrage from concerned scientists that the test detonations of nuclear devices present serious dangers of exposure to radiation, America continued nuclear tests in the Pacific, and Britain was planning more tests. Russell wrote to the *New Scientist*, calling for a ban on all such tests. In spite of criticism from world leaders, the tests continued. Russell wrote an open letter (later appearing in *The New Statesman*) to both Khrushchev and Eisenhower, appealing for a test ban and the elimination of the manufacture and stockpiling of H-bombs. Khrushchev's tone was that of agreement, but the reply from John Foster Dulles (then Secretary of State) expressed contempt for duplicitous Soviet rhetoric and the impracticality of verifiable reductions.

In 1959 Russell managed to dash off *My Philosophical Development*, an excellent retrospective view on lessons of *Principia Mathematica* and his philosophy of Logical Atomism. But more pressing issues loomed. In 1962 the world seemed to be confronting the crisis that he had most feared. Castro had overthrown the Batista dictatorship in Cuba and, in reorganizing the society to communism, he sought economic aid from the Soviet Union. The American government supported an attack at the Bay of Pigs by Florida-based Cuban exiles hoping to regain political power. The attack ended in disaster. In an effort to undermine any further attempt to topple Castro's regime, Cuba redoubled its connections with the Soviets, agreeing to house nuclear missile bases pointed at targets in the United States. President Kennedy ordered a blockade of Cuba and ordered the missile bases dismantled. Russell wrote telegrams to Khrushchev and Kennedy, imploring both to back away from the impending war. He was not taken seriously by either. But, in the end, Russell's suggestion of both sides dismantling missile bases was followed. Both nuclear powers backed down, with agreements that the United States not sponsor further attacks on Cuba[26] and that missile bases be dismantled both in Cuba and in Turkey, where U.S. bases had targeted points in Russia.

Russell's activities in his nineties were as engaged as ever. In 1963 two foundations were established: the Bertrand Russell Peace Foundation and its charitable arm, the Atlantic Peace Foundation. Together with Sartre, Russell played a role in establishing the 1967 International War Crimes Tribunal. Intensely concerned with ending U.S. involvement in Vietnam and Southeast Asia, he was involved in many protests and brought to the press examples of wartime atrocities in his efforts to sway political and public opinion from escalating and continuing the war. Hyperbole on all sides characterized the turbulent times. But there were undoubtedly war crimes. Russell was devoted to the truth, wherever it may lead. In *The Prospects of Industrial Civilization* (1923) he wrote:

> The governors of the world believe, and have always believed, that virtue can only be taught by teaching falsehood, and that any man who knew the truth would be wicked. I disbelieve this, absolutely and entirely. I believe that love of truth is the basis of all real virtue, and that virtues based upon lies can only do harm.
>
> (*PIC*, p. 252)

Life and Work 41

Russell never denied that the world may be discovered to be a horrible place and the universe may be discovered to be unjust. The secret, he said, was to face the fact and not brush it aside, then you can start being happy.[27] Perhaps the prologue of his *Autobiography* best summarizes what he lived for:

> Three passions, simple but overwhelmingly strong, have governed my life: the longing for love, the search for knowledge, and unbearable pity for the suffering of mankind. These passions, like great winds, have blown me hither and thither, in a wayward course, over a deep ocean of anguish, reaching to the very verge of despair.
>
> I have sought love, first, because it brings ecstasy—ecstasy so great that I would often have sacrificed all the rest of life for a few hours of this joy. I have sought it, next, because it relieves loneliness—that terrible loneliness in which one shivering consciousness looks over the rim of the world into the cold unfathomable lifeless abyss. I have sought it, finally, because in the union of love I have seen, in a mystic miniature, the prefiguring vision of the heaven that saints and poets have imagined. This is what I sought, and though it might seem too good for human life, this is what—at last—I have found.
>
> With equal passion I have sought knowledge. I have wished to understand the hearts of men. I have wished to know why the stars shine. And I have tried to apprehend the Pythagorean power by which number holds sway above the flux. A little of this, but not much, I have achieved.
>
> Love and knowledge, so far as they were possible, led upward toward the heavens. But always pity brought me back to earth. Echoes of cries of pain reverberate in my heart. Children in famine, victims tortured by oppressors, helpless old people a hated burden to their sons, and the whole world of loneliness, poverty, and pain make a mockery of what human life should be. I long to alleviate the evil, but I cannot, and I too suffer.

> This has been my life. I have found it worth living, and would gladly live it again if the chance were offered me.
>
> (A, vol. I, p. 3)

Russell died on 2 February 1970 in Penrhyndeudraeth, Wales.

FURTHER READING

Ronald Clark, The Life of Bertrand Russell (New York: Knopf, 1976).

A. G. Grayling, Russell: A Very Short Introduction (Oxford: Oxford University Press, 1996).

Ray Monk, Ludwig Wittgenstein: The Duty of Genius (London: Vintage, 1991).

—— Bertrand Russell: The Spirit of Solitude 1872–1921 (London: Vintage, 1996).

—— Russell (New York: Routledge, 1999).

—— Bertrand Russell: The Ghost of Madness 1921–1970 (London: Vintage, 2001).

Caroline Moorehead, Russell: A Life (New York: Viking Press, 2002).

Alan Ryan, Bertrand Russell: A Political Life (New York: Hill and Wang, 1988).

Miranda Seymour, Ottoline: Life on a Grand Scale (London: Hodder & Stoughton, 1992).

John Watling, Bertrand Russell (Edinburgh: Oliver and Boyd, 1970).

Two

Mathematics and the Metaphysicians

> The fundamental thesis of the following pages, that mathematics and logic are identical, is one which I have never since seen any reason to modify.
>
> *The Principles of Mathematics* Introduction to the 1937 second edition

In a popular children's book *The Number Devil* we are introduced to a "Lord Rustle." The story is about a boy, Robert, struggling to come to appreciate the mysteries of number. In a series of dreams, Robert meets the number devil, who asks him to go easy on his teacher, Mr. Bockel.

> "Many of us," the number devil went on, "have an even harder time than your Bockel, however. One of my older colleagues, the well-known Lord Rustle, once took it into his head to prove that $1+1 = 2$. Look at this proof. This is how he went about it.

$*54.43$. $\vdash :. \alpha, \beta \, \varepsilon \, 1 . \supset : \alpha \cap \beta = \Lambda . \equiv . \alpha \cup \beta \, \varepsilon \, 2$
   Dem.
   $\vdash . *54.26 . \supset \vdash :. \alpha = i'x . \beta = i'y . \supset : \alpha \cup \beta \, \varepsilon \, 2 . \equiv . x \not\equiv y$.
   $[*51.231]$ $\equiv . i'x \cap i'y = \Lambda$.
   $[*13.12]$ $\equiv . \alpha \cap \beta = \Lambda$.   (1)
   $\vdash . (1) . *11 \cdot 11 \cdot 35 . \supset$
      $\vdash :. (\exists x, y) . \alpha = i'x . \beta = i'y . \supset : \alpha \cup \beta \, \varepsilon \, 2 . \equiv . \alpha \cap \beta = \Lambda$ (2)
   $\vdash . (2) . *11.54. *52.1 . \supset \vdash$. Prop

From this proposition it will follow, when arithmetical additon has been defined, that $1 + 1 = 2$.

"Ugh!" said Robert with a shiver. "That's horrendous. And all to show that 1+1 = 2? Something he knew anyway?"

Bertrand Russell's monumental three-volume work *Principia Mathematica* (written with the collaboration of the Cambridge mathematician Alfred N. Whitehead) develops 360 pages before it discusses 1+1 = 2. The proof appears at *110.643 some 86 pages into the second volume. As if with the eyes of a child seeing a logarithm for the first time, some widely read biographers of Russell see the system of *Principia* as one of ". . . quite dizzying complexity. . . . So many definitions and preliminary theorems are needed before arithmetic can get started that, for example, the proposition '1 plus 1 is 2' is arrived at only halfway through Volume II."[1] This is an entertaining story, but in truth Lord Russell, unlike Lord Rustle, was not preoccupied with proving 1+1 = 2. The aim in *Principia* is not arithmetic, but to show the quite wondrous discovery that mathematics consists of the logic of relations without making any appeal to numbers as special metaphysical objects governed by non-logical necessities. In fact, it is not so very difficult to provide a proof within logic of 1+1 = 2. What is very difficult (and in *Principia* impossible) is to find a proof within logic that $1 \neq 2$. This is the heart of the matter. What are numbers?

Russell himself wrote little stories about number devils. One is called "The Mathematician's Nightmare." We are introduced to a Professor Squarepunt, who dozes off after a long day of working in what he took to be a Platonic realm of numbers. In his sleeping thoughts a drama unfolded in which he stood at the center of endless concentric circles of numbers transfigured into passionate, living, breathing beings engaged in a ballet, each presenting its own merits to the conductor with π at the center. Russell wrote:

> Pi's face was masked, and it was understood that none could behold it and live. . . . Throughout the ballet the Professor [Squarepunt] had noticed one number among the primes 137, which seemed unruly and unwilling to accept its place in

the series. . . . At length 137 exclaimed: "There's a damned sight too much bureaucracy here! What I want is liberty for the individual." Pi's masked frowned. But the professor interceded, saying, "Do not be too hard on him. I should like to hear what 137 has to say." Somewhat reluctantly, Pi consented. Professor Squarepunt said: "Tell me, 137, what is the basis of your revolt." . . . At this, 137, burst into excited speech: "It is their metaphysic that I cannot bear. They still pretend that they are eternal, though long ago their conduct showed that they think no such thing. We all found Plato's heaven dull and decided that it would be more fun to govern the sensible world. Since we descended from the Empyrean we have had emotions not unlike yours: each Odd loves its attendant Even; and the Evens feel kindly toward the Odds, in spite of finding them very odd. Our empire now is of this world, and when the world goes pop, we shall pop too."

Professor Squarepunt found himself in agreement with 137. But all the others, including Pi, considered him a blasphemer, and turned upon both him and the Professor. The infinite host, extending in all directions farther than the eye could reach, hurled themselves upon the poor Professor in an angry buzz. For a moment he was terrified. Then he pulled himself together and, suddenly recollecting his waking wisdom, he called out in stentorian tones: "Avant! You are only Symbolic Conveniences."

With a banshee wail, the whole vast array dissolved in mist. And, as he woke, the Professor heard himself saying, "So much for Plato."

(*NEP*, pp. 48–53)

So much, indeed, for Plato's realm of numbers as metaphysical objects residing in a mystical non-physical world and connected to reason by an innate intuition that can only be regarded as occult.[2] The number devil is a Platonist engaging in a mythology about objects that are numbers. We do well to follow Russell's explorations of the benefits of seeing through his deceptions.

NUMBER DEVILS

Cardinal numbers are not strange metaphysical objects. They are quantifiers no different from "all" and "some." To say all things are φ we write "$(\forall x)\varphi x$" To say that something is φ we write "$(\exists x)\varphi x$" To say there are exactly m-many φs we write "$\mathbf{m}_x \varphi_x$". This is the central foundation of the notion that arithmetic is part of the logic of quantification. There may well be substantive mysteries about how we know logic, but there are no new mysteries heaped yet upon them when it comes to our understanding of number. Number is a quantificational notion.

The central notion involved in cardinal number is the notion of one-to-one correspondence. This is a breakthrough due largely to Cantor. The notion is easy to express quantifcationally. The notion is even easier to picture.

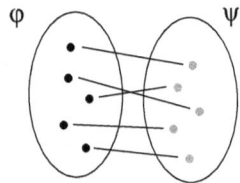

The notion applies whether the φs are finite or infinite and is the foundation of numbering. The objects having the attribute φ are in one-to-one correspondence with those having the attribute ψ just when there is a one-to-one function that assigns to each entity x that is a φ a unique y that is a ψ and to each y that is a ψ a unique x that is a φ. We can abbreviate this writing:

Card$_{x\,y}{}^{\psi y}[\varphi x]$.

This just says that the objects which are φ are in one-to-one correspondence with the objects that are ψ.

For centuries it was wrongly thought that a primitive (unanalyzable) notion of the consecutiveness of a series is at the core of the notion of natural number. The reason lies in taking everyday counting as the exemplar of numbering. Russell explains:

> The logic of counting, as fitted into the new theory is as follows: suppose, for example, that you are counting pound notes. By an act of will, you establish a one-one relation between the several notes and the numbers 1, 2, 3, etc., until there are no notes left. You then know, in accordance with our definition, that the number of notes is the same as the number of numbers that you have mentioned, and, if you have begun with 1 and gone on without skipping, the number of numbers that you have mentioned is the last number that you have mentioned. You cannot apply this process to infinite collections because life is not long enough. But, as counting is no longer essential, that need cause you no alarm.
>
> (*MPD*, p. 72)

In truth, however, counting is derivative from the more fundamental notion of one-to-one correspondence. Russell says:

> While numbers were derived from counting, which takes terms one by one, it was difficult to conceive of the numbers of collections which could not be exhaustively enumerated one at a time. You cannot, for example, come to an end of the finite numbers by counting; however long you go on, there are always larger numbers to come. Therefore, so long as numbers were derived from counting, it seemed impossible to speak of the number of finite numbers. Now, however, it appears that counting is only one way of discovering how many terms there are in a collection, and is only applicable to such collections that are finite.
>
> (*MPD*, p. 71)

Children display the relation of one-to-one correspondence by holding up fingers and saying "This many" in response the question "How many Fs are there?" They correlate each F one-to-one with a distinct finger. No parrot can do this—Alex notwithstanding.[3] When Professor Pepperberg, holding up two key-shaped objects, asks Alex "How many?" the proper reply would be "How many of what?" Contrary to the sleight of hand produced by our

48 Mathematics and the Metaphysicians

surprise in hearing the sound t̄ōō that Alex makes, the response reveals that the parrot is not correlating one-to-one.

The consecutiveness involved in counting is derivative from the more general notion of one-to-one correspondence. Of course, fingers do not make a viable standard for counting by one-to-one correspondence. We readily run out of fingers. Many standards are possible. But Frege quickly realized that the proper standard of correspondence is the numbers themselves. There are exactly two numbers less than or equal to 1, namely 0 and 1. There are exactly three numbers less than or equal to 2, and so on. To say that there are exactly n+1-many Fs is to say that each F is in one-to-one correspondence with the natural numbers less than or equal to n. Details aside, the key is to define the notion of one natural number (as a quantifier) being "less than or equal to" another. We are used to writing:

$m \leq n.$

And of course this means:

$m < n$ or $m = n.$

But in our notation which makes the quantificational nature of number clear, it looks like this:

$\mathbf{m}_x \varphi_x \leq_\varphi \mathbf{n}_x \varphi_x.$

And this means:

$\mathbf{m}_x \varphi_x <_\varphi \mathbf{n}_x \varphi_x$ or $\mathbf{m}_x \varphi_x \equiv_\varphi \mathbf{n}_x \varphi_x.$

It took the genius of Frege to show how to give the quantificational analysis embedded in the definition of:

$\mathbf{m}_x \varphi_x <_\varphi \mathbf{n}_x \varphi_x.$

But let us not pause to explain it here. For the present, it is enough to see that such expressions are quantificational.

How do we express "There are exactly zero many φs" quantificationally? Obviously, to say that there are exactly zero many φs is

Mathematics and the Metaphysicians   49

simply to say that there are no objects that are φ. In symbols, this is written as "$(\forall x)(\sim\varphi x)$." The sign "$(\forall x)(\ldots x \ldots)$" represents the universal quantification "Everything is such that ... it ..." The sign "φx" says that "x is φ." And of course "$\sim$" represents "not." These notions are such manifestly straightforward features of ordinary consciousness that it is not plausible to think of any humans without them. Indeed, it is often said that the Romans did not have the number zero. This is, of course, absurd. What the representational system of Roman numerals lacked was the numeral "0" and the feature of place value. For instance, we write "102" to mean that there are two entities in the one's box, zero in the groups of ten box, and one in the groups of one-hundred box. The numeral "0" is not important for place value. The Romans obviously understood that a box can be empty!

To have the concept zero is to be able to recognize, for some property φ, that nothing is φ. Frege offered a very natural way of analyzing all cardinal number notions in terms of quantificational notions of one-to-one correspondence. Let us introduce the following definition:

$$\mathbf{0}_x \varphi x =_{df} \mathbf{Card}_{xy}^{\,y \neq y} [\varphi x].$$

To say $\mathbf{0}_x \varphi x$ is to say that the objects that are φ are in one-to-one correspondence with the objects that are not self-identical. It follows that:

$$\mathbf{0}_x \varphi x \equiv_\varphi (\forall x)\sim\varphi x.$$

This says that for all properties φ, there are exactly zero many φs if and only if everything fails to be φ.

The sign "$\equiv$" represents "if and only if." It is convenient, as we shall soon see, to hide the universal quantifier ranging over properties φ by subscripting and writing "$\equiv_\varphi$." That is, the expression simply abbreviates "$(\forall \varphi)(\mathbf{0}_x \varphi x \equiv (\forall x)\sim\varphi x)$." Frege goes on to analyze what it is to assert quantificationally that there is exactly one object that is φ. This yields:

50 Mathematics and the Metaphysicians

$$1_x \varphi x =_{df} \mathbf{Card}_{x\,m}{}^{mz\psi z \leq_\psi \, 0z\psi z} [\varphi x].$$

To say that there is exactly one object that is φ is to say that φs are in one-to-one correspondence with numbers less than or equal to zero. It follows that:

$$1_x \varphi x \equiv_\varphi (\exists x)(\varphi y \equiv_y y = x).$$

This says that for all properties φ, there is exactly one φ if and only if something is uniquely φ. Consider the case where φ is the property of being a natural satellite of earth. There is exactly one natural satellite of earth if and only if something (i.e. the moon) is uniquely a natural satellite of earth. The expression "$(\exists x)(\varphi y \equiv_y y = x)$" involves the some quantifier "$(\exists x)(\ldots x \ldots)$" but also involves "$\varphi y \equiv_y y = x$." This uses the convenience of hiding the universal quantifier "$(\forall y)(\ldots y \ldots)$." It abbreviates "$(\forall y)(\varphi y \equiv y = x)$." Similarly, we can go on to the numeric quantifier "exactly two." We have:

$$2_x \varphi x =_{df} \mathbf{Card}_{x\,m}{}^{mz\psi z \leq_\psi \, 1z\psi z} [\varphi x].$$

To say that there are exactly two objects that are φ is to say that φs are in one-to-one correspondence with numbers less than or equal to one, namely zero and one. It follows that:

$$2_x \varphi x \equiv_\varphi (\exists x)(\exists z)((\varphi x \ \& \ \varphi z) \ \& \ x \neq z \ .\&. \ \varphi y \supset_y (y = x.v.y = z)).$$

This says that for all properties φ, there are exactly two φs if and only if something x is φ and some other thing z is φ and everything that is φ is equal to one of those. This holds, for example, where φ is the property of being a natural satellite of Mars. There are exactly two natural satellites of Mars if and only if there are distinct objects (i.e. Phobos and Deimos), both of which are natural satellites of Mars, and everything that is a natural satellite of Mars is equal to either Deimos or to Phobos. The expression "$(\exists x)(\exists z)((\varphi x \ \& \ \varphi z) \ \& \ x \neq z \ .\&. \ \varphi y \supset_y (y = x.v.y = z))$" has the component "$\varphi y \supset_y (y = x.v.y = z)$." The sign "⊃" is for "implies" (where "p implies q" is taken to mean either not p or q). Once again the subscript hides a universal quantifier over y. It abbreviates "$(\forall y)(\varphi y \supset (y = x.v.y = z))$". We can go on in this way indefinitely to form number concepts as quantifiers.

It was not until the pioneering work of Frege that quantificational and numeric statements were discovered to the same in kind. It is a discovery which remains as surprising as Lavoisier's oxygen theory of combustion—a theory that rusting is slow oxidization and fire is rapid oxidization. There is a sort of concreteness achieved by assigning numbers which helps avoid the abstractness of quantification. But numeric quantification is ubiquitous in ordinary arguments. Consider the following: Most S are P; Most S are Q; Therefore, Some P are Q. To find out if it is logically valid, one must be able to understand precisely how it is that the natural language quantifier "most" expresses a numerical concept. Expressed quantificationally, "Most S are P" is this:

$$\text{Card}_{x\,y}^{Sy\ \&\ \sim Py}\,[\varphi x] <_\varphi \text{Card}_{x\,y}^{Sy\ \&\ Py}\,[\varphi x].$$

This says that the cardinal number of entities that are S and are not P is less than the cardinal number of entities that are S and are also P. In offering a diagram and assigning a specific (though unknown) number a to the region in S and out of P and Q and assigning b to the region in S and in P and out of Q the matter becomes clearer.

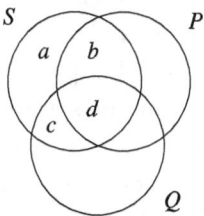

Thus in asserting "Most S are P" we have $(a + c) < (b + d)$. The second premise then can be said to express that $(a + b) < (c + d)$. If the conclusion were false then $d = 0$. A little algebra then yields a contradiction. It is logically impossible for the premises to be true and the conclusion to be false.

Mathematics and the Metaphysicians

One might think to object, as did Piaget, that no child could write out these formulas. Indeed, to write these equivalences down, one must already be able to count; one must grasp the natural numbers and count the number of variables "x," "y," etc. This is correct, but it is not a criticism of Frege/Russell. Understanding the concept of numbering certainly does not involve writing anything. It is a rather deplorable feature of modern education that it is so late that quantificational expressions such as the above are taught in schools. Quantificational thinking is something that is immediate to very young children. Children think numerically because they think quantificationally. They certainly do not discover properties of metaphysical objects that are numbers.

Number devils will, of course, be surprised that addition of natural numbers (understood quantificationally) can be defined without appeal to a primitive notion of a consecutive series of metaphysical objects that are numbers. Such devils are right to point out that arithmetic addition is certainly not the notion of putting objects close together. For all we know, physics might have it that if you get objects close enough together then new particles are generated by the surge in energy! The notion of arithmetic addition is not any better definable in terms of mixing. If you combine one cup of water and one cup of sugar, the result is not two cups of mixture. The sugar is dissolved into the water. What then is the definition of arithmetic addition? It is not anything empirical. All the same, the number devils that imagine numbers to be special objects are not helping matters. As long as natural numbers are imagined to be objects, arithmetic addition will ever remain a Platonic mystery, something tied to the notion of being next in a consecutive series of numbers. With numbers as quantifiers, however, the mystery is solved. The familiar expression

$$1 + 1 = 2$$

is really a convenient way of expressing the more careful and exacting quantificational expression

$(1 + 1)_x \varphi x \equiv_\varphi 2_x \varphi x.$

This says for any property φ, there are exactly 1+1 many φs if and only if there are exactly 2 φs.

If we write this out with all its hidden quantifiers we find the following intimidating formulas:

$(\mathbf{x+y})_x \varphi x =_{df} (\mathbf{x}_z Fz +_{FG} \mathbf{y}_z Gz)_x \varphi x$
$(\mathbf{x}_z Fz +_{FG} \mathbf{y}_z Gz)_x \varphi x = df$
$(\exists F)(\exists G)(\mathbf{x}_x \theta x \equiv_\theta \mathbf{Card}_{xy}^{Fy}[\theta x] :\&: \mathbf{y}_x \theta x \equiv_\theta \mathbf{Card}_{xy}^{Gy}[\theta x] .\&.$
$(\forall x)(Fx \supset \sim Gx) \,\&\, \mathbf{Card}_{xy}^{Fy \vee Gy}[\varphi x]).$[4]

But let us take a simple example. The expression $(1 + 1)_x \varphi x$ says that there 1+1 many φs. The idea is that we can find F and G such that there is exactly one object that is F and there is exactly one object that is G and no Fs are Gs and objects that are φ are in one-to-one correspondence with objects that are either F or G. Arithmetic addition is neither putting objects close together, nor mixing. It is grouping. A group F of exactly one and a group G of exactly one (where nothing is in both groups) is such that the union of the groups yields a group of exactly two. No young child can write it out and the number devil of our children's book made fun of Lord Russell's (Rustle's) even more technical expression of it in *Principia*. But it is not implausible at all that this is precisely what children understand by arithmetic addition. A child might express it by saying, "(Exactly) one of something and (exactly) one of something else make (exactly) two of these things."

Multiplication is naturally more complicated than addition. Multiplication is repeated addition. For convenience we write the familiar expression:

$2 \times 3 = 6.$

This convenient expression hides the quantifiers of the more careful expression:

$(2 \times 3)_x \varphi x \equiv_\varphi 6_x \varphi x.$

54 Mathematics and the Metaphysicians

This says that for any property φ, there are exactly 2 × 3 many φs if and only if there are exactly 6 φs.

The notation $(\mathbf{x} \times \mathbf{y})_x \varphi_x$ says that there are exactly $\mathbf{x} \times \mathbf{y}$ many φs. The full definition, with all its hidden quantifiers, is this:

$(\mathbf{x} \times \mathbf{y})_x \varphi x =_{df} (\mathbf{x}_z Fz \times_{FG} \mathbf{y}_z Gz)_x \varphi x$

$(\mathbf{x}_z Fz \times_{FG} \mathbf{y}_z Gz)_x \varphi x =_{df}$

$(\exists M) (\mathbf{Card}_{x\,y}^{(\exists G)(MzGz\ \&\ Gy)}[\varphi x]\ \&\ (y_z \varphi z \equiv_\varphi \mathbf{Card}_{Fx}^{MzFz}[\varphi x])$
 .&. $(\forall F)(\forall G)((M_x Fx\ \&\ M_x Gx \supset (\forall z)(Fz \supset \sim Gz))\ \&$
 & $(\forall F)(M_x Fx \supset \mathbf{x}_z \varphi z \equiv_\varphi \mathbf{Card}_{x\,y}^{Fy}[\varphi x]))$.

Children learn to multiply by learning to add repeatedly. There are $\mathbf{x} \times \mathbf{y}$ many φs means that we take the cardinal number of the union of a collection M of **y**-many non-overlapping attributes F, G, etc., each of which has exactly **x**-many objects exemplifying it. Once again, it is a bugbear to write out. Children do not write it, they do it.

But what is it to be a natural number? Frege showed how to answer this question. The key is to characterize the notion of a consecutive series without appeal to special intuitions of the numbers themselves. Natural numbers, of course, are paradigmatic of a consecutive series. We have:

0, 1, 2, 3, 4, . . .

The series is structured in such a way that the next after any given number is generated by adding 1. Thus, before Frege the notions of addition and 1 and number and consecutiveness were thought to be primitive and unanalyzable. Frege showed how to understand all these notions quantificationally.

The notion is that one cardinal numbering $\mathbf{b}_x \psi x$ comes immediately after another $\mathbf{a}_x \psi x$ in a consecutive series generated by adding $\mathbf{1}_x \psi x$. The notion is defined as follows:

$a_x\varphi x \; P_\varphi \; b_x\varphi x =df \; (a + 1) \;_x\varphi x \equiv_\varphi b_x\varphi x.$

Frege's genius shows how to go on to quantificationally analyze the notion that one cardinal comes somewhere after another in the consecutive **P** series. This is given by the following definition:

$a_x\psi x <_\psi b_x\psi x =df$
$(\forall F)(a_x\psi x \; P_\psi \; y_x\psi x \supset_y F_\varphi[y_x\varphi x] \; .\&.$
$\quad (F_\varphi[y_x\varphi x] \; .\&. \; y_x\psi x P_\psi \; z_x\psi x : \supset_{x, y} : F_\varphi[z_x\varphi x]) : \supset : F_\varphi[b_x\varphi x]).$

This idea here is that one can arrive at $b_x\psi x$ starting from $a_x\psi x$ by consecutively repeating adding $1_x\psi x$. It is Frege's greatest achievement to have discovered that this idea is definable within logic, requiring no non-logical intuitions of sequence or consecutive infinite series. The notion of a natural number is this:

$N_\varphi[b_x\varphi x] =df \; 0x\psi x <_\psi b_x\psi x \; .v. \; 0_x\varphi x \equiv_\varphi b_x\varphi x.$

The cardinality concept $b_x\varphi x$ is a natural number if it is equal to $0_x\varphi x$ or comes somewhere after $0_x\varphi x$ in the consecutive series defined by the P relation. Natural numbers are the cardinals that are greater than or equal to 0 in the P series. These are the finite cardinals. Indeed, we can define as follows:

$\text{Finite}_x [\psi x] =df \; (\exists a)(N_\varphi[a_x\varphi x] \; .\&. \; a_x\psi x).$

To say that there are finitely many ψs is just to say that some natural number a is such that there are exactly a-many ψs. Infinite is, as expected, the negation of the finite. We have:

$\text{Infinite}_x [\psi x] =df \; \sim\text{Finite}_x [\psi x].$

To say that infinitely many objects have a property ψ is to say that no natural number numbers the ψs. The natural numbers are finite cardinals.

HONEST TOIL OVER THEFT

Dedekind's theory of irrational and real numbers, Russell tells us, brought into prominence the idea of dividing all terms of a series into two classes of which the one wholly precedes the other. Dedekind divided the ratios into two classes, according as their squares are less than 2 or not. All the terms of the one class are less than all in the other. There is no maximum (i.e. the greatest term of the ordering) to the class of ratios whose square is less than 2, and there is no minimum to those whose square is greater than 2. Between these two classes is the Dedekind "gap" where $\sqrt{2}$ ought to be, but there is no term. Russell wrote:

> From the habit of being influenced by spatial imagination, people have supposed that series *must* have limits in cases where it seems odd if they do not. Thus, perceiving there was no *rational* limit to the ratios whose square is less than 2, some allowed themselves to "postulate" an *irrational* limit which was to fill the Dedekind gap. Dedekind . . . set up the axiom that the gap must always be filled, i.e., that every section must have a boundary.
>
> (*IMP*, p. 71)

Russell then quips: "The method of postulating what we want has many advantages; they are the same as the advantages of theft over honest toil" (IMP, p. 71). The deviousness of number devils involves their refusal to explain what numbers are. Frege was first to discover the nature of cardinal numbers—a discovery that Russell made independently some eighteen years later. But what are integers? What are rational numbers and irrational numbers? Not a few mathematicians agonized over these questions, and answers were found. Russell subsumes these discoveries into his logicism, adding some of his own.

There are some equations of natural numbers that have no solutions. Consider the familiar equations from grammar school:

$$m \times 2 = 1.$$

Any teacher will tell you that this equation has a solution in the rationals. But, as a child, I could never quite grasp what a rational could be as a number. I had a reasonable intuition of taking $\frac{1}{2}$ of something. But $\frac{1}{2}$ as a number seemed to be unintelligible to me. Russell would have told me that the above equation is really

$$(\mathbf{m}_z F_z \times_{FG} \mathbf{2}_z G_z)_x \varphi x \equiv_\varphi \mathbf{1}_x \varphi x.$$

This equation has no solution. Mathematicians have constructed a new equation to replace this equation. It is the new equation that has a solution.

To see the construction, let us begin with the following definitions which introduce notations for the relations of natural numbers that give rise to the constructions of the ratios. We have:

$$\left(\frac{p}{q}\right)_{x/y} = df\ x \left(\frac{p}{q}\right) y$$

$$x \left(\frac{p}{q}\right) y = df\ xq = py$$

The expression $\left(\frac{p}{q}\right)_{x/y}$ just says that x bears the relation $\frac{p}{q}$ to y. And our definition defines this to mean that x multiplied by q equals p multiplied by y. For convenience we have hidden quantificational structures essential to the natural numbers. But these could readily be revealed—at the price of tedium.

For example, $x \left(\frac{p}{q}\right) y$ is just a convenient way of avoiding the complications of writing out the complex quantificational structure of

$$x_z F z \left(\frac{p_x F x}{q_x G x}\right)_{FG} y_z G z$$

The convenience does not lead to confusion as long as we accept that we mean to be speaking of natural numbers with our x, y, p, q, etc.

It may be thought that these constructions of rationals seem too narrow. They omit definitions appropriate to expressions such as $\dfrac{\left(\dfrac{1}{2}\right)}{\left(\dfrac{1}{4}\right)}$. Clearly we can repeat the definitions. For example:

$$\dfrac{x}{y}\left|\dfrac{\left(\dfrac{a}{b}\right)}{\left(\dfrac{c}{d}\right)}\right|\dfrac{z}{w} =_{df} \dfrac{x}{y} \times \dfrac{c}{d} = \dfrac{a}{b} \times \dfrac{z}{w}.$$

In this way the needed constructions can be easily accommodated.[5] Indeed we get the familiar result:

$$\dfrac{x}{1}\left|\dfrac{\left(\dfrac{a}{b}\right)}{\left(\dfrac{c}{d}\right)}\right|\dfrac{z}{1} \equiv_{x\,z} x \left(\dfrac{a \times d}{c \times b}\right) z.$$

This is conveniently written as:

$$\dfrac{\left(\dfrac{a}{b}\right)}{\left(\dfrac{c}{d}\right)} = \dfrac{a \times d}{c \times b}.$$

But let us not pause here further for details.

The next step in construction of rationals as ratios is to define a new notion of the "identity" of ratios. We have the following definition:

$$\dfrac{p}{q} = \dfrac{r}{s} =_{df} \left(\dfrac{p}{q}\right)_{x/y} \equiv_{x\,y} \left(\dfrac{r}{s}\right)_{x/y}.$$

Mathematics and the Metaphysicians   59

Thus, for instance, $\frac{1}{2} = \frac{3}{6}$ since for all natural numbers x and y, $2x = 1y$ if and only if $6x = 3y$. As we see, the identity sign between rationals gives way to the biconditional sign and quantification over natural numbers.[6] We can also see that, given our definitions, rational numbers are not distinct from fractions in the present system. It is now straightforward to define "addition" for ratios:

$$\left(\frac{p}{q} + \frac{r}{s}\right)_{e/f} = df \left(\left(\frac{p}{q}\right)_{a/b} + \left(\frac{r}{s}\right)_{abcd} \left(\frac{r}{s}\right)_{c/d}\right)_{e/f}$$

$$\left(\left(\frac{p}{q}\right)_{a/b} + \left(\frac{r}{s}\right)_{c/d}\right)_{e/f} = df \left(\exists\, a, b, c, d\right) \left(\left(\frac{p}{q}\right)_{a/b} \& \left(\frac{r}{s}\right)_{c/d} .\&. \frac{ad + bc}{bd} = \frac{e}{f}\right).$$

Similarly we can define "multiplication" of ratios:

$$\left(\frac{p}{q} \times \frac{r}{s}\right)_{e/f} = df \left(\left(\frac{p}{q}\right)_{a/b} \times \left(\frac{r}{s}\right)_{c/d}\right)_{e/f}$$

$$\left(\left(\frac{p}{q}\right)_{a/b} \times \left(\frac{r}{s}\right)_{c/d}\right)_{e/f} = df \left(\exists\, a, b, c, d\right) \left(\left(\frac{p}{q}\right)_{a/b} \& \left(\frac{r}{s}\right)_{c/d} .\&. \frac{ac}{bd} = \frac{e}{f}\right).$$

These are new notions of addition and multiplication which are related to the definitions for the natural numbers, but they are certainly quite different from them. Quite clearly the multiplication of ratios is not a notion of repeated addition (as in the notion of multiplication of natural numbers). One cannot make sense of, say, $\frac{1}{2} \times \frac{3}{4}$ by saying that it involves adding $\frac{1}{2}$ to itself $\frac{3}{4}$ many times! Multiplication of ratios has a new meaning. Nonetheless, from the new definitions we get the expected theorems:

$$\left(\frac{p}{q} + \frac{r}{s}\right)_{e/f\ ef} \equiv \left(\frac{ps + qr}{qs}\right)_{e/f}$$

$$\left(\frac{p}{q} \times \frac{r}{s}\right)_{e/f\ ef} \equiv \left(\frac{pr}{qs}\right)_{e/f}.$$

Mathematics and the Metaphysicians

It is straightforward to write out these definitions in a way that restores the quantificational structures of the Russellian natural numbers that they hide. As before, ordinary arithmetic languages drop the quantificational understructure and write the convenient expressions:

$$\frac{p}{q} + \frac{r}{s} = \frac{ps + qr}{qs}$$

$$\frac{p}{q} \times \frac{r}{s} = \frac{pr}{qs}.$$

Obviously, it is very convenient to simply write

$$\frac{1}{4} \times \left(\frac{1}{2} + \frac{1}{4}\right) = \frac{3}{16}$$

instead of the cumbersome expression:

$$\left[\left(\frac{1}{4}\right)_{a/b} \times_{abcd} \left(\frac{1}{2} + \frac{1}{4}\right)_{c/d}\right]_{e/f} \equiv_{ef} \left(\frac{3}{16}\right)_{e/f}.$$

But that convenience does not undermine the thesis that the quantificational structures are part of the ordinary meaning (and analysis) of the notions involved.

Now we saw that some equations of natural numbers have no solutions. Our example was the following equation:

$$(m_z Fz \times_{FG} 2_z G_z)_x \varphi x \equiv_\varphi 1_x \varphi x.$$

We can however, replace this equation with another that has a solution in the natural numbers. The new equation looks rather different from the original only when the quantificational structures are depicted. The new equation is this:

$$\left(\frac{p}{q} \times \frac{2}{1}\right)_{x/y} \equiv_{xy} \left(\frac{1}{1}\right)_{x/y}.$$

Mathematics and the Metaphysicians

This equation has many solutions for natural numbers p and q. For example, it holds when $p = 1$ and $q = 2$. It holds as well when $p = 3$ and $q = 6$, and when $p = 4$ and $q = 8$. But all these solutions are "identical" when identity is defined for ratios. That is, $\frac{1}{2} = \frac{3}{6} = \frac{4}{8}$. We can then elevate all the equations for natural numbers, even those that had solutions, to the structure of the ratios. We can put:

$$\text{Natural Ratio}_{xy}\left(\frac{p}{q}\right)_{x/y} =_{df} \text{Ratio}_{xy}\left(\frac{p}{q}\right)_{x/y} \& \, (\exists r)\left(\frac{p}{q} = \frac{r}{1}\right).$$

In virtue of this rewriting, we can say the solution of the new equation

$$\left(\frac{p}{q} \times \frac{2}{1}\right)_{x/y} \underset{xy}{\equiv} \left(\frac{1}{1}\right)_{x/y}$$

is not "in the natural ratios" because $\frac{p}{q} = \frac{1}{2}$. In contrast the equation

$$\left(\frac{p}{q} \times \frac{2}{1}\right)_{x/y} \underset{xy}{\equiv} \left(\frac{6}{1}\right)_{x/y}$$

has a solution "in the natural ratios" since $\frac{p}{q} = \frac{3}{1}$.

The notion of *less than* between ratios is analyzed in the expected way. The following is undoubtedly familiar:

$$\frac{p}{q} < \frac{r}{s} =_{df} (\exists x)(x \neq 0 \,.\&. \, \frac{p}{q} + x = \frac{r}{s}).$$

But it is very misleading. A definition that properly represents the nature of rationals as ratios is this:

$$\left(\frac{p}{q} < \frac{r}{s}\right)_{m/n} =_{df} \left(\frac{p}{q}\right)_{m/n} \underset{mn}{<} \left(\frac{r}{s}\right)_{m/n}.$$

Mathematics and the Metaphysicians

$$\left(\frac{p}{q}\right)_{m/n} < \left(\frac{r}{s}\right)_{m\ n} = df\ (\exists x, y)\left(\frac{x}{y} \neq \frac{0}{1}\ \&\ \left(\frac{p}{q} + \frac{x}{y}\right) = \frac{r}{s}\right).$$

Again, it is convenient to continue the practice of abbreviation which removes all signs of the quantificational structure underlying the constructions. We then have the commonplace expression:

$$\frac{p}{q} < \frac{r}{s}.$$

Of course, we can go on to incorporate a construction of positive and negative (signed) numbers, applying it to signed rationals.

Some important theorems follow from the analysis of rationals if we can be assured that the addition of two natural numbers always yields a new number. (See this section below in this chapter on the number of numbers.) We get:

$$(\forall p, q, r, s)\left(\frac{p}{q} < \frac{r}{s} . \supset . \frac{p}{q} < \frac{p+r}{q+s}\ \&\ \frac{p+r}{q+s} < \frac{r}{s}\right).$$

This then yields the denseness of the rationals:

$$(\forall p, q, r, s)(\exists a, b)\left(\frac{p}{q} < \frac{r}{s} . \supset . \frac{p}{q} < \frac{a}{b}\ \&\ \frac{a}{b} < \frac{r}{s}\right).$$

The denseness of the rationals is essential to the construction of irrational numbers.

What are irrational numbers? Obviously there is no natural number m which can satisfy the equation $m \times m = 2$. But it will not help, in this case, to elevate the equation to ratios, rewriting it as:

$$\left(\frac{p}{q} \times \frac{p}{q}\right) = \frac{2}{1}.$$

No natural numbers p and q form a ratio that solves this equation. A new construction is needed.

Mathematics and the Metaphysicians

Dedekind showed the way. Observe that the series of ratios $\frac{p}{q}$ such that $\frac{p^2}{q^2} < \frac{2}{1}$ has no last term. Because of the denseness of the ratios we can continually get closer to $\frac{2}{1}$ without ever reaching it. The construction in terms of series of ratios can be done generally so that irrational numbers are series of ratios which have no ratio as their last term. This feature of irrationals shows up in the fact that, when expressed in decimal notation, the digits never repeat. (Every repeating decimal represents a ratio.) The structure of the irrational real numbers is introduced by appeal to Russell's improvement of Dedekind's ingenious idea of "cuts" in the series of rationals.

Russell analyzes a Real number as the lower section of a Dedekind cut. It is a series of ratios. For convenience, we shall call Russell's lower-sections "Reals." The Russellian notion is expressed in the present symbolism as follows:

$$\text{Real}_{pq}\{\xi_{p/q}\} = df\ (\exists p, q)\ \xi_{p/q}\ .\&.\ (\exists\ p, q) \sim \xi_{p/q}\ .\&.$$

$$(\forall p, q, r, s) \left(\xi_{p/q}\ .\&.\ \sim \xi_{r/s} : \supset : \frac{p}{q} < \frac{r}{s} \right) .\&.$$

$$\sim (\exists\ p, q) \left(\xi_{p/q}\ \&\ (\forall r, s) \left(\xi_{r/s}\ \&\ \sim \left(\frac{p}{q} = \frac{r}{s} \right) . \supset . \frac{p}{q} > \frac{r}{s} \right) \right).$$

Notations defining less-than and greater-than for Reals follow:

$$\xi_{p/q} <_{pq} \delta_{p/q} = df\ \text{Real}_{pq}\{\xi_{p/q}\}\ \&\ \text{Real}_{pq}\{\delta_{p/q}\}\ \&$$
$$(\exists\ a, b)(\delta_{a/b}\ \&\ \sim \xi_{a/b})$$
$$\xi_{p/q} >_{pq} \delta_{p/q} = df\ \text{Real}_{pq}\{\xi_{p/q}\}\ \&\ \text{Real}_{pq}\{\delta_{p/q}\}\ \&$$
$$(\exists\ a, b)(\xi_{a/b}\ \&\ \sim \delta_{a/b}).$$

Similarly, addition and multiplication for Reals is as follows:

$$(\xi + \delta)_{r/s} = df\ (\xi_{p/q} +_{pq} \delta_{p/q})_{r/s}$$

64 Mathematics and the Metaphysicians

$(\xi_{p/q} +_{pq} \delta_{p/q})_{r/s} = df$
$Real_{pq}\{\xi_{p/q}\}$ & $Real_{pq}\{\delta_{p/q}\}$ &
$(\exists\, a, b, c, d) \left(\xi_{a/b}\ \&\ \delta_{c/d}\ \&.\ \dfrac{r}{s} = \dfrac{ad + bc}{bd} \right)$
$(\xi \times \delta)_{r/s} = df\ (\varphi_{p/q} \times_{pq} \delta_{p/q})_{r/s}$
$(\xi_{p/q} \times_{pq} \delta_{p/q})_{r/s} = df$
$Real_{pq}\{\xi_{p/q}\}$ & $Real_{pq}\{\delta_{p/q}\}$ & $(\exists\, a, b, c, d) \left(\xi_{a/b}\ \&\ \delta_{c/d}\ \&.\ \dfrac{r}{s} = \dfrac{ac}{bd} \right).$

It is readily provable, given there are infinitely many natural numbers, that

$Real_{pq}\{\xi_{p/q}\}$ & $Real_{pq}\{\delta_{p/q}\}\ .\supset.\ Real_{r\,s}\ \{(\xi + \delta)_{r/s}\}$
$Real_{pq}\{\xi_{p/q}\}$ & $Real_{pq}\{\delta_{p/q}\}\ .\supset.\ Real_{r\,s}\ \{(\xi \times \delta)_{r/s}\}.$

Operations of commutation, association, and distribution for addition and multiplication apply to Reals.

We now have expressions in terms of Reals that replace the expressions for natural numbers.

We employ definitions such as the following:

$$0_{p/q} = df\ \dfrac{p}{q} < \dfrac{0}{1}$$

$$1_{p/q} = df\ \dfrac{p}{q} < \dfrac{1}{1}$$

$$2_{p/q} = df\ \dfrac{p}{q} < \dfrac{2}{1}.$$

It is easy to show that all of these are Reals. Next we have expressions such as these:

$(2 \times 3)_{r/s}\ .\equiv_{r\,s}\ .\ 6_{r/s}.$

Writing out the definition, this is:

$$(2_{p/q} \times_{pq} 3_{p/q})_{r/s} \equiv_{r\,s}\ .\ \dfrac{r}{s} < \dfrac{6}{1}.$$

Mathematics and the Metaphysicians   65

Observe, of course, that the real number $\mathbf{0}_{p/q}$ is neither the same as the ratio number $\dfrac{0}{1}$, nor the same as the natural number $\mathbf{0}_x \varphi x$, though they are all related. Similarly, we can rewrite equations for cardinals:

$$(\xi \times 3)_{r/s} \cdot \equiv_{rs} \cdot 6_{r/s}.$$

The solution is now the Real $\mathbf{2}_{p/q}$. It should be noted that, for example, in uses of $\mathbf{1}_{p/q}$ we can fill in all the hidden quantifier expressions showing its genealogy all the way back to the Fregean natural number $\mathbf{1}_x \varphi x$. The "1" appearing in $\mathbf{1}_{p/q}$ is the same as appears in $\mathbf{1}_x \varphi x$. It is not a new number, a "real number 1" as opposed to the "natural number 1" that is involved in the Reals. Nonetheless, the structure is quite different. We just put:

$$\text{Natural Real}_{p\,q}\,\{\xi_{p/q}\} = df\ \text{Real}_{p\,q}\,\{\xi_{p/q}\}\ \&\ (\exists r)\left(\xi_{p/q} \cdot \equiv_{p\,q} \cdot \frac{p}{q} < \frac{r}{1}\right).$$

In like manner, we have:

$$\text{Rational Real}_{p\,q}\,\{\xi_{p/q}\} = df\ \text{Real}_{p\,q}\,\{\xi_{p/q}\}\ \&\ (\exists r, s)\left(\xi_{p/q} \equiv_{p\,q} \frac{p}{q} < \frac{r}{s}\right).$$

Indeed we now have:

$$\text{Irrational Real}_{p\,q}\,\{\xi_{p/q}\} = df\ \text{Real}_{p\,q}\,\{\xi_{p/q}\}\ \&$$
$$\sim (\exists r, s)\left(\xi_{p/q} \cdot \equiv_{p\,q} \cdot \frac{p}{q} < \frac{r}{s}\right).$$

These definitions are expected.

The great value of the structure of Reals is that we can replace equations that had no solutions by analogous equations that do have solutions. We saw that there is no natural number $\mathbf{m}$, such that

$$(\mathbf{m} \times \mathbf{m})_x \varphi x \equiv_\varphi \mathbf{2}_x \varphi x.$$

Mathematics and the Metaphysicians

There is no square root of the natural number 2. We cannot replace the equation with:

$$\left(\frac{p}{q} \times \frac{p}{q}\right)_{r/s} \equiv_{r\,s} \left(\frac{2}{1}\right)_{r/s}.$$

There is no rational number $\frac{p}{q}$ such that $\frac{p^2}{q^2} = \frac{2}{1}$. With the technique of Reals, however, this equation can be replaced by a new equation, namely:

$$(\xi \times \xi)_{r/s} \equiv_{r\,s} 2_{r/s}.$$

Here we have the Real variable $\xi_{p/q}$. There is a Real that satisfies this equation, namely $\frac{p^2}{q^2} < \frac{2}{1}$. That is we put:[7]

$$(\sqrt{2})_{p/q} =_{df} \frac{p^2}{q^2} < \frac{2}{1}.$$

We find that:

$$\{\sqrt{2} \times \sqrt{2}\}_{r/s} \equiv_{r\,s} 2_{r/s}.$$

As always, convenience carries the day, and we write:

$$\sqrt{2} \times \sqrt{2} = 2.$$

But this says that there is a Real, an irrational number $(\sqrt{2})_{p/q}$, which is the square root of the Real $2_{p/q}$. By honest toil, as Russell puts it, we have found our square root of 2.

Of course, we can go further and incorporate definitions for signed (positive and negative) numbers allowing signed Reals. But the idea of the reconstruction should be clear. By replacing all our equations in this way, we generate the so-called "system" of so-called "Real numbers" which in a sense includes the natural numbers, the rationals, and the irrationals. We can go on to define complex numbers (e.g. the square root of -1) as ordered pairs of signed Reals. It is important to realize that these analyses were invented by mathematicians, including Russell. Russell is simply demanding that the analyses be taken seriously as giving the nature of the numbers. The integers, the rationals, and the irrationals and complex numbers are relations. The notion that they are all alike is a useful fiction told to schoolchildren out of fear that the truth is too obscure for them to grasp. But it is high time to tell the truth about "numbers." The number devil's phantasms must be finally revealed.

TAMING THE INFINITE

Unfortunately, the notion of one-to-one correspondence—the very foundation of the notion of cardinality—was more often than not viewed as paradoxical. Its significance was largely missed until Cantor's work. Galileo felt it paradoxical that there is an arithmetic function $fn = 2n$ that pairs off each natural number one-to-one with an even natural number. We are used to being able to infer in practical circumstance that there are more As than Bs if all the As are Bs and some Bs are not As. This, however, relies on there being finitely many Bs. Cantor dissolved such paradoxes by maintaining that the properly arithmetic notion of *more* should not be muddied by empirical experiences with finite groups of physical objects. Cantor offers this:

There are cardinally the same number of As as Bs $(A \approx B) = df$
   The As and Bs are in one-to-one correspondence.
There are arithmetically more Bs than As $(A < B) = df$
   The As are one-to-one with a proper part of the Bs and Bs are not one-to-one with a proper part of the As.

A very important consequence results from applying these notions to rational numbers. Given there are infinitely many natural numbers, there is a rational number between any two rational numbers. This is called the "denseness" of the rational numbers. Nonetheless, Cantor is able to prove that, given his notion of sameness of cardinality, there are the same number of rational numbers as there are natural numbers. That is, there is an arithmetic function that correlates them one-to-one. Intuitively, one can easily see this from an array.

$$N \times N = N$$

```
  0         1         3         6        10
(0,0)─────►(0,1)    (0,2)     (0,3)    (0,4)   ...
  2         4         7        11
(1,0)     (1,1)     (1,2)     (1,3)     ...    ...
  5         8        12
(2,0)     (2,1)     (2,2)     (2,3)     ...    ...
  9        13
(3,0)     (3,1)     (3,2)     (3,3)     ...
 14
(4,0)      ⋮         ⋮         ⋮
  ⋮
```

Since the ratios (rational numbers) are all among the ordered pairs, where (m, n) is just $\frac{m}{n}$ and n is not 0, the array makes it intuitively clear that the rational numbers are in one-to-one correspondence with the natural numbers. But formally what is required is an arithmetic function $f(m, n)$ that yields a one-to-one correspondence between each ordered pair of natural numbers m, n, and a natural number. The function for the above array is this: $\frac{(m+n)(m+n+1)}{2} + m$. Indeed, we can see that once we have this correspondence, it follows that the ordered n-tuples of natural numbers are in one-to-one correspondence with the natural numbers. Any property such that the objects which have it can be put in one-to-one correspondence with the natural numbers is said to be "denumerable."

With these results, one might naturally wonder whether there is a one-to-one correspondence function between natural numbers and numbers such as $\sqrt{2}$, which are irrational. It might be thought,

Mathematics and the Metaphysicians

given our discovery that the ratios are one-to-one with natural numbers, that series of ratios are one-to-one with natural numbers. We know that series of ratios, which repeat when expressed in decimal notation, are one-to-one with natural numbers. But what of series of ratios generally? Cantor showed that every arithmetic function that assigns to each natural number a non-repeating series of ratios will leave some series of non-repeating ratios omitted. So series of ratios are not one-to-one with natural numbers!

Cantor's argument is deceptively simple. Consider just those series of ratios with no last term that are between $\frac{0}{1}$ and $\frac{1}{1}$ and suppose that there is a function that correlates each natural number with a series of ratios that never repeats and leaves no such series out. Here we are using decimal expression for each series of ratios that never repeats. That is $.a_1 a_2 a_3 \ldots a_n \ldots$ etc. represents:

$$\frac{a_1}{10} + \frac{a_2}{100} + \frac{a_3}{1{,}000} + \ldots + \frac{a_n}{10^n} \ldots \text{etc.}$$

As before, an array presents the intuition behind Cantor's diagonal argument.

$$
\begin{array}{ll}
0 & .a1, a2, a3, a4, \ldots \\
1 & .b1, b2, b3, b4, \ldots \\
2 & .c1, c2, c3, c4, \ldots \\
\end{array}
$$

and so on

We can find a series of ratios with no last term (i.e. non-repeating decimal) by following a diagonal path through the array changing a_1 and b_2 and c_3 and so on. Since this decimal never repeats and is distinct from all those in the array, it has been left out of the array! (This intuition relies on numerals, i.e. decimal expressions, for our series of ratios that have no last term. But this is inessential.) Of course, for every natural number there is a unique series of ratios that never repeats. Hence by Cantor's definition there are "more" series of ratios that do not repeat than there are natural numbers. The cardinal number of such series is $2^{\aleph_0}$.

Mathematics and the Metaphysicians

We are now in a position to "tame the infinite," as Cantor would put it. We can understand the notion of the cardinal number of Fs even when infinitely many objects have the property F. For example, the number of natural numbers themselves can be understood. We have:

$$(\aleph_0)_x \varphi x =_{df} \mathbf{Card}_{x\,m}{}^{0z\psi z\,\leq_\psi\,mz\psi z}[\varphi x].$$

That is, $(\aleph_0)_x \varphi x$ says that there are as many objects that are φ as there are natural numbers greater than or equal to 0. We can see that $\aleph_0$ is not one among natural numbers. It is the first infinite cardinal which, following Cantor, is called "aleph naught." The above analysis of arithmetic addition applies to infinite and finite cases. For example, we have:

$$(\aleph_0 + 1)_x \varphi x \equiv_\varphi (\aleph_0)_x \varphi x.$$

This says that for every attribute φ there are exactly $\aleph_0 + 1$ many φs if and only if there are $\aleph_0$ many φs.

We can see why if we recall that there is a one-to-one correspondence between the odd natural numbers together with 0 and the odd natural numbers. Similarly, we have

$$(\aleph_0 + 2)_x \varphi x \equiv_\varphi (\aleph_0)_x \varphi x.$$

since there is a one-to-one correspondence between the odd natural numbers and the odd natural numbers together with 0 and 2. And of course this holds generally, so that for all natural numbers **n**

$$(\aleph_0 + n)_x \varphi x \equiv_\varphi (\aleph_0)_x \varphi x.$$

One cannot increase an infinite cardinality by the inclusion of more objects.

It is possible to multiply infinite cardinals. Indeed, multiplication can be defined so that it applies to both finite and infinite cases. This is defined by appeal to a relation which generates ordered pairs from the two groups being multiplied. We have:

Multiplication

$(\mathbf{a} \bullet \mathbf{b})_x \varphi x = df\ (\mathbf{a}_z Fz \times_{FG} \mathbf{b}_z Gz)_x \varphi x$
$(\mathbf{a}_z Fz \bullet_{FG} \mathbf{b}_z Gz)_x \varphi x = df$
$(\exists F)(\exists G)(\mathbf{a}_x \varphi x \equiv_\varphi \mathbf{Card}_{xy}^{Fy}[\varphi x]\ .\&.\ \mathbf{b}_x \varphi x \equiv_\varphi \mathbf{Card}_{xy}^{Gy}[\varphi x]\ :\&:$
$(\exists R)((R(z,w).\equiv_{z\,w}.\ Fz\ \&\ Gw\ :\&:\ \mathbf{Card}_{x\,uy}^{R(u,\,y)}[\varphi x]))$.

We have a group of **a**-many entities which are F and a group of **b**-many entities which are G. Then we find a relation R which forms ordered pairs <z, w> such that z is an F and w is a G, then we count the cardinal number of such pairs. The definition is easy to understand by examples. Let F contain just the letters a, b, c and let G contain just d, e, f. Then let the relation R form the following ordered pairs:

<a, d>, <a, e>, <a, f>, <b, d>, <b, e>, <b, f>, <c, d>, <c, e>, <c, f>

There are, of course, nine such pairs since $3 \bullet 3 = 9$.

This definition of multiplication applies if there are infinitely many Fs and/or infinitely many Gs. But Whitehead and Russell observed that in cases where infinity comes in, there are times when the existence of the relation generating the ordered pairs might be questioned. How are we to be certain that there is such a relation? If we can find a well-formed formula of the language such that entities satisfy if and only if they fall into such ordered pairs, then comprehension will assure that there is a relation. But it is far from clear how to find such a formula (i.e. a recipe) that does the work. Russell gives a nice example of socks.[8] Suppose we have infinitely many pairs of socks. We need a recipe for choosing exactly one from each pair. But what recipe? Socks are very similar, and so we are at a loss to give a recipe. Whitehead and Russell called the thesis that there is always such a relation that chooses the "multiplicative axiom." It is now more familiarly known as the "axiom of choice."

There are very useful applications of the axiom of choice. Frege held that there are finitely many Fs if and only if some natural number numbers the Fs. To say that there are infinitely many Fs is just to say that the Fs are not finite. In contrast, Dedekind held that to say that there are finitely many Fs is to say that Fs cannot be put into one-to-one correspondence with any group that are a proper subgroup of Fs. The natural numbers are infinite, in Dedekind's sense, because they are in one-to-one correspondence with the even natural numbers—a proper subgroup of them. It requires the axiom of choice to prove that anything infinite in Frege's sense is infinite in Dedekind's sense. This is an important result. Nonetheless, the axiom of choice is controversial. Strange results follow from choice. Banach and Tarski, in the early 1920s, obtained a dissection of a Euclidean sphere into a finite number of pieces—now known to be just five—that could be reassembled by simple affine volume-preserving movements of the pieces into two congruent spheres each of the same volume as the original.

Cardinal numbers must be distinguished from ordinal numbers. Ordinality (i.e. order) has its foundation in ordinal similarity (i.e. isomorphism) of relational structure. The foundation of ordinal numbers is the notion of sameness of structure—a notion that requires that the fields of relations have the same cardinality. It is obvious from the analysis that the notion of an ordinal number is dependent on the notion of a cardinal number. Whenever the field of a relation is finite, we can draw a directed graph of the structural ordering exacted by the relation.

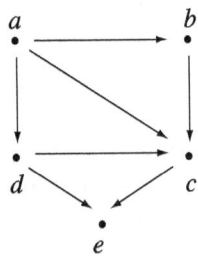

It does not matter to the structure what the entities a b, c, d, e of the field of the relation are. Any entities are ordered in the same structure so long as there is an isomorphism between the two. A two-placed relation R has the same ordinal number as a two-placed relation S if and only if the fields of R and S have the same cardinality under a one-to-one function f, and for all x and y in the field of R, xRy if and only if fx S fy. The field may be changed without changing the structure; the structure may be changed without changing the field.[9] The standard of order type, for ordinal numbers, lies in the notion of a two-placed relation that well-orders its field. This means that the field is in a series (linear)[10] and that for any non-empty grouping of the field, there is a minimal element in that group under the relation. The natural numbers are well- ordered by the relation < (less than). The rationals are not well-ordered by <. Rationals are linearly ordered by <, but some groups of them have no minimal element under the less-than relation. For example, given the infinity of the natural numbers, the group of rationals $\frac{p}{q}$ which are such that $\frac{2}{1} < \frac{p}{q}$ has no minimal element which is less than every other in the group. This is because the rationals are dense and not consecutive. Well-orderings require consecutiveness.

Interestingly, it is consistent to assume as an axiom that a well-ordering relation can always be found, even when the natural ordering involved is not a well-ordering. This well-ordering axiom is equivalent to the axiom of choice. Thus, rational and also real numbers can be well-ordered. Though consistent, the axiom (or its equivalents) was quickly used to generate pseudo-paradoxes. Consider this one by the mathematician Jules Richard. The names in any given language (whose meaningful expressions are finitely long) can be put in one-to-one correspondence with the natural numbers. Since there are more reals than natural numbers, there are, in any naming system, unnamed real numbers. But suppose we exact a well-ordering of the reals and consider the least (under this well-ordering) non-named real. In spite of its satisfying the description of being the least unnamed real, we seem to have named it! Number devils abound.[11]

We used the notation $\text{Card}_{xy}{}^{\psi y}(\varphi x)$ to mean that ψs are in one-to-one correspondence with φs. We can introduce an analogous notation for ordinality, writing

$$\text{Ord}_{xyzw}{}^{xSy}(zRw)$$

to mean that the relation S is ordinally similar to the well-ordering relation R. Recall that the cardinal number zero as a quantificational notion was analyzed in terms of one-to-one correspondence. We have:

$$0_x \varphi x = df\ \text{Card}_{xy}{}^{y \ne y}[\varphi x].$$

The ordinal number 0^r is introduced analogously with the following:

$$0^r{}_{xy}(xRy) = df\ \text{Ord}_{xyzw}{}^{x <^\circ y}(zRw).$$

Here we use the relation:

$$x <^\circ y = df\ x \ne x\ \&\ y \ne y$$

Obviously this is not an interesting ordering of a field since the field is empty (i.e. nothing has the relation). There is no ordinal number 1^r because no order can be exacted on a field of one. The ordinal number 2^r is characterized thus:

$$2^r{}_{xy}(xRy) = df\ \text{Ord}_{xyzw}{}^{x <^2 y}(zRw).$$

This employs the relation:

$$x <^2 y = df\ (\exists z)(\exists w)(z \ne w\ \&\ x = z\ \&\ y = w).$$

We can then say, for a given relation S, that its ordinal number is 2^r as follows:

$$\text{Ord}_{xy}{}^{xSy}(xRy) \equiv_R 2^r{}_{xy}(xRy).$$

Interestingly, finite cardinality of the field of a well-ordering relation determines the finite ordinal number appropriate to it. We have:

$\mathbf{0}^r_{xy}(xRy) \equiv_R (\exists S)(\text{well-order}_{xy}(xSy) \,.\&.$
$(\text{Field}_{xyz}{}^{xSy}(\varphi z) \equiv_\varphi \mathbf{0}_x \varphi x) \,\&\, \text{Ord}_{xyzw}{}^{xSy}(zRw))$
$\mathbf{2}^r_{xy}(xRy) \equiv_R (\exists S)(\text{well-order}_{xy}(xSy) \,.\&.$
$(\text{Field}_{xyz}{}^{xSy}(\varphi z) \equiv_\varphi \mathbf{2}_x \varphi x) \,\&\, \text{Ord}_{xyzw}{}^{xSy}(zRw))$.

And so on. These are all finite ordinals. They are ordinal numbers of well-ordering relations whose fields consist of finitely many objects.

Just as there are infinite cardinals, there are also infinite ordinals. We noted that when the cardinal number of a field is finite, the cardinality alone assures that all well-ordering relations over that field are isomorphic. This fails when the cardinal number of the field of the relation is infinite.

The well-ordering relation < (less than) orders the field of the natural numbers. Consider then a heterogeneous relation of isomorphism between a field of objects and the field of the natural numbers:

$$\omega_{x,y}(xRy) = \text{df Ord}_{xy}{}^<(xRy).$$

Omega is the first infinite ordinal. A relation has ordinal number omega if and only if it orders its field isomorphically with the natural ordering of the natural numbers (generated by the less than relation).

But we can also find ordinal numbers larger than omega. Consider the ordering of the natural numbers in accordance with the following well-ordering relation $<^{+1}$ which orders them this way:

1, 2, 3, 4, 5, ..., n, . . .; 0.

Recall, of course, that there is no end at which to put 0 given that the whole numbers, 1, 2, 3, 4, . . . are infinite. The point is rather that the relation $<^{+1}$ orders its field so that 0 always comes after every other number in the ordering. Now the ordinal number of this relation is larger than that of the relation < in the sense that < orders its field in a way that is isomorphic with a proper part of the ordered field given by $<^{+1}$ and not vice versa. We arrive at the theorem that

$$\omega_{x\,y}(xRy) <_R \omega^{+1}{}_{x\,y}(xRy).$$

Here we define:

$$\omega^{+1}{}_{x\,y}(xRy) =_{df} \text{Ord}_{x\,y}{}^{<^{+1}}(xRy).$$

It is important to note that adding a new member to the field of the relation $<$ does not increase the ordinal number of the relation. As we have seen if we introduce a new entity among the natural numbers, we get a field that has the same cardinality as the natural numbers and can be ordered isomorphically to the ordering of the natural numbers by $<$. This is the basis for saying that the following are consistent:

$$1^r + \omega = \omega$$
$$\omega + 1^r < \omega.$$

The locution can be misleading if we forget that "addition" with respect to ordinals has a technical meaning different from the addition of cardinals. Another well-ordering relation, $<^{+2}$, orders natural numbers this way:

$$1, 2, 3, 4, 5, \ldots\ldots, n, \ldots; 0, 1.$$

And so we have:

$$\omega^{+1}{}_{x\,y}(xRy) <_R \omega^{+2}{}_{x\,y}(xRy).$$

And we can continue thinning in this way, to yield $\omega^{+n}{}_{x\,y}(xRy)$.

But we can also go further with our thinning. We can find well-ordering relations $<^{X2}$ that put all the even natural numbers before the odd numbers. This might be pictured as follows:

$$0, 2, 4, 6, 8, \ldots\ldots; 1, 3, 5, 7, 9 \ldots$$

Here we have yet a new ordinal, namely:

Mathematics and the Metaphysicians

$2\omega_{x\,y}\,(xRy) =_{df} \mathbf{Ord}_{x\,y}^{<^{x_2}}(xRy).$

And clearly, defined in terms of partial isomorphisms, we have:

$\omega_{x\,y}^{+n}\,(xRy) <_R 2\omega_{x\,y}\,(xRy).$

And we can go on still further, finding a well-ordering relation $<^2$, which puts denumerably many numbers after denumerably many numbers, denumerably many times. Pictorially, this is:

1, 3, 5, 7, 9 . . .; 2, 6, 10, 14, . . .; 4, 12, 20, 28, . . .; 8, 24, 40, 56 . . .; . . . .

This takes the odd numbers, then their doubles, then doubles of these, etc. Thus, we have:

$\omega^2_{x\,y}\,(xRy) =_{df} \mathbf{Ord}_{x\,y}^{<^2}(zRw).$

There is no end to this process. Each one of these denumerable series can itself be thinned out to arrive at $\omega^3, \omega^4, \ldots, \omega^\omega, \ldots$, and so on.[12]

Having defined ordinals, we can go on to develop other infinite alephs besides $\aleph_0$. For instance, the cardinal number of distinct well-ordering relations on a field with the cardinality of the natural numbers is $\aleph_1$. (This is the cardinal number of permutations or "thinning" of the natural numbers). Working with the ordinals in this way, we can go on to investigate the alephs. $\aleph_2, \aleph_3, \aleph_4$ etc. Given the infinity of natural numbers, these are clearly larger in cardinality than $\aleph_0$. Clearly, $\aleph_1$ must be either smaller or equal in cardinality to $2^{\aleph_0}$. But there is no known way of proving[13] from the concepts alone whether or not $\aleph_1$ is equal to $2^{\aleph_0}$. The hypothesis that there is no cardinal between $\aleph_0$ and $2^{\aleph_0}$ is called "the continuum hypothesis." The generalized continuum hypothesis is that there is no cardinal between any cardinal c and 2^c.

LOGICISM

Mathematics, wrongly conceived as the science of quantity, appears to study numbers and the necessary relationships governing numbers. No one can reasonably doubt that there are continually new discoveries in mathematics concerning the structural relationships between numbers. Until the rise of the new logic, it was widely held that any theory of structure must be founded on relationships among numbers. And, of course, there are all sorts of numbers: positive and negative, rational, irrational, real, complex (i.e. imaginary), etc. The revolution in logic, however, offered a new way. It provided a foundation for a science of structure. Relations are fundamental to structure. A logic of relations, therefore, trumps all notions of structure that rely on an ontology of objects that are numbers. If mathematics can be understood as an abstract theory of structure, then its fields are branches of logic—the abstract theory of the kinds of structures generated by relations. Russell's views on the ontology of logic evolved from his *Principles of Mathematics* (1903) to *Principia Mathematica* (1910), but he never wavered in his belief that mathematics is a part of logic as the general theory of structure.

This conception of the relationship between mathematics and logic was entirely unknown in 1900. Indeed, the curriculum in grammar and junior high schools still has not caught on to it. It is bewildering that students are not exposed to logic until their first year in college. Perhaps it remains one of the deleterious effects of developmental psychology, whose experiments mistakenly suggested that the level of abstraction necessary for understanding logic is far greater than that required to grasp arithmetic, algebra, geometry, trigonometry, and even calculus! But more seriously, the cause is likely that the revolution in logic took so very long to develop. As late as the eighteenth century, few disagreed with Kant's claim that Aristotelian and medieval syllogistic logicians had discovered everything there was to know about logic. The historian Carl Prantl drew the corollary that any logician after

Aristotle who said anything new was confused, stupid, or perverse. Russell was a tireless campaigner for the new logic and for reforms in the educational curriculum which would put logic in a more foundational role. He was certainly no friend to Aristotelian logic. He spoke rather stridently against it even as a pedagogical tool:

> If you wish to become a logician, there is one piece of advice which I cannot urge too strongly, and that is: do *Not* learn the traditional formal logic. In Aristotle's day it was a creditable effort, but so was the Ptolemaic astronomy. To teach either in the present day is a ridiculous piece of antiquarianism.
>
> (*AofP*, p. 38)

In its efforts to preserve the Aristotelian thesis of an earth at rest in the center of the cosmos, the Ptolemaic system had become an intractable tangle of epicycles. The heliocentric theory of Copernicus supplanted the system entirely, and soon Kepler's improvements broke through the Aristotelian mysticism that circular orbits are metaphysically necessary for heavenly bodies. Boole's pioneering Laws of Thought (1854) is a remarkable advance over Aristotelian and medieval methods. But when it comes to the revolution in logic, it is the mathematician Gottlob Frege who played the role of Copernicus.

Frege's *Begriffsschrift* (1879) offered a new set of structures for quantification theory that entirely supplants the categorical forms of Aristotelian and medieval conceptions of logic. Aristotelian logic accepts four fundamental forms: A, E, I, and O. Validity is about form (i.e. structure). There are exactly two premises in an Aristotelian syllogism. The predicate category P of the conclusion is in the first (major) premise; the subject category S of the conclusion is in

All S are P	**A**	**E**	No S are P
Some S are P	**I**	**O**	Some S are not P

the second (minor) premise. There are only four positions (i.e. "figures") for the middle term M. Thus there are exactly 256 possible syllogistic structures. Medieval logicians found the invalid ones by substitutions for the categorical terms that made the premises true and the conclusion false.

Venn's diagrams of the 1880s supplanted the Aristotelian and medieval rules of the syllogism. Venn uses overlapping circles to demarcate areas. Accordingly, syllogisms can be evaluated quite simply by inspection of the Venn diagrams which depict the structure of the premises (taken together). Boolean Venn diagrams (which permit empty categories) are possible. The class-theoretical interpretation of an A categorical "All S are P" is $S \cap \check{P} = \emptyset$, which says that the intersection of the class S with the complement of P is the empty class. The Venn diagram makes this clear by shading wherever a region is empty.

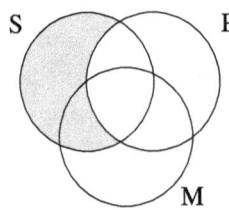

The Venn diagram of the contrapositive "All-non P are non-S" is exactly the same because the statements are logically equivalent. In contrast, the Boolean two-valued (0, 1) algebra interprets the A categorical as $S \times (P - 1) = 0$. In this way, the intersection of classes is represented as multiplication. Union is represented as + (i.e. addition) and complement is multiplication by −1. (This is conveniently written as $P - 1$ instead of $P \times -1$.) The benefit of the algebraic approach is that usual algebraic rules of multiplication can be applied to explain logical inferences. For instance, a common inference (contraposition of an A categorical) is this:

> All S are P.
> Therefore, All non-P are non-S.

Mathematics and the Metaphysicians

The inference is transformed into a Boolean algebra as follows:

$S \times (P - 1) = 0$.
Therefore, $P - 1 \times (S - 1) - 1 = 0$.

Contraposition is thereby understood in terms of the algebraic law of commutation for × together with the rule for multiplication by −1, namely $(n-1) \times -1 = n$.

Boolean algebra replaces categoricals with algebraic statements. Venn diagrams capture them as relationships between classes of entities. Aristotelian Venn diagrams (which exclude empty S, P, and M categories) are also possible. The Aristotelian Venn diagram of "All S are P" appears quite different from the Boolean Venn diagram because of its presumption that the classes S and P and M are not empty. The presumption is represented in a Venn diagram with connecting circles showing that one or another sub-area within each of the categories S, P, and M has a particular (represented with an x) in it. As we can see from the diagram, Aristotelians held that "All S are P" entails that "Some S are P."

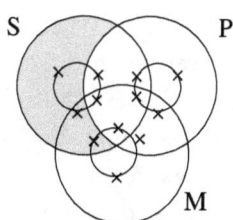

This is denied by Booleans because they accept the empty class. Indeed, presupposing the existence of entities that are S, entities that are P, and entities that are M, Aristotelians accepted as valid some syllogisms that Booleans rejected. We can see the difference in the Aristotelian Venn diagrams. For example, consider the syllogism: All P are M; No S are M; Therefore, Some S are not P. Booleans, accepting empty categories, find it invalid. Aristotelians find it valid.

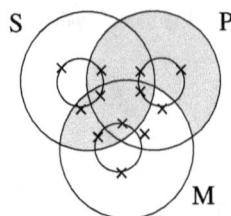

The difference is clear in the Aristotelian diagram. The Boolean notion of an empty class, however, is not so easy to accept, given the notion of a class is a collection of entities. The notion of a class as a collection naturally lends itself to the mistaken view that an empty class is nothing at all. MacColl[14] thought that he had found a compromise by holding that an empty class consists of non-existents and so is merely empty of existents! Following Frege's ideas, Russell's representation of "All S are P" makes it entirely independent of both the Aristotelian and Boolean class-theoretical thinking about it. Russell replaces it with "$(\forall x)(Sx \supset Px)$," which says that everything is such that if it is an S then it is a P. The expression "$Sa \supset Pa$" is taken to have the truth conditions of "either a is not an S or a is a P," and hence no appeal whatsoever is made to the existence of an empty class. On this view, "$(\forall x)(Sx \supset Px)$" is true if nothing is an S. This certainly does not imply that some S are P, which Russellians write as "$(\exists x)(Sx \& Px)$" and read as saying that something is such that it is an S and it is a P.

Following in the footsteps of Boole's two-valued algebra, Schröder realized that mechanical methods were available for determining when a statement invariantly keeps a designated value no matter what values were assigned to its atomic constituents. In Müller's 1909 *Abriss* of Schröder's *Vorlesungen über die Algebra der Logik*, we find a valuation (truth) table used as a decision procedure for determining whether a given formula is a tautology.[15] The formula $(\alpha + \xi) \times (\bar{\alpha} + \xi) = \xi$ is shown to hold no matter what assignment among $(0, 1)$ is given to α and ξ.

Mathematics and the Metaphysicians

$$(\alpha + \zeta)(\bar{\alpha} + \zeta) = \zeta$$

$\zeta =$	0	0	1	1
$\alpha =$	0	1	0	1
$\bar{\alpha} =$	1	0	1	0
$\alpha + \zeta =$	0	1	1	1
$\bar{\alpha} + \zeta =$	1	0	1	1
$(\alpha + \zeta)(\bar{\alpha} + \zeta) =$	0	0	1	1	$=\zeta$

The notion of a tautology owes its origins to these algebraic techniques. A tautologous form is a special statement form built up from atomic formulas by means of sentential logical particles, such as "v" (or), "&" (and), "⊃" (if . . . then . . .), "≡" (if and only if), and "~" (not), which yields the same value no matter what value is assigned to the atomic formulas that compose it. In translation, $(\alpha + \xi) \times (\bar{\alpha} + \xi) = \xi$ becomes $(\alpha \vee \xi) \& (\sim\alpha \vee \xi) .\equiv. \xi$. When viewed as an algebra, logic is a group of fixed rules for operations such as multiplication and addition. Most importantly, the algebraic approach to logic concurs with the Aristotelian view that the conclusion of a deduction cannot go beyond what is contained in the premises.

Aristotelians assumed every sentence could be shoehorned into one or another of the categorical forms. Russell bridled that the assumption, noting that many relational statements cannot be properly captured. Consider this argument:

All men are animals.
Therefore, all heads of men are heads of animals.

No categorical can represent the structural relationship between the premise and the conclusion. A logic of relations is needed, and this became the focus of several intense studies. Boole's *Calculus for Logic* appeared in 1848. Extensions of it to form an *algebra of relatives* were advanced by Schröder and (independently) Peirce.[16] The Peirce/Schröder methods used infinite Boolean sums and products. Russell was not converted. He wrote:

> Peirce and Schröder have recognized the great importance of the subject, but unfortunately their methods, being based, not on Peano, but on the older Symbolic Logic derived (with modifications) from Boole, are so cumbrous and difficult that most of the applications which ought to be made are practically not feasible.
>
> (*PoM*, p. 24)

Algebraic techniques of infinite sum and product are certainly adequate to quantification theory (i.e. the modern predicate calculus with relations). But Frege offered a quite different way to develop quantification theory. His quantifier-free calculus begins from a rule of writing down any instance of the certain forms which serve as axioms, and its inference rule is:

Modus Ponens:
From $p \supset q$ and p infer q.

The quantification theory adds just one more axiomatic form:

$(\forall x)Ax \supset Ay$

where y is free for x in A. The only new rule is this:

Universal Generalization
From $p \supset Ax$ infer $p \supset (\forall x)Ax$

where x is not free in p.

It is a straightforward matter to extend the rules of quantification theory to permit predicate variables such as φ and ψ, demanding that they stay in predicate positions so that $\varphi(x)$ is allowed but $\varphi(\psi)$ is not allowed. Quantification theory for predicate variables simply adds the following axiom schemas:

$(\forall \varphi)A\varphi \supset A\psi$

where ψ is free for φ in A. The only new rule is this:

Universal Generalization
From $p \supset A\varphi$ infer $p \supset (\forall \varphi)A\varphi$

where φ is not free in p.

Mathematics and the Metaphysicians

Peano and his school were stumbling upon similar techniques when Whitehead and Russell attended a congress on their work in 1900. Russell quickly mastered the techniques of much of Peano's school. He only later came to understand and appreciate Frege's discoveries. Interestingly, there is an amusing letter in which Peano writes that some of the rules of quantification theory are yet "abstruse." Peano struggled to find the right quantification rules governing universal generalization under a hypothesis. Frege responds, politely, that he adequately set forth all the needed rules in his *Begriffsschrift*.

Whitehead and Russell's *Principia Mathematica* (section *9) made a further discovery concerning quantification theory. It sketches a demonstration that each line of a proof of a theorem of quantification theory can be proved starting from a quantifier-free tautologous form, generalizing (existentially or universally), switching the order of quantifiers (according to rules) and defining subordinate occurrences of quantifiers in terms of formulas in which all quantifiers are initially placed. *Principia* may be said to reveal that, in an important sense, all the truths of quantification theory are "generalized tautologies."

An unfortunate debate rages to this day about the significance of the difference between Frege's approach to logic and the algebraic approach inaugurated by Boole. It is important to realize that both approaches are equally adequate to quantification theory. Van Heijenoort[17] influenced many, arguing that the algebraic school offers a semantic approach, while the Fregean school takes logic to be a genuine language in its own right. In van Heijenoort's view, this difference explains how it is that Frege maintained that logic is informative, while the algebraic school concurs with the orthodoxy that deduction can never generate anything not already contained in the premises. The algebraic approach is said to be semantic because it offers a formal calculus open to different interpretations and applications of its fundamental signs. The algebraic properties of multiplication, for example, apply to natural numbers, the intersection of classes, and the logical notion of "and." The Fregean school, in contrast, is supposedly antithetical to semantics, demanding that its signs have a fixed meaning as in a language. Van Heijenoort's thesis is misguided. Quantification theory, whether developed as the predicate calculus with relations in the school of Frege and Russell or as the algebra of relatives in the school of Boole, Peirce, and Schröder, is uninformative.

When Frege asserted that his logic is informative in a way that the Boolean algebra is not, he did not have quantification theory (whether for predicate variables or individual variables) in mind. Frege offers a theory of logic that transcends quantification theory. Mathematics is informative because it comprehends ever new kinds of numeric functions. Frege held that logic embraces principles comprehending the existence of ever new kinds of functions, including truth-functions. Russell concurred, though he put it in terms of the comprehension of ever new attributes (properties and relations). The reason that logic is informative and extends knowledge is that it embraces comprehension axioms. Let us call this new logic which transcends quantification theory $^{\varphi}$Logic.

The ever new kinds of attributes comprehended by the axioms of $^{\varphi}$Logic are not just new kinds of attributes of objects. They extend vertically in a hierarchy of levels. Frege explains this vertical hierarchy of levels of attributes (or, more exactly, functions of a certain sort) by appealing to a linguistic analogy and his doctrine that functions (attributes) are "unsaturated" and have only a predicable nature. Accordingly, Frege introduced structured notations to keep function/predicate expressions in function/predicate positions. It is intuitive to think of the higher levels as quantificational structures. Thus, for instance, the quantificational structure $(\forall x)(Fx)$ may be viewed as the "mutual saturation" of a an incomplete (unsaturated) first-level attribute $F(\ )$ falling within an incomplete (unsaturated) second-level quantificational attribute $(\forall x)(\ldots x \ldots)$. In Frege's view, objects fall under first-level functions, while functions of level n mutually saturate (i.e. fall within) functions of

Mathematics and the Metaphysicians

level n+1. The subscripted letter x in $M_x\varphi x$ serves to remind us of this fact. The case is similar as we go up the levels. For example, the quantificational structure

$$(\forall\varphi)(\ldots(\forall x)(\ldots\ldots\varphi x\ldots)\ldots)$$

is displayed in the subscripted letter φ in $\Sigma_\varphi(M_x\varphi x)$.

Comprehension principles for Frege's levels must be stated one at a time since there is no linguistic form in common to the notations for the levels. In a Fregean system we have:

$^{Frege}CP^1$

$$(\exists\varphi)(\forall x_1),\ldots,(\forall x_n)(\varphi(x_1,\ldots,x_n) \equiv A)$$

where φ does not occur free in A. This renders attributes of objects. For instance, if the formula A is $x = x$, then $^{Frege}CP^1$ has the instance:

$$(\exists\varphi)(\forall x)(\varphi x \equiv x = x).$$

This assures the existence of an attribute φ that an object x has if and only if x is self-identical. Frege also embraces comprehension of higher-level attributes:

$^{Frege}CP^2$

$$(\exists M)(\forall\varphi)(M_{x1,\ldots,xn}\{\varphi(x_1,\ldots,x_n)\} \equiv A)$$

where M does not occur free in A. For example, if the formula A is

$$(\forall y)(\varphi y \equiv \varphi y)$$

then $^{Frege}CP^2$ has the instance

$$(\exists M)(\forall\varphi)(M_y\varphi y \equiv (\forall y)(\varphi y \supset \varphi y))$$

This assures the existence of a second-level attribute M that a first level (type) attribute φ has if and only if for all objects y, if y has φ then y has φ. The levels continue vertically.

Frege's logic is not completely axiomatizable. No one consistent axiomatic system can capture all logical truths as theorems. Russellians invented a notation of simple types which enables comprehension for all the levels to be is given as follows:

$$^{\text{Russell}}\text{CP}$$
$$(\exists \varphi^{(t1,\ldots tn)})(\forall x_1^{t1}),\ldots,(\forall x_n^{tn})(\varphi^{(t1,\ldots tn)})(x_1^{t1},\ldots,x_n^{tn}) \equiv A),$$

where $\varphi^{(t1,\ldots tn)}$ does not occur free in A. But, due to Gödel's work of 1931 it is now known that no consistent axiomatization of ^{cP}Logic can capture all logical truths as theorems. Returning to our examples, our attribute of self-identity of objects is assured by:

$$(\exists \varphi^{(o)})(\forall x^o)(\varphi^{(o)}(x^o) \equiv x^o = x^o).$$

Here the superscript o on the variable x^o indicates the lowest type. The superscript (o) on a predicate variable $\varphi^{(o)}$ indicates the type appropriate to a property of individuals. In the next higher type, we have:

$$(\exists M^{((o))})(\forall x^{(o)})(M^{((o))}(x^{(o)}) \equiv x^{(o)} = x^{(o)}).$$

Here the superscript ((o)) on the predicate variable $M^{((o))}$ indicates that it is a property of properties of type (o). For convenience, the following notation using $\varphi^{(o)}$ instead of $x^{(o)}$ can be employed. Thus we have:

$$(\exists M^{((o))})(\forall \varphi^{(o)})(M^{((o))}(\varphi^{(o)}) \equiv \varphi^{(o)} = \varphi^{(o)}).$$

Thus the simple-type symbol o is for objects; the symbol (o) is for attributes of objects; the symbol ((o)) is for attributes of attributes of objects, and so on.

The Russellian notation of simple types is designed to track the Fregean levels in a convenient way. Of course, one might think of attributes in a quite different way. One might hold, for example, that abstractness is a property. This seems like an example of the form $\varphi(\psi)$, and simple types are entirely out of place here. In such cases, φ does not represent a quantificational structure within which ψ occurs in a predicate position. Indeed, if attributes are taken to be entities with an objectual as well as predicable nature, then the motivation for the Fregean symbolism of levels (or Russellian symbolism of simple types) is lost. The motivation

Mathematics and the Metaphysicians 89

was to keep predicate expressions in predicate positions (or track them by simple type indices). The hierarchy of simple types seems to have little justification if one embraces the view that there is a simple property *abstractness* which can hold of other properties.

A simple type-theory of attributes lacks the philosophical pedigree of Fregean levels. The hierarchy of levels of attributes is philosophically justified by the doctrine that attributes have only a predicable nature. Accordingly, Fregean structured variables are necessary for keeping predicate expressions in predicate positions. Indeed, seeing the hierarchy in this way, we can understand why Frege regarded attributes (functions) extensionally. To facilitate comparison with Russell we shall speak of attributes$_e$ or "attributes in extension." Extensionality axioms for the levels of attributes$_e$ would be introduced with axioms such as:

$$\varphi x \equiv_x \psi x .\supset. M_x \varphi x \equiv M x \psi x.$$

The notation $M_x \varphi x$ represents contexts of a structure built up from the logical notations. For example, if $M_x \varphi x$ is the context $(\forall x)\varphi x$ of universal quantification, we have the following instance of the above:

$$\varphi x \equiv_x \psi x .\supset. (\forall x)\varphi x \equiv (\forall x)\psi x.$$

This says that if everything is such that it is φ if and only if it is ψ then everything is φ if and only if everything is ψ. Similar extensionality principles hold for higher levels. We have:

$$M_x \varphi x \equiv_\varphi \xi_x \psi x. .\supset. \Sigma_\varphi(M_x \varphi x) \equiv \Sigma_\varphi(\xi_x \varphi x).$$

Thus, for example, an instance is this:

$$(\forall x)\varphi x \equiv_\varphi \sim(\exists x)\sim\varphi x .\supset. (\forall \varphi)(\forall x)\varphi x \equiv (\forall \varphi)\sim(\exists x)\sim\varphi x.$$

And so on.

In Frege's view, arithmetic truths are truths of ᶜᵖlogic and thus there is no special sort of necessity unique to number. Frege's thesis has come to be called "logicism." Russell held a more radical form

90 Mathematics and the Metaphysicians

of the thesis. In Russell's view, ᶜᴾlogic is the general science of the kinds of structures given by relations. Arithmetic functions on numbers are but one kind among relations. Geometric relations (whether they define a Euclidean space or not) are another kind. In Russell's view, ᶜᴾlogic is the general science of relational structures. Since the branches of mathematics consist in the study of different sorts of number theoretic relations and functions, ᶜᴾlogic subsumes mathematics.

NATURAL NUMBERS AS OBJECTS

To arrive at a logical analysis of numbers as objects, Frege employs a special correlation thesis.[18] Frege assumed that each attribute φ is correlated one-to-one with a unique object źφz. (The object źφz can conveniently be thought of as a class of just those objects that have the attribute.) For example, the correlate of the attribute of being non-self-identical is ź(z ≠ z). This may be thought of as the empty class Λ. Frege defines a relation ∈, which we can think of as "membership," and arrives at the following:

(Correlation) $\varphi v \equiv_v v \in \acute{z}(\varphi z)$.

In Frege's system this enables replacement in accordance with the following:

$$\frac{\varphi v}{v \in \acute{z}\varphi z}.$$

To arrive at the object 0, Frege correlates the quantificational attribute $\mathbf{0}_x \varphi x$ with an object. This happens as follows. Correlation enables φx in $\mathbf{0}_x \varphi x$ to be replaced by $x \in \acute{z}\varphi z$. Thus we get $\mathbf{0}_x (x \in \acute{z}\varphi z)$. This says that źφz has the attribute of being an object u such that $\mathbf{0}_x (x \in u)$. Next, apply the following instance of correlation:

$$\frac{\mathbf{0}_x (x \in v)}{v \in \acute{u}\, \mathbf{0}_x (x \in u)}.$$

Mathematics and the Metaphysicians 91

We have now found the number 0 as an object, namely:

ú $\mathbf{0}_x$ ($x \in u$).

The object correlated with the attribute zero is the class of all classes that have zero many members. It follows that:

$\acute{z}\varphi z \in 0 \equiv_\varphi \mathbf{0}_x \varphi x$.

For all attributes$_e$ φ, the class of all φs is a member of 0 if and only if $\mathbf{0}_x \varphi x$.

Recall that the notion of cardinal number is fundamentally a notion of one-to-one correspondence. It is by correlation that Frege transforms the relation of one-to-one correspondence into a relation between objects. Frege has:

$$\frac{\mathbf{Card}_{xy}{}^{\psi y}[\varphi x]}{\mathbf{Card}_{xy}{}^{y \in \acute{z}\psi z}[x \in \acute{z}\varphi z]}.$$

Similarly, by correlation Frege arrives at:

$$\frac{\mathbf{Card}_{xy}{}^{y \in \acute{z}\psi z}[x \in \acute{z}\varphi z]}{\acute{z}\varphi z \in \text{ú } \mathbf{Card}_{xy}{}^{y \in \acute{z}\psi z}[x \in u]}.$$

Hence, Frege puts:

$\acute{A}$ ($\acute{z}\,\psi z$) = df ú $\mathbf{Card}_{xy}{}^{y \in \acute{z}\psi z}[x \in u]$.

Thus the cardinal number of a class $\acute{z}\psi z$ is the class of all classes whose members are in one-to-one correspondence with the members of $\acute{z}\psi z$. Instead of writing

$\mathbf{0}_x \varphi x \equiv_\varphi \mathbf{Card}_{xy}{}^{\psi y}[\varphi x]$.

Frege can employ an identity between objects, writing

$0 = \acute{A}$ ($\acute{z}\,\psi z$)

This says that 0 equals (is) the cardinal number of ψs.

To find the natural number 1 as an object, Frege uses the fact that correlation has yielded the number 0 as an object. He then considers the attribute of being an object y such that $y \leq 0$. Thus consider

$$\mathbf{Card}_{xy}{}^{y \leq 0}[\varphi x].$$

This is equivalent to:

$$\mathbf{1}_x \varphi x$$

Intuitively, there is just one object less than or equal to 0, namely 0 itself. It follows that:

$$\mathbf{1}_x \varphi x \equiv_\varphi (\exists x)(\varphi y \equiv_y y = x).$$

That is, there is exactly one φ if and only if there is some x which is such that for every y, y is φ if and only if $y = x$. Correlation then gives us the object 1, namely:

$$\acute{u}\, \mathbf{1}_x\, (x \in u).$$

We have:

$$\acute{z}\varphi z \in 1 \equiv_\varphi \mathbf{1}_x[\varphi x]$$
$$\acute{z}\varphi z \in 1 \equiv_\varphi (\exists x)(\varphi y \equiv_y y = x).$$

To find the natural number 2 as an object, observe that we have:

$$\mathbf{2}_x \varphi_x \equiv_\varphi \mathbf{Card}_{xy}{}^{y \leq 1}[\varphi x].$$

Correlation by means of abstraction yields:

$$\acute{u}\, \mathbf{2}_x\, (x \in u)$$

Intuitively, we can see that we can keep on going in this way. The infinity of natural numbers as objects is assured by correlation. By means of correlation, the cardinal number of natural numbers can also be understood as an object. We have:

$$(\aleph_0)_x \varphi x =_{df} \mathbf{Card}_{xy}{}^{0 \leq y}[\varphi x].$$

That is, $(\aleph_0)_x \varphi x$ says that there are as many φs as there are natural numbers greater than or equal to 0. Frege then correlates this with an object, namely:

Mathematics and the Metaphysicians 93

ú $(\aleph_o)_x(x \in u)$.

This is not a natural number, but is the first infinite number which Frege called "endloss" and Cantor labeled $\aleph_o$ for "aleph naught."

Frege's conception of numbers as objects essentially depends upon his notion of correlation together with his logical analysis of numbers in terms of relations of one-to-one correspondence—relations which are not themselves objects. Correlation gave Frege's natural numbers a privileged status among set theoretical objects that all could play the role of natural numbers within set-theory.[19] Unfortunately, in 1901 Russell showed that Frege's correlation thesis is contradictory. Correlation is the thesis that for any condition whatsoever there is an object (or a "class," as we shall call it) of all and only those entities that meet the condition. Some classes, such as the class of all classes, are members of themselves. Other classes, such as the class of all people, are not members of themselves; a class is not a person. But Russell considers the class of all entities that are not members of themselves. Russell arrives at the following instance of correlation:

$v \in \acute{z}(z \notin z) \equiv_v v \notin v$.

For any v, v is a member of the class of all entities that are not members of themselves if and only if v is not a member of itself. But if this holds for all v, it holds for $\acute{z}(z \notin z)$. Thus we have:

$\acute{z}(z \notin z) \in \acute{z}(z \notin z)$

if and only if

$\acute{z}(z \notin z) \notin \acute{z}(z \notin z)$.

This is Russell's paradox of classes (as applied to Frege's correlation thesis).

Russell's paradox of classes (or sets) immediately destroys the naïve notion of a class (or a set). But it is not enough to simply conclude that there are no classes or sets. Consider a town barber who shaves all and only those of the town that do not shave themselves. Does this barber shave himself or not? He shaves himself if and only if he does not. We have a contradiction! In an important sense, the paradox cannot be solved. To solve the barber paradox we would have to accept that there is or can be such a barber and show that the ensuing contradiction can be avoided. This cannot be done. But there is an easy dissolution of the paradox. The sleight of hand is rather apparent. The little trick that traps us is when we naively accept that there is, or better that there could be, such a barber. There is no reason whatsoever to accept this. The trick is more transparent if one says: Consider a man who shaves himself if and only if he does not. There is no reason whatsoever to think there is, or could be, such a man.

Russell's paradox of classes is not like the barber. The reason is that we cannot simply proclaim that there are no classes. Classes (or sets) are used in a great many constructions of mathematics. One must show how to preserve those constructions without them. One might think that we simply need to find the right restrictions which tell us which conditions characterize a set and which do not. Russell struggled for years to find proper restrictions, uncovering along the way the greater part of many ideas current in modern set theories. But in the end, he concluded that there can be no right restrictions. There would be many speculative metaphysical theories of classes or sets, each possibly consistent. This is unacceptable. There can be only one arithmetic, one mathematics, one correct view of what numbers are. A dissolution of the paradox must be found. It is not enough to merely hold that there are no classes/sets. One must show how to do mathematics without classes/sets. We shall explain how Russell did this in Chapter Three. For the present, let us get a glimpse of what it is one has to do. Put in an oversimplified way (which will be expanded in Chapter Three), Russell simply abandons Frege's thesis of correlation. He holds that relational properties, attributes$_e$ of one-to-one correspondence, are themselves the cardinal numbers!

Russell knew that he could parallel Frege's notion of natural numbers as objects in terms of numbers as attributes$_e$. No paradoxes arise here. Thus the natural retreat in the face of paradoxes of concept-correlates (or classes), is to turn to the logical analysis of numbers in terms of attributes$_e$. There are no objects which are classes. Russell offers a no-classes theory of mathematics.

Russell's approach offers a privileged status for its natural numbers. The natural numbers are relational attributes$_e$ of one-to-one correspondence. Mathematics is the science of structure. Russell maintains, however, that structures it studies are not grounded in a realm of Pythagorean (or better, Platonic) objects (e.g. numbers, sets, etc.) with metaphysically necessary essences. Nor are mathematicians drawn by intuitions of the essential metaphysical natures belonging to objects which are numbers, sets, and the like. Unlike object-structuralism, Russell's structuralism does not take mathematics to be a theory of the structures given by objects. Russell holds that the structures studied in arithmetic and mathematics are quantificational structures given by purely logical relations$_e$ themselves. These are higher-level entities which are not objects. This is Russell's epitaph for the number devils of Pythagoras (and Plato).

THE NUMBER OF NUMBERS

One more metaphysical intuition about numbers confronts us. It is a very powerful one from which it is hard to free ourselves. It is the intuition that there are necessarily infinitely many numbers. Now if numbers are quantificational, then this necessity should be a logical necessity. The difficulty is that this necessity seems to be metaphysical and not logical. The quantificational analysis of numbers shows that the number of distinct (i.e. non-coexemplifying) numbers (i.e. quantificational concepts) depends on the number of objects in the world. If that is finite, then there are finitely many natural numbers. This seems very unintuitive at first. Russell struggled for years to avoid this consequence by proving that

96 Mathematics and the Metaphysicians

logic alone assures an infinity of purely logical objects, namely propositions. Ultimately, however, Russell conceded. It may well just not be logically necessary that there are infinitely many natural numbers.

Counting natural numbers (as quantificational concepts) will not assure an infinity of non-coexemplifying natural numbers. Consider, for example, the question of whether there are exactly three φs if and only if there are exactly four φs. In symbols this is:

$$3_x\varphi x \equiv_\varphi 4_x\varphi x.$$

Now clearly this is false. There are many φ that violate this. Consider the case where φ is the property of being a star in the Summer Triangle (Vega, Deneb, Altair). Thus, three and four are not coexemplifying. But suppose there were exactly two objects. If there were exactly two objects then $0_x\varphi x$, $1_x\varphi x$, and $2_x\varphi x$ are not coexemplifying. But no φ would be such that $3_x\varphi x$ and no φ would be such that $4_x\varphi x$. Hence, if there are exactly two objects, then for all φ there are exactly three φs if and only if there are exactly four φs. In short, on the quantificational analysis of numbers, if there were exactly two objects, three would equal four. Indeed, it would also equal five, and so on. Adding one would not always yield a larger natural number.

Both Frege and Russell began their logical analyses of cardinal numbers from the notion of one-to-one correspondence. The striking difference between Russell and Frege, however, is that Russell came (reluctantly) to accept that as a consequence of the logical analysis of number it may (epistemically) well not be logically necessary that there are infinitely many natural numbers! The result is that in *Principia*, the denseness of the rational numbers, the infinity of the primes, etc., and a great many other results require an antecedent clause asserting the infinity of the natural numbers. Though it is not an axiom of *Principia*, this is called the "infinity axiom." It may be stated as follows:

$$\mathbf{Inf} =_{df} (\forall \mathbf{m})(N_\varphi[\mathbf{m}_x\varphi x] \supset (\forall \psi)(\mathbf{m}_x\psi x \supset (\exists x)\sim\psi x)).$$

Thus **Inf** states that for every natural number m, if there are exactly m-many ψs, then there is something which is not a ψ. In *Principia*, we find this:

Infin ax =df$_{*120.03}$ $(\forall \eta^{((0))})$(NC induct $(\eta^{((0))}) \supset \eta^{((0))} \neq \Lambda^{((0))}$).[20]

Translated into our notations, Infin ax is this:

(**Inf ax**) $(\forall n)(N_\varphi[\mathbf{n}_x \varphi x] .\supset. \sim(\mathbf{n}_x \varphi x. \equiv_\varphi \sim(\varphi z \equiv_z \varphi z)))$.

This says that every natural number is exemplified.

What shall we make of this? Much has been made of it—as a criticism of *Principia*. Boolos finds it so perplexing that his best explanation is that Russell had abandoned the spirit of Frege's logicism.[21] Logicism requires, at minimum, that arithmetic necessity is logical necessity. Boolos assumed that the infinity of natural numbers is necessary. What seems startling to Boolos is that *Principia* can blithely go on as if logicism is not doomed by the result that it is not logically necessary that there are infinitely many numbers. A cynic might callously wonder if *Principia* was attempting to hide this from its readers. *Principia*'s first volume appeared in 1910. There are hints of the matter at *50.33 But *infin ax* does not show up fully until *120, some 208 pages into the second volume, which appeared in 1911.

Boolos is not cynical about *Principia*. He thinks that Russell abandoned logicism in favor of a doctrine of "If-thenism," according to which all inference rules involved in mathematics are logical. Kant had famously argued that arithmetic intuitions of series are essentially involved in deriving arithmetic theorems; in geometry, spatial intuitions of figure are essential to deriving the theorems from the axioms and definitions given by Euclid and his followers. As Boolos sees it, If-thenism intends only to show that mathematical theorems can be deduced from mathematical axioms by logical inferences alone. (This requires the expressibility of all mathematical notions in logical symbolism alone.) This is a serious criticism. If-thenism applies to any axiomatic study, be it mathematics or geology. It trivializes logicism.

98 Mathematics and the Metaphysicians

A more charitable interpretation is desirable if it can be found. It can. Russell was not an If-thenist. Surprising though it at first seems, Russell came to think that the infinity of natural numbers may well not be logically necessary. Beatrice Webb, a close friend of Russell, pondered this. She writes:

> Memory recalls my friend Bertrand Russell arguing that the arithmetical proposition that two plus two makes four cannot be proved by pure logic and is merely an empirical truth derived from experience, thus belonging to the visible and not to the invisible world.[22]

Webb's statement is not quite accurate. It is easy to prove that two plus two are four in *Principia*. What cannot be proved in logic is that two plus two are *exactly* four, and so not also three, five, etc. The thesis that it is necessary that there are infinitely many numbers is questionable. The reason was not, as Boolos thinks, because he had abandoned the spirit of Fregean logicism in favor of If-thenism. It is because the analysis of natural number in terms of relations of one-to-one correspondence destroys the ordinary intuition that there are necessarily infinitely many natural numbers.

Principia is unabashed in admitting that it is not the business of logic (mathematics) to decide how many objects there are. Of course, *Principia*'s logic is classical and so assures that there is at least one object (of type o). This, in turn, only assures that there are two non-coexemplifying attributes$_e$ of type (o). In turn, this assures the existence of four non-coexemplifying attributes$_e$ of type ((o)), and so on. We find:

> For the lowest type, we can only prove the existence of at least one object: this is proved in *24.52. For the next type, we can prove the existence of at least two objects, namely Λ and V; these are distinct by *24.1. For the next type, we can prove the existence of 2^2 objects; for the next 2^4, etc. But for the class of individuals we cannot prove, from our primitive propositions, that there is more than one object

in the universe ... We might, of course, have included among our primitive propositions the assumption that more than one individual exists, or some assumption from which this would follow such as

$(\exists \varphi, x, y). \varphi!x . \sim\varphi!y.$

But very few of the propositions which we might wish to prove depend on this assumption, and we have therefore excluded it. It should be observed that many philosophers, being monists, deny this assumption.

(*PM*, p. 333)

The last sentence is a logician's joke. Monism (i.e. the thesis that exactly one object exists) is surely false. But it seems just as surely logically possible. The first volume of *Principia* acknowledges that the question of whether there are infinitely many type o individuals remains open and disputed among philosophers. If philosophical positions such as monism are logically (or metaphysically) possible, then the infinity of natural numbers is not logically necessary. The only necessity for Russell is logical necessity. Hence it is not metaphysically or arithmetically necessary either.

The intuition that necessarily there are infinitely many natural numbers is unquestionably very strong. After all, is it not elementary arithmetic that for any natural number the addition of 1 yields a larger natural number? But what is meant by "addition of 1?" What is meant by one natural number being "larger" than another? There is an analogy with intuitions of geometric necessity. A metaphysician adhering to the thesis that triangles are special sorts of metaphysical objects may well develop the intuition that certain properties are necessary of them. For example, his intuitions of the metaphysical objects that are triangles inform him that it is a necessary truth of these objects that the sum of their internal angles equals the sum of two right angles. If an account is offered that professes to capture geometry, such a metaphysician will evaluate it in terms of these intuitions. If it is proposed that his cherished truths of triangles are not necessary, but rather what is necessary is a conditional whose antecedent may well not be necessary, the metaphysician will scoff. The failure of any theory to produce the essential truths of triangles demonstrates, to the satisfaction of this metaphysician, that proposed theory of geometry is false.

Consider, however, the situation of one who accepts a modern analytic geometry according to which triangles are not objects but relations on ordered pairs of real numbers. It is the theory of relations that now drives intuitions as to what is or is not necessary in geometry. The failure of analytic geometry to capture our metaphysician's metaphysical necessities of triangles is no basis for its rejection. Quite the contrary, our metaphysician's intuitions are the trouble. Russell once quipped: " 'Continuity' " had been, until he [Cantor] defined it, a vague word, convenient for philosophers like Hegel, who wished to introduce metaphysical muddles into mathematics."[23] The metaphysician's necessary truths about numbers are, in Russell's view, another metaphysical muddle.

Modern analytic geometry says that Euclidean geometry is neither logically nor metaphysically necessary. Analytic geometry has abandoned the thesis that there are geometric objects whose essences are known by extrapolating from experiences of ordinary objects. For example, if one takes circles and ellipses to be abstract spatial objects (i.e. figures), then their relationship seems non-logical and metaphysical. But in analytic geometry, there are no objects that are circles and ellipses. A circle is a relation of points (i.e. ordered pairs of numbers) that are equidistant from some given point $<h, k>$. We have:

$$\text{Circle}_{x\,y}\,\{\varphi xy\} = df$$
$$(\exists, h, k, r)(\varphi xy :\equiv_{x\,y} : \frac{(x-h)^2}{r^2} + \frac{(y-k)^2}{r^2} = 1).$$

Mathematics and the Metaphysicians

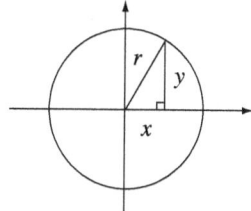

The points constituting a circle in the figure are those that are equidistant from a given point which we have placed at the origin where h and k are 0. The equation for the points constituting a circle, of course, derives from the Pythagorean theorem which, applied here, yields $x^2 + y^2 = r^2$. A little algebra yields $\frac{x^2}{r^2} + \frac{y^2}{r^2} = 1$. The equation for an ellipse gives us the following:

Ellipse$_{x\,y}$ {φxy} =df

$(\exists\, d, c, h, k, r)(\varphi xy :\equiv_{x\,y}: \frac{(x-h)^2}{r^2} + \frac{(y-k)^2}{(d-c)^2} = 1)$.

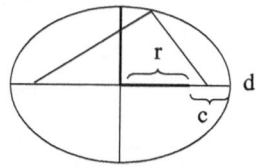

These are relations on numbers.[24] When c = 0, then d = r and the ellipse becomes a circle. Thus, from the nature of these relations we arrive at:

Circle$_{x\,y}$ {φxy} $\supset_\varphi$ Ellipse$_{x\,y}$ {φxy}.

Every circle is an ellipse. (But no ellipse is a circle.) We have a purely logical connection between relations that define circles and those that define ellipses. Similarly, in analytic geometry, lines and triangles are relations on numbers. A line is "straight" when it keeps the same slope. But this is the case on the surface of a sphere

Mathematics and the Metaphysicians

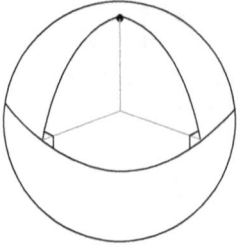

as much as in a Euclidean plane. On the analytic definition of a triangle, it is not necessary that the internal angles of a triangle sum to two right angles. The intuition that it is necessary comes from a notion of triangle as an ideal object abstracted from our experiences of figures in visual space. The intuition is a muddle which vanishes upon analysis.

The dogmatic metaphysician demanded that it is a necessary truth of geometry that every triangle's internal angles sum to two right angles. The analytic geometer discovered that this is not a truth of geometry at all, but rather what is a necessary truth (not an obscure metaphysical necessity but a logical necessity) is the conditional:

> If a metric is Euclidean then
> a triangle in that metric is such that its internal angles sum to
> two right angles.

So it is with Russell's conception of natural numbers quantifiers. The logical analysis frees the notion of number from the metaphysical muddles that haunted it.[25] The dogmatic metaphysician demanded that it is a metaphysically necessary truth of the arithmetic of objects which are numbers that the number n is not the number n+1. Russell discovered that this is not a truth of arithmetic at all. Rather, what is a truth (and indeed a logically necessary truth) is the conditional:

> If there are infinitely many objects, then the number n is not
> the number n+1.

Mathematics and the Metaphysicians 103

This explains why Whitehead and Russell are content in *Principia* to accept conditionals whose antecedent assures an infinity of objects. This is not "If-thenism." The result is independent of logicism. It arises from the analysis of natural numbers as one-to-one correspondence relations. The analysis is fundamental to all analytic conceptions of natural number, including those in modern set theories. The metaphysical postulation of an infinite set does not belong to arithmetic (or mathematics), and the metaphysical postulation that physical space is best modeled as Euclidean does not belong to geometry. Russell's conception of natural number fails to assure—unless there is an infinity of logically necessary objects—that an infinity of natural numbers is logically necessary. But the lessons of analytic geometry should guide us. The intuitions of a metaphysician clinging to the dogma that natural numbers are objects is no basis for rejecting the Frege/Russell structuralist conception of natural number. Once one rejects the metaphysical assumption of natural numbers as objects and accepts analytic arithmetic (with natural numbers as relations of one-to-one correspondence) the intuition that it is necessary that there be infinitely many vanishes.

The school of metaphysicians who divorce numbers from relations of one-to-one correspondence and cling to numbers as special metaphysical objects is left with primitive intuitions of arithmetic addition and the notion of "larger number." But what does "addition of 1 to an object" mean? What does "larger number" mean for this metaphysician? Russell recounted the centuries of conceptual muddles that were produced by such primitive intuitions until Cantor (and Frege) set the world straight. The notion of numbers as relations of one-to-one correspondence reveals a proper understanding of what it is for a number to be "larger than" another and of what "addition of 1" means. But it is here that we discover that the infinity of numbers may well not be necessary.

FURTHER READING

Nino B. Cocchiarella, *Logical Studies in Early Analytic Philosophy* (Columbus: Ohio State University Press, 1988).

Ivor Grattan-Guinness, *The Search for Mathematical Root: 1870–1940: Logics, Set Theories and the Foundations of Mathematics from Cantor through Russell to Gödel* (Princeton, NJ: Princeton University Press, 2000).

Francesco Orilia, *Predication, Analysis and Reference* (Bologna: CLUEB, 1999).

Bertrand Russell, *Introduction to Mathematical Philosophy* (London: Allen & Unwin, 1919).

Alfred North Whitehead, *An Introduction to Mathematics* (London: Oxford University Press, 1911).

Three

Principia Mathematica

> Nevertheless, without a single object to represent an extension, Mathematics crumbles.
>
> *The Principles of Mathematics* (1903)

Returning to *The Number Devil*, Lord Rustle reenters the story when Robert is invited to dine in Number Hell/Number Heaven:

> What they saw was a very old man with snow white hair and a long nose. He was toddling around and around in circles and carrying out a great debate with himself. "All Englishmen are liars," the man mumbled, "but if I say it, what then? I'm an Englishman myself. So I'm lying, too. But then what I've just said—namely, that all Englishmen are liars—is not true. But if Englishmen tell the truth, then what I said before must be true as well. In other words, we are liars.["][1]

There is a minor flaw in Rustle's reasoning: If "All Englishmen are liars" is false, then *some* Englishmen tell the truth. The intended puzzling loop is lost. Rustle should consider "Everything I now say is false," where it is assumed that he now says one and only one thing. More importantly, the number devil should explain how such a seemingly silly mind twister could be thought relevant to understanding the nature of mathematics.

The relationship is this: The comprehension principles of [CP]Logic embrace impredicative loops of quantification. To take one of Russell's now familiar examples, let us grant that Napoleon has all the properties of every great general. Embracing an impredicative loop, we grant that *having all properties of every great general* is itself such a property. The logicist analysis of natural numbers employs impredicativity. And it shows up in the construction of natural numbers, real numbers, and of course in Cantor's work on the infinite. It was by means of such a loop that Cantor was able to prove that the real numbers are not in one-to-one correspondence with the natural numbers. Are impredicative loops of quantification acceptable reasoning or viciously circular and illicit? The famous mathematician Poincaré thought such loops are viciously circular and thus illicit. He demanded that they be avoided, proclaiming that mathematicians obey a "vicious circle principle." Russell's friend Philip Jourdain jokingly[2] put Russell's reply as follows:

> Nearly all mathematicians agreed that the way to solve these paradoxes was simply not to mention them; but there was some divergence of opinion as to how they were to be unmentioned. It was clearly unsatisfactory not to mention them. Thus, Poincaré was apparently of the opinion that the best way of avoiding such awkward subjects was to mention that they are not to be mentioned. But [as Russell put it] "... one might as well, in talking to a man with a long nose, say: 'When I speak of noses, I except such as are inordinately long,' which would not be a very successful effort to avoid a painful topic."[3]

Impredicative loops certainly do walk beside viciously circular confusions of reason, such as Berry's famous paradox of "the least integer not nameable in fewer than nineteen syllables" which seems by its own expression to have defined a number. But we shall see that Russell did not agree with Poincaré. He recognized that impredicative comprehension is the centerpiece of mathematics. Impredicative loops narrowly skirt antinomies produced by subtle confusions—antinomies which have historically been the source of metaphysical muddles introduced by well-meaning philosophers and mathematicians.

PRINCIPIA^L

The system of the 1910 first edition of Principia Mathematica has produced an extensive philosophical debate over that last one hundred years. Part of the cause is that the presentation of the syntax in the work is very informal by modern standards of exactness. Curiously, this was done intentionally so that $\varphi(x)$ can be written instead of having always to print order/type indices such as $\varphi^{(t)}(x^t)$ on the variables of the formal grammar. In a curious letter to Russell during the printing of the work, it suddenly dawned on Whitehead that they should have first set out the formal syntax with order/type indices, and then, with conventions of omitting them, dropped them when convenient.[4] But it was too late, and as presented, it is easy to be misled about the formal syntax intended in the work. Worse, some readers have difficulty distinguishing statements concerning the restoration of the indices and formal logical principles. To see the many issues involved in the debate, let us begin by characterizing two different interpretations of the work. The first aims to be historically faithful to Whitehead and Russell's intent, though it strays from their lackadaisical style. We call it Principia^L. The second is a widely influential interpretation due to Church. We call it Principia^C.

The primitive signs of the language of Principia are v, ~, (,), ' (prime), $\exists$, and $\forall$.[5] The symbol $\forall$ for universal quantification is not used in Principia, but it is very convenient in notations of type theory.[6] Predicate variables and individual variables come with order/type symbols. The individual variables are $x_1^o, x_2^o, \ldots, x_n^o$ (informally x^o, y^o, z^o), and the predicate variables are $x_1^t, x_2^t, \ldots, x_n^t$ (informally $\varphi^t, \psi^t, \theta^t$) where $t \neq o$. A type symbol of simple type theory is defined recursively as follows:

(i) o is a type symbol.
(ii) If $t_1, \ldots, t_n$ are type symbols, then $(t_1, \ldots, t_n)$ is a type symbol.
(iii) There are no other type symbols.

108 *Principia Mathematica*

To generate *Principia*'s ramified types, we proceed by recursively defining the notion of the order of a simple type symbol:

(i) The type symbol o has order 0.
(ii) A type symbol $(t_1, \ldots, t_k)$ has order n+1 if the highest order of the type symbols $t_1, \ldots, t_k$ is n.

The order of an order/type symbol can be determined by counting parentheses from left to right, adding +1 for every left parenthesis and −1 for every right parenthesis. The order is the highest (necessarily non-negative) integer obtained in the counting process.[7]

On the present interpretation, all and only variables are predicative in the sense that their order is the order of their simple type symbol. Thus, all and only variables of the formal language of *Principa* are predicative.[8] As we shall see, Church's interpretation of the system allows more complicated variables whose order indices are not the order of their simple type symbol. It allows non-predicative variables. To see the point, we can make the order of the simple type symbol explicit by writing the order component on the left side of the variable. This yields the following chart (see below). Thus the formula $^1\varphi^{(o/o)}(^o x^o)$ replaces the more simple $\varphi^{(o)}(x^o)$. Similarly, we can write $^2\psi^{(1/(o/o))}(^1\varphi^{(o/o)})$ instead of the more simple $\psi^{((o))}(\varphi^{(o)})$ and so on. Church allows non-predicative variables such as $^3\psi^{(1/(o/o))}$ whose order is not the order of the simple type symbol. But as Church well knows, the historical *Principia* offers a formal language that does not allow non-predicative predicate variables. Nor does it allow terms other than variables.[9]

Simple type + order of type

$\varphi^{(o)}$	$^1\varphi^{(o/o)}$
$\varphi^{((o))}$	$^2\varphi^{(1/(o/o))}$
$\varphi^{(((o)))}$	$^3\varphi^{(2/(1/(o/o)))}$
$\varphi^{(o, o)}$	$^1\varphi^{(o/o, o/o)}$
$\varphi^{(o, (o))}$	$\varphi^{(o/o, (1/(o/o))}$

Principia Mathematica 109

Whitehead and Russell offer section *9 to provide a philosophically satisfactory foundation for the system of quantification theory. The primitive signs of the language of *Principia* are v, ~, (,), ' (prime), $\forall$, and $\exists$. Predicate variables and individual variables come with order/type symbols. The individual variables are x_1^o, x_2^o, ..., x_n^o (informally x^o, y^o, z^o), and the predicate variables are x_1^t, x_2^t, ..., x_n^t (informally φ^t, ψ^t, θ^t) where $t \neq o$. The atomic formulas are of the form:

$$\varphi^{(t1,\,\ldots,\,tm)}(x_1^{t1},\ldots,x_n^{tm})$$

The formulas (wffs) are the smallest set K containing all atomic wffs such that if A, B, C are quantifier-free well-formed formulas (wffs) in K and x^t is an individual variable free in quantifier-free formula C, then $\sim$(A), A v B, and $(\forall x^t)$C are in K. Where p, q, and r are schematic for quantifier-free formulas, and A, B, C are schematic for all wffs, quantifier-free or otherwise, the axiom schema are now as follows:

*1.2 $p \vee p . \supset . p$
*1.3 $q . \supset . p \vee q$
*1.4 $p \vee q . \supset . q \vee p$
*1.5 $p \vee (q \vee r) . \supset . q \vee (p \vee r)$
*1.6 $q \supset r . \supset . p \vee q . \supset . q \vee p$

*9.1 $A[y^t \,|\, x^t] \supset (\exists x^t)A$
where y^t is free for x^t in A

*9.12 $A[y^t \,|\, x^t] \vee A[z^t \,|\, x^t] \supset (\exists x^t)A$
where y^t and z^t are free for x^t in A.

*12.1n
$(\exists \varphi^{(t1,\,\ldots,\,tm)})(\forall x_1^{t1},\ldots,\forall x_n^{tm})(\varphi^{(t1,\,\ldots,\,tm)}(x_1^{t1},\ldots,x_n^{tm}) \equiv A)$,
where $\varphi^{(t1,\,\ldots,\,tm)}$ is not free in A.

The inference rules, in addition to variable rewriting, are:

Modus Ponens:
From A and $A \supset B$, infer B

Universal Generalization:
From A, infer $(\forall x^t)A$

Switch[10]
From $(\forall x^t)(\exists y^v)A(x^t, y^v)$ infer $(\exists y^v)(\forall x^t)A(x^t, y^v)$
where there is a logical particle in A on one side of which all free occurrences of x occur and on the other side of which all free occurrences of y occur.

Definitions include the following:

$x^t = y^t = \text{df}\ (\forall \varphi^{(t)})(\varphi^{(t)}(x^t) \equiv \varphi^{(t)}(y^t))$

$A \supset B = \text{df}\ \sim A \lor B$

$A \& B = \text{df}\ \sim(\sim A \lor \sim B)$

$A \equiv B = \text{df}\ (A \supset B) \& (B \supset A)$.

Where p is quantifier-free and x does not occur free in the formula A and y does not occur free in the formula B, *Principia*'s definitions also include the following:

*9.01 $\sim(\forall x^t)Ax^t = \text{df}\ (\exists x^t) \sim Ax^t$
*9.02 $\sim(\exists x^t)Ax^t = \text{df}\ (\forall x^t) \sim Ax^t$

*9.03 $(\forall x^t)\ Ax^t \lor p = \text{df}\ (\forall x^t)(Ax^t \lor p)$
*9.04 $p \lor (\forall x^t)\ Ax^t = \text{df}\ (\forall x^t)(p \lor Ax^t)$
*9.05 $(\exists x^t)\ Ax^t \lor p = \text{df}\ (\exists x^t)(Ax^t \lor p)$
*9.06 $p \lor (\exists x^t)\ Ax^t = \text{df}\ (\exists x^t)(p \lor Ax^t)$

*9.07 $(\forall x^t)Ax^t \lor (\exists y^v)By^v = \text{df}\ (\forall x^t)(\exists y^v)(Ax^t \lor By^v)$.
*9.08 $(\exists x)Ax \lor (\forall y^v)By^v = \text{df}\ (\forall y^v)(\exists x^t)(Ax^t \lor By^v)$
*9.0x $(\forall x^t)Ax^t \lor (\forall y^v)By^v = \text{df}\ (\forall x^t)(\forall y^v)(Ax^t \lor By^v)$
*9.0y $(\exists x^t)Ax^t \lor (\exists y^v)By^v = \text{df}\ (\exists x^t)(\exists y^v)(Ax^t \lor By^v)$.

This completes the system.

Principia endeavors to demonstrate that the quantification theory of *10 (which has become the standard) can be recovered in the system of *9, which works by employing universal and existential generalizations on tautologies.[11] The theorem schema,

*10.1 $(\forall x^t)A \supset A[v^t \mid x^t]$,
where v^t is free for x^t in A

*10.12 $(\forall x^t)(B \vee A). \supset. B \vee (\forall x^t)A$
where x^t does not occur free in B

together with all instances of *1.2 − *1.6 with quantified formulas in the places of p, q, r were then to be derived on the basis of *9. The intuition behind this is that for any given instance of *10.1 or *10.2, we can imagine finding a proof of it in the system of *9 by working first in reverse order. Move all its quantifiers to initial placement by means of the definitions of *9 and then by creativity find some tautology to generalize to yield the result. By proceeding in this way, the system of section *9 can recover all the principles and inference rules and thus every line of any proof by means of the quantification theory of section *10 of Principia.[12]

This austere system is the edifice that supports the entirety of mathematics. The system is beautiful in its simplicity and clarity. But it was written at a time when grammatical precision did not rule the day in system building. Its articulation in Principia is very informal by modern standards of rigor. This informality, together with the ontological agendas of many a Pythagorean number devil, fueled rival interpretations, some of which are baroque to say the least. Encyclopedia Britannica offers an all too representative characterization of the work:

> Eventually, Russell's attempts to overcome the paradox resulted in a complete transformation of his scheme of logic, as he added one refinement after another to the basic theory. In the process, important elements of his "Pythagorean" view of logic were abandoned. In particular, Russell came to the conclusion that there were no such things as classes and propositions and that therefore, whatever logic was, it was not the study of them. In their place he substituted a bewilderingly complex theory known as the ramified theory of types, which, though it successfully avoided contradictions such as Russell's Paradox, was (and remains) extraordinarily

difficult to understand. By the time he and his collaborator, Alfred North Whitehead, had finished the three volumes of *Principia Mathematica* (1910–13), the theory of types and other innovations to the basic logical system had made it unmanageably complicated. Very few people, whether philosophers or mathematicians, have made the gargantuan effort required to master the details of this monumental work. It is nevertheless rightly regarded as one of the great intellectual achievements of the 20th century.[13]

It is an intellectual achievement indeed. Its reputation for being "bewilderingly complex" and "unmanageably complicated" is entirely undeserved.

PRINCIPIA^C

The system Principia^L contrasts markedly with that of Church, who invented a formal language for Principia which codes a ramified-type structure into the syntax of the predicate variables. Church accepts non-predicative as well as predicative variables and permits cumulation (i.e. an argument to a predicate variable may have an order less than that demanded by the simple-type symbols of the predicate variable). The primitive signs of the language of Principia^C are as before, v, ~, (,), ′ (prime), and ∀. Predicate variables and individual variables come with order/type symbols. The individual variables are $x_1^o, x_2^o, \ldots, x_n^o$ (informally x^o, y^o, z^o), and the predicate variables are $x_1^t, x_2^t, \ldots, x_n^t$ (informally $\varphi^t, \psi^t, \theta^t$) where t ≠ o. Church's system of r-types sets out a recursive definition of r-types as follows:

(i) There is an r-type o to which all and only individuals belong, and whose order is 0.

(ii) If m ∈ ω − {0}, and $t_1 \ldots t_n$ are given r-types, then there is an r-type $(t_1 \ldots t_n)/m$ to which belong all and only n-ary attributes of level m and with arguments of r-types $t_1 \ldots t_n$ respectively.

(iii) The order of such an attribute of r-type $(t_1 \ldots t_n)/m$ is M+m, where M is the greatest of the orders corresponding to the r-types $t_1 \ldots t_n$ (and M = 0 if m = 0). An attribute of r-type $(t_1 \ldots t_n)/m$ is predicative iff m = 1.

Church's notion of level 1 corresponds to the notion of the order of the simple-type symbols in the formation of the notion of an order/type symbol of $Principia^L$. Indeed, if the level is kept always at 1, Church's notation is just a variant of the notation of simple-types (and thus corresponds precisely to the notion of an order/type symbol of $Principia^L$. To illustrate, consider Church's $\varphi^{(o)/1}$. Its order is 1; this is computed by taking the r-type of the symbol o (namely 0) plus the level 1. In the language of $Principia^L$ this is simply the order of the simple-type symbol (o). Church's predicate variable $\varphi^{((o)/1)/1}$ is for an attribute of attributes of individuals. The order is **2**; this is computed by taking the order of the r-type (o)/1 (i.e. 1) plus the level 1. In the terminology of $Principia^L$, this is the order of the simple-type symbol ((o)) (i.e. 2). Similarly, Church takes $\varphi^{(((o)/1)/1)/1}$ to be a predicate variable for an attribute of attributes of r-type ((o)/1)/1. The order here is 3. In the terminology of $Principia^L$ this is the order of the simple type symbol (((o))) (i.e. 3). These are monadic (one-place) attributes. Church uses $\varphi^{(o, o)/1}$ for a dyadic relation of individuals. A predicate variable $\varphi^{(o, (o)/1)/1}$ is for a dyadic heterogeneous relation between an individual and an attribute of r-type (o)/1. Its order is 2. This is computed by taking the order of its highest order of argument, namely that of (o)/1, plus the level. Once again, in the terminology of $Principia^L$ this is the order of the simple type symbol (o, (o)), (i.e. 2). All these attributes are predicative attributes of predicative attributes (or individuals).

Church allows non-predicative variables such as these: $\varphi^{(o)/2}$, $\varphi^{((o)/1)/2}$. These have no analogs in $Principia^L$, because they do not occur in the historical Principia. As we noted, the historical Principia demands that all and only variables be predicative.[14] To characterize the formulas of the language of Principia^C proceed as follows. The atomic formulas are of the form,

$$\varphi^{(t1,\ldots,tn)/m}(x_1^{\beta 1},\ldots,x_n^{\beta n}).$$

where the type of β_i is equal to that of t_i but the order of β_i may be less than or equal to the order of t_i. The formulas (wffs) are the smallest set K containing all atomic wffs such that if A, B, C are wffs in K and x^t is an individual variable free in C, then so are ~(A), A v B, and $(\forall x^t)$C.

Together with *1.2–*1.6, Church construes Principia as having the following axioms governing r-types:

Church(*10.1)
$(\forall x^{t/n}) A \supset A[y^{\beta/n} \mid x^{t/n}]$,
  where $y^{\beta/n}$ is free for $x^{t/n}$ in A, the type of β is that of t and the order is less than or equal to that of t.

Church(*10.12)
$(\forall x^{t/n})(B \vee A). \supset. B \vee (\forall x^{t/n}) A$
  where $x^{t/n}$ does not occur free in B.

Church(*12.1n Predicative$^+$)
$(\exists \varphi^{(t1,\ldots,tn)/m})(\forall x_1^{t1},\ldots,\forall x_n^{tm})(\varphi^{(t1,\ldots,tn)/m}(x_1^{t1},\ldots,x_n^{tm}) \equiv A)$,
  where $\varphi^{(t1,\ldots,tn)/m}$ is not free in A and the bound variables of A are all of order less than the order of $(t_1,\ldots,t_n)/m$ and the free variables and constants of A are all of order not greater than the order of $(t_1,\ldots,t_n)/m$.

Church (*12.1n Reducibility)
$(\forall \theta^{(t1,\ldots,tn)/m}) (\exists \varphi^{(t1,\ldots,tn)/1})$
$(\forall x_1^{t1},\ldots,\forall x_n^{tm})(\varphi^{(t1,\ldots,tn)/1}(x_1^{t1},\ldots,x_n^{tm}) \equiv$
  $\theta^{(t1,\ldots,tn)/m}(x_1^{t1},\ldots,x_n^{tm}))$.

As we see from Church's (*12.1n Reducibility), a predicate variable counts as predicative if and only if its level is 1. This is in stark contrast with Principia^L, which allows no non-predicative variables in its grammar and has *12.1n as its only comprehension axiom. In Principia^L the historical Principia is better represented, for ramification does not appear in its syntax. It appears in the intended nominalistic semantics Whitehead and Russell offered for the formal system. That is, the axiom schema *12.1n is an unwarranted principle in virtue of the intended nominalistic semantics. What is warranted by that semantics is (*12.1n Predicative). Church's formulation of Principia as Principia^C makes ramification a part of its syntax. It allows non-predicative predicate variables and comprehension via (*12.1n Predicative$^+$). Then an explicit principle (*12.1n Reducibility) is added as an axiom schema.

THE NO-CLASSES THEORY

It is remarkable that so much mathematics can be developed from the austere foundation set forth in Principia. Indeed, the foundation develops mathematics without assuming an ontology of classes. To get a glimpse of this, we set out two of Principia's most famous "logical constructions": its theory of definite descriptions and its no-classes theory. The no-classes theory is a recovery of extensional contexts—its emulation of a theory of attributes-in-extension. It thereby recovers, in an ontologically austere way, the more convenient analyses (which simply assumed extensionality) set out in Chapter Two on logicism.

Whether one thinks Principia^L or Principia^C correctly captures Whitehead and Russell's intent, it is important to understand they are not extensional systems. If a system with predicate variables is extensional then for all contexts $A\psi^{(t)}$, coexemplification,

$$(\forall x^t)(\varphi^{(t)}(x^t) \equiv \psi^{(t)}(x^t))$$

is sufficient for substitutivity of the predicate variables so that we arrive at

$$A\psi^{(t)} \equiv A\varphi^{(t)}.$$

Now the grammar of Principia allows the expression of an identity sign flanking predicate variables. In Principia^L we have $\varphi^{(t)} = \psi^{(t)}$ and in Principia^C we have $\varphi^{(t)/m} = \psi^{(t)/m}$. But it is impossible in the system to prove

$$(\forall x^t)(\varphi^{(t)}(x^t) \equiv (\psi^{(t)}(x^t))) \supset \varphi^{(t)} = \psi^{(t)}$$

in Principia^L. (A similar result applies to Principia^C.)

It is also very important to understand that Principia should be taken at its word when it says it is offering a no-classes theory. Unfortunately, the logical constructions of Principia have been interpreted as a form of reductive identity in the spirit of empiricism. For instance, Ayer writes:

> ... when Russell spoke of an object as a logical fiction, he did not mean to imply that it was imaginary or nonexistent ... Similarly, in the period during which Russell held that physical objects were logical constructions, he did not wish to suggest that they were unreal in the way that gorgons are unreal. Logical fictions do indeed exist, but only in virtue of the existence of the elements out of which they are constructed. As Russell put it, they are not part of the ultimate furniture of the world.[15]

In chemistry, heat is reductively identified with mean kinetic molecular motion. The reduction does not show that there is no such thing as heat. Ayer assumes that in Principia classes are "logical fictions" only in the sense that they are reductively identified with attributes.

On this view, there are classes after all! Ayer is mistaken. Principia enables one to emulate the results of a simple type-theory of classes without embracing an ontology of classes. This is not a reductive identity (i.e. the identification of classes with attributes of a certain sort). Classes do go the way of the gorgon sisters.

We begin with the formal theory of definite descriptions. Principia maintains there are no terms besides variables in logic. All the same, the work endeavors to make it appear as though "$\iota x \varphi x$" is a term. Principia has:

*14.01 $[\iota x\varphi x][\psi\,(\iota x\varphi x)] = \mathrm{df}\,(\exists x)(\varphi y \equiv_y y = x.\,\&.\,Bx)$.

In modern notation, what is intended is this:

$[\iota xAx][B(\iota xAx)] = \mathrm{df}\,(\exists x)(Ay \equiv_y y = x.\,\&.\,Bx)$.

As before, I use A and B schematically for formulas of the formal language. Principia uses φ and ψ sometimes as bindable predicate variables and other times as schemas for formulas. I have avoided this, reserving φ and ψ as predicate variables only. Next, Principia has:

*14.02 $E!(\iota xAx) = \mathrm{df}\,(\exists x)(Ay \equiv_y y = x)$.

Whitehead and Russell write: "Whenever we have $E!(\iota x\varphi x)$, $\iota x\varphi x$ behaves, formally, like an ordinary argument to any function in which it may occur."[16] It is important, however, not to be misled by appearances. Principia's ιxAx is not a genuine term.

Unfortunately, the status of ιxAx is obscured by views concerning the general nature of definitions in Principia. It is important to understand that the expression "$\psi(\iota x\varphi x)$" is not a well-formed expression of Principia's formal language. In fact, one may think of the primary scope operator as itself a quantifier, defined thus:

$[\iota xAx][Bx] = \mathrm{df}\,(\exists x)(Ay \equiv_y y = x.\,\&.\,Bx)$.[17]

The sole reason Principia uses $[\iota xAx][\psi(\iota xBx)]$ rather than $[\iota xAx][Bx]$ is to allow the notational convenience of omitting scope markers when smallest scope is intended. Principia's omission of scope markers makes it appear as though definite descriptions are genuine terms. But the convenience is not part of the formal symbolism.

Realizing that "ιxφx" is not a term and "$\psi(\iota x\varphi x)$" never occurs (except by notational convenience) without its scope marker helps immensely to clear up misunderstandings. The syntax of "$E!(\iota x\varphi x)$" does not put "E!" in the predicate position of "ψ" in the formula "$\psi(\iota x\varphi x)$." There is no formula "$\psi(\iota x\varphi x)$" in Principia. Consider:

*14.18 $E!(\iota xAx)\,.\supset.\,(\forall x)Bx \supset B(\iota xAx)$.

Removing abbreviations from *14.18 in a primary scope for B, we have:

$$(\exists x)(Ay \equiv_y y = x) . \supset . (\forall x) Bx \supset (\exists x)(Ay \equiv_y y = x .\&. Bx).$$

It is widely thought that Principia's definitions do not determine an order of application when "$\iota x \varphi x$" is involved. For example, Principia has:

*13.01 $x = y =$ df $(\forall \varphi)(\varphi x \equiv \varphi y)$.[18]

Consider the following:

$\iota xAx = y =$ df $_{*14.01}$ $(\exists x)(Az \equiv_z z = x. \&. x = y)$
$\iota xAx = y =$ df $_{*13.01}$ $(\forall \varphi)(\varphi(\iota xAx) \equiv \varphi y)$.

Which of the two is correct? The confusion disappears once we realize that there is no formula

$\iota xAx = y$

of Principia's object-language. The omission of scope markers is a meta-linguistic convenience. Definitions such as *13.01 formed with free variables, apply only to genuine terms (i.e. free variables) of the language of Principia.

When we have E!(ιxAx) and a truth-functional context C(...), the primary scope [ιxAx][C(Bx)] is equivalent with any secondary scope C([ιxAx][Bx]). For instance, let the context C(...) be ~(...), we have:

E!(ιxAx) . $\supset$. [ιxAx][~ (Bx)] $\equiv$ ~ ([ιxAx][Bx]).

If C is not a truth-functional context, then scopes will not always be equivalent, even when the antecedent condition E!(ιxAx) is met. As we shall see in Chapter Four, the formal apparatus of scope is among Russell's most important contributions to philosophy.

One important use of the theory of definite descriptions in Principia is that it enables the elimination of class abstract terms of the form {y: Ay}, which are read "the class of all and only those entities y that satisfy condition A." In an ontology of classes, we have a comprehension principle for classes which takes the membership sign "∈" as a primitive of the language:

(CP∈) Comprehension Axiom (schema)

$$(\exists x)(\forall y_1 \ldots y_n)(<y_1 \ldots y_n> \in x \equiv A(y_1 \ldots y_n))$$

where y is not free in A. The principle of extensionality is this:

Extensionality axiom for classes

$$x = y \supset (\forall z)(z \in x \equiv z \in y).$$

To see how to avoid class abstract terms of the form {y:Ay}, we have only to notice that we can apply Russell's theory of definite descriptions and use contextual definitions of

$$(\iota x)(y \in x \equiv_y Ay)$$

for the class of all and only those y satisfying the formula A. We arrive at the following:

$$[(\iota x)(y \in x \equiv_y Ay)][Bx] =_{df} (\exists x)(y \in z \equiv_y Ay. \equiv_z. z = x :\&: Bx).$$

Since the extensionality axiom schema assures the uniqueness of the class, we need not trouble over the uniqueness clause in the contextual definition of the definite description. Thus, for primary scope, we have:

$$[(\iota x)(y \in x \equiv_y Ay)][Bx] \equiv (\exists x)(y \in x \equiv_y Ay .\&. Bx).$$

For example, we arrive at:

$$z \in (\iota x)(y \in x \equiv_y Ay) \equiv (\exists x)(y \in x \equiv_y Ay .\&. z \in x).$$

Of course, definite descriptions introduce scope distinctions, and these are tedious. Quine offered contextual definitions for class abstract terms that parallel the results of the theory of descriptions but avoid the attending scope distinctions.[19] In any event, we see that the mere employment of a definite description instead of a class abstract term does not do away with an ontology of classes.

The theory of definite descriptions can be employed by a typed-theory of classes. But it is also perfectly compatible with Zermelo-Frankel set theory, which adopts type-free axioms for set existence that are not logical truths.

So how does this square with Russell's autobiographical comment that the theory of descriptions "... was the first step toward solving the difficulties which had baffled me for so long"?[20] The baffling difficulties, of course, pertained to paradoxes such as that of the class of all and only those classes that are not members of themselves. The solution was Russell's no-classes theory, according to which "classes, are in fact, like descriptions, logical fictions or (as we say) 'incomplete symbols.'"[21] How then is Russell's theory of definite descriptions related to *Principia*'s no-classes theory? To answer this question, one must understand that the no-classes theory of *Principia* has a translation into Russssell's substitutional theory of propositional structure. It was this substitutional theory that Russell developed on the heels of his theory of definite descriptions. But let us answer this question in a subsequent section. It is important to first see that *Principia* is genuinely a no-classes theory.

In spite of Russell's best efforts to be clear in asserting that they are fictions, and almost one hundred years since its appearance, there persists a misguided view that *Principia* identifies classes with attributes (i.e. propositional functions) in intension. For example, Linsky writes:

> Seeing that classes are not objects is enough to resolve the paradox of sets. But this is not to say that classes simply do not exist. To see that they aren't objects is rather to see that they really play the same role as higher-order entities, propositional functions, to which type distinctions do apply.... The technique uses contextual definition, rather than explicit definition, but the effect is not any more of a wholesale ontological elimination than is the theory of definite descriptions.[22]

Perhaps the easiest way to set the record straight—hopefully once and for all—is to point out that if *Principia* identified classes with propositional functions, then the following stipulative definitions for class symbols would be sufficient:

***20.01** $[\hat{y}^t \, Ay^t][B(\hat{y}^t \, Ay^t)] = \text{df} \, (\exists \psi^{(t)}) \, (\psi^{(t)}(x^t) \equiv_{xt} A(x^t) \,.\&. \, B(\psi^{(t)}))$ [23]
***20.02** $z^t \in \varphi^{(t)} = \text{df} \, \varphi^{(t)}$.

But in fact, these are not the only definitions found in *Principia*. To see how the two definitions work, observe that by employing the definitions one immediately gets an analog of the type-theoretical class abstraction:

Abstraction $z^t \in \{y^t : Ay^t\} \equiv_{z\,t} Az^t$.

Principia emulates this with the following theorem schema:

***20.3** $[\hat{y}^t \, Ay^t][z^t \in \hat{y}^t \, Ay^t] \equiv_{z\,t} Az^t$.

This theorem schema is forthcoming because the definitions yield:

$[\hat{y}^t \, Ay^t][z^t \in \hat{y}^t \, Ay^t] = \text{df}_{*20.01, *20.02} \, (\exists \psi^{(t)})(\psi^{(t)}(x^t) \equiv_{x\,t} Ax^t \,.\&. \, \psi^{(t)}(z^t))$.

Hence we have:

$(\exists \psi^{(t)})(\psi^{(t)}(x^t) \equiv_{x\,t} Ax^t \,.\&. \, \psi^{(t)}(z^t)) \equiv_{z\,t} Az^t$.

Thus, the schematic use of type indices enables the definitions to provide for the emulation of classes of entities of whatever type. Thus, if classes were themselves identified with propositional functions (i.e. entities of higher type) then these definitions would be sufficient. But according to *Principia*, these definitions do not render a type-regimented analog of abstraction for classes of classes of entities of type t.

In order to emulate classes of classes of entities of type t, *Principia* offers new definitions. Suppressing type indices for convenience of exposition, we find the following:

***20.08** $[\hat{a}Ba][C(\hat{a}Ba)] = \text{df} \, (\exists \Sigma) \, (\Sigma \alpha \equiv_a B\alpha \,.\&. \, C\Sigma)$ [24]

*20.081 $\alpha \in \Sigma\hat{a} =_{df} \Sigma\alpha$
*20.07 $(\forall\alpha)B\alpha =_{df} (\forall\varphi)B(\hat{y}\ \varphi y)$
*20.071 $(\exists\alpha)B\alpha =_{df} (\exists\varphi)B(\hat{y}\ \varphi y)$.

To understand the definitions, we must examine *Principia*'s use of bound lowercase Greek. Observe that definitions involving lowercase Greek must be applied before any contextual definitions of classes or definite descriptions. We have already seen that definitions framed with genuine variables do not apply to incomplete symbols. Thus, definitions framed with incomplete symbols must be applied before definitions framed with genuine variables. For instance, we find:

*22.03 $\alpha^{(t)} \cup \beta^{(t)} =_{df} \hat{y}^t\ (y^t \in \alpha^{(t)} \lor y^t \in \beta^{(t)})$.

In this definition, $\alpha^{(t)}$ and $\beta^{(t)}$ are schematic and stand in for $\hat{y}^t\ Ay^t$ and $\hat{y}^t\ By^t$, respectively. One must apply *22.03 before applying *20.01. Observe as well that scope markers are not part of the definitions of bound lowercase Greek because Whitehead and Russell intend that the scope of the class symbol be interpreted in its narrowest possible occurrence in the instances of these definitions.

To see how things work, consider the recovery of *Abstraction* for classes of classes. *Principia* has:

$\alpha \in \hat{a}B a \equiv_\alpha B_\alpha$.

Restoring the scope marker, we have:

$[\hat{a}Ba][\alpha \in \hat{a}Ba] \equiv_\alpha B_\alpha$.

To see how the type-theoretical analog of *Abstraction* is a theorem, remove the lowercase Greek by *20.07 to arrive at:

$[\hat{a}Ba][[\hat{y}\ \varphi y][\hat{y}\ \varphi y \in \hat{a}Ba]] \equiv_\varphi B(\hat{y}\ \varphi y)$.

By *20.08, *20.01, *20.02, the left-hand side is:

$(\exists \Sigma) (\Sigma \alpha \equiv_\alpha B\alpha \;.\&.\; (\exists \psi) (\psi x \equiv_x \varphi x \;.\&.\; \Sigma \psi))$.

If the scope were primary in B, then by applying *20.01, the right-hand side is:

$(\exists \psi) (\psi x \equiv_x \varphi x \;.\&.\; B\psi)$.

The expression $\Sigma \alpha \equiv_\alpha B\alpha$ abbreviates:

$[\hat{y}\, \Gamma y][\Sigma(\hat{y}\, \Gamma y)] \equiv_\Gamma B(\hat{y}\, \Gamma y)$.

Putting all this together with a primary scope in B, we have:

$(\exists \Sigma)((\exists \psi) (\psi x \equiv_x \Gamma x \;.\&.\; \Sigma \psi) \equiv_\Gamma (\exists \psi) (\psi x \equiv_x \Gamma x \;.\&.\; B\psi) \;.\&.$
$(\exists \psi) (\psi x \equiv_x \varphi x \;.\&.\; \Sigma \psi))$
$\equiv_\varphi (\exists \psi) (\psi x \equiv_x \varphi x \;.\&.\; B\psi)$.

This is how *Principia* emulates a type-regimented analog of *Abstraction* for classes of classes of type t. The presence of these definitions in *Principia* shows that classes are not entities of any type. *Principia* is genuinely working without an ontology of classes.

The nature of *Principia's* emulation of a type-theory of classes should now be clear. The definition *20.01 emulates classes of all types of entity. But since *Principia's* classes are not entities *20.01 does not emulate classes of classes of entities. Indeed, a similar result applies to *20.08. Although *20.08 emulates classes of classes (of all types of entity), it does not provide for classes of classes of classes of entities. The pattern is nonetheless clear. It is quite straightforward to see that what is needed is a recursive definition with respect to emulating classes. Observe, however, that a general recursive definition neither shows how to emulate classes of relations-in-extension (relations$_e$ of individuals), nor emulates relations$_e$ of classes (of individuals) and the like.

Principia discusses its no-relations in extension (relations$_e$) theory in section *21. The emulation of relations$_e$ is analogous to the emulation of classes set out at *20. We need not go into the details. But let us note that in analogy with *20.02 we find:

*21.02 $a\{\hat{y} \, R \, \hat{u}\}b =_{df} aRb.$[25]

This definition has been wrongly thought to be a comprehension principle for attributes.[26] But it is simply a notational convenience which is better written with the membership sign as follows:

$<a, b> \in R =_{df} aRb.$

No special problems arise for relation$_e$ symbols. Interestingly, the emulation of heterogeneous relations$_e$ (i.e. relations$_e$ between individuals and classes, between classes of different types, etc.) is a central feature of *Principia*'s no-classes (and no-relations$_e$) theory. This is particularly important because it permits us to compare classes of different types. It enables us to prove, for example, that there are exactly as many individuals as there are singleton classes of individuals (i.e. classes with exactly one individual as its member).

PRINCIPIA'S NOMINALISTIC SEMANTICS

In Chapter Two, we sketched the basic features of the logicist construction of the foundations of mathematics. We set it out in a Fregean language of simple types of attributes in extension. Frege held that attributes have only a predicable nature. He made a sharp contrast between concepts (i.e. attributes) and objects. Many of Frege's attributes are quantificational structures, and he certainly has this in mind in arguing for his thesis that attributes are extensional and have only a predicable nature. The quantifier expression "$(\forall x)(\ldots x \ldots)$" fits grammatically with the predicate expression "$\varphi(\;)$" to form "$(\forall x)(\varphi(x))$". Similarly, the quantifier expression "$(\forall \varphi)(\ldots \varphi(\;) \ldots)$" fits grammatically together with "$(\forall x)(\ldots x \ldots)$" to form "$(\forall \varphi)((\forall x)(\varphi(x)))$." Frege demands an extensional language for logic that keeps predicate variables in predicate positions. This respects their fundamentally predicable nature. In this language, it is not possible to formulate Russell's paradox of the attributes R that an attribute φ has if and only if $\sim\varphi(\varphi)$. The paradox requires that a predicate variable occurs in a subject position.

Frege's thesis embodies a theory of simple types of attributes, and the theory is well-motivated independently of any concern to avoid Russell's discovery of the paradox of attributes. This is the bright side. The dark side for Russell is that he could not bring himself to accept Frege's thesis that attributes have only a predicable nature. He thought that the thesis is self-refuting. To assert the thesis is to predicate something of an attribute, and as such the term for the attribute must occur in a subject position. The objection was put to Frege by Benno Kerry in a review of Frege's book *The Foundations of Arithmetic*. On Frege's view, the concept "horse" is not a concept. Kerry found this to be absurd. Russell is in a bind. He cannot accept Frege's thesis that attributes have only a predicable nature. But logic cannot embrace an ontology of attributes regimented by simple type-theory. A theory of logical types of objects is incompatible with the very nature of logic. In our next section we shall chronicle Russell's many struggles to overcome this difficulty. For the present, it is enough to point out that in *Principia*, Russell's solution to the problem is a nominalistic semantics for predicate variables.

The thesis that *Principia* espouses a nominalistic semantics is still hotly debated by scholars. But there is much to be said for it as the best interpretation of the evidence. In *My Philosophical Development* (1959), Russell writes that "[T]he propositional function itself is only an expression" (MPD, p. 82). He goes on to say that "Whitehead and I thought of a propositional function as an expression containing an undetermined variable and becoming an ordinary sentence as soon as a value is assigned to that variable" (MPD, p. 124). These remarks are late and, some think, they can be explained away as the product of a failing memory. But similar remarks are found in earlier works. In *Introduction to Mathematical Philosophy* (1919) Russell is clear that by a "proposition" he means "a form of words" and by a propositional function he means an "expression containing one or more undetermined constituents, such that, when values are assigned to these constituents, the expression becomes a proposition" (IMP, p. 156). This too might be regarded as a change of heart from an earlier realist orientation which accepted an ontology of attributes regimented by orders and types. But we also find the nominalistic orientation in "On the Notion of Cause" (1911–1912) where Russell writes:

> A propositional function is an expression containing a variable, or undetermined constituent, and becoming a proposition as soon as a definite value is assigned to the variable.[27]

And indeed in Principia itself, Whitehead and Russell write:

> By a "propositional function" we mean something which contains a variable x, and becomes a proposition as soon as a value is assigned to x. That is to say, it differs from a proposition solely by the fact that it is ambiguous. It contains a variable of which the value is unassigned.
>
> (PM, p. 38)

There are no propositions in Principia in any ontological sense. Hence, it is quite clear that by a "proposition" Whitehead and Russell can only have meant a formula of the formal language of the work.

The modern formal notion of a nominalistic semantics for predicate variables was entirely unknown at the time Whitehead and Russell wrote, and formal semantics was in its infancy. It awaited the pioneering work of Tarski in the 1930s. Russell is to be forgiven for his inexact expressions of the idea and the use-mention confusions that engulf his expressions of it. But as we shall see, the evidence is incontestable. The intended semantics of the predicate variables of Principia's formal language (i.e. its "propositional functions") is nominalistic. That is, predicate variables are to be interpreted in terms of formulas organized into a hierarchy on the basis of the complexity of the symbols in them. Individual variables, on the other hand, are genuine.

It is important to see that the nominalistic semantics, not

Poincaré's Vicious Circle Principle (VCP), is the philosophical explanation of the ramified-type structure. In 1906 Russell wrote:

> M. Poincaré ... appears not to realize that, if vicious circles ... are to be avoided, some elaborate re-statement of logical principles, more or less resembling my no-classes theory, is absolutely indispensible. We may illustrate this by what M. Poincaré says concerning Richard's paradox. Having first put $E=$ "all numbers definable in a finite number of words," we arrive at a paradox, due says M. Poincaré, to our having included a number only definable in a finite number of words by means of E. This vicious circle he proposes to avoid by defining E as "all numbers definable in a finite number of words without mentioning E." To the uninitiated, this definition looks more circular than ever.
>
> (*InS*, p. 196)

The same lesson occurs in 1908 in "Mathematical Logic as Based on the Theory of Types." Russell writes that Poincaré's VCP is "purely negative in its scope."

> It suffices to show that many theories are wrong, but it does not show how the errors are to be rectified. We cannot say: "When I speak of all propositions, I mean all except those in which 'all propositions' are mentioned"; for in this explanation we have mentioned the propositions in which all propositions are mentioned, which is what we cannot do significantly. It is impossible to avoid mentioning a thing by mentioning that we won't mention it.
>
> (*ML*, p. 71)

In Russell's view, one cannot restrict a variable by adding a clause stating that is restricted. The only escape is to maintain that, while individual variables are genuine (and so unrestricted), predicate variables are not genuine. The restriction thereby comes from the conditions of their significance and is not imposed from without. Russell says that it is "an internal limitation" and "a limitation that does not require explicit statement" (ML, p. 72).

In the introduction to the first edition of *Principia*, Whitehead and Russell have a section called "Why a Given Function requires Arguments of a Certain Type." This offers an informal nominalistic semantics for predicate variables that philosophically justifies and explains the type component of the order/type indices on the predicate variables. They write:

> ... when a function can occur significantly as argument, something which is not a function cannot occur significantly as an argument. But conversely when something which is not a function can occur significantly as an argument, a function cannot occur significantly. Take, *e.g.*, "x is a man" and consider "φŷ is a man." There is nothing to eliminate the ambiguity which constitutes φŷ; there is nothing definite which is said to be a man. A function, in fact, is not a definite object, which could be or not be a man; it is a mere ambiguity awaiting determination, and in order that it may occur significantly it must receive the necessary determination, which it obviously does not receive if it is merely substituted for something determinate in a proposition.*
>
> (*PM*, p. 48)

In a footnote to * we find: "Note that statements concerning the significance of a phrase containing 'φẑ' concerns the symbol 'φẑ' and therefore do not fall under the rule that the elimination of the functional ambiguity is necessary to significance. Significance is a property of signs."[28] What do Whitehead and Russell have in mind in saying that a propositional function is a "mere ambiguity awaiting determination?" They simply mean that a predicate variable is given an assignment in a semantics for the formal language. Their example clearly shows that the semantics they intend is nominalistic. For example, if the predicate variable $\varphi^{(o)}$ is interpreted so that we can replace it by formulas of a language containing, say "x is a man," and if $\psi^{((o))}$ is assigned to "$(\forall x)(\ldots x \ldots)$" then "$\psi^{((o))}(\varphi^{(o)})$" will be assigned to the formula

"$(\forall x)(x \text{ is a man})$."

Taking it the other way around will not result in something meaningful, for we would have

"$(\forall x)(\ldots x \ldots)$ is a man."

The type component of the order/type indices on the predicate variable of *Principia*'s formal language is thereby explained. The explanation sounds much like Frege. But Frege embraced a realism of attributes in extension. Russell avoids the realism by his nominalistic semantics. Russell's types are not types of entities. They are a scaffolding explained in a way that is consistent with Russell's long-held doctrine of the unrestricted variable: the thesis that the language of logic must embrace only one style of genuine variables. Predicate variables are not genuine. Their range is "internally limited" by their significance conditions given in the nominalistic semantics. The genuine variables of the work are the individual variables.

What about the order component of the order/type indices adorning predicate variables? In the introduction to *Principia*'s first edition, there is a section called "Definition and Systematic Ambiguity of Truth and Falsehood." In this section, the philosophical justification and explanation of the order component on the predicate variables is given by appeal to a recursive definition of "truth" and "falsehood." When Russell embraced propositions, properties of truth (obtaining) and *falsehood* (non-obtaining) have to be primitive and unanalyzable. The recursive definition is made possible by *Principia*'s abandonment of Russell's early ontology of propositions. The base of the recursion gives truth-conditions for atomic formulas by means of definite descriptions for purportedly corresponding facts. This is the so-called "multiple-relation theory." In *Principia*, Whitehead and Russell write:

> Owing to the plurality of the objects of a single judgment, it follows that what we call a "proposition" (in the sense in which this is

> distinguished from the phrase expressing it) is not a single entity at all. That is to say, the phrase that expresses a proposition is what we call an "incomplete" symbol; it does not have meaning in itself, but requires some supplementation in order to acquire a complete meaning.[29]
>
> (*PM to *56*, p. 44)

"A proposition," Whitehead and Russell continue, "like such phrases as 'the so and so,' where grammatically it appears as subject, must be broken up into its constituents if we are to find the true subject or subjects (op. cit., p. 48)."[30] In "On the Nature of Truth," Russell intimates that a statement flanked by ". . . is true" is a disguised definite description. He wrote that his new theory of "truth" is ". . . an extension of the principle applied in my article 'On Denoting' [Mind, October, 1905] . . ."[31] This strongly suggests that the theory of definite descriptions is directly involved in Russell's new definition of truth. Russell is neither explicit as to how the analysis is "like" the analysis of definite descriptions, nor does he say what definite description is disguised. But his intent seems clear. The recursive characterization of truth and falsehood is a correspondence theory. The notion of $truth_0$ applicable to wffs[32] that are atomic (i.e. involving no logical constants or quantifiers) is defined in terms of correspondence between a belief and a fact. $Falsehood_0$ is defined as the absence of any corresponding fact. When an atomic wff flanked by the expression ". . . is $true_0$" the formula is to be construed as a disguised definite description. It should be noted that unlike modern formal semantic theories, this allows a formula itself and not a name of a formula to be flanked by ". . . is true." In this way, we can see how the theory of definite descriptions was to play a central role at the base of the recursive definition of "truth" and "falsehood."

We saw that according to section *9 of *Principia*, all formulas in primitive notation have their quantifiers initially placed. The purpose of *9 is to facilitate the recursive definitions of "truth" and "falsehood" as applied to formulas of *Principia*. Details of the multiple-relation theory aside,[33] where $^{e.0}\varphi^{(o)}$ (x_1^o, ..., x_n^o) is an atomic wff, the base of the recursion provides the following:

$^{e.0}\varphi^{(o)}$ (x_1^o, ..., x_n^o) true$_{e.1}$ iff
the fact consisting of the universal assigned to $^{e.0}\varphi^{(o)}$ and the entities assigned to x_1^o, ..., x_n^o in proper order exists.

With the base of the recursion for atomic wffs established, truth-conditions for quantified formulas are given. Whitehead and Russell write:

> That the words "true" and "false" have many different meanings, according to the kind of proposition to which they are applied, is not difficult to see. Let us call the sort of truth which is applicable to φ*a* "first truth." . . . Consider now the proposition (x).φx. If this has truth of the sort appropriate to it, that will mean that every value φx has "first truth." Thus, if we call the sort of truth applicable to (x). φx "*second* truth," we may define "[(x).φx] as second truth" as meaning "every value for φx has first truth," i.e., "(x).(φx has first truth]."[34]

The passage is informal and sketchy. Moreover, there is no clause for molecular wffs. But the intent to offer a recursive definition of "truth" and "falsehood" is absolutely clear. The idea seems to be this. Where *p* is a molecular wff containing exactly n-many subordinate atomic propositional clauses, [~p] true$_{e.n}$ if and only if it is not the case that [p] is true$_{e.n-1}$. Where p and q are molecular and quantifier-free wffs, [p ⊃ q] is true$_{e.a+b}$ if and only if either [p] is false$_{e.a}$ or [q] is true$_{e.b}$. Where Ax is a quantifier-free wff, [(∀x)Ax] is true$_{1.1;\ e.n}$ if and only if every entity x is such that [Ax] is true$_{1.o;\ e.n}$.

The truth conditions *Principia* gives for general judgments (i.e. quantified wffs) is important. According to the recursive characterization of the *Principia*, the truth of a quantified wff lies in its correspondence with several facts. Whitehead and Russell are explicit:

And generally, in any judgement (x). φx, the sense in which this judgment is or may be true is not the same as that in which φx is or may be true. If φx is an elementary judgment, it is true when it *points to* a corresponding complex. But (x). φx does not *point to* a single corresponding complex: the corresponding complexes are as numerous as the possible values of x.[35]

The recursive characterization of "truth" and "falsehood," founded upon the multiple-relation theory of judgment and its abandonment of propositions (and their accompanying primitive properties of truth and falsehood), are central features of Russell's philosophical explanation of order in the ramified type-theory of Principia.

To see this, we must understand how the recursion applies when predicate variables are involved. Order indices on the predicate variables track the hierarchy of senses of truth and falsehood as applied to wffs at a level (i.e. order) in a fixed hierarchy. The levels are determined by the complexity of the wffs involved. For instance, level L_1 contains formulas with bound and free individual variables and no formulas with higher order variables. Level L_2 contains L_1 and allows formulas with bound and free predicate variables of order 1 but no higher. To illustrate how order indices on predicate variables are explained in the semantics, let us introduce fine-grained order indices. For instance, instead of Principia's predicate variable

$$\varphi^{(o)}$$

whose type is (o) and order is 1, consider the following variable:

$$^{1.m;e.a}\varphi^{(o)}.$$

This is a predicate variable of type (o) which in the nominalistic semantics is such that only wffs that contain exactly m-many bound individual variables and a-many quantifier-free propositional subordinate clauses can be substituted for its occurrences. Arguments to this predicate variable are individual variables of the form $^{\circ}x^{\circ}$. Following Russell's example, the recursively defined hierarchy of truth and falsehood contains clauses such as the following. Where A is wff containing the variable $^{1..n;e.b}\varphi^{(o)}$ free, and where d is the number of occurrences of the bound predicate variable $^{1..n;e.b}\varphi^{(o)}$ in predicate positions in the formula A, we have:

$[(\forall^{1.n;\ e.b}\varphi^{(o)})A]$ is true $_{z.\ w;\ \ldots;\ 1.m;\ e.a}$ iff every formula A* is true $_{z.\ w;\ \ldots;\ 1.m\ +\ (n\ \times\ d);\ e.a\ +\ (b\ \times\ d)}$ where A* is obtained by replacing each occurrence of the variable $^{1.n;e.b}\ \varphi^{(o)}$ in A by a formula B containing exactly n-many bound individual variables, and b-many elementary (molecular) sub-formulas.

An example will be helpful. Consider:

$[(\forall^{1.n;\ e.b}\varphi^{(o)})(^{1.n;\ e.b}\varphi^{(o)}(y^{\circ}))]$ is true $_{2.1;\ 1.0;\ e.1}$.

This wff is true in the sense 2.1; 1.0; e.1 because of the following. It is 2.1 because it contains one level 2 quantifier $(\forall^{1.n;\ e.b}\varphi^{(o)})$ over a level 1 predicate variable $^{1.n;\ e.b}\varphi^{(o)}$. It is 1.0 because it contains zero many level 1 quantifiers over individual variables y°. It is e.1 because there is exactly one occurrence of an atomic subordinate wff it, namely $^{1.n;\ e.b}\varphi^{(o)}(y^{\circ})$.

Now the recursion defines this notion of true $_{2.1;\ 1.0;\ e.1}$ by appeal to the assertion that for every wff B of level 1.n, e.b, the result of properly putting B for the predicate variable $^{1.n;\ e.b}\varphi^{(o)}$ in $^{1.n;\ e.b}\varphi^{(o)}(y^{\circ})$ yields a wff that is true in sense $1.0 + (n \times d);\ e.1 + (b \times d)$. In this case $d = 1$ (since the predicate variable $^{1.n;\ e.b}\varphi^{(o)}$ has exactly one occurrence in predicate position). To see this, consider the case where the formula B is:

$(\forall x^{\circ})(^{1.0;\ e.1}\psi^{(o)}(x^{\circ}) \supset\ ^{1.0;\ e.1}\psi^{(o)}(z^{\circ}))$.

The result of the replacement, putting y° in the position of z°, is $B(y^{\circ})$. That is:

$(\forall x^{\circ})(^{1.0;\ e.1}\psi^{(o)}(x^{\circ}) \supset\ ^{1.0;\ e.1}\psi^{(o)}(y^{\circ}))$.

As we can see, this is true in sense $1.0 + (1 \times 1)$; e.$1 + (2 \times 1)$. That is, it is true in sense 1.1; e.2.

The recursive definitions of "truth" and "falsehood" provide the philosophical explanation of the order component of the order/type indices on Principia's predicate variables. The order indices track the recursively defined senses of "truth" and "falsehood" as applied to wffs of Principia.

Happily, not all the details of the number as well as the order of the quantifiers in a given formula are reflected in the order/type indices of Principia's predicate variables. Whitehead and Russell explain that for convenience, there is no need to burden the notation in this way. Whitehead and Russell write:

> First order propositions are not all of the same type, since as was explained in *9 two propositions which do not contain the same number of apparent variables cannot be of the same type. But owing to the systematic ambiguity of negation and disjunction, their differences of type may usually be ignored in practice. No reflexive fallacies will result, since no first-order proposition involves any totality except individuals.[36]

Nonetheless, we see clearly how Principia's philosophical explanation of order/type indices relies on its informal nominalistic semantics for predicate variables.

The success of Principia's *9 as a quantification theory justifies the Wittgenstein/Ramsey claim that quantification theory consists of "generalized tautologies." It does not, of course, yield a decision procedure for logical truths of quantification theory. Church (1936) showed that quantification theory is undecidable.[37] But the success of *9 as a quantification theory corroborates Wittgenstein's thesis that quantification theory is not a science which extends knowledge. The comprehension axiom schema *12.1n of Principia, however, is another matter entirely. It is precisely comprehension that makes logic a genuine science (i.e. informative) in a way that quantification theory is not. Wittgenstein and Ramsey noticed that unlike the logical truths of quantification theory, *12.1n cannot be reached by generalizing tautologies. But more importantly, the comprehension principle *12.1n is impredicative and as such it is not valid in Principia's intended nominalistic semantics! The comprehension principle that is validated by such a semantics is the following weaker "predicative" comprehension principle:

*12.1n (Predicative)
$(\exists \varphi^{(t1, \ldots, tm)})(\forall x_1^{t1}, \ldots, \forall x_n^{tm})(\varphi^{(t1, \ldots, tm)}(x_1^{t1}, \ldots, x_n^{tm}) \equiv A)$,
where $\varphi^{(t1, \ldots, tm)}$ is not free in A and the bound variables of A are all of order less than the order of $(t_1, \ldots, t_n)$ and the free variables and constants of A are all of order not greater than the order of $(t_1, \ldots, t_n)$.

Of course, the adoption of *12.1n captures all instances of *12.1n (Predicative) and thus obviates having two comprehension principles. But this is no mere convenience. When seen from the perspective of what is validated by the intended nominalistic semantics, comprehension principle *12.1n is an unwarranted Reducibility principle which assures that order vanishes altogether in extensional contexts in favor of the impredicative comprehension of simple type-theory. The failure of *12.1n to be valid in the intended nominalistic semantics of Principia is a serious flaw in the semantics. It is a problem that is quite independent of Wittgenstein's thesis that logic is not a science. This is a serious problem for Russell even if one accepts that logic is a genuine science. Wittgenstein and Ramsey can accept a predicative comprehension principle because it is valid in a nominalistic semantics. The semantics makes it consonant with their conception of logic as consisting of generalized tautologies. But they cannot accept the impredicative *12.1n.

FROM *PRINCIPLES* TO *PRINCIPIA*

The historical evolution of the ramified type-theoretical structure of Principia Mathematica is complicated. Simple type theoretical structure blocks Russell's paradoxes of classes and attributes. It blocks the Burali-Forti paradox of ordinals and a host of other such paradoxes. How then did Russell find himself in the predicament of having a nominalistic semantics which cannot support the fundamental comprehension principles of the theory?

The orthodox answer, captivating the minds of scholars for almost one hundred years, is that Russell thought that both the semantic paradoxes of naming and definability (e.g. those of Berry, Richard and König/Dixon and the Epimenides Liar) stem from a source in common with the paradoxes of classes and attributes. This traditional answer is mistaken. To understand the reasons why it is mistaken we must walk the long and winding journey Russell took to solve the paradoxes plaguing logicism by an analysis of the variables of quantification.

Fundamental to Russell's conception of the language for pure logic is the notion that there is only one style of genuine variables of quantification: individual variables. Special variables for different kinds of entities, predicate variables, propositional variables, and class variables are on a par with special variables for dogs as opposed to cats and snakes. None should be part of the language of pure logic. Logic treats all entities alike and applies equally to whatever there is. There can be to logical types of entities. Let us call this thesis about logic "Russell's doctrine of the unrestricted variable." It is the centerpiece of *The Principles of Mathematics*.

When Russell discovered his paradox of classes (i.e. the class of all entities not members of themselves) and the paradox of attributes (i.e. the attribute an attribute exemplifies if and only if it does not exemplify itself) he at once recognized the tension between a type-theoretical dodge of the paradoxes and the doctrine of the unrestricted variables of the language of logic. At first he worked to find logical principles for determining what classes (and attributes) there are. But no such principles of logic could be found to separate the good classes (and attributes) from the bad and ugly. He concluded that pure logic must get along without the assumption that there are comprehension principles for classes and attributes.

Russell's plan for solving the paradoxes was to emulate a hierarchy of simple types of attributes (and thereby the classes which are their extensions) without employing any comprehension principles for attributes or classes. Thus was born Russell's substitutional theory of propositional structure. Logic, Russell thought, is the synthetic a priori science of structure: the theory of the structure of propositions. *Principles* was to have a second volume, working out in a technically formal way the doctrines of the first volume which free mathematics from the metaphysicans, the number devils who make it appear as if there are special non-logical necessities governing entities which are numbers. The substitutional theory was to be its centerpiece. Since logic treats all entities alike as individuals (i.e. entities, logical subjects) the language of the theory has individual variables as its only variables.

This has not been very well appreciated by the orthodox interpretation of Russell. The reason is that Russell's notion of a proposition was misunderstood. Let me put the point starkly: *There are no paradoxes of the quantification theory of propositions*. The orthodox interpretation failed to see this because of confusions about Russell's views on propositions. But archival manuscripts (i.e. an analog of the Dead Sea Scrolls) finally began to be understood in the 1980s, and an entirely new perspective emerged. Russellian propositions are not *about* anything in the semantic sense in which we say a thought is about something. They are mind- and language-independent intensional entities that are akin to states of affairs, some of which are obtaining (i.e. are true) and others of which are non-obtaining (i.e. are false).

The early Russellian language of propositions uses the horseshoe sign "$\supset$" in a way that is quite different from its use in *Principia* and in modern logic. Let me use the sign "$)$" to mark the distinction. Thus, where x and y are individual variables, "$x \,) \, y$" is a well-formed formula read "x implies y." The sign "$)$" is a relation sign.

It is flanked by terms to form a formula. Thus "x **)** {y **)** x}" is to be read as saying "x implies y's implying x." Using the horseshoe in the modern way, "x ⊃ y" is quite ungrammatical. The modern sign "⊃" is a statement connective which is flanked by formulas to form formulas. We have to write "A ⊃ B," where A and B are formulas, not terms. Thus we read the modern expression "A ⊃ B," as saying "if A then B." The modern expression "A ⊃ B" is expressed in the language of substitution as "{A} **)** {B}." One must transform (i.e. nominalize) a formula A into a term {A} since the sign "**)**" is flanked by terms. The syntax is a bit confusing, especially because it is tedious to use braces. Russell allows subject position to mark a nominalizing transformation, using dots for punctuation. For instance, he allows "x . **).** y **)** x" instead of the more exacting "x **)** {y **)** x}." Similarly, he allows "A . **).** B **)** A" instead of the more exacting "{A} **)** {{B} **)** {A}}."

The other logical particles of the theory of propositions are defined in terms of the relation of implication. As expected, Russell has:

$\alpha \equiv \beta = df\ (\alpha\ )\ \beta) \cdot (\beta\ )\ \alpha)$.

The sign "•" is not for conjunction in the modern sense. Russell has:

$\alpha \cdot \beta = df \sim (\alpha\ )\ \sim\beta)$
$\sim\alpha = df\ (\forall z)(\alpha\ )z)$.

Thus "∼α" says that α implies everything and "α • β" says that α's implying β's implying everything implies everything. This is quite different than the ordinary modern notion of conjunction. Indeed, Russell allows "x • y," which is complete gibberish if the sign were for conjunction. We can see this by realizing that Russell's logical rule of simplification cannot be:

From α • β infer α.

This would have as an instance the incoherent:

From Russell • Frege infer Russell.

Only a well-formed formula can be inferred. Confusion on this matter has led some to read Russell's "α • β" as "α is true and β is true." That way, simplification would yield the formula "α is true." But this is misguided. There is no predicate "true" in the formal logic of propositions. In the language of propositions, the rule of simplification is this:

From {A} • β infer A.

The logical particles should not be confused with the modern logical connectives.

One intriguing feature of Russell's theory of propositions is that it embraces a consistent form of ontological self-reference. Russell embraces general propositions. General propositions quantify over everything, including themselves. Every instance of the following logical axiom of universal instantiation is accepted.

$(\forall x)Ax \;.\;).\; A\{(\forall x)Ax\}.$

For example, consider the following:

$(\forall x)(x = x) \;.\;).\; \{(\forall x)(x = x)\} = \{(\forall x)(x = x)\}.$

This form of quantificational self-reference involves circularity, but it is not a source of paradox. There are no paradoxes of the quantificational logic of Russellian propositions. Confusion on this point abounds in the literature on Russell, and for a great many years it made it impossible to understand the historical origin and nature of *Principia*'s so-called "ramified type theory."

Russell's quantificational logic of propositions allows ontological self-reference which is not problematic or viciously circular in any way. Indeed, in a manuscript of 1905 Russell considered whether there is a propositional Liar paradox that arises with the following general proposition:

$\{(\exists x)(\text{I now assert } x \;.^{\bullet}.\; \sim x)\}.$

This did not deter him from going forth with his conception of logic as a theory of the structure of propositions. Russell seems to have recognized that the propositional Liar is not part of the quantificational logic of propositions. It involves contingent entities (i.e. persons) and psychological theories which assume that minds stand in relations of assertion (or alternatively belief, etc.) to propositions. The orthodoxy might appeal to Russell's comments in *Principles*, suggesting that there is a logical (non-psychological) notion of assertion. But in his Appendix A he demurs and says that assertion is never part of a proposition (PoM, p. 504). The orthodoxy proclaims that semantic properties of truth and falsehood are essential to Russellian propositions. But this misunderstands Russell's horseshoe, as if "x ⊃ y" has to be interpreted to mean "if x is true then y is true." This wrongly conflates Russell's early use of the horseshoe sign with the modern use of the sign. The confusion persists to this day, and with it comes the mistaken view that Russellian propositions are somehow involved in semantic paradoxes, such as the Epimenides Liar, which arises with "This proposition is false". No propositional Liar can be formulated in spite of the rampant form of ontological "self-reference" allowed in Russell's early quantificational theory of propositions. Russell embraced the ontological self-reference of general propositions unhesitatingly. There are no paradoxes of propositions—yet.

Russell's substitutional theory endeavors to emulate a simple type theory of attributes (and so also classes). The expression $p\frac{x}{a}!q$ says that (proposition) q is structurally exactly like p except containing x where p contains a. (An alternate notation for this is $p/a;^x!q$.) To emulate bound predicate variables $\varphi^{(o)}$ Russell uses two individual variables p and a. For example,

$$(\forall \varphi^{(o)})(\exists x^o)\ \varphi^{(o)}(x^o)$$

is emulated by writing:

Principia Mathematica

$$(\forall p)(\forall a)(\exists x)(\exists q)\left(p\frac{x}{a}!q \mathbin{.\!^\bullet.} q\right).$$

Russell next employs definite descriptions for propositions. He writes "$p\frac{x}{a}$" to abbreviate the definite description "$(\iota q)\left(p\frac{x}{a}!q\right)$." This enables the substitutional language to parallel more closely the notions of simple type theory. For example, the expression

$$(\forall \varphi^{(o)})(\forall x^o)(\varphi^{(o)}(x^o) \supset \varphi^{(o)}(x^o))$$

is translated into the language of propositions as follows:

$$(\forall p)(\forall a)(\forall x)\left(p\frac{x}{a}\right) p\frac{x}{a}.$$

Removing the abbreviation of definite descriptions, we have:

$$(\forall p)(\forall a)(\forall x)(\exists q)\left(p\frac{x}{a}!r \equiv_r r = q \mathbin{.\!^\bullet.} q\right) q.$$

The number of bound individual variables increases as we ascend logical types. The expression $s\frac{p,\,a}{t,\,w}!q$ says that q is structurally exactly like s except containing p wherever s contains t and containing a wherever s contains w. Russell writes "$s\frac{p,\,a}{t,\,w} q$" to abbreviate the definite description "$(\iota q)\left(s\frac{p,\,a}{t,\,w}!q\right)$." The substitutional theory emulates binding a predicate variable of type $\psi^{((o))}$ by using three individual variables s, t, and w. For example, the expression

$$(\forall \psi^{((o))})(\forall \varphi^{(o)})(\psi^{((o))}(\varphi^{(o)}) \supset \psi^{((o))}(\varphi^{(o)}))$$

is translated into the language of propositions as follows:

$$(\forall s)(\forall t)(\forall w)(\forall p)(\forall a)\left(s\frac{p,\,a}{t,\,w}\right) s\frac{p,\,a}{t,\,w}.$$

Removing the abbreviation of the definite description, we have:

$$(\forall s)(\forall t)(\forall w) \; (\forall p)(\forall a)(\exists q)\left(s\frac{p,a}{t,w} \; !r \equiv_r r = q. \&. q\right) q\right).$$

As we see, a hierarchy of types of attributes is emulated by the number of individual variables employed.

These examples suggest that anything expressible in the language of the simple-type theory of predicate variables has a straightforward translation into the type-free language of the substitutional theory of propositions. The expression $\varphi(\varphi)$, which violates simple-type theory, cannot be emulated in either language. In the language of substitution it would require the ungrammatical expression

$$p\frac{x,y}{a} \; !q.$$

It is meaningless to speak of substituting two entities x and y for one entity a in a propositional structure. The substitutional theory of propositional structure is not a theory of types of entities. Rather, it emulates a theory of types of attributes (and thus classes as their extensions) in type-free theory. It therefore affords a genuine solution of the paradoxes of attributes and classes from within pure logic itself. The only genuine variables are individual variables.

The historical connection between the substitutional theory of propositional structure, the theory of definite descriptions, and the no-classes theory of *Principia* can now be made clear. Prior to the discovery of definite descriptions, Russell struggled with the ideas developed in *Principles* to formulate a substitutional theory that offers a bridge from Aristotelian categorical logic to the variables of the new quantification theory. The theory of denoting concepts in *Principles* was to have been the bridge from categorical logic to the new quantification theory. On that early theory, denoting concepts, such as *all A*, *some A*, *the A*, and *an A* occur as constituents of propositions. The bridge explains individual variables by means of the substitution of one entity for another in a proposition. The bridge emulating predicate variables involved substituting one denoting concept for another in a proposition. Russell hoped that the bridge would also yield insights into solving the paradoxes of attributes. The paradoxes involve using bound predicate variables for attributes. The legitimate cases of using predicate variables would be revealed by the substitutional analysis and this, Russell hoped, would show how the paradoxes of attributes (and thereby also the paradoxes of classes) can be solved.

It was in his struggle to work out a viable theory of substitution of one denoting concept for another that Russell discovered this new theory of definite descriptions. The argument has come to be called the "Gray's Elegy" argument. It appears in "On Denoting," and in a manuscript of June 1905 titled "On Fundamentals." The argument has baffled commentators for decades. But the crux is this. Russell came to believe that the theory of denoting concepts of *Principles* generates a hopelessly obscure notion of propositional structure. The pristine theory of propositional structure involves things and concepts (i.e. properties and relations). Things can only occur in a proposition "as logical subject" (i.e. "as term"). It is in virtue of such an occurrence in a true proposition that an entity is said to have a property (or stand in a relation). Thus all entities occur as terms in true propositions. Concepts are entities; thus they occur as term. But concepts have the capacity for an indefinable two-fold occurrence. Consider the following proposition:

Socrates is human.

The property *being human* occurs in it as concept (predicatively). Socrates occurs in it as term. Socrates is a thing; things cannot occur as concept in a proposition. The concept (property) *being human* occurs as term in the following proposition:

Socrates exemplifies (the property of) *being human*.

It is the relation *exemplifies* that occurs as concept. The unity of a proposition lies in the occurrence of a property or relation in it as concept.

The case of denoting concepts, however, raises special concerns. The fundamental law of denoting is this (PoM, p. 75):

> A denoting concept involving a property F denotes an entity x only if {x is an F} is a true (obtaining) proposition.

In the law, the true proposition {x is F} is one in which the entity x occurs as term. It is only in virtue such an occurrence that an entity exemplifies F. Thus for example, *every man* denotes Socrates only if {Socrates is a man} obtains. Adhering to the law of denoting, it is clear that denoting concepts must themselves be capable of the twofold occurrence distinctive of concepts generally. Otherwise, it would be impossible for one denoting concept to denote another. The denoting concept

> the denoting concept occurring in the proposition {Every man is mortal}

denotes *every man* only if *every man* occurs as term in a true proposition predicating the property of being a denoting concept occurring in {Every man is mortal}. So it is clear that denoting concepts must be able to occur as term. But consider the structure of the proposition

> {Every man is mortal}.

How does the denoting concept *every man* occur? If it were to occur as term, the proposition would be (as it were) about the denoting concept *every man* and it is not. It is about each man, Socrates, Plato, Aristotle, Newton, Darwin, Einstein, etc. Hence its occurrence is more akin to an occurrence as concept. But the way a denoting concept occurs as concept is a new beast for Russell's zoo, and he failed to find a way to accommodate it. Of course, ordinary language permits the grammatical replacement of the expression "every man" in the sentence "Every man is mortal" by the expression "Socrates." The result is the sentence "Socrates is mortal." But ontological structure is violated by the substitution of Socrates for *every man* in the proposition {Every man is mortal}. The lessons Russell drew from this were monumental. Ordinary grammar does not always reflect propositional structure.

In 1905, Russell abandoned all hope of forging a bridge from categorical logic to the new quantification theory of individual variables by appeal to substitution. He adopted the individual variables as primitive, leaving the constituents of propositions named by nominalized general formulas unsettled. But the benefit was worth the loss. With the new theory of definite descriptions, a substitutional theory emulating type-regimented predicate variables at last became viable. It was therefore, as Russell put it, the "first step" toward the solution of the paradoxes plaguing logicism. The elimination of denoting concepts and the theory of definite descriptions made the structure of propositions intelligible. Moreover, the scope distinctions afforded by the theory of definite descriptions showed how to construct extensional contexts (i.e. emulate classes) from non-extensional contexts. Thus, with the collaboration of Whitehead assured, everything was in place by the end of 1905 for a second volume of *Principles*. All that remained, as Russell put it, "was to write the book out."

Then came crisis. Russell knew well enough that paradoxes of propositions will arise if we pair the theory of propositions with a theory of classes. Indeed, even a theory of types of classes is powerless to block it. In Appendix B of *Principles*, Russell sets out a paradox that results if comprehension of classes yields a class w such that:

$$(\forall x)(x \in w \equiv (\exists m)(x = \{y \in m\,)_y\, y\} \,.\bullet.\, x \notin m)).$$

After existential instantiation, and a use of identity principles for propositions, we arrive at the following contradiction:

$$\{y \in w\,)_y\, y\} \in w \equiv \{y \in w\,)_y\, y\} \notin w.$$

The source of this contradiction is that it is in violation of Cantor's power-class theorem that there can be no function from entities onto classes of entities. The existence of propositions assures that there is such a function. To each class m there is a unique proposition $\{y \in m\ )_y\ y\}$. We have a violation of Cantor's power theorem. It is important to see, however, that this is not a pure paradox of propositions. It involves pairing the ontology of propositions with an ontology of classes. Russell justifiably dismissed it, for his solution to the paradoxes of classes was a no-classes (i.e. no comprehension principles for classes) theory.

A similar paradox arises when Russell's theory of propositions is paired with a standard[38] theory of attributes (or even a type-theory of attributes). In manuscripts and letters to Frege of 1904, Russell sets out a paradox that arises with the comprehension of an attribute φ such that:

$$(\forall x)(\varphi x \equiv (\exists \psi)(x = \{\psi y\ )_y\ y\} \cdot \bullet \cdot \sim \psi x)).$$

After an application of the identity principles for propositions, we arrive at the contradiction:

$$\varphi (\{\varphi y\ )_y\ y\}) \equiv \sim \varphi (\{\varphi y\ )_y\ y\}).$$

This violates a form of Cantor's power-class theorem. There is no function from objects onto attributes of objects. Yet for each attribute ψ there is clearly a unique proposition $\{\psi y\ )_y\ y\}$. Once again we have paradox. Once again this is not a pure paradox of propositions. Russell justifiably dismissed it. His solution to the paradox of attributes is a no-attributes (i.e. no comprehension axioms for attributes) theory.

In his 1905 paper "On Some Difficulties in the Theory of Transfinite Numbers and Order Types," Russell came to the conclusion that no logical principles justifying restrictions on the comprehension of classes (or attributes) can be found. To find a genuine solution of the paradoxes of classes and attributes, one must get along without such comprehension principles. Of course a type-theory of entities is not a solution either. Russell's solution to the paradoxes plaguing logicism was to emulate a simple-type structure of attributes (and thereby classes) in a type-free theory of propositions. In 1906 he added a footnote to the publication of the paper, reporting: "From further investigation, I now feel hardly any doubt that the no-classes theory affords the complete solution of all the difficulties stated in the first three sections of this paper" (OT, p. 164). The impure paradoxes of propositions showed Russell that his no-classes substitutional theory of propositions must emulate a simple-type theory of attributes (and classes) in such a way as to stay out of trouble with Cantor.

It is not easy to stay out of trouble. In 1906, Russell discovered a pure paradox of propositions. It is not a paradox of the quantificational theory of propositions. It is a paradox embedded in his substitutional emulation of the structure of a simple type theory of attributes. Let us call it Russell's "p_o/a_o paradox." The new p_o/a_o paradox of propositions is not in any way akin to the Liar. It stems from a fundamental tension between the substitutional theory and the diagonal method used by Cantor to generate his power-class theorem.[39] In the substitutional theory every pair p/a represents an attribute (and through the emulation of extensional contexts also a class). At the same time, it is clear that there is a one-to-one function which assigns to every pair of entities p and a a unique entity $\{p\ )\ a\}$.[40] We have only to let the function be such that $f(x, y) = \{x\ )\ y\ \}$. This yields contradiction. Consider the pair of entities p_o and a_o such that:

$$(\forall x)\left(p_o \frac{x}{a_o} \equiv \left\{(\exists p, a)\left(x = \{p\ )\ a\}\ .\bullet.\ \sim\left(p\frac{x}{a}\right)\right)\right\}\right).$$

This readily yields:

$$p_o \frac{\{p_o\ )\ a_o\}}{a_o} \equiv \sim\left(p_o \frac{\{p_o\ )\ a_o\}}{a_o}\right).$$

We have a contradiction.

There are different ways to generate such a contradiction in the substitutional theory.[41] Instead of using $\{p \supset a\}$ as we have above, Russell originally used $\left\{p\dfrac{b}{a}!q\right\}$. Consider the pair of entities p_o and a_o such that:

$$(\forall x)\left(p_o\dfrac{x}{a_o} \equiv \left\{(\exists p, a)\left(x = \left\{p\dfrac{b}{a}!q\right\} . \bullet . \sim\left(p\dfrac{x}{a}\right)\right)\right\}\right).$$

We now have the contradiction:

$$p_o\dfrac{\left\{p_o\dfrac{b}{a_o}!q\right\}}{a_o} \equiv \sim\left(p_o\dfrac{\left\{p_o\dfrac{b}{a_o}!q\right\}}{a_o}\right).$$

In 1907 Russell admitted to his former student Ralph Hawtrey that the paradox "pilled" the substitutional theory. In his letter (see below), Russell explains that he tried several ways to solve the paradox, but it kept on being resurrected in various new forms. It is unfortunate that nothing was known of its existence for so many years. Historians of *Principia* went on blithely thinking that Russell had embraced types (and orders) of entities and that ramification was due to thinking that logical and semantic paradoxes (e.g. the Liar) have a common source (and so a common solution). Indeed, even when it became known in the 1970s, the confusion that early Russellian propositions require a semantic truth predicate marginalized its importance for understanding the evolution of Russell's philosophy of mathematics. The paradox plays the role of the Rosetta Stone, enabling us to read the ancient Egyptian hieroglyphics. It is not a semantic paradox, but it is a purely logical paradox unique to the substitutional theory. To "pill" is not to kill. The substitutional theory, retrofitted with a theory of orders of propositions to block the paradox, survived in Russell's 1908 work "Mathematical Logic as Based on the Theory of Types." Russell was very resistant to abandon the substitutional theory since it dissolves

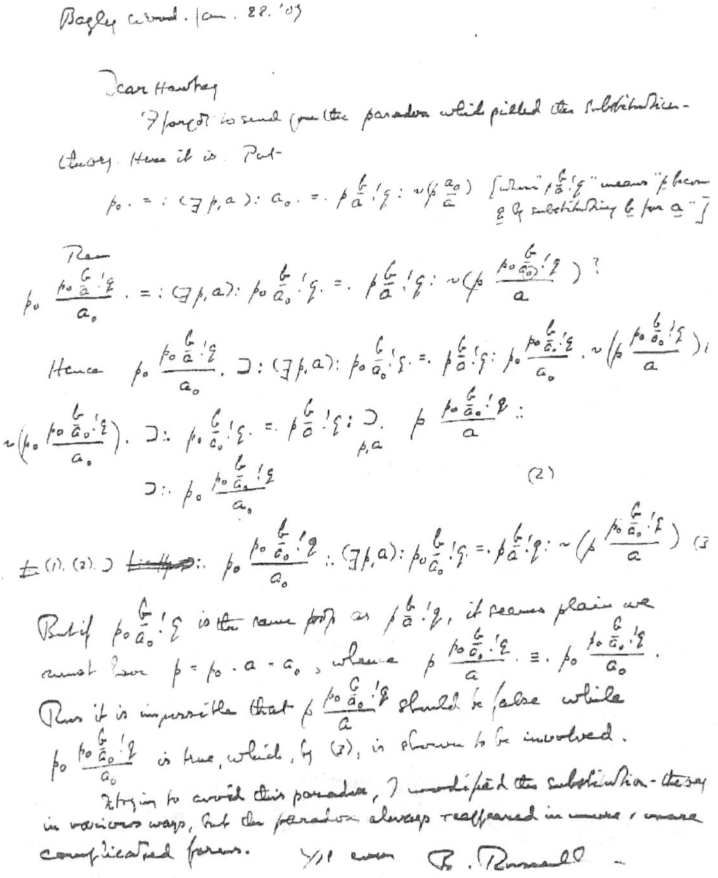
Bagley Wood. Jan. 22. '07

Dear Hawtrey

I forgot to send you the paradox which pilled the substitution-theory. Here it is. Put

$p_0 .=: (\exists p, a): a_0 .=. p\frac{b}{a}!q : \sim(p\frac{a_0}{a})$ [where "$p\frac{b}{a}!q$" means "p becomes q by substituting b for a"]

Then

$p_0\frac{p_0\frac{b}{a_0}!q}{a_0} .=: (\exists p, a): p_0\frac{b}{a_0}!q .=. p\frac{b}{a}!q : \sim(p\frac{p_0\frac{b}{a_0}!q}{a})$?

Hence $p_0\frac{p_0\frac{b}{a_0}!q}{a_0} . \supset : (\exists p, a): p_0\frac{b}{a_0}!q .=. p\frac{b}{a}!q : p_0\frac{p_0\frac{b}{a_0}!q}{a_0} . \sim(p\frac{p_0\frac{b}{a_0}!q}{a})$,

$\sim(p_0\frac{p_0\frac{b}{a_0}!q}{a_0}) . \supset :. p_0\frac{b}{a_0}!q .=. p\frac{b}{a}!q : \supset_{p,a} . p\frac{p_0\frac{b}{a_0}!q}{a} ::$

$\supset :. p_0\frac{p_0\frac{b}{a_0}!q}{a_0}$ (2)

$\vdash (1).(2). \supset :. p_0\frac{p_0\frac{b}{a_0}!q}{a_0} :. (\exists p, a): p_0\frac{b}{a_0}!q .=. p\frac{b}{a}!q : \sim(p\frac{p_0\frac{b}{a_0}!q}{a})$ (3)

But if $p_0\frac{b}{a_0}!q$ is the same prop as $p\frac{b}{a}!q$, it seems plain we must have $p = p_0 . a = a_0$, whence $p\frac{p_0\frac{b}{a_0}!q}{a} . \equiv . p_0\frac{p_0\frac{b}{a_0}!q}{a_0}$.

Thus it is impossible that $p\frac{p_0\frac{b}{a_0}!q}{a}$ should be false while $p_0\frac{p_0\frac{b}{a_0}!q}{a_0}$ is true, which, by (3), is shown to be involved.

In trying to avoid this paradox, I modified the substitution-theory in various ways, but the paradox always reappeared in more & more complicated forms.

Yrs ever B. Russell

the paradoxes plaguing logicism. Its abandonment in *Principia* reveals that he thought he had found a new dissolution: a new, ever more ontologically austere way to emulate classes. *Principia* is not a ramified type-theory of entities; it emulates the structure of a theory of classes, without the ontology of numbers, classes, attributes, or propositions. This paradox is the conceptual linchpin for any proper understanding of *Principia*.

Why was the p_0/a_0 paradox so bewildering? The answer is that within the logic of substitution it can be traced to the fact that the axioms governing propositions in the substitutional theory yield the following theorem schema:

$$(\exists p, a)\, (\forall x)\left(p\frac{x}{a} \equiv \{Ax\}\right)$$

where p and a are not free in A. Given Russell's ontology of propositions this seems to be logically true. To see this, let the proposition p be {Aa}. We have:

$$(\forall x)\left(\{Aa\}\frac{x}{a} \equiv \{Ax\}\right).$$

Recall that $\{Aa\}\frac{x}{a}$ abbreviates the definite description $(\iota q)\left(\{Aa\}\frac{x}{a}!q\right)$. And observe that the proposition q that results from substituting x for a in {Aa} is usually the proposition {Ax}. So we have:

$$(\forall x)(\exists q)\left(\{Aa\}\frac{x}{a}!r \equiv_r r = q \,.\, \bullet \,.\, q \equiv \{Ax\}\right).$$

This is read as follows:

> For all x there is a unique proposition q resulting from substituting x for a in {Aa}, and q is equivalent to {Ax}.

This certainly seems to be a truth of the logic of propositions. Russell was shocked and dismayed by its yielding a contradiction.

The "theory of types" of 1906 is not theory of types of entities. It is the name Russell applied to his "no-comprehension principles for attributes" and "no-comprehension principles for classes" theory which makes use of definite descriptions for propositional substitutions and thereby emulates a theory of types of attributes (and classes). Russell first heralded this "substitutional" theory in "On the Theory of Transfinite Numbers and Order Types" (1905). The theory was developed more fully in a little-known paper called "On the Substitutional Theory of Classes and Relations." Russell's enthusiasm for the theory was at its zenith. The concluding paragraph reads:

> It [the substitutional theory] affords what at least seems to be a complete solution of all the hoary difficulties about the one and the many, for while allowing that there are many entities, it adheres with drastic pedantry to the old maxim that "whatever is, is one."
>
> (*STCR*, p. 189)

Curiously, in that paper Russell wrote:

> The only serious danger, so far as appears, is lest some contradiction should be found to result from the assumption that propositions are entities; but I have not found any such contradiction, and it is very hard to believe that there no such things as propositions.
>
> (*STCR*, p. 188)

The paper "The Substitutional Theory of Classes and Relations" (STCR) was withdrawn from publication at the last minute precisely because Russell discovered the p_0/a_0 paradox. Russell tells the story in a letter of 10 October 1906 to his friend the mathematician Jourdain:

> I'm glad you feel attracted by the no-classes theory. I am engaged at present in purging it of metaphysical elements as far as possible, with a view to getting the bare residuum on which its success depends. . . . I decided not to publish the paper I read at the London Mathematical [Society] in May; there was much in it that wanted correction, and I preferred to wait till I got things into more final shape.
>
> (*GG*, p. 93)

The paradox is unique to Russell's no-classes (substitutional) recovery of mathematics within a theory of propositions. The paradox is not a paradox of the quantificational logic of propositions.

It arises only within Russell's substitutional theory. Its existence and significance went largely unknown for some seventy years.

Historical events then conspired to obscure for many years to come a proper understanding of Russell's solution to the paradoxes plaguing the logical foundations of mathematics. Henri Poincaré, perhaps the most prominent mathematician of the day, launched a diatribe against the notion of "impredicative definition" involved in the diagonal arguments of Cantor. A simple example of an impredicative characterization of a class is given as follows. Consider the class A whose members are the just the classes {a} and {a, b}. The intersection of A, is characterized as:

"the class of all entities that are in *every class* in A."

Now the intersection of A is the class {a} and it is itself a member of A. The characterization of the intersection of A is impredicative because it involves the quantifier expression "every class" that refers to classes, including the intersection of A itself. There is no controversy about this when the cases in question are finite. In the present example, we can avoid the quantifier expression "every class" that is involved in our impredicative characterization of the intersection of A by just listing the classes in question. But when the case involves infinitely many classes, impredicative characterizations are often important.

An impredicative characterization is essential to Cantor's famous power-class theorem that no function correlates each member of a class A with a subclass of A in such a way that does not leave any sub-classes of A out of the correlation. This leads directly to Cantor's paradox of the greatest cardinal. Moreover, since the Real numbers are in one-to-one correspondence with the class of all subclasses of the natural numbers, it leads as well to the result that there is no function correlating each finitely long name definable in a fixed vocabulary with a Real number in such a way that leaves no Real out of the correlation. König concluded from this that Reals are not well ordered. If one could well order the Reals, there would then be a first among those not definable; and yet we just defined it. It was not long, however, until the theory of classes generated a proof that the Reals can be well-ordered. Meanwhile, there was also the Burali-Forti paradox of the class of all ordinals and Russell's paradox of the class of all classes not members of themselves. Poincaré's diagnosis: "*There is no actual infinite;* the Cantorians have forgotten this, and they have fallen into contradiction."[42] In Poincaré's view, the paradoxes involve vicious circularity. The solution lies in the following VCP:

> Whatever involves an apparent variable [quantifier] must not be among the possible values of the variable [quantifier].

One must reject "impredicative definition" as viciously circular, self-referential definition.

Russell was eager to reply to Poincaré and herald his substitutional theory as a genuine solution designed so that it ". . . avoids all known contradictions, while at the same time preserving nearly the whole of Cantor's work on the transfinite."[43] But he preferred to wait until he had some avenue for solving his newly discovered substitutional paradox of propositions. In a letter of 15 May 1907 to the mathematician Couturat, Russell explains:

> I have retired here [Providence House, Clovely] alone for nearly two months, in order to get through my work a little faster than usual. I still believe that my solution to the contradictions is good, but it seems to me that it need to be extended to propositions, that is to say that the latter, likes classes and relations, cannot replace ordinary entities. To say, for example that the law of excluded middle is not red, would be to utter nonsense, and not a truth. I will follow your advice in replying to M. Poincaré. For this reason I will not reply quickly, because I would like to get into order what I have to say about the solution of the contradictions.
>
> (*Letters*, p. 301)

Russell's eventual reply to Poincaré is a work of genius, and together with STCR it is probably most important for a proper understanding of his philosophy of mathematics. Published in 1906, it has a wonderful and boldly descriptive title: "On 'Insolubilia' and Their Solution by Symbolic Logic" (InS).[44]

There is a long history of scholars interpreting Russell as agreeing with Poincaré, banishing impredicativity and holding that all the paradoxes derive from viciously circular self-reference. In truth, Russell sides with Cantor against Poincaré in the debate. The Burali-Forti, Cantor's paradox of the greatest cardinal, his own paradoxes of classes, and attributes are regarded as genuinely requiring a radical rethinking of the first principles of logic. Other paradoxes, such as Richard's paradox and Berry's paradox of the least integer not nameable in less than nineteen syllables, are dismissed.

Unfortunately, Russell's views were lost for some seventy years. The publication of Principia Mathematica overshadowed his paper InS, in which the complicated p_o/a_o paradox is not discussed. Moreover, couched within Russell's theory of propositions, it is all too easy to mistakenly conflate propositions (as mind and language independent states of affairs) with linguistic entities (or meanings) of some sort. This makes it seem as though paradoxes of nameability and Liar paradoxes are formulable within Russell's logic of propositions. We have already noted Russell's comments to Couturat about the law of excluded middle. Writing to his friend Pippa in a letter dated 9 July 1906, Lytton Strachey reports that Russell is now grappling with the proposition "All Cretans are Liars" in his effort to solve the paradoxes:

> Bertie informs me that he has now abolished not only "classes," but "general propositions"—he thinks they're all merely fantasies of the human mind. He's come to this conclusion because he finds it the only way in which to get round the Cretan who said that all Cretans are liars.[45]

Happily, the volumes of work notes Russell left have revealed an entirely new perspective.

In Russell's view, the structure of a theory with special variables restricted to types of classes, orders of general propositions, and the like must be emulated in a no-classes and no-general propositions theory whose only genuine variables are the individual variables of pure logic. He writes:

> It is important to observe that the vicious-circle principle is not itself the solution of vicious circle paradoxes, but merely the result which a theory must yield if it is to afford a solution of them. It is necessary, that is to say, to construct a theory of expressions containing apparent [bound] variables which will yield the vicious-circle principle as an outcome. It is for this reason that we need a reconstruction of logical first principles, and cannot rest content with the mere fact that paradoxes are due to vicious circles.
>
> (*InS*, p. 205)

Russell offers the following "reconstruction of logical first principles":

(1) a substitutional no-classes theory which emulates a simple-type theory of attributes (and thereby classes);

(2) a reconstruction of quantification theory without an ontology of general propositions and an new "mitigating axiom" assuring the existence of certain non-general propositions which are to do duty in the absence of general propositions;

(3) a recursive correspondence theory of truth for general statements.

All paradoxes of classes (and attributes) are dissolved by (1). The unique p_o/a_o paradox is dissolved by (2). The paradoxes of "nameability" and "definability" and the Liar paradoxes are not genuine paradoxes calling for amendments within logic. They are treated by noticing that notions of nameability and definability are intelligible only if a fixed set of symbols is first set forth. To be "nameable" is relative to fixed symbols. The idea is akin to the notion, later adopted by Alfred Tarski, of a hierarchy of languages. Russell writes:

... but *definable* is relative to some given set of fundamental notions, and if we call this set of fundamental notions I, "definable in terms of I" is never itself definable in terms of I. . . . It is easy to define "definable in terms of I" by means of a larger apparatus I'; but then "definable in terms of I' " will require a still larger apparatus I" for its definition, and so on. Or we may take "definable in terms of I" as itself part of our apparatus, so that we shall now have an apparatus J consisting of I together with "definable in terms of I". In terms of this apparatus J, "the least ordinal not definable in terms of I" is definable, but "the least ordinal not definable in terms of J" is not definable. Thus the paradox of the least indefinable ordinal is only apparent.

(*STCR*, p. 185)

Paradoxes of nameability and definability are thus dispatched. Impredicative characterization is not, as Poincaré held, impredicative "definition." To think it is a definition confusedly blurs the distinction between mind- and language-independent entities and the formulas of a given language that we use to talk about them. The two unsung papers STCR and InS are absolutely central to a proper understanding of Russell's philosophy of mathematics.

Poincaré proclaimed that vicious circles of self-reference are involved in "impredicative definitions." Russell disagreed, but he preferred to wait to reply until he had worked out what to say about the p_o/a_o paradox. In "On 'Insolubilia' and Their Solution By Symbolic Logic" Russell finally published his reply to Poincaré and was still fully wedded to substitution. To deal with his troubles with the p_o/a_o paradox, Russell thought he could simply abandon his ontology of general propositions. Only quantifier-free formulas A of the formal language of substitution can be nominalized to generate terms {A} which refer to propositions. Thus

$$\left\{(\exists\, p,\, a)\left(x = \left\{p\frac{b}{a}!q\right\} \mathbin{.\cdot.} \sim\left(p\frac{x}{a}\right)\right)\right\}.$$

and all its variants are not well formed. Russell recognizes that a radical restructuring of the quantification theory is required. Consider, for instance, the following:

$\{(\forall x)Ax\} \supset \{A\alpha/x\}$.

With general propositions abandoned, this foundational axiom schema of the quantification theory is not even well formed. To rectify this, Russell adopts "∃" as a primitive sign of his new quantification theory of propositions. He defines all subordinate occurrences of quantifiers by certain formulas with all the quantifiers initially placed. The following is now an axiom schema:

$(\exists x)(\{Ax\} \supset \{A\alpha/x\})$

where α is free for x in A. In his way, he recovers quantification theory of propositions without general propositions. With general propositions abandoned, Russell requires an account of truth and falsehood for general formulas. Thus he offers recursive definitions of "truth" and "falsehood" as applied to formulas involving quantifier symbols. The recursion is such that the truth-conditions for syntactically compound quantified sentences depend on the truth conditions for quantifier-free formulas.

Hoping to avoid the technicalities of the substitutional theory, Russell does not take up the p_o/a_o paradox explicitly in his reply to Poincaré. Even worse, Russell illustrates his abandonment of general propositions by considering a propositional liar: a man who says "I'm now asserting a false proposition." Since there are no general propositions, Russell tell us, there is no entity referred to by a nominalization of this sentence. Hence there is no contradiction. There is no proposition being affirmed, and for this reason the man says something false. Unfortunately, Russell's discussion of the propositional Liar obscures the fact that his abandonment of general propositions was not at all motivated by a Liar paradox. The fog confounded historians for generations. But matters became yet worse.

Shortly after publication of InS, Russell noticed that his plan of abandoning general propositions did not work! To recover mathematics, the system of InS requires new "mitigating" axioms postulating the existence of certain non-general propositions. Without general propositions, the substitutional axiom schemas yield:

$$(\exists p, a) \left((\forall x) \left(p \frac{x}{a} \equiv \{Ax\} \right) \right)$$

where p and a are not free in Ax and Ax is quantifier-free. Russell's mitigating axioms restore strong theorem schemas such as:

$$1906(CP)_{sub} \quad (\exists p, a) \, (\forall x) \left(p \frac{x}{a} \equiv Ax \right)$$

where p and a are not free in Ax. Russell hoped that the p_o/a_o paradox relies on contexts such as identity, and so requires the nominalization of a general formula. But he was mistaken. His mitigating axiom reintroduces the paradox. An instance is this:

$$(\forall x) \left(p_o \frac{x}{a_o} \equiv (\exists p, a) \left(x = \left\{ p \frac{b}{a} \, ! \, q \right\} \therefore \sim \left(p \frac{x}{a} \right) \right) \right).$$

The mitigating axioms of Russell's proposed "solution of the 'insolubilia' by symbolic logic" are worthless.[46]

Chagrined, Russell concluded that orders of propositions must be introduced if the substitutional theory is to consistently emulate a simple-type theory of attributes. This is the substitutional theory embedded in Russell's 1907/8 paper "Mathematical Logic as Based on the Theory of Types."[47] Russell returns to his ontology of general propositions. But now Russell imagines propositions ramified into orders. Ramification of propositions demands that propositional variables and terms come with order indices. Using subscripts, we can nominalize a formula of the language to make a term $\{A\}_v$ in accordance with the following rule. If n is the highest order index on any variable occurring in A, then $v = n + 1$ if the variable is bound and $v = n$ if the variable is free. Russell's new regimentation on the formulas of the language of substitution now demands that we have:

$$p_{m+n} \frac{x_n}{a_n} ! \, q_{m+n}$$

$$s_{m+n+1} \frac{p_{n+1}, a_n}{t_{n+1}, w_n} ! \, q_{m+n+1}.$$

This is the source of *Principia*'s thesis that the order must be at least order of the simple type. (This is something Church's interpretation captures with the notion of level.) The order is the order of the simple type (see the chart below). In the substitutitonal theory, there is no such thing as type since the type of an attribute is emulated in a no-comprehsion principles for attributes theory which builds simple type distinctions into the number of substitutions involved. But the substitutional theory is now regimented by order indices on its variables. The regimentation demands that Russell introduce axiom schemas that enable a reduction of propositional order. For instance he has:

1908 (Reducibility $CP_1)_{sub}$

$$(\forall p_n, b_o)(\exists p_1, a_o)(\forall x_o)\left(p_1 \frac{x_o}{a_o} \equiv p_n \frac{x_o}{b_o}\right).$$

These axioms of reducibility enable Russell to recover from the crippling effect that ramification (i.e. orders of propositions) has on the emulation of classes in the theory.

Attention to the historical evolution of Russell's ideas reveals that Russell had no qualms about the allegedly "circular self-reference" of impredicative comprehension that so animated Poincaré. The

Simple type + order of type		Substitution + Order	
$\varphi^{(o)}$	$^1\varphi^{(o/o)}$	p/a	p_1/a_o
$\varphi^{((o))}$	$^2\varphi^{(1/(o/o))}$	$q/p, a$	$q_2/p_1, a_o$
$\varphi^{(((o)))}$	$^3\varphi^{(2/(1/(o/o)))}$	$j/q, p, a$	$j_3/q_2, p_1, a_o$

whole point of Russell's 1908 reducibility axiom for propositions was to recover his substitutional emulation of the full impredicative comprehension of simple types of attributes, while at the same time staying out of trouble with Cantor. The orders of propositions avoids troubles with Cantor's power theorem. But it must be remembered that Russell found a standard theory according to which attributes have only a predicable nature unacceptable. He also found an ontology of simple type-stratified attributes unacceptable. His official solution had been to emulate impredicative comprehension of simple types of attributes by means of the techniques of his substitutional theory of propositions. But with propositions now split into orders, the substitutional theory emulates a ramified type-theory of attributes. To assure the recovery of the emulation of the impredicative comprehension of attributes within this new substitutional theory retrofitted with orders of propositions, Russell adds to the system an axiom of reducibility for propositions. Once the axiom of the reducibility of propositions is in place, all the mathematical uses of impredicative comprehension of attributes are recovered and mathematics is restored.

Interestingly, the language of Church's Principia^C can be translated into the language of substitution most faithfully. That is, the constructions of the substitutional theory of "Mathematical Logic" are able to emulate the non-predicative variables of Church's system. For example, Church allows a variable $^2\varphi^{(o/o)}$, which he writes as $\varphi^{(o)/2}$. The substitutional theory emulates this by using the matrix p_2/a_o. Similarly, Church allows a variable $^3\varphi^{(1/(o/o))}$, which he writes as $\varphi^{((o)/1)/2}$. This is emulated by use of q_3/p_1, a_o, and so on. It best fits Russell's remarks in "Mathematical Logic" that the language of predicate variables is but a convenient notation, replaceable by the more exacting language of the substitutional theory (ML, p. 77). Perhaps this is what Principia would have been like had Russell stuck to his original plans for a second volume of Principles.

The proposed second volume of Principles was never written.

Instead, there is *Principia Mathematica*. Russell contemplated putting the substitutional theory in an appendix to *Principia*, but this never happened. The reason is that Russell abandoned his ontology of propositions. The logical particles of *Principia* are statement connectives in just the modern sense, not signs for relations between propositions. Russell found the hierarchy of orders of propositions impossible to philosophically justify. Instead of the purely syntactic emulation of predicate variables of the substitutional theory, *Principia*'s formal language allows predicate variables adorned with order/type indices (suppressed for notational convenience). These variables, unlike the individual variables, are not genuine. They are not restricted but internally limited by their conditions of significance given by *Principia*'s nominalistic semantics for predicate variables. The nominalistic interpretation involves recursive definitions of "truth" and "falsehood" intended to philosophically justify and explain the order component of the order/type indices on predicate variables. Ramification is the untoward byproduct of this semantics. But the positive outcome was that in *Principia* there are no types or orders of entities. Whatever is (be it universal, particular, or fact), is an individual. The individual variables are the only genuine variables.[48]

FURTHER READING

Charles, Chihara, *Ontology and the Vicious Circle Principle* (Ithica, NY: Cornell University Press, 1973).

William Hatcher, *The Logical Foundations of Mathematics* (Oxford: Pergamon, 1981).

Gregory Landini, *Russell's Hidden Substitutional Theory* (Oxford: Oxford University Press, 1998)

Bernard Linsky, *Russell's Metaphysical Logic* (Stanford, CA: CSLI, 1999).

W. V. O. Quine, *Set Theory and Its Logic* (Cambridge, MA: The Belknap Press, 1969).

Four

The Philosophy of Logical Atomism

> Every philosophical problem, when it is subjected to the necessary analysis and justification, is found either to be not really philosophical at all, or else to be, in the sense in which we are using the word, logical.
> *Our Knowledge of the External World*

Echoing Plato, Russell wrote that "whoever wishes to become a philosopher will do well to acquire a considerable knowledge of mathematics."[1] Russell's work in *Principia* endeavored to show that there is no uniquely mathematical notion of necessity. The necessity of mathematics is that of ᶜᵖlogic. This led to a bold new scientific conception of philosophy. Russell called it "Logical Atomism," and its fundamental thesis is this: The only necessity is logical necessity.

In Russell's view, scientific philosophy involves a re-conceptualization and reconstruction of concepts which reveal that the only necessity is logical necessity. Schools of philosophy, Russell tells us, should be characterized rather by their logic than their metaphysics (LA, p. 323).

Just as the only necessity is logical necessity, the only proper philosophical ontology for Russell is the ontology of logic. Ontology is generated by attempts to account for necessary relationships. In Russell's view, non-logical ontological theories derive from confusions that make it appear that there are non-logical necessities unique to mathematics, physical science, metaphysics, ethics, and so on. The most fundamental feature of Russell's new Logical Atomism is that philosophical problems can be solved (i.e. dissolved) by abandoning the ontology of the rival philosophical theory and offering a logical reconstruction of the laws within the ontological framework of logic.

This interpretation of Russell's philosophy of Logical Atomism is revisionary. It contrasts starkly with an orthodox interpretation that construes the "atomism" of Russell's Logical Atomism as epistemically accessible building blocks out of which the metaphysical and the physical world is composed. It is a form of metaphysical zoology, a philosophical inventory of the kinds of metaphysical complexes that there are together with an investigation into their atomic constituents. Russell is interpreted as holding that philosophy comprises a body of knowledge that is gained by exploring a metaphysical world of atoms and complexes of them found by logical analysis and acquaintance. Pears writes that, "Russell believed that the logician's task is to carry out a survey of 'logical objects,' some of which are forms while others are the real counterparts of the logical connectives."[2] The current orthodox interpretation has it that Russell's philosophy of Logical Atomism is committed to an epistemic theory of acquaintance which finds the logical atoms to include be sense-data. Pears writes:

> 'Logical atomism' is Russell's name for the theory that there is a limit to the analysis of factual language, a limit at which all sentences will consist of words designating simple things ... His theory of knowledge led him to claim that the only simple particulars that we know are sense-data, and that the only simple qualities and relations we know are certain qualities and relations of sense-data. Their simple qualities and relations are those with which we have to achieve acquaintance in order to understand the words designating them. This fixes the character of his logical atomism. It is a version of empiricism and it uses a criterion of simplicity based on the

> exigencies of learning meanings.... The doctrine of forced acquaintance is the foundation of Russell's logical atomism.[3]

On the present revisionary interpretation, the orthodox interpretation is mistaken. Russell's theory of sense-data is not an ontological theory. Sense-data are contingent physical particulars hypothesized as part of a contingent theory to explain physical laws governing physical continuants persisting through time.

Part of the confusion stems from the corruption of the word "ontology." The corruption comes originally from the neo-empiricist Quine, who, in criticizing Carnap's positivist thesis that metaphysics and philosophical ontology is "meaningless," offered a new meaning for the word "ontology." In Quine's view, there are no uniquely philosophical ontological questions. There are only ordinary empirical questions of what there is: questions that are settled empirically by the natural sciences. Russell disagrees with Quine. He uses the term "ontology" as Carnap did. He is concerned with the uniquely philosophical ontologies that are introduced to explain allegedly non-logical metaphysical necessities in mathematics, physical science, ethics, and the like. Russell's Logical Atomism is a research program to show that the only necessity is logical necessity and that all ontological assumptions of speculative metaphysics outside the domain of logic are spurious.

Russell's Logical Atomism should not be identified with any of the particular epistemological theories couched within it. It certainly is not committed to the existence of acquaintance with sense-data. Russell would come to adopt different epistemic theories within this research program. Indeed, in his very first lectures on Logical Atomism, he already indicates that he is on the verge of adopting neutral monism and abandoning acquaintance (as a dyadic relation) and sense-data (as physical objects of sensation). In its place, he has sensation as a brain/nervous system process causally linked to other physical processes outside the body. Russell altered his views over the years. He rejected material continuants enduring through time and methodological solipsism (*Our Knowledge of the External World as a Field for Scientific Philosophy*, 1914). He adopted neutral monism which rejects sense-data, acquaintance, and self, and he rejects Brentano's principle of intentionality (*The Analysis of Mind*, 1921). He advocated naturalizing the study of mind, borrowing from experimental (behavioristic) psychology (*Outline of Philosophy*, 1927). He subsumed Minkowski's interpretation of Einstein's general relativity into his neutral monism (*The Analysis of Matter*, 1927), revising his account in *Our Knowledge* accordingly. He adopts a causal theory of indexicals (*An Inquiry Into Meaning and Truth*, 1940). He evaluates different accounts of probability and finds empiricism limited (*Human Knowledge: Its Scope and Limits*, 1948). None of these changes mark any alteration whatever to Russell's philosophy of Logical Atomism.

What then, it might be asked, is the "atomism" of Russell's Logical Atomism? Russell calls his philosophical program "Logical Atomism" not because it is built from ontological atoms (neither sense-data, nor any other sorts of atoms), but because he rejects building metaphysical systems of the world which are, in his opinion, inspired by misguided religious, moral, or self-oriented conceptions of what the world must be like. The following passage nicely captures this attitude:

> Intellectually, the effect of mistaken moral considerations upon philosophy has been to impede progress to an extraordinary extent. I do not myself believe that philosophy can either prove or disprove the truth of religious dogmas, but ever since Plato most philosophers have considered it part of their business to produce "proofs" of immortality and the existence of God. . . . In order to make their proofs seem valid, they have had to falsify logic, to make mathematics mystical, and to pretend that deep-seated prejudices were heaven-sent intuitions. All this is rejected by the philosophers who make logical analysis the main business of philosophy. . . . For this renunciation, they have been rewarded by the discovery that

> many questions formerly obscured by the fog of metaphysics, can be answered with precision, and by objective methods ... Take such questions as What is number? What are space and time? What is mind, and what is matter? I do not say that we can here and now give definitive answers to all these ancient questions, but I do say that a method has been discovered by which, as in science, we can make successive approximations to the truth ...
>
> (*HWP*, p. 835)

Russell's approach is piecemeal. It is in stark contrast with previous philosophical systems exemplified by philosophers, such as Hegel, who were inspired by religious and ethical desires to build a metaphysics tailored to human nature. Russell writes:

> To build up systems of the world, like Heine's German professor who knit together fragments of life and made an intelligible system out of them, is not, I believe, any more feasible than the discovery of the philosopher's stone. What is feasible is the understanding of general forms, and the division of traditional problems into separate and less baffling questions.[4]

To emphasize this piecemeal approach, Russell proclaims that there are no propositions of which the universe is the subject. He writes: "The philosophy which I wish to advocate may be called Logical Atomism or absolute pluralism, because, while maintaining that there are many things, it denies that there is a whole composed of those things."[5] The revisionary interpretation of Russell's philosophy as Logical Atomism is the interpretation we shall adopt in this book, marking, where we can, its heretical nature.

Russell explains that it was the work in *Principia* on mathematics that formed the foundation for his new logical atomist research program in philosophy.[6] The work on the foundations of mathematics grew into a supreme maxim for scientific philosophizing. Russell states the maxim as follows: "Wherever possible, logical constructions are to be substituted for inferred entities" (RSDP,

p. 115). Russell gave many examples of his maxim for scientific philosophy. He writes:

> Some examples of the substitution of construction for inference in the realm of mathematical philosophy may serve to elucidate the use of this maxim. Take first the case of irrationals. In old days, irrationals were inferred as the supposed limits of series of rationals which had no rational limit . . . We now define an irrational number as a certain class of ratios, thus constructing it logically by means of ratios, instead of arriving at it by a doubtful inference from them. Take again the case of cardinal numbers. Two equally numerous collections appear to have something in common: this something is supposed to be their cardinal number. But so long as the cardinal number is inferred from the collections, not constructed in terms of them, its existence must remain in doubt, unless in virtue of a metaphysical postulate ad hoc. By defining the cardinal number of a given collection as the class of all equally numerous collections, we avoid the necessity of this metaphysical postulate, and thereby remove a needless element of doubt from the philosophy of arithmetic. A similar method, as I have shown elsewhere, can be applied to classes themselves, which need not be supposed to have any metaphysical reality, but can be regarded as symbolically constructed fictions.
>
> (RSDP, p. 116)

Russell heralds Frege's analysis of the notion of cardinal number as "the first complete example" of "the logical-analytic method in philosophy."[7] In *Principia* we find constructions of classes, rational numbers, and real numbers (construed as lower sections of Dedekind cuts). What is of central importance to the constructions is that there are no classes, no natural numbers, no (positive and negative) integers, no rational numbers, and no real numbers. The laws of mathematics are recovered without assuming an ontology of such entities. It was in adopting an ontology of such objects that metaphysicians brought non-logical essences and necessities, and with them many of the traditional problems of philosophy, into mathematics.

Metaphysical conundrums arise because ordinary (and quasi-scientific) notions such as space, time, matter, motion, limit, continuity, change, and the like are hybrid notions whose logical components have not been properly separated from their empirical/physical components. Russell's philosophy of Logical Atomism aims at a separation of these components. This is accomplished by means of a logical analysis running side by side with advancements and discoveries in mathematical and physical science. In the process, a new, more exacting account which supplants the earlier account emerges. Russell describes his new program as making logic the essence of philosophy.

WAYS OF PARADOX

In "On Denoting," Russell wrote that,

> A logical theory may be tested by its capacity for dealing with puzzles, and it is a wholesome plan, in thinking about logic, to stock the mind with as many puzzles as possible, since these serve much the same purpose as is served by experiments in physical science.
>
> (*OD*, p. 110)

Of course, it not just any "puzzles" Russell has in mind; it is those puzzles that rise to the level of significant paradoxes. Paradoxes might best be characterized as an apparently unacceptable conclusion derived by apparently acceptable reasoning from apparently acceptable premises.[8] Russell would certainly agree that more than once in history the discovery of paradox has been the occasion for major reconstruction at the foundation of thought. The development of nineteenth-century analysis (i.e. Zeno's paradoxes), set theory (e.g. Russell, Cantor, and Burali-Forti paradoxes), Gödel's incompleteness theorems and Tarski's semantics (i.e. Liar paradoxes), and Einstein's special theory of relativity (i.e. Michelson-Morley paradox) are captivating examples.

Perhaps everyone knows the puzzle of the proof that 2 = 1. Here is one version of the argument:

(1) If $m = n$ then $(m + n)(m - n) = n(m - n)$

(2) If $(m + n)(m - n) = n(m - n)$ then $\dfrac{(m + n)(m - n)}{m - n} = \dfrac{n(m - n)}{m - n}$

(3) If $\dfrac{(m + n)(m - n)}{m - n} = \dfrac{n(m - n)}{m - n}$ then $\dfrac{m + n}{1} = \dfrac{n}{1}$

(4) If $m = n$ then $\dfrac{m + n}{1} = \dfrac{n}{1}$.

But now just take the case where m and n are 1 and we get:

$$\dfrac{1 + 1}{1} = \dfrac{1}{1}.$$

Hence, 2 = 1. It is often said that the argument fails because division by zero is "undefined" or somehow illicit. Why is it illicit? Well, it might be said, if it were allowed, that one could prove 2 = 1. Surely this is not an explanation. We want to know what logically has gone wrong in the argument. The proper explanation is that the algebraic law of cancellation is this:

If $v \neq 0$ then $\dfrac{m \times v}{v} = \dfrac{m}{1}$.

Thus, the third line of the argument is false. It should be:

If $m - n \neq 0$ then if $\dfrac{(m + n)(m - n)}{m - n} = \dfrac{n(m - n)}{m - n}$ then $\dfrac{m + n}{1} = \dfrac{n}{1}$.

As it is, it misapplies the algebraic law.

The paradox is an occasion to clarify the algebraic law. It is also an occasion to ask whether, in fact, there is a ratio $\dfrac{m}{0}$. Russell's logicism accepts that for every natural number m and n, there is a relation $\frac{m}{n}$. A ratio is a relation between natural numbers x and y such that

$$x \left(\frac{m}{n}\right) y$$

if and only if x × n = m × y. Some ratios are interesting; others are not. The ratio $\frac{0}{m}$ is interesting since $\frac{0}{m} = \frac{0}{1}$. The ratio $\frac{m}{0}$ is uninteresting and worth ignoring.

The paradox of division by zero is not very deep, though it holds a few lessons. Some paradoxes, however, raise deep problems with mathematical, scientific, and metaphysical conceptions of the world. Many important paradoxes arise from importing intuitions wrought from experience with physical objects into the realm of mathematics, and vice versa. Here is an old paradox. Suppose we divide a line segment AC in half. Now there is no such thing as cutting a point in half, for by definition, points have no length. But then if we are to cut a line in half, in which half is the midpoint? If the length of a line is determined by its points, then if the midpoint is in line segment AB and not in line BC, then AB is longer than BC since it has one more point. Hence, physical intuition suggests that we have not divided the line in half.

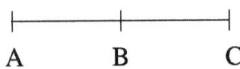

A   B   C

The paradox is solved by realizing, as Cantor did, that every line segment has the same cardinal number of points and that the length of a line is defined not by the number of the points but by the structural ordering of the points. In the following figure there is a one-to-one correspondence between points P on line segment CD and points P′ on the shorter line segment AB. Intuitively, for any physical objects which could be associated with this figure, the

The Philosophy of Logical Atomism

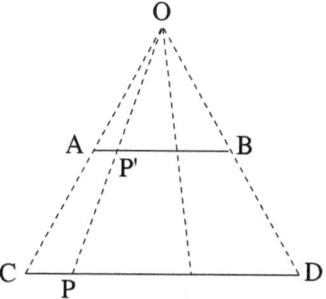

sticks laying along from P to P′ would have width, and each would overlap more of AB than CD. Sticks do not intersect at points. But mathematically lines and points have no width, and so we have a one-to-one correspondence of points on CD with points on AB, even though the line segment AB is shorter than the line segment CD. Once again, the paradox is dissolved when we divorce the mathematical notion of length of a line segment from intuitions based on experiences with physical sticks and pebbles.

What are points? Modern analytic geometry, following Descartes, takes them to be pairs of numbers. A straight line, in the mathematical sense, is a mathematical function. It is a relation R of a special sort such that, for some numbers m, b, and for all numbers x, y, either xRy if and only if $y = mx + b$ or for some number c, we have $mx = c$.&. $y = y$ (see figure overleaf). Points on a line (i.e pairs of numbers) obviously have no length at all. As we saw, the mathematical notion of length is not determined by the number of points, but by the ordering of the points. That is, the ordering of the pairs of numbers by a relation R (i.e. the one line) is structurally similar to just a proper part of the ordering by the relation S (i.e. the other line). The sleight of hand that produces the paradox of dividing a line in half lies in thinking about lines and points the way we think about physical sticks and pebbles.

Applying our abstract mathematical ideas to the world is no simple task. Is the notion of exactly half of a stick intelligible? And is there any physical sense in which sticks have infinitely many

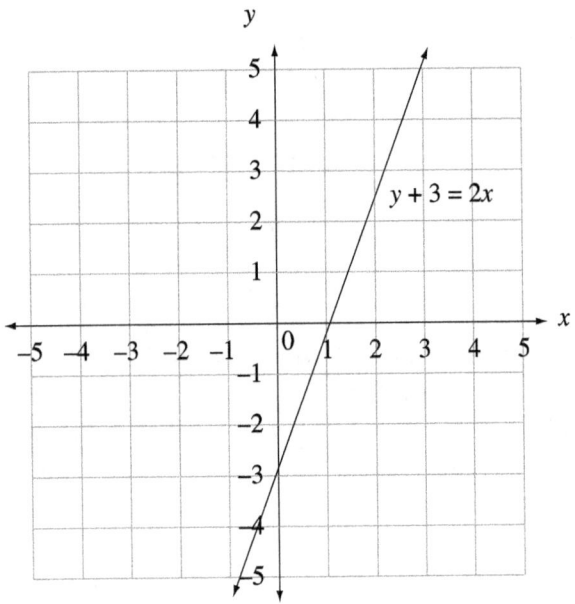

parts? The answer to such questions depends on whether physical events overlap sufficiently so that physical correlations (given by light interactions) of parts of those events are fine enough to be modeled by the dense structure of rational numbers. (The rationals are dense in the sense that for any two there is one in between them.) Physical correlations enable workable approximations of measuring a given distance by the denseness of the ratios. For example, by rotation on a lathe, a stick can be scribed with marks that approximate being equidistant from one another. By appeal to such physical correlations, we can improve our accuracy of measurement to any degree modeled by the structure of the ratios.

But what about physical sticks and pebbles? Zeno of Elea is most famous for paradoxes that arise when mathematical notions are applied to the world. One of his popular paradoxes is known as Achilles and the Tortoise. The argument aims to show that if, in a race, the tortoise starts some distance ahead, Achilles (the very fastest of Greek runners) would be powerless to catch up. Achilles has to transverse a greater distance than the tortoise, so it seemed to Zeno that if he catches the tortoise at some time, he has to have transversed more measurement points than the tortoise in the same amount of time. Of course, we can see that in the mathematical sense the distances traveled by both Achilles and the tortoise have the same cardinal number of points (i.e. denumerably many points) even though Achilles's distance is greater. The difference in distance is not due to a difference in the cardinal number of points. There is a one-to-one correspondence between the points of the distance Achilles runs and the distance the tortoise runs. The cardinal number of points on any line segment of any length is the same as that of any other. Russell likens the situation to his paradox of Tristram Shandy, who, in writing a very detailed autobiography, falls further and further behind the events of his life. Nonetheless, if Tristram lives a life with as many days as there are natural numbers, there is a one-to-one correspondence between his life events and entries in his autobiography.[9]

Naturally, we think of Achilles has having consecutively added segments of the physical distance to the tortoise during his run. One of Zeno's worries is that consecutively adding will never add any distance to Achilles's starting point because to add any distance he must consecutively add each distance (measured in the rationals) less than that distance. Zeno reasons that to begin his process of consecutively adding, he must start by first adding the least distance between his starting point and any given distance, say $\frac{9}{10}$ of the way to the tortoise. But since the rationals are dense—between any two there is a distinct rational—there is no least distance. If motion is to be modeled as consecutive addition, then neither Achilles nor the tortoise can move.

The reply to Zeno is that motion is not properly modeled as consecutive addition. Indeed, no consecutive addition will enable the sum of infinitely many increments. To see this point, consider

174 The Philosophy of Logical Atomism

summing consecutively as follows. Begin with $\frac{9}{10}$ and then add to that sum $\frac{9}{100}$ and then add to that sum $\frac{9}{1,000}$ and then $\frac{9}{10,000}$ and so on. The astute philosopher will point out that these consecutive additions towards infinity do not equal 1. Fair enough. But it is a naïve philosopher who thinks that $.\overline{9}$ is not equal to the ratio $\frac{1}{1}$. The definition is this:

$$.\overline{9} = df \lim_{n \to \infty} \sum \frac{9}{10^{n+1}}.$$

Weierstrass showed how to define the arithmetic sum of the series without any appeal to consecutive additions or infinitesimal quantities. Consider the following series:

$$\frac{9}{10}, \frac{9}{100}, \frac{9}{1,000}, \frac{9}{10,000}, \frac{9}{100,000}, \ldots$$

The function that determines the series (i.e. its general term) is $\frac{9}{10^{n+1}}$ since the assignment of n consecutively to 0, 1, 2, 3, etc. yields the series. How can one define the notion of the arithmetic sum of this series? Weierstrass defines[10] the limit of the series as follows:

$$\lim_{n \to \infty} \sum \frac{9}{10^{n+1}} = \frac{L}{p} = df$$

$\frac{L}{p}$ is the ratio such that for all ratios $\frac{e}{q} > \frac{0}{1}$ one can find a ratio $\frac{N}{r} > \frac{0}{1}$ which is such that

for all n, $\frac{Lq - pe}{pq} < \frac{9}{10^{n+1}} < \frac{Lq + pe}{pq}$.

The arithmetic sum of our series is $\frac{1}{1}$. With his logical analysis of the notion of a limit, Weierstrass liberated the calculus from the notions of "completing an infinity" or "reaching a point by getting infinitely close to it." In Russell's view, philosophers have paid too little attention to his breakthrough.

Russell's work in philosophy was inspired by the great advances made by mathematicians and physical scientists.[11] His exuberance is apparent in the following:

> Zeno was concerned, as a matter of fact with three, each presented by motion, but each more abstract than motion, and capable of a purely arithmetic treatment. These are the problems of the infinitesimal, the infinite and continuity. To state clearly the difficulties involved, was to accomplish perhaps the hardest part of the philosopher's task. This was done by Zeno. From him to our own day, the finest intellects of each generation in turn attacked the problems, but achieved, broadly speaking, nothing. In our own time, however, three men—Weierstrass, Dedekind and Cantor—have not only merely advanced the three problems but have completely solved them. The solutions, for those acquainted with the mathematics, are so clear as to leave no longer the slightest doubt or difficulty. This achievement is probably the greatest of which our age has to boast; and I know of no age (except the golden age of Greece) which has a more convincing proof to offer of the transcendent genius of its great men. Of the three problems, that of the infinitesimal was solved by Weierstrass; the solution of the other two was begun by Dedekind, and definitively accomplished by Cantor.
>
> (MM, p. 64)

The new mathematics of the infinite eventuated in new logical analyses of notions such as number, continuity, limit, space, and time. With Cantor, the notion of continuity, which seemed impossible to render by any notion of magnitude, depends only on the notion of order. The derivative and the integral became, through the new definitions of "number" and "limit," not quantitative concepts, but ordinal concepts. Continuity lies in the fact that some classes of discrete units form a dense compact class. "Quantity," wrote Russell, ". . . has lost the mathematical importance which it used to possess, owing to the fact that most theorems concerning it can be generalized so as to become theorems concerning order."[12] In Russell's view, Cantor's work on the transfinite put to rest centuries of speculative metaphysics surrounding the infinite and the notion of continuity. Russell writes,

> Continuity had been, until he [Cantor] defined it, a vague word, convenient for philosophers like Hegel, who wished to introduce metaphysical muddles into mathematics. . . . . By this means a great deal of mysticism, such as that of Bergson, was rendered inadequate.
>
> (*HWP*, p. 829)

In his *A History of Western Philosophy* Russell added yet more examples of logical analyses. "Physics," Russell tells us, "as well as mathematics, has supplied material for the philosophy of philosophical analysis. What is important to the philosopher in the theory of relativity is the substitution of space-time for space and time" (HWP, p. 832). Experience with sticks makes it seem that the notion of physical length is intuitively clear as an intrinsic, non-relational property of a body. Of course, scientists knew that temperatures and pressures deform sticks, even those of iron and steel and concrete. But this did not jeopardize the traditional concept of physical length as an intrinsic property. With the proper caveats of a fixed temperature, pressure, etc., a standard metrical physical length is readily established. But Einstein maintains that, given we accept Maxwell's equations and the invariance of the propagation of electromagnetic energy in a vacuum, the concept of physical length is a relational property and not an intrinsic property. Protagoras said that "man is the measure of all things (physical)." Einstein says that the measure of all things physical is the invariant behavior of electromagnetic energy (i.e. light). The result is a philosophical transformation of traditional physical concepts of space and time into space-time. Russell's discussion in *The ABC of Relativity* remains today one of the best explications of Einstein's theory, showing (contrary to a host of popular discussions still present today) that the theory is about the world itself and not merely about practices of measurements by observers. Russell sees clearly that it is a theory of the relativity of physical length, not a theory that lengths contract under accelerations approaching light speed.

Turning to quantum theory, Russell writes: "I suspect that it will demand even more radical departures from the traditional doctrine of space and time than those demanded by the theory of relativity."[13] Russell approvingly cites the new work in quantum theory as important for logical analysis of matter. And he counts Einstein's thesis that "simultaneity" has to be defined as just such a separation of the logical from the empirical (*HWP*, p. 832). Just as Einstein reconceptualizes Maxwell's laws for the propagation of light without the aether, Russell's Logical Atomism abandons the non-logical ontological necessities of former speculative philosophies, offering a re-conceptualization and logical reconstruction (where possible) of the laws of the earlier theory. Many successes of the earlier theories are retained by the reconstruction. Retention, however, is always partial. Some processes and mechanisms of earlier theories are treated as flotsam. The supplanting tradition may come to regard the terms of the earlier theories as non-referential or regard earlier ontologies as idle wheels that serve no explanatory purpose.

Conspicuous by its absence is any mention of an epistemic agenda. Admittedly, in his article "Logical Atomism" Russell stated his supreme maxim for scientific philosophy in an epistemic form: "Wherever possible, substitute constructions out of known entities for inferences to unknown entities."[14] But if we read carefully we find that what he has in mind are the lessons, exacted from the constructions of *Principia*, which show how to (by and large) recover the laws of an earlier theory without its problematic ontological commitments. He writes:

> Given a set of propositions nominally dealing with the supposed inferred entities, we observe the properties which are required of the supposed entities in order to make these propositions true. By dint of a little logical ingenuity, we then construct some logical function of less hypothetical entities which has the requisite properties. This constructed function we substitute for the supposed inferred entities, and thereby obtain a new and less doubtful interpretation of the body of propositions in question. This method, so fruitful in the philosophy of mathematics, will be found equally applicable in the philosophy of physics, where, I do not doubt, it would have been applied long ago but for the fact that all who have studied this subject hitherto have been completely ignorant of mathematical logic. I myself cannot claim originality in the application of this method to physics, since I owe the suggestion and the stimulus for it entirely to my friend and collaborator Dr. Whitehead, who is engaged in applying it to the more mathematical portions of the region intermediate between sense-data and the points, instances, and particles of physics.
> (ORSP, p. 116; see also LA, p. 326)

Russell endeavors to abandon the traditional conception of matter as a physical substance enduring and changing through time. In *The Analysis of Matter* (1925), Russell says that knowledge of physics is confined to structural and mathematical properties, not intrinsic natures of physical substances.[15] In *Outline of Philosophy* Russell says that "our knowledge of the physical world is purely abstract: we know certain logical characteristics of its structure, but nothing of its intrinsic character."[16] Matter, a continuant persisting through time, is a logical fiction.

Unfortunately, the logical constructions of *Principia* have been interpreted as a form of reductive identity rather than as an elimination. For example, in a reductive identity, when it is said that a rock is a swarm of molecules, we do not say that there are no rocks. When we say that heat is mean kinetic energy, we do not proclaim that there is no such thing as heat. If, thanks to Watson and Crick, molecular biology identifies a gene with a segment of deoxyribonucleic acid (DNA), we do not say that there are no genes. In contrast, the history of science also provides examples of elimination. We do say that there is no caloric fluid, no phlogiston, and no luminiferous aether. There are no demonic possessions; there are, rather, epileptic seizures. For many years *Principia* was interpreted as a reductive identity. But a proper understanding of *Principia* undermines this interpretation completely. We have seen that it makes no assumption of classes, natural numbers, integers, rationals, and reals. At first it seems preposterous to say that there is no matter, no trees, rocks, and the like. But we shall see in subsequent chapters that an eliminativist approach to matter is not as shocking as it may at first appear. Russell had long been captivated by Zeno's famous paradoxes of motion and McTaggart's puzzles of the nature of time itself. Russell was a four-dimensionalist; a bit of matter is not a continuant persisting through time. It is rather constituted by a series of events (i.e. stages), each of which is transient (if not momentary). In physical change, we do not have literally the same object gaining and losing properties—something McTaggart thought incoherent. Change is to be understood as eliminating the material object in favor of stages, each of which has a given property at a time. Russell offered the following amusing passage as early as 1901:

> Weierstrass, by strictly banishing from mathematics the infinitesimal, has at last shown that we live in an unchanging world, and that the arrow in its flight is truly at rest. Zeno's only error lay in inferring (if he did infer) that, because there is no such thing as a state of change, therefore the world is in the same state at any one time as at any other. This is a consequence which by no means follows; and in this respect, the German mathematician is more constructive than the ingenious Greek.[17]

In the 1920s the new theory of relativity (and the then fledgling quantum theory) seemed to Russell to conclusively corroborate the view. We should take Russell at his word when he applies the techniques of *Principia* to physics of points, instances of time, and particles (i.e. material continuants persisting in time). They do not exist.

On Russell's conception, philosophy becomes every bit as technical as mathematics and physical science. Indeed, it makes philosophical analysis inseparably tied to both. Ontological questions are distinctive because they inspire speculative ontologies and necessities outside of logic. Logical Atomism aims to sort out the interplay of logical/mathematical and empirical scientific notions that have created the logical mirages which mislead philosophers—not ordinary people—into imagining metaphysical (i.e. non-logical) necessities. It cannot do this from an armchair. The separation of logical/mathematical notions from physical/empirical notions awaits advances in both mathematical fields and empirical scientific fields, such as physics, chemistry, biology, and psychology.

Of course, in principle, one can discover all the possible logical forms from an armchair. But one cannot be in a position to assign to a sentence a given logical form unless one has empirical and sometimes very technical knowledge of the world. Understanding the meaning (in the sense of being a competent speaker of English) is not a sufficient condition for assigning the correct logical form (i.e. finding the correct truth-conditions). This is because ordinary communication is not concerned with ontology. Ordinary meaning (in the service of successful communication) plays little role in questions of logical form, and ontological concerns are largely out of place in ordinary communication. Ordinary statements of a language may, in fact, have very complicated truth-conditions that are entirely unknown to the speakers of the language. These complications are certainly rarely required for success in ordinary communication. If I say to my son Ansel that the temperature outside is 98 and rising, he will understand that he should not wear a coat. He can understand this without understanding anything of the scientific nature of temperature. To reveal the mirages that inspire metaphysical (i.e. non-logical) necessities and muddles, philosophers must walk in the muddy empirical streets with the scientists.

To illustrate the point, consider the complicated interplay of mathematical and empirical physical concepts involved in the ordinary sentence: The temperature is 98 degrees and rising.[18] In the hands of a (very) naïve philosopher, the English surface grammar inspires a metaphysics of entities that are temperatures and numbers which rise. Russell enjoins us to sort out the physical, logical, and arithmetic notions involved in the ordinary language statement. The analysis certainly does not neglect facts about how ordinary language is used to communicate. But it involves much more. Logical analysis must ask "What is temperature in the physical sense?" not simply "How is the word 'temperature' used in practical circumstances?"

Hand-waving more than a little bit, physics tells us that the temperature of an object is the kinetic energy of the molecules composing the object relative both to fixed parameters of pressure and volume and a reference frame. When confined to a tube that fixes a standard of pressure and volume, the molecules of mercury are known to be predictably sensitive to the kinetic motions of objects they are in contact with. Increase in the molecular motions of the mercury causes its volume to increase in the tube. By scribing marks on a tube containing mercury and fixing two fiduciary marks (as in the Celsius scale, when the tube is immersed in ice and in boiling water) we can scribe the tube with marks from 0 to 100. Now we can say that there are ninety-eight marks that are (or would be) reached at time t after the cessation of the expanding of mercury in a standard tube in contact with O. That is, we say that the temperature of O at t is 98 degrees. To say the temperature of O is rising at t brings in the notion of rate of change relative to the change in time. If we want rate of change to be measured "at an instant" we will have to bring in the notion of the calculus to define "rising" (i.e. changing at an instant of time). Accommodating this involves the notion of the limit in the calculus and will further complicate the technical expression of the simple ordinary language statement. But in any event, once the proper logical forms (i.e. truth-conditions) are given (i.e. once we write the technically accurate sentence that makes perspicuous the interplay of physical and mathematical properties), the technical language expressing the truth-conditions will obviously dismantle the inclination our naïve philosopher may have toward the adoption of temperatures or rising numbers.

Russell explains the need for a technical language in philosophy in an amusing passage in which he objects to a then current trend among some philosophers attempting to dismantle philosophical inquiry by appeal to an "ordinary" use of words. He writes:

> They are persuaded that common speech is good enough not only for daily life, but also for philosophy. I, on the contrary, am persuaded that common speech is full of vagueness and inaccuracy, and that any attempt to be precise and accurate requires modification of common speech both as regards vocabulary and as regards syntax. Everybody admits that physics and chemistry and medicine each require a language which is not that of everyday life. I fail to see why philosophy, alone, should be forbidden to make a similar approach towards precision and accuracy. Let us take, in illustration, one of the commonest words of everyday speech: namely, the word "day." The most august of this word is in the first chapter of Genesis and in the Ten Commandments. The desire to keep the Sabbath "day" has led orthodox Jews to give a precision to the word "day" which it does not have in common speech: they have defined it as the period from one sunset to the next. Astronomers, with other reasons for seeking precision, have three sorts of day: the true solar day; the mean solar day; and the sidereal day. These have different uses: the true solar

day is relevant if you are considering lighting-up time; the mean solar day is relevant if you are sentenced to fourteen days without the option; and the sidereal day is relevant if you are trying to estimate the influence of the tides in retarding the earth's rotation. All these four kinds of day—decalogical, true, mean and sidereal—are more precise than the common use of the word "day." If astronomers were subject to the prohibition of precision which some recent philosophers apparently favor, the whole science of astronomy would be impossible.

For technical purposes, technical languages differing from those of daily life are indispensable. I feel that those who object to linguistic novelties, if they had lived a hundred and fifty years ago, would have stuck to feet and ounces, and would have maintained that centimeters and grams savor of the guillotine.

(*MPD*, p. 242)

Russell's remarks allude to the dark history of our imprisonment by dogmatisms hostile to the advancement of thought. In his *Dialogue Concerning Two Chief World Views* Galileo makes a fool of Simplicius, the defender of geocentrism, and insults Pope Urban VIII by having Simplicius utter the Pope's own position that the false heliocentric theory is but convenient artifice for practical calculation. The Pope, formerly a staunch supporter of Galileo's research into "practical" calculation, did not take ridicule lightly, and summoned him to stand trial for heresy in 1633. He was found guilty and forced to renounce his views under threat of imprisonment. His works were banned and he lived constantly under suspicion and forced contrition. Only recently has the Church expressed regret for how Galileo was treated for the "heretical" thesis that the sun is the center of the universe and that the earth moves.

Eppur si muove (And yet it moves). Ontology, as it was practiced by the Aristotelians—with metaphysical necessities grounded in objects and their essences, entelechies, natural states and motions, vital forces, and the like—is to be rejected in philosophy as steadfastly as it was rejected by Newtonian empirical science. In its place, Russell demands that philosophers separate empirical concepts from logical concepts to uncover the analyses which reveal that the only necessity is logical necessity. In analysis, it is not enough to philosophers to explore our concepts and their meaning relationships. Moreover, the quest for logical form is not an empiricist endeavor to show that ontology is meaningless. It is the endeavor to get the ontology right. What, then, is the right ontology? For Russell, just as only necessity is logical necessity, the only ontology is that of pure logic. The rest is produced by mirage.

RUSSELL'S PARADIGM: DEFINITE DESCRIPTIONS

Perhaps the greatest challenge to any thinker is stating the problem in a way that will allow a solution.[19] In Russell's words,

> ... often the most difficult step in the discovery of what is true is thinking of a hypothesis which may be true; when once the hypothesis has been thought of it can be tested, but it may require a man of genius to think of it.[20]

In an amusing opening to his influential paper "On What There Is," Quine writes:

> A curious thing about the ontological problem is its simplicity. It can be put in three Anglo-Saxon monosyllables: "What is there?" It can be answered, moreover, in a word—"Everything"—and everyone will accept this answer as true. However, this is merely to say that there is what there is. There remains room for disagreement over cases; and so the issue has stayed alive down the centuries.[21]

The curious thing about this opening is that it is so very far from Russell's views on the nature of ontology. Russell considers existential commitments to be ontological only if they concern metaphysical objects that play a role in necessary truths (i.e. necessary truths of logic, mathematics, causation, ethics, etc). Russell holds that the only necessity is logical necessity; the proper ontology then is just the ontology of logic.

Quine holds that ontological questions are simply questions of what exists. Quine makes no distinction between questions of philosophical ontology and ordinary questions of happenstance, such as whether there are black swans, whether Shakespeare wrote *Hamlet*, or whether there is any water now left in the Aral Sea. The question of whether there are prime numbers above googolplex is on a par with the question of whether there are coelacanths in the Chalumna River off South Africa.

The new quantificational logic, which Russell made central to ontological analysis, shows up surreptitiously when Quine cagily answers "Everything" to the question "What is there?" Russell set forth the connection between ontology and quantification long before Quine coined the maxim "To be is to be the value of a variable."[22] Russell and Quine maintain that commitments to what there is are not properly given by a predicate "... exists," but by the variables of quantification. But, in Russell's view, this is not to say that they reveal ontological commitments. Russell's point was that in mistaking "... exists" as a genuine predicate, philosophers were led to make ontological commitments to special objects with essential properties. Pegasus, some philosophers thought,[23] must necessarily be in order that he has the property of not existing. Hence, "being"—though not "existence"—must necessary belong to whatever can be an object of thought. After 1905, Russell does not accept the question "What is there?" It is just a variant of "What exists?" and this has no truth-conditions. It is a pseudo-question.

The problem of the objects of thought is very old, dating at least to Plato's *Theaetetus*. It concerns the paradoxical matter of thinking about what is not. Plato writes:[24]

Socrates: Then he who thinks of that which is not, thinks of nothing?
Theaetetus: Clearly.

> Socrates: And he who thinks of nothing, does not think at all?
> Theaetetus: Obviously.
> Socrates: Then no one can think that which is not, either as a self-existent substance or as a predicate of something else?
> Theaetetus: Clearly not.

One of Russell's achievements in philosophy is to show that the question "How do we think about what is not?" is a complex question. A question is complex when the presuppositions that are required for its intelligibility are false or do not apply to the case at hand. Suppose a child who is not afraid of the dark is asked "How did you overcome your fear of the dark?" There is no way to answer. To answer is to attempt to maneuver within the parameters set by the presumptions of the question. It is the applicability of the presumptions that must be challenged. But in philosophy, background presumptions are often hidden and difficult to challenge. One of the presumptions of the question as to how we think about what is not is that we do think about what is not. In Russell's view, we do not think about what is not. We think by using quantifiers such as "all" and "some."

Russell provided a general means of finding truth-conditions for natural language sentences involving an ordinary proper name or definite description without presuming that the name or description has a reference. It has come to be called his "theory of definite descriptions." It was set forth in 1905 in a paper called "On Denoting," and it came to be a paradigm of Russell's new philosophy of logical analysis.[25]

Russell's theory of definite descriptions can be presented in terms of the following steps toward finding truth-conditions. The steps are these:

> Step 1: Replace the given ordinary proper name with an ordinary definite description "the A."

The Philosophy of Logical Atomism   187

Step 2: Determine the intended scope of the definite description involved.

Step 3: Represent the truth-conditions for the scope quantificationally.

We have seen how Frege's new quantification theory supplanted the medieval categorical forms. Russell is offering a new extension which enables a transcription of "the A is B" as

$(\exists x)(Ay \equiv_y y = x .\&. Bx)$

This is read as "Something is such that it is uniquely A and it is a B."

For convenience we can invent a quantifier expression for this, abbreviating as follows:

$[\iota x A x][Bx] =df (\exists x)(Ay \equiv_y y = x .\&. Bx)$.

Thus, in addition to the quantifiers

$(\forall x)(...x...)$
$(\exists x)(...x...)$

we have

$[\iota x A x][...x...]$.

In this way, the language of logic remains pure. The only terms are variables. No names or descriptions occur. Nonetheless, Russell prefers a notational convenience that makes it appear as if "the A" is a term in the language of logic, though it is really a quantifier. For this reason, Russell defines as follows:

$[\iota x A x][B(\iota x A x)] =df (\exists x)(Ay \equiv_y y = x .\&. Bx)$.

Thus instead of a quantifier

$[\iota x A x][...x...]$

Russell invents the quantifier

$[\iota x A x][...\iota x A x...]$.

The benefit is that when one intends the narrowest scope possible we can drop the quantifier and simply write $B(\iota x A x)$.

A very important result of the theory of definite descriptions concerns the conditions when a primary scope and a secondary scope are equivalent. The following scope law is provable:

$$(\exists x)(Ay \equiv_y y = x) . \supset . [\iota x A x][C(Bx)] \equiv C([\iota x A x][Bx])$$

where C is any truth-functional context (e.g. those built up from the logical particles). Indeed, the centerpiece of Russell's theory of definite descriptions is its capacity to render quantificational scope syntactically (by means of the apparatus of the bound variables of quantification). This is the great advantage of giving quantificational representations of the truth-conditions of ordinary sentences involving proper names or definite descriptions. Russell offers an entertaining example by taking up the question as to whether the present king of France is or is not bald. We have two scopes:

(Scope 1) Something is uniquely King of France at present and not bald.
$[\iota x P x][\sim B x]$.
(Scope 2) It is not the case that something is uniquely King of France at present and bald.
$\sim[\iota x P x][B x]$.

By the scope law, the two scopes are equivalent if something is uniquely King of France at present. But, of course, there is no present King of France. The question is intractable if one accepts that to decide the issue we must examine an intentionally inexistent present king of France—an object of thought which is supposedly referred to by "the present King of France." How are we to choose which, among the myriad possible present nonexistent kings of France (some of which are bald and others of which are not bald), is the proper referent of "the present King of France"? Poking fun at Hegel's notion that history progresses by synthesizing contradictories, Russell retorts that, "Hegelians who love a synthesis will probably conclude that he wears a wig."[26]

Consider the question as to whether Pegasus is a horse. In finding the truth-conditions Russell asks us to replace the ordinary name "Pegasus" with an ordinary definite description appropriate to the origins of the name "Pegasus." Let us, therefore, use

> The winged horse who according to Greek myth
> was born from the beheaded Medusa.

This yields the new sentence:

> The winged horse who according to Greek myth
> was born from the beheaded Medusa is a horse.

Next we give the truth-conditions quantificationally:

> Some unique winged horse who according to Greek myth
> was born from the beheaded Medusa is a horse.

This is false since, of course, there is no such horse. Naturally enough, however, conversational use of the proper name "Pegasus" offers a more charitable interpretation. One may intend to say the following:

> According to Greek myth,
> the winged horse who was born from the beheaded
> Medusa is a horse.

Giving the truth-conditions quantificationally yields a somewhat obvious truth:

> According to Greek myth,
> some unique winged horse born from the beheaded
> Medusa is a horse.

The different readings can be understood as differences in the scope of the quantifier "some."

When the truth conditions begin with "some unique ..."

the scope is said to be primary. Otherwise, it is said to be secondary.

In some cases only a primary scope is available. Consider, for example, whether Pegasus is self-identical. Russell's method for finding truth-conditions renders the truth-conditions of "Pegasus is self-identical" quantificationally as follows:

> Some unique winged horse who according to Greek myth was born from the beheaded Medusa is identical to itself.

This is false since there is no such horse. There is no secondary scope available. Contrast "Pegasus is not self-identical." We now have an ambiguity between primary and secondary. A secondary scope yields:

> It is not the case that some unique winged horse who according to Greek myth was born from the beheaded Medusa is identical to itself.

This is true. The primary scope yields:

> Some unique winged horse who according to Greek myth was born from the beheaded Medusa is such that it is not self identical.

This, of course, is false since there is no such horse.

In natural language, scope of quantifiers can be clumsy and often rely heavily on context of usage. For example, the sentence "All that glitters is not gold" is used (poetically) to mean that not everything is such that if it glitters then it is gold. It is not typically used to mean that everything is such that if it glitters it is not gold. Very often in natural language scope is not represented by syntactic markers at all. It is achieved by a speaker's reliance on her listener's pragmatic knowledge of salient features of the context of her utterance. This is especially manifest when definite descriptions are used. Russell writes:

> I have heard of a touchy owner of a yacht to whom a guest, on first seeing it remarked: "I thought your yacht was larger than it is"; and the owner replied, "No, my yacht is not larger than it is." What the man meant was, "The size that I thought your yacht was is greater than the size your yacht is".
>
> (*OD*, p. 115)

Pragmatic circumstances of utterances constrain viable interpretations. An utterance of,

> I thought (the length of) your yacht is larger than it is,

does not strike listeners as irrational because it is charitably taken to mean that your yacht has some unique length and I thought erroneously that your yacht has a larger length. Similarly, if a man says,

> I dreamt that the inventor of bifocals did not invent bifocals,

listeners would not take him to be an idiot, but rather take him to have intended to say that some unique inventor of bifocals was the subject of a dream in which the inventor did not invent them. The intended scope is given by pragmatic assumptions of a shared understanding between speaker and listener.

Speakers typically bring a great deal of descriptive information to bear when they use ordinary proper names in communication. But the apparatus of using and understanding proper names in communication involves something quite different from simply replacing the ordinary proper name with a definite description. To see this, let us first observe that communication with ordinary proper names does not produce the sorts of ambiguities of scope that are involved in describing objects. This feature of communication became a favorite of Kripke, who was working on systems of modal logic involving statements of possibility and necessity.[27] There seems to be no ambiguity in understanding a speaker who asserts:

> It is possible that Gödel did not discover that arithmetic is incomplete.

But ambiguity certainly arises if we replace the name "Gödel" with the definite description "the discoverer that arithmetic is incomplete," arriving at:

> It is possible that the discoverer that arithmetic is incomplete did not discover that arithmetic is incomplete.

This admits of two scopes. The secondary is:

> It is possible that some unique discoverer that arithmetic is incomplete is such that he did not discover that arithmetic is incomplete.

Of course, no charitable listener would take the speaker to have intended this secondary scope. They would interpret the speaker as intending to say:

> Some unique discoverer that arithmetic is incomplete is such that it is possible that he did not discover that arithmetic is incomplete.

The secondary scope makes the speaker irrational. Listeners will naturally adopt the primary scope.

But it will not do to say that the communicative rule for using proper names is one of replacement with a definite description together with a particular convention on determining scope. To see this, we need only invoke a case of an actual discovery so that we cannot use a modal context to produce scope. No irrationality seems to accompany the claim that scholars now believe that, according to the Bible, David did not kill Goliath. But if the scholars took "Goliath" to be short for "the Philistine killed with a slingshot by David," they *are* irrational. We cannot state their new interpretation as saying:

> Biblical scholars now believe that David did not kill the Philistine killed with a slingshot by David.

Scope distinctions of definite description seem powerless to correct the situation. The new interpretation is not properly expressed in a primary scope by a Biblical scholar saying:

> Some unique Philistine killed with a slingshot by David is such that Biblical scholars now believe that David did not kill him.[28]

Obviously, Biblical scholars did not take "Goliath" to simply mean "the Philistine killed with a slingshot by David." Upon hearing a new wave Bible scholar utter "David did not kill Goliath," the listener cannot proceed by using a replacement rule for proper names that tells him to replace "Goliath" with the definite description "the Philistine killed with a slingshot by David" and adjust for scope.

One might hope to salvage a replacement rule of communication with proper names by arguing that, upon hearing the utterance involving a proper name, listeners are to perform a replacement with a more exacting rendition of the definite description associated with the name. That is, Bible scholars really never took "Goliath" to mean "the Philistine killed with a slingshot by David," but rather the more exact description "the Philistine whom a part of the Bible suggests was killed with a slingshot by David." Communication with definite descriptions, after all, may itself involve inexact expressions and even indexicals and demonstratives. (For example, the definite description "the man over there" employs the demonstrative "there" together with a descriptive component.) If we are allowed a retreat to a more exacting description, it may be possible to save some form of a replacement rule of communication.

Be this as it may, there is no reason to suppose that speakers of a natural language must always have specific definite descriptions in mind when they communicate with ordinary proper names. The situation is analogous to the use of pure indexical words such as "I" and "now" and use of demonstratives such as "here," "this," and "that." A speaker must understand something of the attitudes, beliefs, and perspectives of his or her audience in order to communicate successfully with such words. Communication requires an understanding of the shared rules of a community of speakers. If a thunderous lightning strikes during a speech in which the speaker was saying "Did you hear that noise?" the demonstrative "that" refers to the thunder because the rules of communication demand that listeners are to find the most salient auditory event close to the speech act.[29] The speaker must accept this even if in the case in question he or she was lecturing about white noise and intended to refer to the hum of the computer. In understanding the rules, the speaker is often thinking descriptively about many aspects of his or her environment. But no definite description may be properly said to replace (or provide the meaning of) the demonstrative "that." The meaning is given by the rules for the proper use of the word. Communication does not involve a simple replacement rule.

Does this show that there is something wrong with Russell's theory of definite descriptions? Certainly not. The theory does require that we replace proper names by definite descriptions in the quest to render truth-conditions quantificationally. But this is neither an endeavor to provide a theory of communication, nor a theory of what is before a speaker's mind in communication. Though it has been appropriated to the ends of a theory of communication and an empiricist epistemology, the theory of descriptions is non-partisan. It belongs to no theory of reference. Russell's theory of definite descriptions is a quest to give careful truth-conditions that get the ontology right—minimizing, wherever possible, speculative philosophy.

Philosophers contrive ontological commitments everywhere. Many derive from the problems of intentionality and thus engage us in questions of the nature of mind and thought. But Russell's concern in advancing his theory of definite descriptions was not to develop a theory of reference in communication.[30] Rather, he hopes to preserve what he calls a "robust sense of reality" and disabuse philosophers of their fanciful inclinations toward the non-existent. Consider the following:

> I thought of something I would like to buy you for Christmas but I couldn't get it because it doesn't exist.[31]

At first blush, it may seem that we are pushed into holding that some object of thought is such that it does not exist. But an escape is available. We can put:

> Some property is such that I thought of buying you something that has that property for Christmas, but I didn't because everything fails to have that property.

Engaging examples of such "objects of thought" abound. Consider this:

> Sherlock Holmes is more famous than any other detective.

Replacing "Sherlock Holmes" with the definite description "the master detective living at 221B Baker Street according to the Conan Doyle stories," we might try the following:

> More people have employed the property of being a master detective living at 221B Baker Street according to the Conan Doyle stories in directing their thoughts than they have employed any property that some detective uniquely has.

Finding the right paraphrase is often difficult for want of an adequate philosophy of mind. But our robust sense of reality carries the day.

To investigate whether an argument is deductively valid (i.e. whether the truth-conditions of the premises guarantee the truth-conditions of the conclusion), one must first provide a structural representation of the truth-conditions of the premises and conclusion. This can pose quite a challenge, especially when contexts involving intentionality are involved. The following argument is valid:

> Ponce de Leon finds the fountain of youth.
> Therefore, some unique fountain of youth is such that Ponce de Leon finds it.

Observe, however, that its natural language structure is the same as that of the invalid argument:

> Ponce de Leon thinks about the fountain of youth.
> Therefore, some fountain of youth is such that Ponce de Leon thinks about it.

The truth-conditions of the respective premises of these arguments are quite different. In this sense, the two arguments do not have the same logical form, though they have the same natural language form. The truth-conditions for "Ponce de Leon thinks about the fountain of youth" are quite different from what they naively appear to be. What those truth-conditions are, however, eludes philosophers and scientists to this day. Knowing how to successfully communicate in practical circumstances does not require an exacting knowledge of truth-conditions of the sentences used. Speakers aware of the meaning difference between "finds" and "searches for" will not make the erroneous generalization in the case of Ponce's search. Only a philosopher caught up in a theory would insist that thinking of the fountain of youth entails that there is a fountain of youth about which one thinks. The application of Russell's theory of definite descriptions as a tool for finding exacting truth-conditions, like the application of Newton's laws to the tides or Einstein's equations to the perihelion of Mercury, is complicated and may await the discovery of new empirical and philosophical theories. But the robust among philosophers will surely adhere to the Russellian research paradigm.

The endeavor to uncover the truth-conditions for a given statement is a quest to uncover what Russell calls "logical form." In evaluating an inference as deductively valid or invalid, we are concerned with logical form of the truth-conditions, not the grammatical form of the sentences involved. Validity is about structure, not the content of what is said. The content of what is said, however, plays a very important role in exacting the structure, and this is where empirical sciences and mathematics frequently come into play. Consider the argument:

> Timber wolves are disappearing.
> Rushka is a timber wolf.
> Therefore, Rushka is disappearing.

What is being said by the first premise? The truth-condition for "Timber wolves are disappearing (during temporal interval t in region R)" is this:

> The number of timber wolves born during t in region R is less than the number of timber wolves that died during t in region R.

To be sure, if we take the premise to be saying,

> everything is such that if it is a timber wolf then it is disappearing,

then we could apply it to Rushka and yield:

> If Rushka is a timber wolf then Rushka is disappearing.

But the premise does not have this truth-condition. In the sense in which it is true that timber wolves are disappearing, we see that "Rushka is disappearing" is ungrammatical.

The statement "Men are numerous" has a form similar to the statement "Timber wolves are disappearing." Consider the argument:

> Men are numerous.
> Socrates is a man.
> Therefore, Socrates is numerous.

The odd conclusion could only follow from the premises if we adopt the perverse reading that "Men are numerous" is true just when everything is such that if it is a man then it is numerous! The truth-condition is that the number of men is much greater than zero.[32] This is a numeric statement. Similarly, consider:

> Men are existing.
> Socrates is a man.
> Therefore, Socrates is existing.

Russell maintains that once again it would be perverse to think that the truth condition of,

> Men are existing,

is that everything is such that if it is a man then it is existing. The truth condition is that the number of men is not zero.

In Russell's view, the truth-conditions for sentences asserting or denying existence are numeric. Russell follows the lead of Frege's *Foundations of Arithmetic* (1884). Frege wrote:

> In this respect existence is analogous to number. Affirmation of existence is in fact nothing but the denial of the number nought. Because existence is a property of concepts the ontological argument for the existence of God breaks down. But oneness is not a component characteristic of the concept "God" any more than existence is. Oneness cannot be used in the definition of this concept any more than the solidity of a house or its commodiousness or desirability, can be used in building it along with the beams, bricks and mortar.[33]

Accordingly, if we say, "The winged horse doesn't exist,"

we are saying the number of the concept of being winged and a horse is zero. This is true since there are exactly zero many winged horses.

But Frege does not explain in this passage how to give truth-conditions for statements of existence made with ordinary proper names. It would not be of help to be told that the truth-conditions for,

Pegasus exists,

are that the number of the concept being equal to Pegasus is not zero. "Pegasus" still occurs in the phrase. Frege's approach was to introduce a chosen object, say 0, for proper names that do not refer, and then just evaluate the truth conditions in virtue of it. But on that view, "Pegasus exists" and "Pegasus is a number" would be true, while "Pegasus is a horse" is false. Russell felt that this approach is "plainly artificial."[34]

Russell's theory of definite descriptions shows how to avoid this problem entirely. Frege is correct that statements of existence property belong to properties (i.e. concepts), not proper names. But on Russell's view, to give the truth-condition for

Pegasus exists

we replace the ordinary name "Pegasus" for a definite description involving A and then assert

$(\exists x)(Ay \equiv_y y = x)$

which says that the number of objects that are A is exactly one. Logic does not transcribe "Pegasus exists" as "E(Pegasus) for ". . . exists" is not transcribed into the language of logic as a predicate. Russell does allow the following definition:

$E!(\iota x Ax) =_{df} (\exists x)(Ay \equiv_y y = x)$.

This, however, is simply a convenient notation to avoid writing a complicated expression. It certainly does not reintroduce a property of existence.

Russell's account of the nature of statements of existence is an insight that dispenses with a great tendency for speculative philosophy—some of cosmological significance. Russell made this point in his radio debate with Father Copleston[35]:

> Copleston: But are you going to say that we can't, or we shouldn't even raise the question of the existence of the whole of this sorry scheme of things—of the whole universe?
>
> Russell: Yes. I don't think there's any meaning in it at all. I think the word "universe" is a handy word in some connections, but I don't think it stands for anything with meaning.

The sentence "Why does the universe exist?" is just a figurative way to phrase the sentence "Why does something exist?" which has no truth-conditions. This is not to say, however, that there are no truth-conditions for "Why does anything with mass exist?" One can, with trepidation about the physical nature of mass, ask why something has mass. But the question of the existence of something is lost to incoherence. A philosophical conundrum captivating minds for centuries is but a pseudo-question.[36]

One famous application of Russell's theory is in dispensing with St. Anselm's ontological argument for the existence of God. Russell never addressed Anselm's version. He took up Descartes's form of the ontological argument. Descartes writes that ". . . it is in truth necessary to admit that God exists, after having supposed him to possess all perfections, since existence is one of them."[37] In "On Denoting" Russell follows Leibniz's discussion of Descartes and dismisses the argument as follows:

> "The most perfect Being has all perfections; existence is a perfection; therefore the most perfect Being exists" becomes: "There is one and only one entity x which is most perfect; that one has all perfections; existence is a perfection; therefore that one exists." As a proof this fails for want of the premise "there is one and only one entity x which is most perfect."
>
> (*OD*, p. 117)

It is unclear, however, how Russell imagined representing the argument symbolically. On the official view of *Principia*, "existence" is not a logical predicate. Instead, he suggests that the argument's first premise begs the question.

This diagnosis is awkward. Much later, in *A History of Western Philosophy*, Russell explains:

> There is, therefore, or there can be conceived, a subject of all perfections, or most perfect Being. Whence it follows also that He exists, for existence is among the number of the perfections. Kant countered this argument by maintaining that "existence" is not a predicate. Another kind of refutation results from my theory of descriptions.
>
> (*HWP*, p. 586)

This passage suggests that even if one accepts existence as a property, the argument fails. This naturally raises the question as to when Russell first came to maintain that statements of existence are to be transcribed into logic quantificationally. In a manuscript of 22 December 1905 Russell's position is clear. There is no known earlier explicit passage. But in the July 1905 issue of *Mind*, prior to the appearance of "On Denoting" in October 1905, Russell published a paper called "On the Existential Import of Propositions." Russell proclaims that symbolic logic does not care a "pin" about the ordinary sense of "exists" as applied to individuals.[38] This suggests that he thinks that existence statements are not transcribed into symbolic logic by means of an existence predicate.

How then can a Russellian formulate the Descartes/Leibniz version of the ontological argument? Let us use "Gx" for "x is perfect." Perhaps the following is best:

$(\forall \psi)(\text{Perfection}(\psi) \supset \psi(G))$
Perfection $\{(\exists x) \, \hat{\varphi} \, x\}$
Therefore $(\exists x)Gx$.

The first premise says that the property G (i.e. the property of being perfect) has every perfection property. The second premise says that being exemplified is a perfection property. The conclusion is that the property G is exemplified. We now define as follows:

Perfection(ψ) =df $[\iota x Gx][\varphi x] \supset_\varphi \psi(\varphi)$.

The property ψ is a perfection property if and only if every property φ of God (i.e. the perfect being) exemplifies it. Now this construal captures Russell's hint in "On Denoting" that the argument begs the question (in an interesting way). Supplying the definition of Perfection(ψ) in the first premise yields:

$$(\forall \psi)([\iota x Gx][\varphi x] \supset_\varphi \psi(\varphi) .\supset. \psi(G)).$$

Now observe that the definite description "the perfect being" has a secondary scope. This secondary scope is logically equivalent to the following primary scope:

$$[\iota x Gx][(\forall \psi)(\varphi x \supset_\varphi \psi(\varphi) .\supset. \psi(G))].$$

This is a bit surprising. Indeed, one might wonder how one arrives at E!(ιxGx) from the weaker conclusion (∃x)Gx. The answer is that we have:

Perfection $\{[\iota x Gx][\hat{\varphi}x]\}$.

That is, we have:

$$[\iota x Gx][\varphi x] \supset_\varphi [\iota x Gx][\varphi x].$$

Hence from this and the first premise, we have [ιxGx][Gx]. This entails E!(ιxGx). It is in virtue of the logical equivalence of the scopes that the argument begs the question.

Anselm's ontological argument is different from the Descartes/Leibniz version. Anselm's idea is that the God-concept, by its nature, directs us to think of a being who exists. In short, Anselm takes it to be a thesis that, for any formula A:

> Conceiving of God as A is conceiving of God as both A and as existing.

Anselm then arrives that the following instance of his thesis:

> Conceiving of God as not existing is conceiving of God as both not existing and existing.

Anselm then points out that the consequent is false since it is impossible to conceive of a contradiction. Thus, conceiving of God as not existing is impossible. Hence, if conceptual powers track what is logically possible, God necessarily exists.

Interestingly, Anselm takes the name "God" to be a stand-in for the definite description "the being a greater than which cannot be conceived." (Let us use "Gx" for "x is a being a greater than which cannot be conceived.") Putting aside Anselm's views about conceivability, one might try to state the argument in terms of logical possibility (abbreviated with $\lozenge$). The Russellian diagnosis is a follows. Anselm seems to begin with the thesis that for any formula A:

$\lozenge$ A($\iota z G z$) $\supset$ $\lozenge$ (A($\iota z G z$) & E!($\iota z G z$)).

But this very strong thesis is unacceptable to Russell. If the definite description has a secondary scope in the formula A, then existence E!($\iota z G z$) is not assured. For example, let A($\iota z G z$) be:

good($\iota z G z$) or I am unhappy.

The scope of the definite description is this:

[$\iota z G z$][good (z)] or I am unhappy.

This says that either something is uniquely G and it is good or I am unhappy. This is true since I am unhappy. It certainly does not imply that God exists. To avoid this problem, one might try to represent Anselm's fundamental thesis as this:

($\forall \varphi$)($\lozenge$ φ($\iota z G z$) $\supset$ $\lozenge$ (φ($\iota z G z$) & E!($\iota z G z$))).

Since φ is a predicate variable, only a primary scope for the definite description with respect to φ is available. Making the scope clear, we have:

($\forall \varphi$)($\lozenge$ [$\iota z G z$][φz] $\supset$ $\lozenge$ ([$\iota z G z$][φz] & E!($\iota z G z$))).

Russell would certainly accept this premise as logically true. But the derivation of [] E!($\iota z G z$) cannot proceed. In *Principia*, "non-existence" is not a property and so cannot be involved in a universal instantiation. Russell's expression $\sim$E!(ιzGz) is certainly not of the form $\varphi(\iota z Gz)$. Thus we see that a Russellian can formulate the argument, accept Anselm's conceptual truth that there is something special about the property G, and yet reject the ontological argument because existence is not a property.

Realizing this diagnosis of the flaw in Anselm's argument, it might be said that Russell's thesis that "existence" and "non-existence" are not properties is not needed to block Anselm's ontological argument. Suppose that there is a property of existence (written E). Imagine universally instantiating to arrive at:

$$\Diamond\,[\iota z Gz][\sim Ez] \supset \Diamond\,([\iota z Gz][\sim Ez]\,\&\,E!(\iota z Gz)).$$

The consequent is a contradiction and hence, by *modus tollens*, we have $\sim\Diamond\,[\iota z Gz][\sim Ez]$.

Anselm's derivation is blocked. Attention to scope reveals that the conclusion is not equivalent to saying that necessarily one and only one entity is G. Rather, it asserts:

$$\sim\Diamond\,(\exists z)(Gy \equiv_y y = z\,.\&.\sim Ez).$$

This is equivalent to:

$$[]\,(\forall z)(Gy \equiv_y y = z\,.\supset. Ez).$$

This says that necessarily everything is such that if it is uniquely G then it exists. In light of the issues of scope, one might say that it is attention to the scope of a definite description, not the rejection of existence as a property, that forms the essence of a Russellian diagnosis of the flaw in Anselm's ontological argument.[39]

Be this as it may, it must be understood that the thesis that existence is not a property is an integral part of Russell's view that quantification is the inmost secret of the paradox of the directedness of intentionality. The problem of the directedness of intentionality was a famous subject of Alexius Meinong (1853–1920), an Austrian psychologist working at the University of Graz. Meinong become infamous for maintaining that "there are objects of which it is true to say they are not." In 1894 he founded an institute of experimental psychology and supervised the promotion of Christian von Ehrenfels, the founder of Gestalt psychology. Meinong held a strident form of the principle of intentionality he adopted from his mentor Franz Brentano. Intentionality is the distinctive mark of the mental, Brentano maintained, since thoughts represent and are directed toward (i.e. are about) objects other than themselves. Meinong held that the phenomenology of intending relies on a principle of the independence of *sosein* from *sein*. He thought that this is the only way to assure the directedness of intentionality. The *sosein* of the object of the intentional act of thinking, say, of the existing golden mountain assures an existing golden mountain—in spite of the fact that the existing golden mountain does not exist. In "On Denoting" Russell's naturally points out that Meinong's principle is "apt to infringe the law of contradiction." But Meinong replied that existing as a "determination of so-being" (*sosein*) is not the same as existence (which is a "determination of being"). The bemused Russell had "no more to say on this head."[40]

Russell's theory of definite descriptions is a technique for unraveling the truth-conditions of sentences in a way that avoids appeal to new speculative philosophical ontologies. Though it is not designed to be part of a theory of reference or communication, it has an interesting implication for a theory of mind. When we think that Pegasus does not exist, surely we do not stand in some mysterious relation to a non-existent Pegasus. Our thought's structure should be represented quantificationally, for example, as:

Everything fails to be uniquely both winged and a horse.

In affirmation of existence, we think quantificationally by means of employing the quantifier "something" and in denying existence; we think quantificationally by employing the quantifier "everything" together with negation. Russell's explanation of the directedness of intentionality rejects Meinong's principle of the independence of *sosein* from *sein*. It suggests that thinking is fundamentally quantificational. In thinking that Pegasus does not exist, we are not thinking about Pegasus. How then do we think about what is not? We do not.

THE LOGICAL MIRAGE

For any given occurrence of an ordinary proper name or definite description, Russell's theory of definite descriptions enables truth-conditions to be given without presupposing a referent of that name or definite description. This, together with the scope distinctions that it produces, is particularly useful in solving paradoxes. It is worth illustrating some of its more famous uses here.

The ordinary use of definite descriptions as genuine singular terms produces what Russell calls a "logical mirage." The mirage is that the universal laws apply. Russell's analysis rejects the naïve principle for the application of universal laws. The naïve principle is this:

From $(\forall x)Cx$ infer Ca

where a is a term (including a name or a definite description).[41] Russell has:

From $(\forall x)Cx$ infer Cy

where y is a variable.[42] From this, Russell arrives at the theorem:

$E!(\iota x Ax)$ & $(\forall x)Cx .\supset. [\iota x Ax][Cx]$.

This is a very important change to the formal system for logic.

Russell's adjustment to the application of universal laws applies to the laws of identity. The universal law of identity is this:

$(\forall x)(\forall y)(x = y .\supset. Px \supset Py)$

where Py results by replacing one or more free occurrences of x in Px by free occurrences of y.

In applying Russell's principle of universal instantiation to the universal law of identity, we have:

E!(ιxAx) & (∀x)(∀y)(x = y .⊃. Px ⊃ Py) .⊃.
[ιxAx] [(∀y)(x = y .⊃. Px ⊃ Py)].

where Py results by replacing one or more free occurrences of x in Px by free occurrences of y.

The following is also valid:

[ιxAx][ιyBy][x = y] ⊃ ([ιxAx][Px] ⊃ [ιyBy][Py]).

From here one can arrive at two forms:

Argument form A
[ιxAx][ιyBy][x = y]
Some x is uniquely Ax and some y is uniquely By and x = y

[ιxAx][D(Cx)]
Some x is uniquely Ax and it is such that D(Cx).

Therefore, [ιyBy][D(Cy)].
Some y is uniquely By and it is such that D(Cy).

Argument form B
[ιxAx][ιyBy][x = y]
Some x is uniquely Ax and some y is uniquely By and x = y.

D[ιxAx][Cx]
D(Some x is uniquely Ax and it is such that Cx).

Therefore, D[ιyBy][Cy].
D(Some y is uniquely By and it is such that Cy).

Argument form A is valid. The conclusion is provable from the premises because the definite description has primary scope. Argument form B, however, is not valid. The conclusion follows only when D is a truth-functional context.

We now have a template to diagnose a host of arguments that are based on the logical mirage produced by misapplying the universal law of identity to definite descriptions. Let us begin with a notorious argument whose conclusion is the striking result that if there are facts then there is at most one Great Fact which is the truth maker for every empirical sentence! The argument aims to demonstrate very easily that the ontology facts are useless to a correspondence theory of truth. The argument has come to be called a "slingshot" by analogy to David's supposed success in toppling Goliath with a very simple tool.

For concreteness, let R say that Saturn's atmosphere is mostly hydrogen and let S say Venus's atmosphere is mostly carbon dioxide. These are both true and surely made true by quite different facts. Let "fact R" mean the fact or facts that make it the case that R. Hence, intuitively fact R ≠ fact S. Proponents of the slingshot hope to show (minimally) that for any true empirical formulas R and S, fact R = fact S. For convenience in explaining the argument, let us use "Rxz" for "$x = z$.&. R" and "Sxz" for "$x = z$.&. S". Now observe that:

"R" is logically equivalent to "$(\forall z)([\iota x\ Rxz]\ [x = z])$"
fact R = fact $(\forall z)([\iota x\ Rxz]\ [x = z])$

"S" is logically equivalent to "$(\forall z)([\iota y\ Syz][y = z])$"
fact S = fact $(\forall z)([\iota y\ Syz]\ [x = z])$.

The second of each pair holds since logical equivalents have the same empirical facts as truth makers (if any). Noting that R and S are both true, the slingshot next proceeds as follows:

$(\forall z)([\iota x\ Rxz]\ [\iota y\ Syz]\ [x = y])$
fact R = fact $(\forall z)([\iota y\ Ryz]\ [x = z])$
Therefore, fact R = fact $(\forall z)([\iota y\ Syz]\ [x = z])$.

The slingshot would have us conclude that fact R = fact S. But the argument above (after universally instantianting the first premise) has form B and is invalid. The definite description has a secondary scope. It is certainly intuitive that features of different ways of describing an object have no bearing on the constituents of the empirical fact described. But this by no means warrants the inference. A logical mirage is produced by inattention to the scope of the definite description.

A version of the following paradox is due to Frege. We are to imagine a time before astronomers first discovered that the planet Venus is responsible for the appearance of a very bright star (i.e.

heavenly body) always near the sun, but it appears some parts of the year in the morning and other parts of the year in the evening. We have:

> The morning star is identical to the evening star
> Socrates believed that the morning star is a planet.
> Therefore, Socrates believed that the evening star is a planet.

The puzzle is that the conclusion seems to follow deductively by the universal law of identity. A naïve application of the law to the case at hand assigns the context $P(...)$ to:

> Socrates believed that ... is a planet.

Thus one can apparently conclude that if this holds of the morning star, it holds of the evening star. If Socrates believed the morning star is a planet then Socrates believed that the evening star is a planet. Applying Russell's theory to Frege's belief paradox, we let Mx be "x is a morning star" and Ex be "x is an evening star," and let D be the context "Socrates believed ..." and C be the context of "... is a planet." The following has the invalid form B:

> $[\iota x\, Mx][\iota y Ey][x = y]$
> Socrates believed that $[\iota x\, Mx][x$ is a planet$)]$
> Therefore, Socrates believed that $[\iota y\, Ey][y$ is a planet$]$.

Presenting definite descriptions quantificationally so clearly shows the fallacy that it is hard to imagine how it could have eluded logicians for so long. It eluded them because of the logical mirage produced by the ordinary language appearance of definite description as genuine singular terms. When the truth-conditions are properly represented, the universal law of identity cannot be applied to generate the paradox.

Russell's logical mirage thesis demands a fully syntactic approach to the belief paradox. That is, the paradox is due to a failure to properly match the proper inference pattern for applying universal principles. This approach does not, however, require a position on the truth-conditions for ascriptions of belief. In "On Denoting" Russell maintains that although a mind can be directly acquainted with universals, thought about physical objects, people, and the like is always descriptive. These features of his theory play a role in representations of secondary occurrences of definite description. Consider "Socrates believed that the morning star is a planet." We have:

Socrates believed that [ɩxMx][x is a planet].

This says that Socrates believed that some unique morning star is a planet. But if Socrates's thought must be descriptive, what would be a primary scope? A straightforward rendition of the primary scope yields:

[ɩxMx][Socrates believed that x is a planet].

This says that some unique morning star is such that Socrates believed of it that it is a planet. But this rendition of primary scope relies on a semantic distinction between "believing that" and "believing of." The former is akin to a direct quote which represents the actual sentence the believer used and thereby reveals the concepts the believer herself employed. In contrast, "believing of" is akin to a freely indirect report which leaves what sentence the believer used and what concepts the believer employed entirely open.

Ascriptions of belief to another are often *de dicto* (i.e. they are sensitive to the structure of the sentence believed). At the same time, we do make ascriptions of belief to others without knowing the precise nature of structure of the sentences believed. We have indirect speech. These belief ascriptions are said to be *de re* (about the thing) because the person ascribing the belief to another describes the object of the other's belief in his or her own way, not in the way the other thinks of it. How then can a Russellian advancing the logical mirage thesis represent *de re* belief ascriptions? To capture a primary scope that requires Socrates's belief to be descriptive, we have:

$(\exists x)(My \equiv_y y = x)$ & $(\exists \varphi)(\varphi x \equiv_x Mx$.&. Socrates believed that $[\iota x \varphi x][x \text{ is a planet}])$.

This says that something is uniquely a morning star and some property φ is such that a thing has that property if and only if it is a morning star and Socrates believed that something uniquely has that property and is a planet. This better fits with Russell's mirage diagnosis and his efforts to find a syntactic solution to the paradox. The natural result is that, in the primary scope, we may now (given the identity of the morning star and the evening star) infer that something is uniquely an evening star and some property φ is such that a thing has that property if and only if it is an evening star and Socrates believed that something uniquely has that property and is a planet.[43] But this is no mere application of the law of identity.

Mirages of a similar sort occur when it comes to the metaphysics of necessity and possibility. Let us use "[](...)" to abbreviate "It is necessary that ...". In Quine's view, quantified modal logic was born in the sin of confusion of use and mention. One of Quine's arguments is that "9" is not referential in the context of "[](9 > 7)." Modal logicians who take it to be referential allegedly cannot diagnose the fallacy in the following argument:

(1) 9 = the number of planets
(2) [](9 is greater than 7)
Therefore, [](the number of planets is greater than 7).

Quine holds that "[](9 > 7)" is not about the number 9. It is about the sentence "9 > 7." Thinking that the sentence "[](9 > 7)" is about the number 9 is every bit as confused as thinking that since "cat" occurs in "cattle" the sentence

"cattle" has six letters

is about a cat. Interestingly, it is common to reply to Quine by using the distinctions of scope made possible by Russell's theory of definite descriptions. Let "Px" mean that x numbers the planets of our solar system. (Of course, we are neglecting the recent official demotion of Pluto to an asteroid.) The derivation wrongly assumes that the following inference can be performed by means of the universal law of identity:

$[\iota x Px][9 = x]$
$[](9 > 7)$
Therefore, $[][\iota x Px][x > 7]$.

Russell's theory reveals that there is no such instance of the law of identity.

It is, however, somewhat ironic that Russell's theory of definite descriptions has been appropriated to undermine Quine's argument. Quine holds that ascriptions of necessity are properly about sentences. Russell disagrees. Nonetheless, there is a deep agreement between them. Both maintain that necessity is a matter of structure and is not about the inner essence of objects. Because of this, there is something seriously wrong with quantifying into the context of necessity when it binds an individual variable. It should be meaningless. There is a quite different approach to Quine's argument that reveals the logical mirage involved in it. This approach applies a Russellian account of the nature of natural numbers as quantifiers. Rendering the truth-conditions in accordance with Russell's account, we have a rather starkly different structure rendering the truth-conditions:

(1) $\text{Card}_{xy}^{Py}[\varphi_x] \equiv_\varphi 9_x[\varphi_x]$
For all φ, φs are in one-to-one correspondence with planets of our solar system if and only if there are exactly nine φs.

(2) $[] (9_x \varphi_x >_\varphi 7_x \varphi_x)$
Necessarily for all φ, exactly nine φ's is a greater number of φs than exactly seven φs.

Therefore, $[] (\text{Card}_{xy}^{Py}[\varphi_x] >_\varphi 7_x[\varphi_x])$.

Necessarily for all φ, exactly as many φs as planets of our solar system is a greater number of φs than exactly seven φs.

It is now obvious that no application of the law of identity applies. The logical mirage is clearly the source of confusion. There is, in fact, no identity statement at all!

The central question, however, remains. Is quantificationally binding an individual variable in the context $[](...)$ legitimate? An important consequence of allowing such quantification is that the universal law of identity would yield:

$$(\forall x)(\forall y)(x = y \supset [](x = x) \supset [](x = y)).$$

If we accept the truth of $(\forall x)[](x = x)$, which says that every entity is necessarily self-identical, we arrive at:

$$(\forall x)(\forall y)(x = y \supset [](x = y)).$$

This is not too surprising a result given that we focus on the nature of the variables of quantification. But if some names designate rigidly and non-descriptively—names such as "Hesperus" and "Phosphorus"—one can use this result to arrive at the doctrine that there are non-logically metaphysically necessary truths, such as $[](\text{Hesperus} = \text{Phosphorus})$, which are known a posteriori. This is precisely the position Kripke arrived at.

Since there is a unique number of planets of our solar system, the following argument involving primary occurrence of the definite description would be allowed if binding individual variables in the context of necessity were allowed:

$[\iota x Px][9 = x]$
$[](9 > 7)$
Therefore, $[\iota x Px][[](x > 7)]$.

The conclusion says that there is a unique number of planets of our solar system, and necessarily it is greater than 7. This agrees that there need not be 9 planets, but it says the number of planets (i.e. 9) is such that its essence is to be greater than 7. Russell would bridle at this essentialism just as violently as Quine. It heralds a collapse, perhaps not to Aristotelian entelechies, but certainly to essences which are fundamentally non-logical, metaphysical necessities. Aristotelians imagined that certain kinds of objects have internal essences: the number 9 essentially greater than 7, man essentially rational, stars essentially in circular motion, and the earth essentially at rest. Aristotelian essentialism was upturned by the Copernican revolution and the rise of Newtonian empirical science. In Russell's view, Aristotelian essentialism, and metaphysical necessities in general, are antithetical to modern science. Friends of binding individual variables in the context of necessity fundamentally disagree with Russell on the nature of necessity. For Russell, all necessity is logical necessity, and logical necessity is a fundamentally structural notion. It is true in terms of the structure, not true in terms of the inner essence of an object. Quantificationally binding an individual variable in the context of necessity undermines the structure. Russell and Quine therefore agree that it should be excluded as grammatically ill formed.

Russellians require logical form that rejects binding individual variables in the context $[](\ldots x \ldots)$ and yet permits a sort of *de re* quantification that preserves the view that necessity is a matter of structure. Looking for a replacement for

$$(\forall x)[](x = x)$$

we cannot put:

$$(\forall \varphi)([]([\iota x \varphi x][x = x]).$$

This says that for every property φ it is necessary that some unique entity is φ and self-identical. It is false since for some property φ it is certainly not necessary that there be a unique entity which is φ. A better candidate is this:

$$(\forall \varphi)([](E!(\iota x \varphi x) \supset [\iota x \varphi x][x = x])).$$

This says that for every property φ, it is necessary that if some unique entity is φ then some unique entity is φ and self-identical. But there is no expression which replicates the import of:

$(\forall x)(\forall y)(x = y \supset [](x = y))$.

The following is not a theorem:

$(\forall \varphi)(\forall \psi)([\iota x \varphi x][\iota y \psi y][x = y] \supset [](E!(\iota x \varphi x) \& E!(\iota x \psi x) .\supset.$
$[\iota x \varphi x][[\iota y \psi y][x = y])))$.

This is obviously false for it rules out contingent identifications. The closest we can come is this:

$(\forall \varphi)(\forall \psi)([\iota x \varphi x][\iota y \psi y][x = y] \supset$
$(\exists F)(\varphi x \equiv_x Fx \& (\exists G)(\psi x \equiv_x Gx .\&. [](E!(\iota x Fx) \& E!(\iota x Gx) .\supset.$
$[\iota x Fx][[\iota y Gy][x = y]])))$.

This is trivial for we have only to let F be the same property as G.

For Russell, the question of whether something is necessary or possible cannot be answered until one exacts the logical structure of the truth-conditions of the statement in question. Consider the sentence "◊(Pegasus exists)," which says it is logically possible that Pegasus exists. Given the truth-conditions for "Pegasus exists" we have:

$◊(\exists x)(Wy \equiv_y y = x)$.

Here we use "Wy" for "y is winged and a horse." In Russell's view, the truth conditions for the modal statement are given by removing the predicate letter "W" and replacing it with a predicate variable which is existentially bound in widest scope. We get:

$(\exists \varphi)(\exists x)(\varphi y \equiv_y y = x)$.

Since this is actually true, Russell regards it to be logically possible that Pegasus exists. Observe that on this view, the truth-conditions of "Possibly Pegasus exists" have nothing to do with Pegasus. Indeed, the very same truth-conditions apply to the sentence

"Possibly Francesca exists." Francesca is a person, but the truth-conditions have nothing to do with her.

Next consider a sentence asserting that it is necessary that if Ben Franklin exists then he invented bifocals. Replacing "Ben Franklin" with "the inventor of bifocals" and using "Ix" for "x invented bifocals," we have an ambiguity of scope. One disambiguation is this:

$$[](E!(\iota xIx) \supset [\iota xIx][Ix]).$$

This says: "Necessarily if the inventor of bifocals exists then the inventor of bifocals invented bifocals." Applying Russell's procedure, this becomes:

$$(\forall \varphi)(E!(\iota x \varphi x) \supset [\iota x \varphi x][\varphi x]).$$

This says "For every property φ, if the thing that is φ exists then the thing that is φ is φ." This is, of course, true.

What of a *de re* rendition of scope? If quantifiers are allowed to bind individual variables within the context of $[](...)$, we might try to capture the *de re* with this:

$$[\iota yIy][[](E!(\iota xIx) \supset Iy)].$$

This is false. It says that there is some unique y who invented bifocals and who is such that necessarily if there is a unique inventor of bifocals then y invented bifocals. But we have seen that Russell would not allow binding an individual variable in this way. It violates his thesis that logical necessity is fundamentally a feature of structure. For the *de re* scope, the Russellian approach would be to bind a predicate variable. Thus:

$$E!(\iota xIx) \,\&\, (\exists \psi)(\psi y \equiv_y Iy \,\&\, [](E!(\iota x \psi x) \supset [\iota x \psi x][Ix])).$$

There is now no problem applying Russell's technique. We get:

$$E!(\iota xIx) \,\&\, (\exists \psi)(\psi y \equiv_y Iy \,\&\, (\forall \varphi)(E!(\iota x \psi x) \supset [\iota x \psi x][\varphi x]).$$

This is false.

Russell's thesis is that the only necessity is logical necessity and logical necessity is an issue of structure. Formally stated, Russell's thesis concerning logical necessity as applied to formulas not containing bound predicate variables is this:

$$[]A \text{ if and only if } (\forall \varphi_1)\ldots(\forall \varphi_n)(\forall x_1)\ldots(\forall x_k)(A^*),$$

where A contains no predicate variables or individual constants (names) and its only free individual variables are $x_1, \ldots x_k$ and A^* results by replacing all the predicate letters $F_1, \ldots, F_n$ in A with predicate variables $\varphi_1, \ldots, \varphi_n$. The case of $\Diamond A$ is defined as $\sim[]\sim A$, and thus involves the existential quantifiers $(\exists \varphi_1)\ldots(\exists \varphi_n)(\exists x_1)\ldots(\exists x_k)(A^*)$. Cocchiarella has shown that (for the first-order formulas) Russell's approach parallels the semantic approach of Tarski, making logical necessity coincide with logical truth as a fundamentally structural (*de dicto*) notion.[44]

Whitehead once quipped that it is nice when all enemies have one neck. We have seen that the theory of definite descriptions dissolves a host of philosophical problems in one and the same way. They are all produced by a logical mirage. Russell's theory of definite descriptions is an important paradigm for solving puzzles. From puzzles about numbers to the Augustinian mysteries of God and creation, it continues to this day to be one the most successful and powerful philosophical tools for avoiding the ontological reveries and dogmatisms of philosophers.

FURTHER READING

Nino B. Cocchiarella, *Logical Studies in Early Analytic Philosophy* (Columbus, OH: Ohio State University Press, 1988).

James Griffin, *Wittgenstein's Logical Atomism* (Seattle: University of Washington Press, 1969).

Saul Kripke, *Naming and Necessity* (Cambridge, MA: Harvard University Press, 1980).

Leonard Linsky, *Oblique Contexts* (Chicago: University of Chicago Press, 1983).

Francesco Orilia, *Ulisse, il quadrato rotondo e l'attuale re di Francia* (Pisa: Edizion Ets, 2002).

Hans Reichenbach, *The Rise of Scientific Philosophy* (Berkeley, CA: University of California, 1951).

Five

Scientific Epistemology

> It has been common among philosophers to begin with how we know and proceed afterwards to what we know. I think this is a mistake because knowing how we know is one small department of knowing what we know.
>
> *My Philosophical Development* (1959)

Given our characterization of Russell's Logical Atomism as a research program to show that the only necessity is logical necessity, it should be no surprise to discover that the theories developed within Logical Atomism orient themselves to the best sciences of the day. We have seen that there is an a posteriori (empirical) component in the philosophy of Logical Atomism. In order to show that the only necessity is logical necessity, one must know something about the actual world—about physics, chemistry, biology, psychology, and the like.

Russell applied his new scientific philosophy of Logical Atomism to the venerable question of how to reconcile our knowledge of physics with epistemology. The topic was addressed most famously by Kant (1724–1804), who was concerned with reconciling Newton's physics with the epistemological skepticism produced by Hume's associationist psychology. In Russell's day, the question was formed in terms of the new physics of Einstein and the current psychological theories involving Watson's behaviorism.

On the heels of his series of Lowell lectures at Harvard, entitled "Scientific Method in Philosophy" (1914), he wrote the book

Our Knowledge of the External World as a Field for Scientific Method in Philosophy.[1] The orientation Russell takes is complicated, and naturally there are many debates about the proper interpretation of his views. Traditional epistemology begins from Descartes's notion of methodological doubt. It begins from the standpoint of the person evaluating the extent of his or her knowledge and investigates the sort of justification she may have in making knowledge claims. Only the data available to reflective mediation can be taken as the starting point for epistemology. This is called "methodological solipsism." It does not suppose solipsism (i.e. I alone exist), but rather supposes that epistemology begins only from one's own experiences.

In the *Problems of Philosophy* (1912) Russell's notion of Logical Atomism as a method for scientific philosophy was in its infancy. In the work, there are passages that suggest that Russell embraces methodological solipsism as his epistemic starting point. He writes that "[w]e must therefore, if possible, find in our own purely private experiences, characteristics which show, or tend to show, that there are in the world things other than ourselves and our private experiences" (P, p. 21). *Our Knowledge* was thus interpreted as a form of phenomenalism, an empiricist and methodologically solipsist construction of matter in terms of mental states. In *Problems*, Russell was not clear about the status of these private experiences as sense-data. But it was not long until he went on record with the thesis that sense-data are physical entities, not mental entities. And in *My Philosophical Development* Russell confutes the interpretation of his epistemology as methodologically solipsist:

> The method of Cartesian doubt, which appealed to me when I was young and may still serve as a tool in the work of logical dissection, no longer seems to me to have fundamental validity. Universal skepticism cannot be refuted, but also cannot be accepted. I have come to accept the facts of sense and the broad truth of science as things which the philosopher should take as data, since, though

their truth is not quite certain, it has a higher degree of probability than anything likely to be achieved in philosophical speculation.

(*MPD*, p. 207)

Russell's approach to epistemology, at least from 1914 onward, is not a methodological solipsism. It employs information from empirical fields such as evolutionary biology, physics, chemistry, and psychology, applying them to give an account of how an organism's cognitive processes, together with the data it receives from perception, enable it to successfully engage its environment.

To understand Russell's approach to epistemology, one must appreciate that his construction of matter is not motivated by empiricism. Our *Knowledge* was modified several times, as Russell incorporated into it more and more of the current science of the day. The scientific method in philosophy that Russell is applying is theory of four-dimensionalism which rejects the existence of matter (as continuants persisting in time) in favor of series of transient physical particulars (i.e. sensations and sensibilia) which are its stages. This four-dimensionalism would later be buttressed by Minkowski's interpretation of Einstein's theory of Relativity. The proper orientation to Russell's epistemology is that it is articulated from a position outside of any knower. Russell explains:

> Sense-data at the times when they are data are all that we directly and primitively know of the external world; hence in epistemology the fact that they are *data* is all-important. But the fact that they are all we directly know gives, of course, no presumption that they are all that there is. If we could construct an impersonal metaphysics independent of the accidents of our knowledge and ignorance, the privileged position of the actual data [sense-data] would probably disappear, and they would probably appear as a rather haphazard selection from a mass of objects more or less like them. In saying this, I assume only that it is probable that there are particulars with which we are not acquainted. Thus the special importance of sense-data is in relation to epistemology, not to metaphysics. In this

respect, physics is to be reckoned as metaphysics: it is impersonal, and nominally plays no special attention to sense-data. It is only when we ask how physics can be known that the importance of sense-data re-emerges.²

Contrary to a long history of interpretation, we shall find that Russell's approach is in league with the naturalization of epistemology.

THE PROBLEMS OF PHILOSOPHY

On the heels of the completion of *Principia*, Russell was commissioned by Gilbert Murray to write a book on the principles of mathematics. Murray was one of three general editors of the Home University Library, a series of short hardcover books designed to bring the best minds to a widely uneducated audience at the shocking price of only one shilling. Russell at first resisted, but Murray pressed him repeatedly. "Tell me," he argued,

> of another philosopher who is 1. completely alive and original; 2. democratic, so that he wants to communicate his thought to shop assistants; 3. sharp-eyed and not wobbly or sloppy in thought, and then I shall cease to persecute you.³

Russell agreed. *Problems of Philosophy*, the "Shilling Shocker," as it came to be called, was born. It was written in part during a period in which Russell was in love with Lady Ottoline Morrell. They read Leopardi's poems⁴ and studied Spinoza's concept of the "intellectual love of God," which frees one from the self-imposed prison the world's indifference to our interests produces. Russell imagined writing a book with Ottoline which might be called "Prisons." Some of their ideas found their way into *Problems*. The value of philosophy, apart from its role in giving unity to and systematizing the sciences by offering a critical examination of the grounds of our convictions, beliefs and prejudices, lies in "... the greatness of the objects which it contemplates, and the freedom from narrow and personal aims resulting from this contemplation"

(P, p. 157). Philosophical contemplation frees us from self-interest so that

> the free intellect will see as God might see, without a here and now, without hopes and fears, without the trammels of customary beliefs and traditional prejudices, calmly, dispassionately, in the sole and exclusive desire of knowledge—knowledge as impersonal, as purely contemplative, as it is possible for man to attain.
>
> (P, p. 160)

Otherwise we are trapped. "Unless we can so enlarge our interests as to include the whole outer world, we remain like a garrison in a beleaguered fortress ... if our life is to be great and free, we must escape this prison and this strife" (P, p. 157). The book so admirably succeeds in bringing the value and the main problems of philosophy to beginners that it is still widely read today in and out of the academy.

Problems focuses its attention on the longstanding debate between rationalism and empiricism. It offers its own unique solution, which is intended to rival that of Kant. The debate centers on status of arithmetic and geometry. Ignorant of the new logic, most every philosopher before Frege thought that arithmetic sentences such as

$$2 + 2 = 4$$

and geometric sentences such as,

> All triangles are such that their interior angles sum to two right angles,

are not part of logic. These truths advance knowledge. But logic was thought to be analytic and uninformative.

The empiricist Hume was never quite sure precisely how to understand the notion analytic. He spoke of "relations of ideas." He contrasted these with the associations of distinct ideas that are forged by an organism's developing habits of expectation. Russell explains the notion of an association of ideas amusingly in the following text:

And this kind of association is not confined to men; in animals it is also very strong. A horse which has been often driven along a certain road resists the attempts to drive him in another direction. Domestic animals expect food when they see the person who usually feed them. We know that all these rather crude expectations of uniformity are liable to be misleading. The man who has fed the chicken every day throughout its life at last wrings its neck instead, showing that more refined views as to the uniformity of nature would have been useful to the chicken.

(*P*, p. 63)

Associations of ideas are easily explained by the development of habits that are reinforced by the repetition of some experiences. The notion of a relation of ideas is given a more precise expression by Kant. Analytic truths are trivial because they are true in virtue of meaning alone. The law of self-identity

$A = A$

is analytic in the sense that it is not informative. Aristotelian categorical logic renders the logical forms statements can have. Hence, a categorical sentence is analytically true when the predicate term's meaning is contained in the meaning of the subject term's meaning. For example,

All unmarried men are unmarried

is analytically true in virtue of a relation of the ideas "unmarried man" and "unmarried." The meaning of "man" is contained in the meaning of "unmarried man." All such analytic truths are uninformative and knowable a priori (i.e. independently of empirical investigation, testing, etc.). This yields the following definition:

Analytic$_K$ = df true in virtue of the law of self-identity or
in virtue of the meaning of the non-logical words.

The "logical words" for Kant were the categorical forms. Arithmetic and geometry are not analytic$_K$. They are informative, so Kant thought they must be synthetic and a priori.

The rejection of categorical forms and the development of the new ᶜᵖlogic of Frege and Russell changed both the terminology and the conception of "analytic." In *The Principles of Mathematics*, Russell put the point starkly:

> ... Kant never doubted for a moment that the propositions of logic are analytic, whereas he rightly perceived that those of mathematics are synthetic. It has since appeared that logic is just as synthetic as all other kinds of truth.
>
> (*PofM*, p. 457)

Mathematics and logic are not analytic in Kant's sense. But the new informative ᶜᵖlogic offers a new meaning for "analytic." We have:

Analytic$_R$ = df$_{Russell}$ true in virtue of logical structure.

In this sense, we can express Russell's view by saying that mathematics is analytic$_R$. This is just the thesis of logicism. But there is yet another non-Kantian notion of analytic. This is the notion set out by the new positivistic empiricists who rejected the old Aristotelian categorical logic in favor of the new quantification theory but remained uncommitted to ᶜᵖlogic. They offered this:

Analytic$_p$ = df true in virtue of the meaning of the logical particles of the new quantification theory.

For example, consider this sentence:

Everything is such that if it is unmarried and a man then it is unmarried.

The form of this is:

Everything is such that if it is A and B then it is A.

This holds in virtue of the logical words alone. While this is an improvement on Kant, it falls well short ᶜᴾLogic and Logicism.⁵ Quantification theory cannot capture mathematics and geometry as being Analytic$_R$.

Arithmetic and geometric truths are not analytic$_K$, and so Kant, as Hume before him, was baffled by how it is that we know they are necessary. Knowledge gained by sense experience would, it seems, at best secure a very high probability. It never could convince us that something is necessary. We don't have a degree of justification in arithmetic. It is necessary. Heroic attempts by John Stuart Mill aside, it is not by induction from past successes in combining (i.e. mixing, stirring, or bringing close together) that we come to conclude that $2 + 2 = 4$. Empiricists are therefore at a lost to explain the necessity of mathematics and how we come to know it. For Empiricists, there are no further sources of knowledge. All non-analytic knowledge is gained by means of sense experiences.

Rationalists, following Socrates and Plato, maintained that there is another source of synthetic knowledge. This source explains how we know synthetic and yet necessary truths. Some synthetic ideas, such as those of arithmetic and geometry, are innate. In this way, they are known a priori (i.e. independent of empirical investigation by means of the senses). The Socratic method, perhaps the most popular method of teaching in law schools to this day, has its foundation in the doctrine of innate ideas. The method is to assist the student in coming to focus on a form of knowledge that is at once both about the world and yet given a priori. Plato's dialogue *The Meno* offers an excellent example. By drawing a picture, Socrates endeavors to demonstrate that a wholly uneducated slave boy innately knows how to find the length of the side of a square which is double in area of a given square (see the figure overleaf).⁶ Platonic explanation of the source of this knowledge is the Socratic doctrine of *Anamnesis* (recollection). Plato maintains that we have innate knowledge of arithmetic and geometric Forms and that recollection of those Forms is elicited (in varying degrees) on the occasion of certain sense experiences.

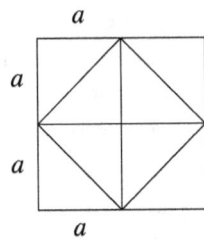

The relation of a mind to Platonic Forms seems occult, and the theory of anamnesis strains credulity. But how then could a mind, without appeal to sense experience, come to have such ideas which are about the world? Rationalists were willing to live with the mystery; empiricists were not. But both were in serious epistemic trouble. Without justification of mathematics and geometry, knowledge—whether synthetic a posteriori or otherwise—is impossible. Kant showed a way to re-conceptualize the entire matter. The mind does not stand in a relationship to a realm of ideas (i.e. Platonic Forms) or any other realm in its having innate ideas. How then are synthetic a priori truths possible? Kant characterizes his answer as revolutionary—every bit as revolutionary as Copernican heliocentrism. Space and time are not discovered in the world by empirical investigations of a passive mind receiving sense-experiences. The mind (i.e. cognition) is active, not passive. It imposes structures on the data of sense-experience. Kant's idea has thrilled psychologists ever since.

The structures, "pure empirical (aesthetic) intuitions" as Kant calls them, are those of space and time. Euclidean geometry is the product of the activity of the mind in spatially structuring the data of sense. According to Kant, we can only understand geometry if we appeal to our sense experiences of spatial figures. Many of Euclid's proofs depend essentially on appeals to spatial intuitions of motion and superposition (e.g. in the definition of congruence) or the concept of a point occurring spatially between other points on a line. Similarly, by making time a scaffolding for the very possibility of thought, Kant is able to provide a foundation for arithmetic. The consecutive sequence (of time) constitutes the notion of natural numbers because that notion is the notion of consecutive series. The arithmetic of addition of 1 is just the notion of the next in a consecutive sequence. Geometry and arithmetic are necessary and knowable a priori (i.e. without appeal to empirical discoveries) because they are the product of the active structuring of experience by the mind. Nothing which is not so structured can be experienced.

Kant's views do have a prima facie plausibility. Think how odd it would be to imagine a new scientific breakthrough reported in the headlines: "New concept discovered: Time. Henceforth, please consecutively order your thoughts in terms of before and after." This is not just odd; it is unintelligible. Our thoughts are given to consciousness with a temporal order. Kant maintains the order is given by some pre-conscious mechanism doing the consecutive sequencing—a scaffolding for thought. One might object: It is nature's events that are in a fixed temporal consecutive sequence. Our thoughts simply follow the sequence. But do they? Are the events of nature in a fixed consecutive (or dense or continuous) sequence? What is the physical foundation for such a fixed, absolute ordering of physical events? How could such physical laws be known? We are certainly not aware of any judgments of such order. And the very contents (i.e. meanings) of our thoughts would be lost in the process if we were continually in the process of coming up with, by trial and error, orderings that make the best theory about the way the world is.

Certainly visual images of non-Euclidean spaces seem impossible. But by the 1820s, János Bolyai and Nikolai Lobachevsky separately wrote treatises on hyperbolic geometry denying Euclid's parallel postulate. Bolyai ends his work by mentioning that it is not possible to decide through mathematical reasoning alone if the geometry of the physical universe is Euclidean or non-Euclidean; this is a task for the physical sciences. Bernhard Riemann, in a famous lecture in 1854, founded the field of Riemannian geometry, discussing in particular the ideas now called "manifolds," "Riemannian metric," and "curvature."

Faced with the new non-Euclidean geometries developed in the nineteenth century, neo-Kantians maintained that they are intelligible only in terms of projective geometries and the groups defined by invariances in transformation that are discussed in the Erlangen program of Felix Klein. Triangles projected onto the surface of, say, a sphere, have their internal angles sum to more than two right angles. If "straight" means constancy of slope, then lines projected onto a geodesic are straight. The surface of a sphere is not a Euclidean plane, but locally the laws of the Euclidean plane geometry are good approximations of the metric. The simplest model for elliptic geometry is a sphere, where lines are "great circles" (e.g. the equator or the meridians on a globe). In the elliptic model, for any given line l and a point *A*, which is not on l, all lines through *A* will intersect l. A model showing the consistency of hyperbolic geometry was found by Eugenio Beltrami in 1868. He showed that a surface called the "pseudosphere" has the appropriate curvature to model a portion of hyperbolic space.

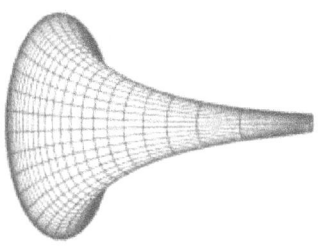

partial pseudosphere

In a second paper in the same year he defined the "Klein model," the "Poincaré disk model," and the "Poincaré half-plane model," which model the entirety of hyperbolic space. He then used this to show that hyperbolic geometry was logically consistent if Euclidean geometry is. (The converse follows from the horosphere model of Euclidean geometry.) Projections of this sort are consistent with

Kant's view. They maintain that it is only by projection or algebra that non-Euclidean structures can be made intelligible to consciousness. There are no non-Euclidean spatial intuitions.

Kant offered a metaphysical foundation for the very possibility of Newtonian science, which was widely taken to be the final physical theory and a complete knowledge of nature's processes. In Kant's day, absolute time and Euclidean space were thought to be fundamental to Newtonian science. When Russell wrote in 1912, the world of mathematics and science had changed dramatically. The new geometry opens the way to a rejection of the claim that Euclidean geometry is necessary of physical space, and Einstein's special relativity (1905) made physical time relative to the invariance of the propagation of electromagnetic energy (i.e. light). These discoveries largely destroyed Kant's proposed resolution of the debate between rationalists and empiricists.

In Problems, Russell presents a new solution to the long suffering philosophers grappling with the old impasse between rationalism and empiricism. Russell's replacement was based on a theory of acquaintance with universals. The theory of acquaintance allows a form of direct contact between a self-conscious mind and universals, and structural features given by relations among universals—features of the world that would remain if all conscious beings ceased to exist. Russell's thesis is that acquaintance relates a self to universals (i.e. properties and relations) and also to relations among universals which are neither mental objects (e.g. ideas, images, thoughts, etc.), nor physical objects (i.e. continuants persisting through time). By means of acquaintance with logical relations of universals, we know the foundational parts of mathematical logic. Acquaintance enables knowledge of mathematics.

Russell's doctrine of acquaintance concurs with rationalism's thesis that at least some of mathematics and geometry are knowable a priori. But in Russell's view, rationalists floundered because at best they seemed forced to accept a mysterious relation (e.g. Plato's anamnesis) between mind and abstract particular objects of mathematics (i.e. numbers) and geometry (i.e. spatial figures). They did not realize that a priori knowledge of mathematics and geometry could find its ground in the ᵠlogic of relations between universals.

Russell maintains that all a priori knowledge is derived from acquaintance with logical relations between universals (P, p. 103). Interestingly, Russell includes foundational principles of probability as knowable a priori. He writes:

> Principles such as the law of gravitation are proved, or rather are rendered highly probable, by a combination of experience with some wholly a priori principle, such as the principle of induction. Thus our intuitive knowledge of truths, is of two sorts: pure empirical knowledge, which tells us of the existence and some of the properties of particular things with which we are acquainted, and pure a priori knowledge, which gives us connections between universals, and enables us to draw inferences from the particular facts given in empirical knowledge.
>
> (P, p. 149)

This view may at first seem surprising because it shows that, in Russell's view, the foundational principles of probability are part logic. But Russell's view is clear. It is in virtue of being grounded in relations among universals that a truth has the status of being knowable a priori. The phrase "relations among universals" is not used innocently by Russell. He means that, like mathematics and geometry, it has a foundation in pure logic. Russell even goes so far as to say that the principle of induction is a logical principle:

> In addition to the logical principles which enable us to prove from a given premise that something is *certainly* true, there are other logical principles which enable us to prove, from a given premise, that there is a greater or less probability that something is true. An example of such principles—perhaps the most important example—is the inductive principle . . .
>
> (P, p. 73)

To understand this, we must realize that Russell states the "principle of induction" as follows:

> It must be conceded, to begin with, that the fact that two things have been found often together and never apart does not, by itself, suffice to *prove* demonstratively that they will be found together in the next case we examine. The most we can hope is that the oftener things are found together, the more probable it becomes that they will be found together another time, and that, if they have been found together often enough, the probability will amount *almost* to certainty.
>
> (*P*, p. 65)

Stated in this way, the principle of induction is a mathematical principle concerning the nature of probability. It is in that form that it makes sense of its being a truth of logic.

Curiously, Russell thanks Keynes in the Preface of *Problems* for discussions on probability. It is not known how much Keynes influenced Russell in thinking that there is a form of induction that is a logical principle. His statement of the principle of induction does seem to parallel that which eventually appears in Keynes's *Treatise on Probability* (1921), and Russell would certainly have been aware of the mathematics of probability (often illustrated by rolling dice under idealized physical conditions). Russell's ^{CP}Logic can capture fundamental theorems in the mathematical theory of probability, such as the law of large numbers[7] proved by Bernoulli in 1713 and the central limit theorem[8] proved by Kyapunov in 1901. But a detailed discussion of probability would await Russell's book *Human Knowledge: Its Scope and Limits* (1948), and by then he had a change of heart.

We can see that Russell has very strong rationalist sympathies in *Problems* due to the foundations of logic and mathematics. Russell admits that, when many cases are observed, a result may be reached and only later will the a priori connection between universals subsequently be uncovered. Russell illustrates this with the geometric example that perpendicular lines from the sides of a triangle to opposite angles always meet at a point.

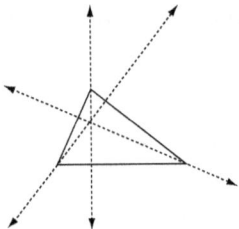

He remarks that,

> ... it would be quite possible to be first led to this proposition by actually drawing perpendiculars in many cases, and finding that they always met in a point; this experience might lead us to look for the general proof and find it. Such cases are common in the experience of every mathematician.
>
> (P, p. 107)

Thus, the principle of probability involved in Russell's statement of induction might find its way into logic. Interestingly, Russell includes (with hesitation) some ethical principles as knowable a priori. He writes, "It would seem, also, though it is more disputable, that there are some self-evident ethical principles such as 'we ought to pursue what is good' " (P, p. 112). It is intriguing to imagine how this principle could be more precisely formulated as a logical relation between universals.

Russell's rationalist tendencies are tempered, however, when he adds a twist which makes very important concessions to empiricism. In Russell's view, knowledge of physical continuants persisting through time can only be obtained by means of description from the data of sensory experiences present to us. All the knowledge a person has of a given physical continuant must be based on the judgments that person makes as to what is the best causal explanation of his or her present and past sensory-data emanating from the physical continuant. To take Russell's favorite example, a table is a physical continuant persisting through time that presents a vast array of sense-data, one for each position and perceiver in space causally related to it. Consider the structure of the light reflected from the surface of a table. If we consider positions in space around the table keeping a fixed distance (i.e. positions closer to the table or farther away), the structure of the light reflected changes dramatically. Each position with respect to the table is a location which would offer a sensible datum for an organism capable of engaging with the light reflected; it is a minimally perceivable configuration of the light reflected from the table in a region of space at a time. In *Problems* Russell holds that it is the sense-data of a table that provides the entirety of our knowledge about the physical continuant we call the table. Russell's concession to empiricism consists in his view that all knowledge of the existence of physical continuants is by description founded upon sense-data. Thus, for example, a table in front of a person S at a time can only be known to S by means of a definite description such as "the physical continuant which has a very high probability of being causally responsible for the present and remembered sense experiences presented."

Traditional empiricists and rationalists alike accepted a solipsistic starting point for epistemology. That is, they maintained that a theory of what we know must begin from a theory of how we know. Descartes set the stage. He maintained that a mind has special infallible non-inferential access to the nature of its own mental states. Descartes put it by saying "*Cogito ergo sum*" (I think, therefore I am). But his point is not to draw an inference from a premise. His point is perhaps better expressed by saying "I am [aware that I am now] thinking [so and so]." A mind cannot be deceived about the nature of the states it takes itself to have. Error can arise as to whether, for example, a table is before me, but not as to whether it seems to me now that I see a table. This generates a solipsistic starting point in epistemology that takes the foundational data to be experiences as mental states.

Descartes was a rationalist and so espoused sources of synthetic a priori knowledge about what is outside his mind apart from the mental experiences he has. Traditional empiricists such as Locke,

Berkeley, and Hume exclude such sources of knowledge, but they concur with Descartes that mental experiences are the starting point for all empirical knowledge of what is outside of one's mind. Russell offers something completely new to both schools concerning empirical knowledge. He holds that a mind has acquaintance with something outside it, namely sense-data. By means of acquaintance with sense-data, together with acquaintance with the universals inhering in them and logical structures (i.e. relations of universals), Russell assures the possibility of knowledge by description of physical continuants (persisting in time).

Descartes's rationalism as well as Locke's empiricism held a thesis called "representative realism." To understand this, consider this old question: If there were no sentient creatures and a tree were to fall, would it make a sound? A representative realist would say that there are two senses of "sound" involved. One is a compression wave in the atmosphere produced by the tree sweeping though the air. Another is the qualitative experience produced in a mind of a sentient creature as a representation of that compression wave. Only the first exists in the situation imagined. Similarly, when we see a red patch, the color is a representation produced by the mind in reaction to the object seen. The object's surface reflects waves (or photons on a particle theory of light) which impinge on the retina and produce patterns of neural activity in the brain and nervous system. But the qualitative aspects of color-experiences are in the mind. The same holds for other sensory qualities, smells, tastes, and textures. There is some debate about whether common sense sides with representative realism. Most people would be inclined to say that the odor of rotting fish is not in the fish but is produced in the mind in response to activities in the nose and brain brought about by particles the rotten fish has spewed into the air. Common sense offers similar accounts for tastes, though it is usually more cautious about sounds, textures, and colors. Common sense may suggest that the fish must have some color, but it recognizes that the observed color on a given occasion is often as much a product of the mind's reaction to the light as it is a product of the object itself.

Scientific Epistemology

It is quite easy to arrive at representative realism from even the most cursory common sense features of every day experience. I look at bodies moving in complicated ways similar to my own body and conclude that some of them have minds like mine making judgments about the information coming to their bodies from objects which stimulate them in various ways. The spiking of neurons in a friend's tongue is caused by its contact with particles of a lump of sucrose ($C_{12}H_{22}O_{11}$) crystals. I observe that this is the data from which my friend judged that a sweetness and odor is in the lump. But I can see that only the vibratory motions of the lump engage her tongue. Similarly, I investigate the way light emitted from an object causes my friend's retina to be stimulated and I recognize that her visual judgments can only be made on the basis of the data coming to her brain from her retina. The vibratory motions of light reflected to her retina from a surface were represented in her mind as if a color on the surface. I then compare her judgments and the state of her body with the physical continuants I see about her and I conclude that she is mistaken. She was naively realistic. The sweetness is somehow her mind's reaction to the sucrose and the color is her reaction to the light, which affects her only as radiant energy. I conclude that her judgments about shapes, sizes, and motions are roughly on the right track, but her judgments of color, taste, smell, texture, and pitch are not on the right track. Generalizing from such cases, I conclude that other people make judgments about physical continuants from a solipsistic starting point. They begin from the mental representations of the data of their senses.

A curious analogy ensues. Let me voice the analogy in the first person. I discover that others can only make perceptual judgments on the basis of their bodies being impinged upon by waves (or particles) which cause patterns of neural activity in their brains and nervous systems. I then make an analogy to my own case, concluding that I am in the same epistemic situation. In this way, a representative realism applies to me as well.

This argument by analogy is worrisome. My analogy would not

be warranted if I begin from a solipsistic starting point. My analogy assumes empirical knowledge of other bodies and the ordinary physical objects engaging them. If the analogy were apt, this assumption is unwarranted. Berkeley rejected representative realism. He noticed that arguments from perceptual relativity in favor of representative realism (i.e. arguments that colors, tastes, textures, sounds, and smells are products of mind while shapes and motions are in the world) cannot be justified solipsistically. From the first person, I have no greater reason to hold that color, sound, taste, texture, and smell experiences are less faithful in representing the nature of the world's objects than I have for shape experiences or experiences of motion. From the first person, I can only compare some experiences I have to other experiences I have, noting incompatibilities. Given the empirical assumption that there is a material object outside of my mind which persists as the same through the different perceptual experiences I have, I conclude that if it persists through time my perceptual experiences cannot all represent it correctly. For example, the coin looks oval from one perspective and round from another, but surely it cannot be both. The color looks different in different light, but the object cannot be both colors. But from the first person, all such experiences equally stand or fall as representations. Rationalists like Descartes might proclaim that it is synthetic and a priori that shapes and motions belong to the mind-independent world. Empiricists have no such recourse. Traditional empiricism maintains that all non-analytic knowledge of the world is obtained by means of inference from observations made possible by sense experiences. Paired with a demand for a solipsistic starting point in epistemology, representative realism is questionable.

Empiricists are in more trouble still. Traditional empiricists, following Locke, hold a conceptual thesis—a verificationist theory of empirical meaning—according to which the meaning of an empirical concept lies in its implications for actual and anticipated sense-experiences. Given this conceptual thesis, it is not possible to speak of a material object *causing* a representation in a mind. The concept of cause is itself an empirical concept. Its meaning is derived from sense-experiences alone. Berkeley's empiricism concludes that Locke's representative realist concept of matter as that which causes mental sense-appearances is not viable because it is not intelligible. Berkeley's empiricism offers a reconceptualization of the notion of matter. Matter is to be understood in terms of sense representations themselves. Berkeley's famous dictum was this: *Esse est percipi aut percipere* (To be is to be perceived or to perceive). This position is a form of what is called "phenomenalism." According to Berkeley, this new notion of matter better fits with the ordinary common sense notion that colors, textures, pitches, tastes, and smells are just as much a part of matter as are shapes, sizes, motions, and numbers.

In *Problems* Russell offers a unique way to avoid these consequences. He agrees with the empiricists that matter (i.e. material continuants persisting through time) cannot be known by acquaintance. But he disagrees with Berkeley's reconceptualization of matter. He thinks that matter can be known by means of a description such as "the cause of our sense-data." Russell offers a unique escape from Berkeley's problem of the unintelligibility of a physical (i.e. material) thing causing something mental. Sense-data are not (all) mental.

Russell permits acquaintance with universals and sense-data, both of which are outside of the mind. Thus, unlike traditional empiricists, empirical knowledge does not begin from one's mental objects. Russell writes:

> Berkeley was right in treating the sense-data which constitute our perception of the tree as more or less subjective, in the sense that they depend upon us as much as upon the tree, and would not exist if the tree were not being perceived. But this is an entirely different point from the one by which Berkeley seeks to prove that whatever can be immediately known *must* be in a mind. For this purpose

arguments of detail as to the dependence of sense-data upon us are useless.

(P, p. 41)

Russell rejects Berkeley's argument that only what is mental can be an object of thought. Russell writes:

> It is necessary to prove, generally, that by being known, things are shown to be mental. This is what Berkeley believes himself to have done. It is this question, and not our previous question as to the difference between sense-data and the physical object, that must now concern us.
>
> (P, p. 41)

Berkeley confuses a mental act with its object. Russell distinguishes the sensation, which is a mental act of awareness, from the sense-datum, which can be the object of such an act (P, pp. 12, 14). He holds that "acquaintance with objects essentially consists in a relation between the mind and something other than the mind" (P, p. 42). In *Problems* Russell hints that some sense-data are physical. He observes that ". . . among the objects with which we are acquainted are not included physical objects (as opposed to sense-data), nor other people's minds" (P, p. 52). If by "physical object" Russell means a physical continuant such as a table persisting through time, then the clause "as opposed to sense-data" is intended to include acquaintance with those physical objects—the fleeting, perspectival, subjective ones that do not persist—that are sense-data.

In *Problems* Russell does not explicitly say that sense-data are physical. He was explicit, however, in 1913.[9] And he was absolutely emphatic about this point thereafter. Sense-data are physical objects, but they are not physical continuants (i.e. matter). Sense-data last only for the duration of whatever is the minimal period of perception. Sense data are subjective because they are as highly sensitive to us (in our position in space) as they are to the physical continuant from which they emanate.

Scientific Epistemology 239

This has a direct bearing on the question as to whether Russell accepts a solipsistic starting point for epistemology in *Problems*. There is a sense in which Russell is conceding something to the solipsistic starting point for epistemology. By appealing to what we know about perception from a physical and psychological point of view, he concludes that it is acquaintance with the physical sense-data presented that provides the foundation of one's empirical knowledge of matter (i.e. physical continuants). But this is not the traditional conception of methodological solipsism. The traditional problem of empirical knowledge was formulated as the problem of explaining how a mind, sequestered in a realm of its own mental states, comes to have knowledge of what is outside of it. Since Russell holds that at least some sense-data with which we are acquainted are physical, he does not embrace traditional methodological solipsism.

Russell thinks there are limits to philosophy's critical analysis of how we know. He writes that we are powerless to refute an absolute skeptic who, placing himself or herself outside of all knowledge, simply demands (without justifying his or her doubts) that a telling argument be made that he or she knows something. Russell explains that

> ... all refutation must begin with some piece of knowledge which the disputants share; from blank doubt, no argument can begin. Hence the criticisms of knowledge which philosophy employs must not be of the destructive kind, if any result is to be achieved. Against this absolute skepticism, no logical argument can be advanced. But it is not difficult to see that skepticism of this kind is unreasonable.
>
> (*P*, p. 150)

Russell does not regard Descartes's methodological doubt as a destructive form of skepticism. Methodological doubt was employed by Descartes to find an indubitable foundation for all knowledge. Descartes thought that methodological doubt entails methodological solipsism. Russell seems to disagree. The method requires that we offer arguments for each of our doubts individually—arguments which, as Russell put it, "begin from some piece of knowledge which the disputants share." If Russell thinks this shared knowledge is empirical, then of course Russell rejects methodological solipsism.

What then would Russell say of Descartes's famous "dream argument?" In a dream we have experiences that are qualitatively indistinguishable from veridical sense-experiences. Is this not sufficient reason for Russell to doubt acquaintance with anything physical? If sense-data are physical as Russell thinks, Descartes's dream argument would only show that one cannot know by introspection whether a given sense-datum is physical or mental. Moreover, we cannot know from the qualitative content alone whether a given sense-datum is a manifestation of a physical continuant persisting in time. This, however, does not warrant a solipsistic starting point for epistemology. This fact about physical sense-data is itself an empirical discovery!

In *Problems* Russell offers a survey of the sources of our knowledge. We have immediate knowledge (by acquaintance) of particulars (e.g. sense-data and perhaps the self) and universals (including logical relations between universals). Russell explains:

> Our immediate knowledge of things, which we called *acquaintance*, consists of two sorts, according as the things known are particulars or universals. Among particulars, we have acquaintance with sense-data and (probably) with ourselves. Among universals, there seems to be no principle by which we can decide which can be known by acquaintance, but it is clear that among those that can be known are sensible qualities, relations of space and time, similarity, and certain abstract logical universals.
>
> (*P*, p. 109)

In contrast to knowledge by acquaintance, Russell says we have derivative knowledge. He continues as follows:

Scientific Epistemology

> Moreover, we have immediate and derivative knowledge of truths. Our derivative knowledge of things, which we call knowledge by *description*, always involves both acquaintance with something and knowledge of truths. Our immediate knowledge of *truths* may be called *intuitive* knowledge, and the truths so known may be called *self-evident* truths. Among such truths are included those which merely state what is given in sense, and also certain abstract logical and arithmetic principles, and (though with less certainty) some ethical propositions. Our derivative knowledge of truths consists of everything we can deduce from self-evident truths by the use of self-evident principles of deduction. . . . If the above account is correct, all our knowledge of truths depends on intuitive knowledge.
>
> (*P*, p. 109)

We have knowledge of matter by description—the entity causing sense-data so and so. This, it would seem, is the best explanation for the data of sense (i.e. the permanence and coherence of our sense-data and our passivity in sensation).

In Russell's view, intuitive knowledge is the foundation of all knowledge. It presents to the mind "self-evident" principles. One very important point Russell emphasizes about self-evidence is that it comes in degrees. Russell writes:

> Truths of perception and some of the principles of logic have the very highest degree of self-evidence; truths of immediate memory have an almost equally high degree. The inductive principle has less self-evidence than some of the other principles of logic, such as "what follows from a true premise must be true." Memories have a diminishing self-evidence as they become remoter and fainter; the truths of logic and mathematics have (broadly speaking) less self-evidence as they become more complicated. Judgments of intrinsic ethical or aesthetic value are apt to have some self-evidence, but not much.
>
> (*P*, p. 117)

Scientific Epistemology

Degrees of self evidence are important in the theory of knowledge because a proposition may enjoy self-evidence in some degree and yet be false.

The following passage is central to Russell's account of knowledge because it shows that although acquaintance—in particular, acquaintance with sense-data and logic—is the foundation of all knowledge, the largest body of what is commonly called "knowledge" should be regarded as probable opinion. He writes:

> From what has been said it is evident that, both as regards intuitive knowledge and as regards derivative knowledge, if we assume that intuitive knowledge is trustworthy in proportion to the degree of its self-evidence, there will be a gradation in trustworthiness, from the existence of noteworthy sense-data and the simpler truths of logic and arithmetic, which may be taken as quite certain, down to judgments which seem only just more probable than their opposites. What we firmly believe, if it is true, is called *knowledge*, provided it is either intuitive or inferred (logically or psychologically) from intuitive knowledge from which it follows logically. What we firmly believe, if it is not true, is called *error*. What we firmly believe, if it is neither knowledge nor error, and also what we believe hesitatingly, because it is, or is derived from, something which has not the highest degree of self-evidence, may be called *probable opinion*. Thus the greater part of what would commonly pass as knowledge is more or less probable opinion.
>
> (P, p.139)

Indeed, Russell goes on to say that most of our ordinary empirical knowledge is probable opinions justified by coherence:

> In regard to probable opinion, we can derive great assistance from *coherence*, which we rejected as the *definition* of truth, but may often use as a *criterion*. A body of individually probable opinions, if they are mutually coherent, become more probable than any one of them would be individually. It is in this way that many scientific

hypotheses acquire their probability. They fit into a coherent system of probable opinions, and thus become more probable than they would be in isolation. The same thing applies to general philosophical hypotheses. Often in a single case such hypotheses may seem highly doubtful, while yet, when we consider the order and coherence which they introduce into a mass of probable opinion, they become pretty nearly certain. This applies, in particular, to such matters as the distinction between dreams and waking life. If our dreams, night after night, were as coherent one with another as our days, we should hardly know whether to believe the dreams or the waking life. As it is, the test of coherence condemns the dreams and confirms the waking life. But this test, though it increases probability where it is successful, never gives absolute certainty, unless there is certainty already at some point in the coherent system. Thus the mere organization of probable opinion will never, by itself, transform it into indubitable knowledge.

(P, p. 140)

In *Problems* the notion of degrees of self-evidence and a coherence theory of the justification of empirical statements are central components in Russell's theory of knowledge. Degrees of self-evidence play a role in Russell's arguments that immediate memory can be taken as reliable in building empirical knowledge. It also plays a role in Russell's conception of philosophical analysis as engaged with empirical science. "Philosophical knowledge," Russell explains, ". . . does not differ essentially from scientific knowledge; there is no special source of wisdom which is open to philosophy but not to science, and the results obtained by philosophy are not radically different from those obtained from science" (P, p. 146). In Russell's view, the epistemic question of how we have knowledge of physical continuants is a theory articulated within a broad knowledge of physics and psychology.

OUR KNOWLEDGE OF THE EXTERNAL WORLD

In 1914, Whitehead was working on the projected fourth volume of *Principia* on geometry. He persuaded Russell of a way to avoid the difficulties encountered in *Problems* when it came to justifying knowledge (by description) of the existence of material objects persisting in time as the best explanation of the data of sense. This afforded an occasion for Russell to apply his new analytic method in philosophy. He writes:

> The central problem by which I have sought to illustrate method is the problem of the relation between the crude data of sense and the space, time, and matter of mathematical physics. I have been made aware of the importance of the problem by my friend and collaborator Dr. Whitehead, to whom are due almost all the differences between the views advocated here and those suggested in *The Problems of Philosophy*. I owe to him the definitions of points, the suggestion for the treatment of instants and "things," and the whole conception of the world of physics as a construction rather than an *inference*. What is said on these topics here, is, in fact, a rough preliminary account of the more precise results which he is giving in the fourth volume of *Principia Mathematica*. It will be seen that if his way of dealing with these topics is capable of being successfully carried through, a wholly new light is thrown on the time-honoured controversies of realists and idealists, and a method is obtained of solving all that is soluble in their problem.
>
> (*OKEW*, p. vi)

Russell says that constructive techniques so well employed in *Principia* are possible for the construction of spatial points, instants of time, and material particulars (i.e. continuants persisting through time). We can get along without inferring the existence of matter from the data by means of a logical reconstruction from the transitory physical objects that are sense-data. Russell explains his motivations as follows:

> In physics, as ordinarily set forth there is much that is unverifiable: there are hypotheses as to (α) how things would appear to a spectator in a place where, as it happens, there is no spectator; (β) how things would appear at times when, in fact they are not appearing to anyone; (γ) things which never appear at all. All these are introduced to simplify the statement of causal laws, but none of them form an integral part of what is known to be true in physics. . . . If physics is to consist wholly of propositions known to be true, or at least capable of being proved or disproved, the three kinds of hypothetical entities we have just enumerated must all be capable of being exhibited as logical functions of sense-data.
>
> (OKEW, p. 116)

Russell lays down the following definition: "Things are those series of aspects which obey the laws of physics" (OKEW, p. 115). Whether there are such series is, of course, an empirical question settled by experimental physics itself. In virtue of this logical re-conceptualization of the notion of a physical continuant, Russell shows that experimental science is in a position to gain empirical evidence for or against particular material objects. Our Knowledge marks a radical departure from Problems. In Problems matter (i.e. physical continuants persisting in time) was postulated as the cause of physical sense-data—the most likely explanation of the data. We now see that, shocking as it may first appear, Russell's view in Our Knowledge is that physical continuants persisting in time do not exist!

Another innovation in the theory is that the physical sense-data out of which the laws of matter (i.e. continuants) are to be reconstructed include unperceived sense-data, as well as those perceived. Russell explains:

> In the *Problems of Philosophy* and in all my previous thinking, I have accepted matter as it appears in physics. But this left an uncomfortable gulf between physics and perception, or, in other language, between mind and matter. In my first enthusiasm on

> abandoning the "matter" of the physicist, I hoped to be able to exhibit the hypothetical entities that a given percipient does not perceive as structures composed entirely of elements that he does perceive. . . . This first exposition was in a paper called "The Relation of Sense-Data to Physics," published in *Scientia* in 1914. In the paper I said: "If physics is to be verifiable we are faced with the following problem: Physics exhibits sense-data as functions of physical objects, but verification is possible if physical objects can be exhibited as functions of sense-data.
>
> (*MPD*, p. 104)

Russell came to hold that the data, namely the actual sense-data that have been perceived by all people up to now, are insufficient for the reconstruction of the physical laws of matter. Russell recalls the moment when the breakthrough of how to do this first occurred to him:

> There were several novelties in the theory as to our knowledge of the external world which burst on to me on New Year's Day 1914. The most important of these was the theory that space has six dimensions and not only three. I came to the conclusion that what, in the space of physics, counts as a point, or, more exactly, as a "minimal region", is really a three dimensional complex of which the total of one man's percepts is an instance. Various considerations led me to this view. Perhaps the most cogent is that instruments can be constructed which, at places where there are no living percipients, will make records of the sort of things that a man might perceive if he were at those places. . . . It follows that, in one tiny region of physical space there is at every moment a vast multiplicity of occurrences corresponding to all the things that could be seen there by a person or recorded by an instrument. These things, moreover, have spatial relations to each other which correspond more or less accurately with the correlated objects in physical space.
>
> (*MPD*, p. 105)

Scientific Epistemology

In *Our Knowledge* Russell expands the data to those physical sense-data actually perceived and sensibilia (i.e. physical sense-data that exist but are not actually perceived by anyone). Matter (i.e. physical laws governing continuants in time) is to be constructed from physical sense-data and sensibilia (i.e. unperceived sense-data). Obviously, *Our Knowledge* does not proceed from a solipsistic starting point for epistemology. It takes for granted that there are physical objects: sense-data. It accepts the meaningfulness of the notion of causal laws governing the ordering of sense-data.

Russell is not taking a solipsistic starting point for his epistemology of matter. Russell writes:

> It may be said—and this is an objection which must be met at the onset—that it is the duty of the philosopher to call in question the admittedly fallible beliefs of daily life, and to replace them by something more solid and irrefragable. In a sense this is true, and in a sense it is effected in the course of analysis. But in another sense, and a very important one, it is quite impossible. While admitting that doubt is possible with regard to all our common knowledge, we must nevertheless accept that knowledge in the main if philosophy is to be possible at all. There is not any superfine brand of knowledge, obtainable by the philosopher, which can give us a standpoint from which to criticize the whole of the knowledge of daily life. . . . Philosophy cannot boast of having achieved such a degree of certainty that it can have authority to condemn the facts of experience and the laws of science.
>
> (OKEW, p. 74)

Russell's rejection of methodological solipsism in *Our Knowledge* is especially evident from the fact that his reconstruction of the laws of physical continuants relies on the existence of the sense-data of other minds. Russell writes:

> The hypothesis that other people have minds must, I think, be allowed to be not susceptible of any very strong argument support

> from the analogical argument. At the same time, it is a hypothesis which systematizes a vast body of facts and never leads to any consequences which there is reason to think false. There is therefore nothing to be said against its truth, and good reason to use it as a working hypothesis. When once it is admitted, it enables us to extend our knowledge of the sensible world by testimony, and thus leads to the system of private worlds which we assumed in our hypothetical construction.
>
> (*OKEW*, p. 103)

The traditional argument for other minds is the argument from analogy: some material bodies move similarly to my own body when I have thoughts, feel pains, and feel emotions; by analogy I conclude that these bodies must be directed by thoughts, feelings, and emotions similar to my own. The argument from analogy is, of course, consistent with a solipsistic starting point in epistemology. But Russell accepts the existence of other minds and their private worlds as part of his construction of matter. This certainly would not be allowed if he accepted a solipsistic starting point for epistemology. The argument from analogy presupposes that there are material bodies! Rejecting a solipsistic starting point, Russell allows himself to say that a general doubt about the existence of other minds is not worthy of significant concern. Russell can therefore accept, by and large, a system of many private worlds of sense-experience from which, together with unperceived sense-data, we can construct the public world of physical space and the laws of physical matter.

Our *Knowledge* is not a theory in the spirit of Berkeley's phenomenalism which constructs matter out of mental sensory ideas. Russell's theory of matter is a four-dimensionalist view that material objects are tubes of similar stages spread out in time, with their temporal parts or stages occurring at each instant of time.[10] This characterization, however, begins from the assumption that there are temporal instants which form a continuous series and that events occur at instants in the temporal series. This is not Russell's characterization since Russell is not committed to the existence of temporal instants. Though Einstein was not himself a four-dimensionalist about matter, Eddington's investigation convinced Russell that physical time is itself a construction from the physical correlations made possible by light interactions between overlapping events.

In applying the differential calculus to model change of position of a moving object over time, we have a ratio of time to position. This ratio is made by correlations between parts of events which overlap. The events that inform the construction of the notion of velocity at a spatial point and instant of time are ordinary, ongoing processes of everyday experience. These are processes we naturally describe by employing reference to ordinary material continuants (e.g. the flowing of the Mississippi into the Louisiana delta, the melting of the glaciers, light reaching the earth from the sun, and the expansion of the universe). These are quite ordinary overlapping events whose parts are naturally supposed to be ordinary material objects persisting in time. Consider the case where one event is the motion of the hands of a clock and the other is the motion of the physical continuant across the field whose ground is scribed with (roughly) equidistant hash marks. When the clock's second hand was at x the object was at hash mark y, etc. The definition of a velocity at a temporal moment is made possible only by appeal to the limit of the function characterizing the changes in the ratio of distance to time in the overlapping correlations of the events of the motion of the object. (It is now common to illustrate this in analytic geometry as an application of the problem of finding the tangent to a curve at a point.)

The notion of instantaneous velocity is the derivative (i.e. a limit) of a function. On Weierstrass's reconceptualization of the notion of the limit of a function, the limit does not involve infinitesimals. Weierstrass's notion of the limit requires a neighborhood some of whose ratios of distance to time are future to the point to be constructed and some whose ratio of distance to time are before it. The notion of the leading point of an ongoing motion cannot be defined. It is possible to speak (by Weiserstrass's construction) of an event (e.g. of having a velocity) at an instant only in virtue of the presence of overlapping ordinary events involving physical continuants. A cautionary note is in order. In Russell's view, it is a contingent empirical matter whether the physical correlations by light interactions of ordinary overlapping events are fine enough to enable the construction of talk of "temporal instants." In his essay "On Order in Time" (1936) Russell sets out the parameters needed for the construction and notes that ". . . the existence of instants requires hypotheses which there is no reason to suppose true—a fact which may be not without importance in physics."[11]

Now integration in the calculus is the inverse of the tangent problem. Once again, there are no infinitesimal instantaneous velocities which, taken together, reconstitute the motion of an object in space. Infinitesimals do not return to haunt physics when we apply the calculus. We speak legitimately of matter being constituted by events of minimal duration only in the way we speak of the composition of the integral. It finds its legitimacy in virtue of Weierstrass's notion of the limit. Both are constructions from ordinary ongoing events which overlap in time with one another. If Russell imagined his reconstruction of matter to parallel what may be said by way of applying the calculus to physical processes, then one may feel, at first, that there is a circularity in the construction. The events out of which matter is to be constructed are themselves abstractions from light correlations of continuants occurring in ordinary events. The apparent circularity, however, is explained away by Russell's abandonment of methodological solipsism. The data, at first accepted uncritically, is the data of events involving continuants persisting in time. We then apply the calculus to construct minimal events not involving continuants in time but which are such that, by a process of integration, we can reconstruct the continuant in question. Just as an area under a curve might be said to be constructed by adding together a non-denumerable infinity of infinitesimal areas, we say that a bit of matter at a time is a "sum" of the events that "it" causes at that time.

RUSSELL'S LOST BOOK: *THEORY OF KNOWLEDGE*

What is the definition of "knowledge?" In Plato's dialogue Theaetetus, knowledge is defined as justified, true belief. As with Plato before him, Russell imagines examples to show that true belief is not sufficient for knowledge. Edmond Gettier is often credited with being the first to demonstrate that if the highest possible degree of justification is logically compatible with the falsehood of the belief in question, then no degree of justification of a true belief is sufficient for knowledge.[12] Is a fourth condition for knowledge required? The matter is complicated. Gettier merely offered a few cases of a somewhat justified true belief which falls short of knowledge. This certainly does not show the general negative result. Being frustrated by failed attempts to find a way to draw a figure without lifting one's pencil or retracing does not show that it cannot be done.

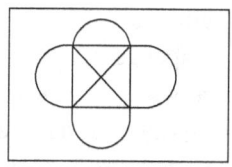

In Problems Russell's first example is of a person who believes that the late Prime Minister's name begins with a "B." He believes this proposition because he has the false belief that the late Prime Minister is Mr. Balfour. In truth, the late Prime Minister was Sir Henry Campbell Bannerman. In his second example, Russell imagines a person who believes a newspaper report on the outcome of a battle. The news agency made an intelligent guess well before the outcome was determined and it happened to be true (P, p. 132). The person has a false belief that the newspaper report is reliable, though the person's false belief seems justified by his evidence of the general reliability of the news agency. In *Human Knowledge* Russell offers yet another example. By looking at a clock on the wall that had been working normally, a person has a true belief of what time it is. But unbeknownst to him, the clock has stopped and it shows the correct time by sheer accident. In the newspaper and clock cases it seems that Russell would credit the persons involved with some degree of justification in their false beliefs. In *Problems* Russell draws the following lesson: "It is clear that a true belief is not knowledge when it is deduced from a false belief" (P, p. 132). Perhaps Russell only meant to offer a requirement, together with true belief, for a degree of justification high enough to suffice for knowledge. But perhaps he beat Gettier to the intuition by over fifty years: knowledge requires a fourth condition.

In any case, there is much to be said in favor of the Russell's lesson. It has not been popular with epistemologists because of apparent Gettier problems which seem to skirt the Russellian approach. Suppose a very reliable and respected newspaper, say *The New York Times*, prints a correct story of an event, and a janitor S, pulling the paper from the incineration bin reads the paper and knowing its reliability concludes correctly the event has happened. Unbeknownst to S, the newspaper read was one of a very few that escaped destruction. In endeavoring to prevent the event from becoming public immediately, the president persuaded the editors of all news agencies to postpone the report a few days for national security. Did S reason essentially through a false premise? It may seem not, and yet S does not have knowledge.[13] But what premise did S employ in concluding that the event happened? Was it *just* that *The New York Times* is very reliable and printed the story or did it also include that the newspaper read was officially sanctioned by the editors and not a printing pulled before circulation? Though widely bypassed, Russell's approach is enjoying something of a revival.[14]

On the heels of *Problems*, one might have imagined that the question of the nature of knowledge would play a central role in Russell's new book project of 1913: *The Theory of Knowledge*. But,

Scientific Epistemology

having resoundingly dismissed pragmatist and coherence definitions of "truth," the book became preoccupied with giving an analysis of truth as correspondence to fact. It is not often appreciated that *Principia* offered an informal semantics which was intended to philosophically justify the order component of the order/type indices adorning *Principia*'s predicate variables. The theory defines "truth" and "falsehood" recursively. The truth-conditions of complex statements are given by a recursion whose base case (i.e. atomic case) lies in the notion of a belief-state (itself a fact) corresponding to a fact. That is, the base case of the recursion relies on Russell's multiple-relation theory of judgment. Russell worked steadfastly on the theory in 1913, but he eventually shelved this part of the project to work on another aspect of his theory of knowledge project: the nature of matter in physics. He had accepted an invitation from Harvard University to deliver the 1914 Lowell lectures on the subject. This work would become *Our Knowledge of the External World*. Russell's second chapter of the work shows that the multiple-relation theory was still alive. But, as we shall see, it was certainly not well.

Written in earnest at a pace of some ten pages a day, Russell had reached page 350 of his book project *The Theory of Knowledge* by the end of Cambridge's Easter term. Its foundation is the theory of acquaintance and the multiple-relation theory of judgment. Difficulties with the view soon began to appear and Russell was eager to correct them. The faltering multiple-relation theory was revised in *Problems* and revised again and worked out in some detail in *Theory of Knowledge*. It would be the second book Russell attempted during the splendor of his relationship with Lady Ottoline. And as with the first book *Prisons*, the book was abandoned.

Facts and Russellian propositions are like men and dinosaurs: they never coexisted. This is very often missed even by scholars of Russell's philosophy. In *The Principles of Mathematics* Russell endorsed a theory of propositions. Propositions are akin to states of affairs insofar as their obtaining (truth) or non-obtaining (falsehood) are primitive, unanalyzable notions. Russell held that universals have a "two-fold" capacity. Thus, for example, the universal *loves* occurs "as concept" in the proposition:

Desdemona loves Cassio.

This provides the unity of the proposition. The universal *loves* occurs "as term" in the proposition:

Desdemona and Cassio exemplify love.

The unity of this proposition is provided by the occurrence in it as concept of the universal *exemplification*. The capacity of a universal to occur as concept in a proposition is Russell's solution to the problem of unity of the proposition. In work that quickly became famous, the idealist philosopher F. H. Bradley had argued that the former proposition requires the existence of the latter to account for its unity. He maintained that there is a vicious infinite regress in such an analysis of unity. There is an infinity of distinct and logically related propositions. In addition to the above, there is also

Desdemona and Cassio and *love* exemplify *exemplification*.

And so on to infinity, with each failing to analyze the unity of the other. Accepting that there are infinitely many logically related propositions, Russell solved the problem by maintaining that the unity of the one proposition is not dependent upon the existence of the other. The occurrence of a universal in a proposition as concept is what provides the unity (*PoM*, p. 50). In this way, Russell deftly solves Bradley's famous regress argument by appeal to the indefinable capacity of a universal to occur as concept in a proposition.

While there are propositions, "truth" (obtaining) is indefinable. Russell abandoned it in *Principia* when he offered a definition of "truth" in terms of correspondent with fact. It is sometimes said that a fact is a true proposition, but this wholly misunderstands what Russell is up to. The notion of a true fact is unintelligible. The statement "Desdemona loves Cassio" is true when there is a fact corresponding to it and false when there is no such fact. The fact

Desdemona's loving Cassio

exists insofar as the relation *loves* actually relates the constituents Desdemona and Cassio together. But in the proposition

Desdemona loves Cassio

the relation *loves* occurs in the proposition as concept even if the proposition is false (non-obtaining). The notion that the relation *loves* occurs as concept is wholly dissimilar to the notion of its relating constituents to generate a fact. It does not relate the constituents even when the proposition is true. Nonetheless, it occurs in the proposition as concept.

The unity of a fact lies in the occurrence in it of a universal relating the constituents. Bradley's regress cannot be applied to Russellian facts. Indeed, Russell no longer even accepts that there are infinitely many facts whose existence is logically connected. There is a fact:

Desdemona loving Cassio.

But nothing in Russell's theory of facts assures that there exists a fact:

Desdemona and Cassio exemplifying *loves*.

Facts are composed of entities structured by a relating relation (or universal). That they are structured entities tied by a relating relation is precisely what makes is possible to recursively define "truth" and "falsehood."

A map helps depict the structure of a fact. Russell uses hyphens to compose names of facts. The expression "a-in-the-relation-R-to-b," or more tersely "a-R-b," is used to name a fact. For example, there is the fact named by "Desdemona-in-the-relation-*loves*-to-Cassio." We have used the expression "Desdemona's loving Cassio" because it emphasizes the point that such an expression is a term and not a formula. There is another fact with a quite different structure but composed (Russell thinks) of the very same constituents.[15] Obviously, Cassio's loving Desdemona is a new fact. Once again, a map helps depict the different structure involved.

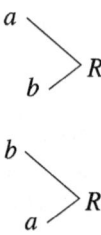

Again, Russell uses hyphens to form a name of such a fact, depicting its structure. He has "b-R-a" as a name of this fact. There are many worries one can have about the nature of the differences between these two facts. Of central concern is how a relation produces the differences in structure between the two facts. This is of special concern when non-spatial facts involving intentional relations such as *loves* are concerned. In a spatial relationship we might think of constituents closer or farther away from another, but this makes no sense with love.

Russell holds that there are belief (understanding or judging) complexes. When a person m has a belief (or makes a discursive judgment), say that a bears R to b, there is a belief (understanding or judgment) complex consisting of the mind m related by belief to the entities *loves* and a and b. This complex (or fact) is structured by the relation *believes*. We can name this complex "m-believing-with-respect-to-(a, R, b)." Its structure may be represented in a map. In contrast, when a person m has a belief that b bears R to a there is a complex (or fact) with the same constituents but structured differently by *believes*. We can form a name for this with "m-believing-with-respect-to-(b, R, a)." It has a different map (see figure overleaf). All facts are structured complexes. This is at the foundation of Russell's theory, and it applies to belief-complexes in every bit the

$$m\text{-}B \underset{\diagdown b}{\overset{\diagup a}{\text{——}}} R$$

$$m\text{-}B \underset{\diagdown a}{\overset{\diagup b}{\text{——}}} R$$

same way as other complexes. The structure is important, not just the constituents.

As we can see, Russell's multiple-relation theory holds that belief (judgment or understanding) is not a dyadic relation between a mind and a proposition (state of affairs), but a multiple-relation whose relata (in the atomic case) include the constituents of a would-be corresponding fact. It is important not to be misled. Russell's theory is not that there is a relation *believes* such that for a mind m, and entities a and b and relation R,

believes(m, a, R, b) if and only if m believes that a bears R to b.[16]

This makes "believes(m, a, R, b)" a formula (or a sentence if m, a, R and b are constants). As we saw, Russell's expression "m-believing-with-respect-to-(a, R, b)" is a term (or a name) of an entity. Russell's theory is a correspondence theory. Belief-complexes (i.e. facts) correspond, when true, to other facts.

Now the theory of definite descriptions plays a foundational role in Russell's correspondence theory (i.e. his recursive definition) of truth and falsehood. The essence of the idea is that when a declarative sentence such as "a loves b" flanks the predicate ". . . is true" it acts like a definite description:

"the fact corresponding to m-believing-with-respect-to-(a, loves, b)."

Accordingly, truth consists in there being a complex

a-loves-b

which corresponds to the belief complex

m-believing-with-respect-to-(a, loves, b).

That is, there is a fact consisting of a, loves, and b structured in the right way.[17] Falsehood consists in there being no corresponding fact.

Russell's multiple-relation theory faces a difficulty that has come to be called the "narrow direction problem."[18] G. F. Stout objected that the theory could not distinguish the belief that *a loves b* from the quite different belief that *b loves a*.[19] It must be understood, however, that the problem is not to explain what distinguishes belief-complexes. Russell assumed from the onset that complexes are structured entities and that distinct complexes can have precisely the same constituents. There is thus no special difficulty with belief-complexes in this regard. The narrow direction problem is not the problem of how to explain structure. The problem is to explain why the belief-complex m-believing-with-respect-to-(a, loves, b) points only to a-loves-b as its would-be corresponding fact, while m-believing-with-respect-to-(b, loves, a). points only to b-loving-a as its would-be corresponding fact. It is the problem of explaining correspondence.

Russell was quick to acknowledge the problem. In "On the Nature of Truth and Falsehood" Russell says that in the belief-complex m-believing-with-respect-to-(a, loves, b) the subordinate relation loves ". . . must not be abstractly before the mind but must be before it as proceeding from a to b rather than from b to a." On this view, the subordinate relation as it enters into the belief-state has a "sense" and in the corresponding complex it must have the same sense.[20] Russell soon came to admit, however, that this proposal does not succeed. As he later put it in his manuscript *Theory of Knowledge* (1913), relations do not come with a "hook" at one end and an "eye" at another.[21] When a relation occurs as a substantive—as is the case when it occurs as a constituent of a belief-complex—it is not relating, and the so-called "sense" of the subordinate relation is lost.

Scientific Epistemology   259

In *Problems* Russell thought he had the narrow direction problem solved by employing the idea of a partial isomorphism of structure. Though a relation does not come with a hook and an eye, the complex in which it occurs as a relating relation is structured. Russell writes:

> If Othello believes truly that Desdemona loves Cassio, then there is a complex unity, "Desdemona's love for Cassio," which is composed exclusively of the objects of the belief, in the same order as they had in the belief, with the relation which was one of the objects occurring now as the cement that binds together the objects of the belief. On the other hand, if Othello believes falsely, there is no such complex unity composed of the objects of the belief.[22]

A picture may help see the partial isomorphism.

$$m\text{-}B \overset{a}{\underset{b}{\diagup\!\!\diagdown}} R \overset{a}{\underset{b}{\diagdown\!\!\diagup}} R$$

It is the partial isomorphism of structure that assures that the belief-complex points to exactly one would-be corresponding complex. A belief complex such as m-believing-with-respect-to-(a, loves, b) has a structure—an order of occurrence of its constituents generated by the relating relation *belief*. It is in virtue of this that *a-loving-b* is its appropriately corresponding fact, for this fact alone has the constituents *a*, *b*, and *loves*, and has a structural ordering of these constituents that is partly isomorphic to their structural order in the belief-complex.

In *Theory of Knowledge* Russell came to reject this plan. The notion of the order of the constituents of a complex relies upon a spatial or sentential analogy. In the complex *a-loving-b*, it not proper to say that the constituent *a* occurs "first" and *b* occurs "second." Complexes do indeed have structures, but the structure is not always spatial, and certainly it does not track the linear order of the expressions of a statement. In *Theory of Knowledge* Russell gave his last attempt to solve the narrow direction problem. He introduced what he calls "position relations." An entity a has a determinate position in a complex even though one may not legitimately order the positions by "first," "second," and so on. For example, Russell tells us that in the complex a-similarity-b there is only one position that both a and b occupy. He calls this complex "symmetrical." The complex a-loving-b, on the other hand, is unsymmetrical since (as was the case of Russell and Ottoline) a might well love b without b loving a. In such a case, a and b occupy two distinct positions. It is structurally possible for distinct a and b to occupy one another's positions in the complex. Accordingly, Russell calls it "homogeneous" with respect to these positions. In a complex such as Socrates' being human, the positions occupied by Socrates and humanity are quite different. The complex is unsymmetrical. But in this case it is not structurally possible for Socrates to occupy the predicational position of humanity in the complex. Socrates is not a universal (and so lacks a predicational nature). The complex is both unsymmetrical and heterogeneous (i.e. non-homogeneous). Russell calls such complexes "non-permutative." A complex is "permutative" with respect to the two of its constituents when those constituents occupy distinct positions and when those positions are homogeneous.[23]

Russell's characterization of unsymmetrical and non-permutative complexes depends upon distinctions of type*.[24] One must be on guard not to confuse this notion with Principia's notion of type theory. The difference in type* is not coded into Principia's logical grammar. Universals are values of the individual variables (type 0) of Principia. Type* distinctions occur between individuals, universals, particulars, and complexes which are not distinct in simple type. Complexes cannot occur as constituents of entities that are not complex, and universals are of a different type* from concrete complexes (facts) and entities that are not complex. Types* are not the types or orders of Principia. The notion of type*, unlike the notion of order/type, was perfectly legitimate to Russell. Indeed, Russell had long held that the difference between universal and particular is an unanalyzable and primitive logical notion. Universals have

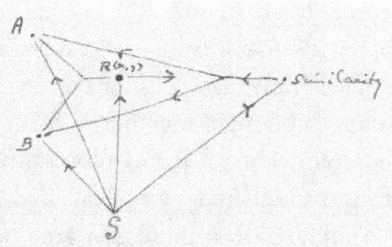

In this figure, one relation goes from S to the four objects; one relation goes from R(x,y) to similarity, & another to A & B, while one relation goes from similarity to A & B. This figure, I hope, will help to make clearer the map of our five-term complex.

both a predicable and an individual nature, and, quite independently of the direction problem, this is essential to the viability of the multiple-relation theory. In addition to the new notion of an entity's "position in a complex," Russell amends the multiple-relation theory in *Theory of Knowledge* by maintaining that in mental complexes of belief, judgment, and understanding there occurs a cognitive act of logical intuition (i.e. acquaintance) with logical forms. As we have seen, Russell tells us that the complex *a-similarity-b* is symmetrical and therefore has only one position: it is identical with the complex *b-similarity-a*.[25] The complex *a-before-b*, on the other hand, is distinct from the complex *b-before-a*, but all these concepts have the same logical form, namely the form of a dual complex (of two-place predication). Russell maintains that position relations are not determined by the logical form of a complex but by the relating relation of the complex. An object has a position in a complex. Russell sometimes expresses the logical form of a dyadic complex using "R(x,y)." His notation and ideas about the nature of logical forms are in flux, but at one point in the book he attempts a map of the complex relational structure of a person S understanding that A is similar to B (see facsimile above). One thing is certain: the inclusion of logical forms makes complexes of belief and understanding complicated in structure. In any event, it is very important to understand that Russell eventually comes to hold that the logical form of a complex (fact) is not a template which depicts where the terms are to be fitted together to form the purportedly corresponding complex. Logical forms play a different role. They are introduced to provide the content of our understanding of the classification of complexes into those that are "permutative" and those that are "non-permutative." Belief or judgment requires an understanding of the form of the purported corresponding complex. In Russell's view, it is acquaintance with logical form that is essential for, and logically prior to, understanding words such as "predicate," "relation," and "dual complex" and logical words such as "or," "not," "all," and so on.[26]

For example, understanding the sentence "a is red" requires more than being acquainted with a and the universal "redness." It presupposes an understanding of predication, the form of a monadic complex (i.e. fact). According to the multiple-relation theory, when the statement "a is red" is flanked by ". . . is true" it is a disguised definite description. Extrapolating from the modifications of the theory in Theory of Knowledge, the definite description now is this:

"the fact corresponding to m-believing-with-respect-to-(a, redness, **P**)"

where **P** is the logical form of monadic predication. The statement "a is red" (and so also the belief-complex) is true if and only if there is a complex consisting of a and the universal "Redness"—namely, a's-redness. In this simple case, the direction problem does not arise. The corresponding complexes are non-permutative.

In contrast, consider the truth conditions for "a loves b." The would-be corresponding complex is permutative, and consequently Russell's characterization of the notion of correspondence is indirect. The truth conditions of this statement cannot be given simply by stating that it is true just when there is a fact consisting of a and b and the relating relation loves. The order is central. To capture

Scientific Epistemology 263

the order, Russell makes an appeal to his new view that the relation *loves* fixes two position relations: C_1 and C_2. Accordingly, the statement "*a* loves *b*," when it occurs flanked by the predicate "is true" disguises the following definite description:

"the α such that $a\ C_1\ \alpha$ and $b\ C_2\ \alpha$."[27]

In short:

[*a* loves *b*] is true if and only if
there is a unique fact α such that $a\ C_1\ \alpha$ and $b\ C_2\ \alpha$.

At first blush, this may seem to simply push the problem back. The truth-conditions for "$a\ C_1\ \alpha$" and "$b\ C_2\ \alpha$" must be given. But according to Russell, these do not involve the direction problem. That is, [*a* has C_1 in α] is true if and only if there is a fact consisting of *a* and C_1 and α. The complex asserted to exist is non-permutative. Thus the truth-conditions which involve indirect correspondence with permutative complexes such as *a-loving-b* will be defined recursively from the truth-conditions that involve direct correspondence with non-permutative complexes such as a-C_1-α and b-C_2-α. Russell's account assumes that there is a type* distinction between a fact (i.e. complex) α and an entity *a* that is not a complex. The relata of a position relation C_1 must differ in type*. A fact cannot have a position in an entity that is not complex. With type* distinctions in place and logical forms taken to be constituents of belief-complexes, the narrow direction problem cannot arise.

The Theory of Knowledge does not address the problem of the truth-conditions for ascriptions of propositional attitudes. Russell shelved and then aborted his book project which made the theory of knowledge rest on the multiple-relation theory of truth and falsehood. There is much speculation on what Russell might have had in mind. But it is rather easy to see how his ideas would be extended to form a theory. To properly define the correspondence (truth) conditions of "S believes that *a* loves *b*," Russell must form a definite description which captures the structural order of the belief-complex:

m-believing-with-respect-to-(a, loves, b, $\mathbf{R}^2$).

(I use $\mathbf{R}^2$ as the logical form of dyadic predication.) Of course, the narrow direction problem arises once again.[28] But one can apply Russell's solution to the narrow direction problem in such cases. We are to find position relations E_1, E_2, E_3, and E_4 fixed by the relating relation believes. The statement "S believes that a loves b," when it is flanked by the truth predicate would, on this view, be interpreted as disguising the following definite description:

"the fact α such that a has E_1 in α and b has E_2 in α and loves has E_3 in α and $\mathbf{R}^2$ has E_4 in α."

Accordingly, we have:

[S believes that a loves b] is true if and only if there is a fact α such that a has E_1 in α and b has E_2 in α and loves has E_3 in α and $\mathbf{R}^2$ has E_4 in α.

In this way, Russell hoped at last to have solved the narrow direction problem.

The question of the ontological nature of logical forms, however, vexed Russell. This is particularly the case for those grounding our understanding of logical words. In Theory of Knowledge Russell was tentative when it came to the question of what sort of entities logical forms are to be. In a chapter entitled "Logical Data" he notes that "logical objects cannot be regarded as entities, and therefore what we shall call 'acquaintance' with them cannot really be a dual relation."[29] There must be kinds of acquaintance. Universals, concrete particulars, and complexes differ logically, and "relations to objects differing in logical character must themselves differ in logical character."[30] Whatever the ultimate analysis, Russell decides that something like logical experience or logical intuition is required for the understanding of logical words like "particular," "universal," "relation," "dual complex," and "predicate." Russell regards logical intuition as a kind of immediate knowledge obtained through a process of abstraction and generalization carried to its utmost limit. Every logical notion is a *summum genus*, the limit of this process of abstraction.

Finally, Russell comes to a decision in *Theory of Knowledge*. "If possible," he writes, "it would be convenient to take as the form something which is not a mere incomplete symbol." Logical forms are to be identified as abstract general facts "with no constituents." Russell explains:

> ... the form of all subject-predicate complexes will be the fact "something has some predicate"; the form of all dual complexes will be "something has some relation to something."
>
> ... the logical nature of this fact is very peculiar. For "something has some relation R to something" contains no constituent except R, and "something has some relation to something" contains no constituent at all. It is therefore suitable to serve as the "form" of dual complexes. In a sense, it is simple, since it cannot be analyzed. At first sight, it seems to have structure, and therefore not to be simple; but it is more correct to say that it *is* a structure.
>
> (*TK*, p. 114)

In Russell's view, abstraction and generalization direct the mind in such a way that it becomes acquainted with a logical form. Construed as abstract fact with no constituents, logical forms are puzzling entities. But in any event, it is clear that logical forms do not contain ontological counterparts of logical particles, quantifiers, or variables. They contain no constituents at all! Russell is explicit. He remarks that ". . . a molecular form is not even the form of any actual particular; no particular, however, complex, has the form 'this or that,' or the form 'not-this'."[31]

Consider the belief ascription made by a person S that m believes that every human is mortal. Extrapolating from the *Theory of Knowledge*, Russell's approach would take the ascription to be true in virtue of the existence of the following corresponding belief complex:

m-believing-with-respect-to-(humanity, mortality, **GEN**).

A constituent of this belief state is the logical object **GEN**, acquaintance with which grounds our a priori knowledge of the logical notion of the subordination of one universal under another. The logical form **GEN** is to be identified as this abstract general fact:

some-universal-being-subordinate-to-some-universal.

The person believes truly, however, when every human is mortal. The truth-conditions of the statement "Every human is mortal" are rendered by Principia's recursive definition, not by correspondence with this logical form (construed as an abstract general fact). In this way, Russell's account of the content of our understanding of logical notions is compatible with Principia's recursively defined hierarchy of senses of truth and falsehood. A similar account applies where the understanding of logical particles is involved. Consider an ascription made by a person S that m believes a is red or b is white. The ascription is true in virtue of the existence of a complex belief-fact, namely:

m-believing-with-respect-to-(a, redness, b, whiteness, **OR**).

The logical notion **OR** which is a constituent of this belief state is not a relation that the logical particle for which "v" stands. The logical particles of Principia do not stand for relations. They stood for relations when Russell embraced an ontology of propositions. But Principia is a no-propositions theory. The logical form **OR** is rather a logical object, acquaintance with which is to account for our a priori knowledge of the nature of disjunction. Russell was uncertain as to what sort of object it might be, but his comments in Theory of Knowledge suggest that he identifies it with an abstract general fact such as the following:

some-universals-being-such-that-one-or-another-of-them-is-exemplified.

It is important to realize that it is not in virtue of the existence of a molecular fact containing an ontological analog of the logical particle "v" that a person m believes truly that *a* is red or *b* is white. Rather, the person believes truly because *a* is red or *b* is white. That is, the truth conditions of "*a* is red or *b* is white" are given in accordance with Principia's recursive definition. There are no molecular facts containing ontological counterparts of logical particles.

It is important to realize that Theory of Knowledge is consistent with Principia's recursive theory of truth. The recursive theory of truth requires that all facts (that are truth-makers) be atomic and logically independent. The exemplification of one universal (which occurs in such a fact that is a truth-maker) never excludes exemplification of another. According to Principia, the existence of many facts is what provides truth-makers for general statements. This is essential to Principia's hierarchy of senses of truth and falsehood, and it is this hierarchy which provides the philosophical justification of the order component of the order/type indices on predicate variables. Thus the abstract general facts of Theory of Knowledge are not truth-makers.

Russell's Theory of Knowledge manuscript is inclined toward embracing abstract general facts. But in his 1918 Logical Atomism lectures Russell goes much further. He argues on behalf of both partly general facts and even negative facts.[32] These positions are compatible with Principia's recursive definitions of "truth" and "falsehood." Unfortunately, their compatibility has gone largely unnoticed. Interpreters frequently read Russell's later inclinations toward general facts and negative facts into Principia. The mistake lends itself to the view that in Principia Russell held that the logical particles are relation signs and that general facts are the truth-makers for general statements. The interpretation obliterates the role that the recursive definitions of "truth" and "falsehood" plays in Principia's philosophical explanation of order indices on predicate variables. It ignores the recursive nature of its definitions of "truth" and "falsehood" and, accordingly, it must construe the VCP as providing the philosophical justification for ramified types.[33]

This also undermines a proper understanding of the criticisms Wittgenstein had of Russell's theory.

Russell's version of the multiple-relation theory in his *Theory of Knowledge* manuscript was surely intended to be consistent with *Principia*'s recursive theory of truth. In the manuscript, Russell reluctantly embraced a theory that explains knowledge of logical notions as a form of acquaintance between a mind and certain logical forms. He tentatively assumes that there is a faculty of pure logical intuition which acquaints the mind with the logical forms grounding our understanding of notions such as "all," "some," "not," "or," and "if . . . then." He reified logical forms, identifying them (albeit tentatively) with abstract general facts. This was his plan for an account of our a priori knowledge of logical notions and for our grasp of abstract logical structure. But Russell's identification of logical forms with abstract general facts could not reasonably have been entertained by Russell if it undermines the recursive nature of the correspondence theory of truth set forth in *Principia*. It is perfectly coherent for Russell to hold a recursive definition of "truth" which requires that no facts contain ontological counterparts of the logical connectives and yet maintain that the mind can be acquainted with purely logical objects such as universal, particular, not, or, dyadic relation, all and some, and so on.

By 1914 Russell had lost confidence in the multiple-relation theory. He came to believe that the notion of acquaintance as a dyadic relation between a mind and an object (e.g. logical form, sense-datum, etc.) was too simplistic. In his Logical Atomism lectures, Russell says that the truth-conditions of a general formula $(\forall x)Ax$ require more than the truth of each among Ax_1 through Ax_n. It requires the general fact that $x_1, \ldots . x_n$ are *all* the entities.[34] But it certainly does not follow that this general fact is itself the truth-maker for the general formula. Russell seems ready to abandon the multiple-relation theory at the base of the recursion, but he is surely not prepared to abandon *Principia*'s recursive theory of truth itself. As we have seen, that theory provided the philosophical justification for *Principia*'s hierarchy of orders. It requires the thesis that the logical particles do not stand for relations (or properties) and demands that general facts are not truth-makers for general formulas. Indeed, Russell explicitly states in his Logical Atomism lectures that the logical particles do not stand for relations that occur as constituents of facts.[35] "In a logically perfect language," he writes, "the words in a proposition should correspond one by one with the components of the corresponding fact, with the exception of such words as 'or,' 'not,' 'if,' 'then,' which have a different function."[36]

Reflecting on the matter some forty years later in *My Philosophical Development*, Russell explained that:

> ... I had, later, to abandon this theory because it depended upon the view that sensation is an essentially relational occurrence—a view which ... I abandoned under the influence of William James. ... I abandoned this theory, both because I ceased to believe in the "subject," and because I no longer thought that a relation can occur significantly as a term, except when paraphrase is possible in which it does not so occur.[37]

In short, it was Russell's adoption of neutral monism, together with the thesis that universals have only a predicable nature, that led him to abandon the multiple-relation theory.

It seems odd that Russell does not mention Wittgenstein's influence. Russell's letters of 1912–1913 suggest that Wittgenstein's criticism played a significant role in Russell's abandonment of the multiple-relation theory. On 27 May 1913 he wrote to Ottoline of the progress on his new *Theory of Knowledge* book:

> ... we were both cross from the heat—I showed him a crucial part of what I have been writing. He said it was all wrong, not realizing the difficulties—that he had tried my view and knew it wouldn't work. I couldn't understand his objection—in fact he was very inarticulate—but I feel in my bones that he must be right, and that

> he has seen something I have missed. If I could see it too I shouldn't mind, but as it is, it is worrying, and has rather destroyed the pleasure in my writing . . .[38]

What did Russell feel in his bones was right? Was it Wittgenstein that caused Russell to abandon the multiple-relation theory or was it, as Russell later reflected, his conversion to neutral monism?

The correct answer is that it was both. In his lectures on Logical Atomism, Russell wrote of ". . . the impossibility of putting the subordinate verb on a level with its terms as an object term in the belief," and concludes that the multiple-relation theory was "a little unduly simple" because it does treat the object verb as if one could put it as just an object like the terms, ". . . as if one could put 'loves' an a level with Desdemona and Cassio as a term for the relation 'believe'."[39] Russell's phrase "a little unduly simple" is an understatement. He has come to think that in a statement such as "S believes that a loves b" the subordinate verb "loves" somehow retains an assertoric force for otherwise the statement does not indicate whether it is to be the fact of a's loving b or the fact of b's loving a that is to make the belief true. It must, as Russell puts it, appear in a complex as a relating relation. And yet, it cannot be assertoric for the belief statement does not assert that the relation "loves" actually relates a to b. In his Logical Atomism lectures Russell wrote that in judgment

> . . . both verbs have got to occur as verbs, because if a thing is a verb it cannot occur otherwise than as a verb. The subordinate verb is functioning as a verb, and seems to be relating two terms, but as a matter of fact does not when a judgment happens to be false. That is what constitutes the puzzle about the nature of belief. The discovery of this fact is due to Mr. Wittgenstein.[40]

In Russell's estimation, Wittgenstein has revealed "a new beast for our zoo."[41] This is a beast indeed, for surely no atomic sentence can have two verbs occurring assertorically.[42]

That universals have both a predicable and an individual nature had long been central to Russell's philosophy. But Russell was softening. Perhaps Wittgenstein is right that a deeper analysis (revealing that all proper contexts are extensional) might dissolve many of the outstanding philosophical problems plaguing *Principia*'s logicism. Russell had been resisting his attraction to neutral monism since 1907, and we now know that it was discussed in early chapters of Russell's *Theory of Knowledge* manuscript, which Wittgenstein read. Wittgenstein was becoming convinced that Russell's work had not gone far enough to analyze logical and semantic notions such as truth and belief. The doctrine of acquaintaince with logical objects in *Theory of Knowledge* was, in his view, a step backward. All theories of types, including Russell's types*, must be done away with! As Wittgenstein's sees it, Russell's multiple-relation theory relies on the employment of pseudo-concepts in its effort to exclude nonsensical belief.

Russell reported to Wittgenstein that he was "paralyzed" by this criticism.[43] It should be emphasized that Wittgenstein was offering a general objection to the very idea of a theory of truth and was not just objecting to Russell's theory. Wittgenstein's demands have force against every theory that attempts to do semantics. To state the nature of the correspondence relations that characterize truth requires the employment of notions that Wittgenstein regards as pseudo-concepts. Facts (i.e. complexes) cannot be named or described. A name of a fact, such as Russell's "the-redness-of-this" or "*a*-in-the-relation-*R*-to-*b*," fails to show the predicable nature of the relating property (or relation). Forming a definite description fares no better. In attempting to avoid the narrow direction problem and characterize the proper correspondence relation grounding truth, Russell had offered a description of the appropriate fact that is to be the truth-maker. Wittgenstein's criticism is that any characterization of the correspondence relation must ultimately say that there is a universal that relates the constituents of the purported fact that is to correspond to the belief state. But to speak of the universal (i.e. the relating relation)—to put a sign for it in a subject position in a descriptive clause—is to fail to represent its universal nature. The notion of being a universal is a logical notion; it must be given in the syntax by keeping signs for universals in predicate positions. Notions such as universal, particular, predication, and the like have logical content and are pseudo-concepts. Wittgenstein accuses Russell's work in *Theory of Knowledge* as betraying the research program of logical analysis.

At times Russell found Wittgenstein's philosophical tirades barely intelligible, but it was clear enough to him that Wittgenstein was right about a much deeper logical analysis being needed. Russell described the abandonment of *Theory of Knowledge* as "an event of first-rate importance in my life" which "affected everything I have done since." Wittgenstein held that Russell's constructions had not gone far enough, and Russell was more than willing to believe this. In 1924, Ramsey wrote to Wittgenstein with the following assessment of the influence he had on Russell. "Of all of your work," says Ramsey, "he seems now to accept only this: that it is nonsense to put an adjective where a substantive ought to be which helps in the theory of types."[44] Ramsey was not far off. It must be understood, however, that this seemingly small point is quite important. It challenges one of Russell's most sacred doctrines. That is, the thesis that universals are capable of a twofold occurrence: a predicational occurrence and also an individual occurrence.[45] If universals are not capable of occurring otherwise than predicationally, an entirely new way of thinking of metaphysics, logic, and knowledge is required. Acquaintance and logical intuition would require a complete reconstruction. The task is daunting. From this perspective, it is not at all surprising to find that Russell turned to neutral monism and behaviorism for help. Russell needed help. A wholly new set of analyses, more extensive than ever, would have to be uncovered.

ACQUAINTANCE AND LOGIC

Russell's Logical Atomism has been interpreted as if it were a part of a project within British empiricism. Russell allegedly operates with a criterion of simplicity that allows him to identify logical atoms as things with which we are familiar, namely sense-data and their properties.[46] The foundation of Russell's atomism, on this view, is an empiricist principle of acquaintance. It takes mental sense-data as its logical atoms and offers an empiricistic reduction of all factual language (i.e. empirical statements) to statements about sense-data.

Russell's many examples of logical atomistic analysis do not corroborate the interpretation that atomism involves ontological reduction to known entities with which a mind may be acquainted. Russell's examples (i.e. Frege, Cantor, Weierstrass, Einstein, and the new quantum physics) are not cases of an empiricist analysis of factual language—as if Weierstrass's reconstruction of limits is an analysis of the ordinary of the word "limit" or Einstein's theory of space-time is an analysis of the nineteenth-century factual language of "simultaneity." The thesis that acquaintance is the cornerstone of Russell's Logical Atomism has produced a sort of blindness to this.

Acquaintance is not the cornerstone of Russell's philosophy of Logical Atomism. Logical analysis is the cornerstone. Acquaintance, in one form or another, is the cornerstone of Russell's epistemology. But his epistemology is articulated from the standpoint of physics and psychology, not from a metholodologically solipsistic standpoint with acquaintance at its foundation. Indeed, Russell offered different analyses of the nature of acquaintance. It is far from an Archimedean foundation from which all analysis begins.

My *Philosophical Development* (1959), Russell reflected on his theory of acquaintance in the following passage:

> I have maintained a principle, which still seems to me completely valid, to the effect that, if we can understand what a sentence means, it must be composed entirely of words denoting

things which we are acquainted or definable in terms of such words.

(*MPD*, p. 125)

This lends itself to the picture that acquaintance is foundational in all of Russell's philosophy. In truth, however, Russell's notion of acquaintance underwent rather dramatic changes as his logical analyses expanded. In "On Denoting" (1905) Russell embraced an ontology of atomic, molecular, and general propositions (as mind- and language-independent, obtaining or non-obtaining states of affairs). The principle of acquaintance is stated as follows:

> In every proposition that we can apprehend (i.e., not only in those whose truth or falsehood we can judge of, but in all that we can think about), all the constituents are really entities with which we have immediate acquaintance.[47]

Propositions in this sense were abandoned in *Principia* (1910), never to reappear. In "Knowledge by Acquaintance and Knowledge by Description" (1910–1911) and in *Problems* (1912) Russell renders the principle of acquaintance as follows: "Every proposition which we can understand must be composed wholly of constituents with which we are acquainted."[48] Quite obviously the notion of a proposition has changed. Moreover, the notion of acquaintance itself changes. In the 1917 Logical Atomism lectures, Russell begins to worry that acquaintance is not a simple relation. "Understanding a predicate," Russell writes,

> is quite a different thing from understanding a name.... To understand a name you must be acquainted with the particular of which it is a name, and you must know that it is the name of that particular. You do not, that is to say, have any suggestion of the form of a proposition, whereas in understanding a predicate you do.[49]

Russell had come to maintain that universals have only a predicable nature. Consequently, acquaintance with a universal is not simply as a relation with a mind as one of the relata a universal as another.[50]

Russell's Logical Atomism did not begin from an epistemic principle of acquaintance that "fixes the nature" of logical atoms as sense-data. In the atomism lectures themselves, Russell already admits that he is on the verge of embracing neutral monism. He writes:

> I feel more and more inclined to think that it [neutral monism] may be true. I feel more and more that the difficulties that occur in regard to it are all of the sort that may be solved by ingenuity.
>
> ... One is the question of belief and the other sorts of facts involving two verbs. If there are such facts as this, that I think may make neutral monism rather difficult, but as I was pointing out, there is the theory that one calls behaviourism, which belongs logically with neutral monism, and that theory would altogether dispense with those facts containing two verbs, and would therefore dispose of that argument against neutral monism.
>
> (*PLA*, p. 279)

Russell's adoption of neutral monism pushed him to abandon the self (i.e. the conscious subject), and this put an end to his theory that physical sense-data are the immediate objects of mental acts of sensation. The cognitive act of sensation is no longer distinct from the physical sense-datum.[51] The results of this change were striking. Russell explained that

> ... new problems, of which at first I was not fully conscious, arose as a consequence of the abandonment of "sense-data." Such words as "awareness," "acquaintance," and "experience," had to be re-defined, and this was by no means an easy task.[52]

Russell attempts to replace "acquaintance" and offers an analysis of knowing in sympathy with some of the ideas of behaviorism, which he regards as the natural ally of neutral monism.[53]

Undue emphasis on an epistemic theory of acquaintance as

definitive of Logical Atomism obscures this. For example, Tully writes: "The most notable feature of Russell's conversion to neutral monism from Logical Atomism (as he called his position in 1914) was the abandonment of acquaintance or awareness as the cornerstone of his metaphysics and epistemology."[54] If a primitive relation of acquaintance with sense-data was definitive of Russell's Logical Atomism, then Russell's "conversion to" neutral monism would be an abandonment of Logical Atomism in favor of neutral monism. But in fact Russell regarded neutral monism as a theory within Logical Atomism.[55]

Russell's willingness to employ psychology and the new physics in his analysis of acquaintance immediately raises questions as to how we know logic. If logic is the foundation of all analysis, knowledge of logic has to be exempt from naturalization by appeal to psychology and physics. How can this tension be resolved in Russell's philosophy of Logical Atomism?

In reading Russell, we do well to keep in mind that there are different senses of "logic" at work in his writings. Questions as to whether knowledge of logic is self-evident began to appear in Russell's philosophy with the discovery of the logical paradoxes at the foundations of mathematics. The orthodox tradition has it that logic consists in the rules of the categorical syllogism and in the law of identity and the law of contradiction. Mistakes in logic were thought to be impossible because logical truths are self-evident and uninformative. This conception carries over to the new quantification theory (viewed in some sense as generalized tautologies). In *Problems*, knowledge of the new quantification theory logic is a priori and explained by an indefinable cognitive faculty of acquaintance with universals and their structural relationships. This position persists into *Our Knowledge of the External World*. But the new informative ^{cp}logic which embraces axioms for the comprehension of ever new functions (i.e. attributes) is quite another matter. Frege included an axiom assuring that each function/attribute is correlated with a unique extension (i.e. class). He admitted that this axiom of correlation[56] lacks the highest degree of self-evidence. "I have never concealed from myself," Frege wrote, "its lack of the self-evidence which the others possess, and which must properly be demanded of a law of logic ..."[57] Though it enjoyed some reasonable degree of self-evidence, Russell showed that it is false as it leads to contradiction.

Russell held that there are parts of ᶜᵖlogic where re-construction of first principles is involved. These parts, unlike the new quantification theory, have a quite different epistemic status. In 1906, Russell explains the point as follows:

> The method of logistic is fundamentally the same as that of every other science. There is the same fallibility, the same uncertainty, the same mixture of induction and deduction, and the same necessity of appealing, in confirmation of principles, to the diffused agreement of calculated results with observation. ... In all this, logistic is exactly on a level with (say) astronomy, except that, in astronomy, verification is effected not by intuition but by the senses. The "primitive propositions" with which the deductions of logistic begin should, if possible, be evident to intuition; but that is not indispensible, nor is it, in any case, the whole reason for their acceptance. The reason is inductive, namely that, among their known consequences (including themselves), many appear to intuition to be true, none appear to intuition to be false, and those that appear to intuition to be true are not, so far as can be seen, deducible from any system of indemonstrable propositions inconsistent with the system in question.
>
> (*InS*, p. 194)

Russell was then immersed in the problem of dissolving the paradoxes plaguing logicism. He held that some elaborate revision to logical principles resembling simple-type structure is absolutely indispensible (InS, p. 196). The epistemic justification of this revision, however, can only be given inductively and a posteriori—no less so than physics and astronomy.

In Principia this point recurs. The cause of this odd epistemic situation lies in the discovery of the logical paradoxes. "In formal logic," Whitehead and Russell write, "the element of doubt is less than in most sciences, but it is not absent, as appears from the fact that the paradoxes followed from premises which were not previously known to require limitation" (PM to *56, p. 59). Principia adopts an axiom of reducibility which enables the emulation of a type-stratified theory of classes without assuming the existence of classes. This axiom is not fully self-evident. But Russell explains that self-evidence is not a guide when it comes to the foundational principles of the new logic:

> That the axiom of reducibility is self-evident is a proposition which can hardly be maintained. But in fact self-evidence is never more than a part of the reason for accepting an axiom, and is never indispensible. The reason for accepting an axiom, as for accepting any other proposition, is always largely inductive, namely that many propositions which are nearly indubitable can be deducted from it, and that no equally plausible way is known by which these propositions could be true if the axiom were false, and nothing which is probably false can be deduced from it. If the axiom is apparently self-evident, that only means, practically, that it is nearly indubitable; for things have been thought to be self-evident and have yet turned out to be false. . . . In the case of the axiom of reducibility, the inductive evidence in its favor is very strong, since the reasonings which it permits and the results to which it leads are all such as to appear valid.
> (PM to *56, p. 59)

The a posteriori status of some parts of the ᶜᴾlogic is emphasized again in Russell's 1924 discussion of his philosophy of Logical Atomism. Russell puts the point as follows:

> The epistemological question: "Why should I believe this set of propositions?" is quite different from the logical question: "What is

the smallest and logically simplest group of propositions from which this set of propositions can be deduced?" Our reasons for believing logic and pure mathematics are, in part, only inductive and probable, in spite of the fact that, in their logical order, the propositions of logic and pure mathematics follow from the premises of logic by pure deduction. I think this point important, since errors are liable to arise from assimilating the logic to the epistemological order, and also, conversely, from assimilating the epistemological to the logical order. The only way in which work on mathematical logic throws light on the truth or falsehood of mathematics is by disproving the supposed antinomies. This shows that mathematics may be true. But to show that mathematics is true would require other methods and other considerations.

(*LA*, p. 326)

Principia offers a theory of logical form which endeavors to save mathematics from ruin (by "disproving" the antinomies). Whether or not this theory of logical form (and its axiom of reducibility) is actually true can only be discovered inductively and probabilistically —by its results.

FURTHER READING

Alberto Coffa, *The Semantic Tradition from Kant to Carnap: To the Vienna Station* (Cambridge: Cambridge University Press, 1993).

Nicholas Griffin, "Russell's Multiple-Relation Theory of Judgment," *Philosophical Studies* vol. 47 (no. 2), (1985), pp. 213–247.

Gregory Landini, *Wittgenstein's Apprenticeship With Russell* (Cambridge: Cambridge University Press, 2007).

Lydia and Timothy McGrew, *Internalism and Epistemology: The Architecture of Reason* (New York: Routledge, 2006).

David Pears, *The False Prison*, Vol. I (Oxford: Clarendon Press, 1987).

Six

Mind and Matter

> The gap between mind and matter has been filled in, partly by new views of mind, but much more by the realization that physics tells us nothing as to the intrinsic character of matter.
>
> *Outline of Philosophy* (1927)

In *Our Knowledge of the External World* (1914) Russell advocated a four-dimensionalist theory of material continuants persisting in time. By 1918 he was prepared to argue for a much broader form of four-dimensionalism. Not only material continuants persisting in time are to be constituted by series of transient physical particulars, but minds (as "selves" persisting in time) are also to be so constituted. This expansive four-dimensionalism is the key to understanding Russell's neutral monism. As we shall see, it makes it unique. Russell is endeavoring to transcend the traditional distinction between minds (as continuants) and matter (as continuants), constructing both out of orderings of the physical events that are their stages.

Spinoza (1632–1667) famously accepted Descartes's view that mechanical explanations alone are admissible in the new science of matter. At the same time he held that there is only one substance. The duality lies not in the substance, but in the attributes of substance: thought and extension. The apparatus of causal explanation within the attribute of extension is mechanical, rigid body impacts. The apparatus of causal explanation within the attribute of thought is will, desire, and intellection. The incommensurability lies in the sorts of properties (i.e. modes) predicable of objects within an attribute. Characterized by the duality of attributes of thought and extension, we cannot speak of mind and body causally interacting since cause is within an attribute. We can only speak of there being a kind of parallel. But understood as being undergirded by one substance,[1] the parallel is certainly no fortuitous accident.

Spinoza's substance monism at first seems to strain credulity. Viewed in a Cartesian way, mental properties (e.g. phenomenal colors, sounds, tastes, smells, and textures) are so completely disparate from material properties (e.g. shape, size, and motion) that it seems inconceivable that one substance can undergird both. Thomas Nagel famously argued that while it might be true that a mental process (e.g. experiencing an object by the auditory profile of its echo) is constituted by a physical process (e.g. neural events in one's brain and nervous system), it is inconceivable *how* it could be true. Nagel reminds us that if bats have experiences of echolocation, then although we can understand the wave mechanics of echoes and the chemical mechanics of transmission across synapses, we have no access to what it is like to experience as a bat does. The subjective qualitative nature of a bat's consciousness, Nagel concludes, is simply closed off from physical explanation, though it might well be physical.[2]

Mind and body do interact—as if to spite the philosophers. Because of the obviousness of interaction, we can see why someone might adopt neutral monism in spite of the apparent inconceivability of how it can be true. Consider the analogy with light, which displays properties of transverse electro-magnetic waves (e.g. in polarization and interference patterns in propagation through slits) and yet can also display properties of particles. The history of the science of light is a history of arguments over whether a wave model or a particle model best fits the data. In modern times, and especially with the successes of quantum theory, physics seems reconciled to the duality in spite of its inconceivability—a substance neutrality of light with respect to wave and particle.

William James's neutral monism is quite different from that of Spinoza. In his essay entitled "Does Consciousness Exist" (1904) James writes that the "self" is a non-entity. He proclaims that "[t]hose who still cling to it are clinging to a mere echo, the faint rumor left behind by the disappearing 'soul' upon the air of philosophy."[3] James made an important contribution to the thesis of neutral monism because of his thesis that consciousness is active and fluid, like a stream, ever in motion. This opens the way to think that properly speaking it is an organism proceeding through time that is properly said to be conscious in virtue of its interactions with its environment and with its own internal states. With his book *Theory of Knowledge* abandoned, Russell published one of its chapters as "On The Nature of Acquaintance" (1914). In it he praises James's views on consciousness, but he rejects neutral monism.

By 1915, however, Russell is beginning to chip away at the traditional distinction of mental and physical. In a letter to the editor of *The Journal of Philosophy, Psychology and Scientific Methods* Russell writes that ". . . my whole philosophy of physics rests on the view that the sense-datum is purely physical . . . . a particular which is a datum is not logically dependent upon being a datum."[4] Russell goes on in his letter to imagine how one might go about defining "mental." Noting that a world without minds contains no relations such as perceiving, remembering, desiring, enjoying, and believing, he writes: "This suggests that no *particulars* of which we have experience are to be called 'mental,' but that certain facts, involving certain relations, constitute what is essentially mental in the world of experiences."[5]

In short, Russell's neutral monism merges a four-dimensionalism with respect to matter (i.e. continuants persisting in time) with James's thesis that consciousness is a process: Conscious selves persisting through time, no less than physical continuants, are series of space-time events. It is worth quoting at length from the opening of *The Analysis of Mind*:

On the one hand, many psychologists, especially those of the behaviourist school, tend to adopt what is essentially a materialistic position, as a matter of method, if not metaphysics. They make psychology increasingly dependent on physiology and external observations, and tend to think of matter as something much more solid and indubitable than mind. Meanwhile, the physicists, especially Einstein and other exponents of the theory of relativity, have been making "matter" less and less material. Their world consists of "events," from which "matter" is derived by a logical construction. Whoever reads, for example, Professor Eddington's Space, Time and Gravitation (Cambridge University Press, 1920), will see that an old-fashioned materialism can receive no support from modern physics. I think that what has permanent value in the outlook of the behaviorists is the feeling that physics is the most fundamental science at present in existence. But this position cannot be called materialistic, if, as seems to be the case, physics does not assume the existence of matter. The view that seems to me to reconcile the materialistic tendency of psychology with the anti-materialistic tendency of physics is the view of William James and the American new realists, according to which the "stuff" of the world is neither mental nor material, but a "neutral stuff," out of which both are constructed.

(AMi, p. 5)

Succinctly put, Russell says that the old distinction between soul and body (i.e. mind and matter) has evaporated quite as much because matter has lost its old solidity as because mind has lost its spirituality (R&S, p. 133). Russell accepts the interpretation of the physicist Sir Arthur Eddington that relativity eliminates the traditional notion of matter in favor of series of events in space-time. In 1915 Einstein's general theory of relativity bested Newton's theory of gravitation in finally providing an adequate explanation of the perihelion of the planet Mercury. By 1919 an expedition led by Eddington confirmed general relativity's prediction for the deflection of starlight by the sun, making Einstein famous. Russell even retrofitted *Our Knowledge* in 1926 with the new view, replacing physical sense-data at the basis of the construction by events in space-time.

Russell's neutral monism is sketched in *The Analysis of Mind* (1921) and makes an appearance in the new Appendix C of the second edition of *Principia Mathematica* (1925), where Russell investigates its implications for the extensionality of belief. It looms large in Russell's 1925 paper "Logical Atomism" and in Russell's books of the period: *The ABC of Relativity* (1925), *Outline of Philosophy* (1927), and, of course, *The Analysis of Matter* (1927).

MATTER: THE PROBLEM STATED[6]

The problems of mind and matter arise in the following way. Aristotelian explanations of nature, the standard for thousands of years, encourage appeal to teleological functions (i.e. purposes and ends) that objects play in a harmonic process to sustain life and order in the cosmos. Each natural kind (roughly, species) has its proper purpose in this great harmony, just as the organs of a body each have their purpose in sustaining the life of an organism. The Copernican revolution destroyed Aristotelianism in physical science. If the earth moves, motion has every bit the claim to being as natural as rest. The arrow's flight does not require, as Aristotle thought, a sustaining drive pushing the arrow. Its natural state is not rest. The proper question is not, as Aristotle would have it, what sustains the arrow's flight, but rather what brings it to a stop. A rock does not roll downhill because of an Aristotelian entelechy—a force, drive, disposition, or will like conatus in the rock to reach its natural place (at the center of the cosmos at earth's center). A plant does not orient its leaves to the sun by a vital force within.

Accepting the Copernican revolution, Descartes endeavored to provide the foundations for a new non-Aristotelian philosophy of science. He advanced a substance dualism, according to which there are two fundamentally distinct substance types: *res cogitans* (i.e. thought, mind) and *res extensa* (i.e. volume, body). Substance dualism requires that a hypothesis counts as scientific only if it is given quantitatively and solely in terms of mechanical laws governing motions in the material substance. The admissible terms from which these explanations are to be generated consist of the quantitative notions of shape, size, number, and motion—just the qualities that representative realism regarded as primary. The very notion of the "mechanical" was defined by Descartes by means of its contrast to the mental (i.e. *res cogitans*). The Cartesian scientists found Galilean forces, acceleration and gravitational attractions, to be every bit as occult as Aristotelian entelechies. Agency does not belong in science. The loadstone magnet does not attract iron. Perhaps, the mechanist conjectures, it sends out shaped particles which, permeating the iron, drive the iron to it by the mechanics of the screw.

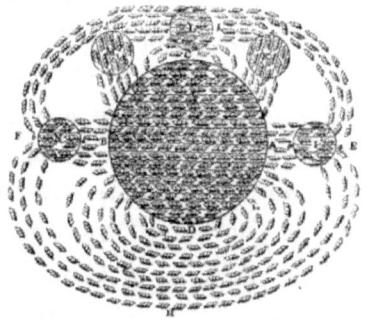

The sun does not exert a "force at a distance" upon the planets. Our solar system is one of many vortices of swirling particles. Cartesian science demarcates the physical by reference to its incommensurability with the mental. The Cartesians thought that there is no other way to provide the foundation for the intelligibility of a non-Aristotelian physics.

The Cartesian perspective launched a wonderful new way to see the world. In Descartes's *Traité de l'homme* he described the human body as a machine. William Harvey had discovered the circulation of the blood, but he was an Aristotelian and regarded systole, the heart's contraction which pushes the blood through its ventricles, as being generated in the heart by its purpose in sustaining the life of the organism. Eager to show that a mechanical explanation is all that is warranted, Descartes imagined the heart to be a pump operating like a tea kettle, with compression due to heating in the chambers of the heart pushing the blood through the arteries and returning it in condensation by the veins. In *La description du corps humain*, he endeavored to replace the notion of life and Harvey's *epigenesis*, the vital forces directing the egg to produce an organism, with mechanical processes.

Newton's empiricist philosophy of science rejected the purely mechanical perspective of the Cartesians. It offers a compromise between the Cartesian demand for a mechanical and quantitative science and the Galilean forces, which were so useful in characterizing the law of inertia at the core of the new science of celestial and terrestrial dynamics. Newton's philosophy of science accommodates such forces if and only if they can be articulated by some quantitative law and corroborated by his experimental method. Gravitational force even "at a distance" (without contact) between objects with mass m_1 and m_2 is legitimated on this model. It is legitimate because it is governed by a quantitative law

$$F = G \frac{m_1 \times m_2}{d^2}$$

which can be empirically tested. The force F is equal to a constant G multiplied by the product of the masses of the objects divided by the square of their distance. This force is an action at a distance involving no contact between the objects. It is regarded as occult by the mechanical science. Nonetheless, it counts as scientific on the Newtonian model. On the other hand, Aristotelian teleology, with its entelechies, natural states, and places, does not fit the model. On the Newtonian model, it is appealing to quantitative law and empirical testability (i.e. verification) in observation that sets the foundation for the new non-Aristotelian science of physics.

The Newtonian model of the requirements for a hypothesis being genuinely scientific rules out Aristotelian entelechies and teleological modes of explanation because such conjectures cannot, typically, be characterized quantitatively and thereby empirically tested. The Aristotelian notion that nature abhors a vacuum imagines nature as if it were an agent with a desire and purpose in acting. By putting marks on a tube open at only one end, Pascal can test his conjecture that air has a weight which exerts a pressure by comparing the height of the water in his simple barometer at the bottom of Puy de dôme and at the top. The relationship of altitude to pressure can be measured and expressed quantitatively, thus supporting further predicated observations, whose outcomes corroborate the conjecture. Agency, on the other hand, does not easily fit the model of testability; one has to lay down strict parameters on what agents can do, and even then it seems hopeless to offer quantitative laws concerning their behavior. As Pascal pointed out with his Puy de dôme experiment on barometric pressure, we are at a loss as to whether to say nature abhors a vacuum at the top of a mountain more than at the bottom. Newton's model for science was readily applicable to chemistry, and the new genetic biology could be viewed as not far out of line. With Newton, the new science of physics no longer relies on substance dualism. The Newtonian model makes it at least intelligible—contra Descartes—to incorporate a science of psychology in a unified scientific conception of the world.

The history[7] of psychology, however, is a history of fledgling pseudo-sciences—at least according to John Broadus Watson, an American psychologist who took his Ph.D. at the University of Chicago in 1903. He demanded that psychology adhere to a strictly mechanical model. All attempts at psychology which deal with consciousness are useless and vicious, nothing but the survival of the discredited vitalism and the theological notion of the soul. Watson claimed that psychology should not be concerned with the notion of mind or with human consciousness. Instead, psychology should be concerned only with behavior. Watson published what is now sometimes considered his manifesto, the article "Psychology as the Behaviorist Views It" (1913). Watson's work was based on the experiments of Ivan Pavlov, who had studied animals and associative learning. In Pavlov's best-known experiment, each time the dogs heard a bell they were fed, and after a period of training the ringing of the bell would elicit salivation in the dogs, anticipating the food. They had been conditioned to salivate at the sound of a bell. Pavlov believed, as Watson was later to emphasize, that all animals, including humans are subject to reflexive conditioning in this way. He hoped to found a new psychology on the basis of explaining behavior by means of conditioned response. Modern behaviorism, of course, is associated with B. F. Skinner, whose early work *The Behavior of Organisms: An Experimental Analysis Of Behavior* (1938) is classic. Skinner's studies led him to modify Watson's almost exclusive emphasis on reflexes and conditioning. Like Watson before him, Skinner maintained that for psychology to become a genuine science, it must not appeal to notions of mind or consciousness in its explanations of behavior. Instead, reinforcements and "operant conditioning," as he called it, should be the foundation of any science of psychology.

Descartes himself held no hope for a science which employs the notion of consciousness and mind. Descartes would certainly have accepted behaviorism as a genuine science—a mechanical science of the animal body—since reflex and conditioning is certainly within his conception of the material. Indeed, a careful behaviorist need never pronounce that there is no consciousness or mind; he or she need only exclude such concepts as antithetical to the possibility of a genuine science of psychology. Unfortunately, a purely mechanical science of psychology places very austere demands on psychology. Many psychologists today reject behaviorism, hoping to rehabilitate the concept of mind (and consciousness) adhering not to a mechanical method, but to a loosely articulated Newtonian model of science. Does Freudian psychoanalysis, with its notion of the preconscious, Oedipal complexes, and the like, fit the Newtonian model of a genuine science? Disputes rage even to this day.

The followers of Descartes's mechanical conception of science demanded that physical explanations appeal only to the motions of colliding rigid bodies. Mechanical atomism, as it came to be called, produces an unbridgeable gap between mind and matter. When construed as impacting rigid bodies, mechanical processes cannot constitute a thought, a color sensation, etc. Conversely, a thought to move my arm, which is not extended in space, cannot push on the rigid bodies in my arm to bring about its motion. Descartes rejected this consequence. He rejected atoms, appealing instead to a sort of fluid dynamics: compression and waves in the fluid which is the *res extensae*. But no one seems to have agreed with him that this helps in the least to allow for mind–body interactions. The result, as Russell's aunt had once told him, is this: "What is mind? No matter. What is matter? Never mind!"[8] As we'll see, Russell did not believe her.

NEUTRAL STUFF: IS IT REALLY NEUTRAL?

We have seen that there is a school of interpreters of Russell who take *Our Knowledge* to be a work set squarely in the tradition of British empiricism; it is a form of phenomenalism. The fact that Russell explicitly maintains that sense-data are physical is a dark secret for them. This school takes heart, however, when Russell adopts neutral monism, for the mental/physical distinction supposedly collapses. Neutral monism might be brought into the camp of empiricism and phenomenalism. The connections to Eddington's views on relativity seem no impediment to such an interpretation. After all, Einstein was clearly influenced by the positivist views of Ernst Mach, whose empiricism (and verificationism) is famous.

There are no physical facts of motion, Mach argued, outside of what is verifiable by measurements. Newton's notion of absolute motion is empirically meaningless. Ptolemy's frame of reference was the earth, and in Mach's view, this is every bit as legitimate as Copernicus's frame which is the sun. The debate between them is empirically meaningless. In walking, it is perfectly legitimate to describe the situation as the universe rolling beneath my feet so that my muscular efforts are to slow my body and thereby arrive across the room. No empirical measurements could reveal otherwise. Mach was well aware of Newton's arguments that accelerated and non-uniform motion offer telling grounds for the absoluteness of motion. Imagine a universe with just a spinning bucket of water. The water will rise up the sides. Newton held that we are left without a physical explanation for the rise of the water if we take the water as being at rest and the bucket spinning. Mach resisted Newton's thought experiments. An imagined universe with one bucket of water is not a physical universe. In our universe, gravitational forces are covariant. The water is at rest, and the entire universe with all its galaxies spins about it, pulling the water up the sides of the bucket. In this way, Mach argues that the principle of relativity of motion is immune to empirical disconfirmation.

Einstein's views have often been interpreted as verificationist. The behavior of light is fixed and used for all physical measurements of time and even for the metric of spatial distances. As a consequence, matter (e.g. clocks, meter sticks, etc.) have no reference frame-independent properties (e.g. rigidity and length) which would enable measurement with them to trump the behavior of light. The verificationist contends that there is no physical meaning to the notion of simultaneity apart from what can be verified by the measured behavior of light. Consider the following passage from *The ABC of Relativity*:

> The theory of relativity, apart from convention, tells us that events in the universe have a four dimensional order, and that, between any two events which are near together in this order, there is a relation called "interval," which is capable of being measured if suitable precautions are taken. It tells us also that "absolute motion," "absolute space," and "absolute time" cannot have any physical significance; laws of physics involving these concepts are not acceptable. This is hardly a physical law in itself, but rather a useful

rule to enable us to reject some proposed physical laws as unsatisfactory.

(*ABC*, p. 128)

At the time Russell wrote, positivist (verificationist) interpretations of relativity were still in vogue. Both Eddington and Mach are neutral monists. Their neutral monism was contrived to fit positivism in physics. Putting all this together makes it seem as if neutral monism fits squarely in the camp of British empiricism. The neutral stuff are phenomenal qualitative states which, because phenomenal, naturally constitute minds, but also constitute material continuants persisting in time.

In light of the difficulties of characterizing neutral monism, let us offer the following provisional distinctions:

(A) Neutral monism without four-dimensionalism (James? Spinoza?):
There is a neutral stuff which underlies both matter and mind.
(B) Neutral monism with four-dimensionalism (Russell, Mach):
  (1) The neutral stuff are physical events in space-time, some series of which constitute material objects persisting in time and other series of which constitute minds persisting in time. The different series have many events in common, but some events may occur only in minds and some may occur only in material continuants.
  (2) The neutral stuff are phenomenal qualitative states, some series of which constitute material objects persisting in time and other series of which constitute minds persisting in time. The different series have many events in common, but some states may occur only in minds and some may occur only in material continuants.

Can B1 and B2 be collapsed? In Chapter Five we found that four-dimensionalism with respect to matter is not circular—though it is true that in order to speak of a physical stage we must appeal to the physical (i.e. material) continuant of which it is a stage. The same may be said to hold for the notion of a phenomenal stage in a four-dimensionalist analysis of mind. Admittedly, the characterization of something being "phenomenal" is intelligible only with respect to a mind (i.e. a self persisting in time with consciousness). There is no circularity, however. Thus, it may seem that the division between B1 and B2 collapses. A neutral monist may say that a given stage may well be described as "phenomenal," alluding to its being a stage of a series which constitutes a mind or described as "physical," alluding to its being a stage of a series that constitutes a material object.

At first this seems promising, but there can be no collapse of B1 and B2 if we are to do justice to the notion of the phenomenal in a sense in which it is connected to the notion of the qualitative aspects of consciousness. Thus B1 and B2 are distinct forms of neutral monism. In both, the "neutral" stuff is not so neutral after all. In both, there is neutral stuff, but the neutrality consists in that it can occur among the series which are continuants persisting through time, whether material or mental.

Of course, few spoke in terms of phenomenal characters (i.e. qualia) in the heyday of neutral monism. John Searle describes the issue as follows:

> Consciousness so defined is an inner, first-person, qualitative phenomenon . . . . all conscious phenomena are qualitative, subjective experiences, and hence are qualia. There are not two types of phenomena, consciousness and qualia. There is just consciousness, which is a series of qualitative states.[9]

Searle maintains that the problem of mind is the problem of consciousness (i.e. qualia). Few saw the issue this way in the heyday of behaviorism, which made consciousness" peripheral to what is wanted in an explanation of mind. Russell writes:

> Man has developed out of the animals, and there is no serious gap between him and the amoeba. Something closely analogous to

knowledge and desire as regards its effects on behaviour, exists among animals, even where what we call "consciousness" is hard to believe in; something equally analogous exists in ourselves in cases where no traces of "consciousness" can be found. It is therefore natural to suppose that, whatever may be the correct definition of "consciousness," "consciousness" is not the essence of life or mind. In the following lectures, accordingly, this term will disappear until we have dealt with words, when it will re-emerge as mainly a trivial and unimportant outcome of linguistic habits.

(*AMi*, p. 40)

Given what Russell says about consciousness, we best not follow Searle's definition.

Neutral monism requires that a mind or self be construed as a series of stages. The question before us is whether phenomenal characteristics (qualia) are intrinsic to a stage. Consider the following passage from Mach's "The Analysis of Sensations" (1886):

A colour is a physical object so long as we consider its dependence upon its luminous source, upon other colours, upon heat, upon space and so forth. Regarding, however, its dependence upon the retina . . . it becomes a psychological object, a sensation.[10]

Mach suggests that the stage in question is psychological (a sensation of) color insofar as it occurs in a series which may be described as dependent on the retina, and it is physical color insofar as it is described in terms of a series including stages of reflection of light from the surface of an object. In designating the stage as a "psychological object," Mach appeals only to the stage being among a series of retinal, brain, and nervous system stages studied by psychology. That certainly makes it part of the domain of behavioristic psychology. But behaviorism is notorious precisely because it ignores what is phenomenal, subjective, and conscious. Phenomenal color, as something intrinsic to a stage, seems to have been lost. A stage surely does not acquire phenomenal character in virtue of its occurrence in a series that constitutes a mind.

In the *Analysis of Mind*, Russell cites Mach approvingly (*AMi*, p. 144). But Russell's use of the word "sensation" is more complicated. Russell's form of neutral monism allows for stages of matter that cannot be brought under psychological laws and thus do not occur in the series that are minds; it allows stages of minds ("images") that Russell thinks may not be quite able to be brought under physical laws and so do not occur in the series that are matter. This is clear in the following passage:

> The stuff of the world, so far as we have experiences of it, consists, on the view that I am advocating, of innumerable transient particulars which as occur in seeing, hearing, etc., together with images more or less resembling these, of which I shall speak shortly. If physics is true, there are, besides the particulars that we experience, others, probably equally (or almost equally) transient, which make up that part of the material world that does not come into the sort of contact with a living body that is required to turn it into a sensation.
>
> (*AMi*, p. 143)

Consider the following wonderfully blunt statement of neutral monism:

> Physics and psychology are not distinguished by their material. Mind and matter alike are logical constructions; the particulars out of which they are constructed, or from which they are inferred, have various relations, some of which are studied by physics, others by psychology. . . . The two most essential characteristics of the causal laws which would naturally be called psychological are subjectivity and mnemic causation; these are not unconnected, since the causal unit in mnemic causation is the group of particulars having a given passive place at a given time, and it is by this manner of grouping that subjectivity is defined . . . Habit, memory and thought are all

developments of mnemic causation. It is probable, though not
certain, that mnemic causation is derivative from ordinary physical
causation in nervous (and other) tissue.

(*AMi*, p. 307)

Russell suggests that a "sensation" is a stage of a process in a living body. The images that are central to mnemic causation are stages of neural processes. But if images are stages of neural processes, so are sensations—if by "sensations" Russell means those stages of the processes in the living body when matter impinges upon it.

In the *Analysis of Mind* Russell collapses his former distinction between the mental act of sensation and the physical sense-datum which is the object of that act. He writes:

> When I see a patch of colour, it seemed to me that the colour is not psychical, but physical, while my seeing is not physical, but psychical. Hence I concluded that the colour is something other than my seeing of the colour. This argument, to me historically, was directed against Idealism; the emphatic part of it was the assertion that colour is physical, not psychical. I shall not trouble you now with the grounds for holding as against Berkeley that the patch of colour is physical; I have set them forth before, and I see no reason to modify them. But it does not follow that the patch of colour is not also psychical, unless we assume that the physical and the psychical cannot overlap, which I no longer consider a valid assumption. If we admit—as I think we should—that the patch of colour may be both physical and psychical, the reason for distinguishing the sense-datum from the sensation disappears, and we may say that the patch of colour and our sensation in seeing it are identical.

(*AMi*, p. 142)

Russell's collapse of his former distinction between sensation and sense-datum is difficult to understand. The unsensed physical sense-data of *Our Knowledge* are not abandoned. With the distinction between the mental act of sensing and the object (sense-data) abandoned, Russell cannot speak of unsensed sense-data as "unsensed sensations." Thus the term "sensation" is unfortunate. It is more proper to say that some stages (i.e. transient particulars) occur in series which constitute matter and also may occur in series that constitute minds. When they occur in series constituting minds, they are called "sensations." When they do not, Russell has no expression for them besides "transient particulars" and should not call them "sensations." Thus, Russell speaks loosely when he says that "sensations are what is common to the mental and physical worlds; they may be defined as the intersection of mind and matter."[11] Stages, or "transient particulars," as Russell calls them, are sensations simply in virtue of occurring in series that constitute minds.

There is another difficulty in the collapse. In *Our Knowledge*, matter is constructed in terms of series of sense-data, whether sensed or unsensed. Thus, for example, in *Our Knowledge* the sense-datum which is a patch of color—understood as a stage of the process which we normally regard as the reflection of light waves from a surface of a tree—is a constituent in a series of stages that constitutes the tree. But Russell now says that ". . . the sensation that we have when we see a patch of colour simply *is* that patch of colour, an actual constituent of the physical world, and part of what physics is concerned with" (*AMi*, p. 142). Now we may say that the transient particular which, in virtue of it occurring in a series which constituted a mind, is a sensation. It also occurs in a series which constitutes neurons firing in a brain (a material object). In this sense, the transient particular is both mental and material. But it certainly seems odd to think, carrying over the lesson from *Our Knowledge*, that it occurs in the series of stages that constitute the material object that is the table! We are used to thinking of tables as independent from brains. Nonetheless, this is Russell's position. Some trees—the ones that are never experienced by any mind—have no stages in common with brains. Others have transient particulars in common with brains.

In any case, Russell's collapse of the sensation/sense-datum distinction does not determine whether he held the B1 or the B2 form of neutral monism. Given that it is the very same transient particular that may or may not occur in a series that constituted a mind, it seems that Russell holds B2. Though it is a very strange view, it is possible that Russell held that transient particulars have qualitative states intrinsic to them even if they never occur in series that constitute minds. But I doubt this could have been Russell's position. Hence, we shall proceed with the view that Russell's neutral monism adopts B1. Transient particulars are without intrinsic phenomenal character just as were the physical sense-data of *Our Knowledge*.

Are there qualia? At first, it seems outrageous to deny them. Daniel Dennett has done about as good a job as is possible in softening the shock of holding such a position. He puts the matter as follows:

> Nothing, it seems, could you know more intimately than your own qualia; let the entire universe be some vast illusion, some mere figment of Descartes's evil demon, and yet what the figment is made of (for you) will be the qualia of your hallucinatory experiences. Descartes claimed to doubt everything that could be doubted, but he never doubted that his conscious experiences had qualia, the properties by which he knew or apprehended them. . . . So when we look one last time at our original characterization of qualia, as ineffable, intrinsic, private, directly apprehensible properties of experience, we find that there is nothing to fill the bill. In their place are relatively or practically ineffable public properties we can refer to indirectly via reference to our private property-detectors—private only in the sense of idiosyncratic. And insofar as we wish to cling to our subjective authority about the occurrence within us of states of certain types or with certain properties, we can have some authority—not infallibility or incorrigibility, but something better than sheer guessing—but only if we restrict

ourselves to relational, extrinsic properties like the power of certain internal states of ourselves to provoke acts of apparent re-identification. So contrary to what seems obvious at first blush, there simply are no qualia at all.[12]

At times, Russell's neutral monism seems to flirt with this view.

Russell's neutral monism pushed him to a naturalization of mind that rejects phenomenal qualia as being intrinsic to transient particulars. It did not, however, push Russell to the abandonment of qualia, not at least in his later work. In *Outline of Philosophy* (1927) Russell suggests that qualia can be retained within his neutral monism. He coins the word "chrono-geography" for the science which begins with events (i.e. transient particulars) having space-time relations and so does not assume at the outset that certain strings of them can be treated as persistent material units or as minds. He then asks himself the following question: Is matter emergent from events? That is, can the science of matter, as it appears in physics and chemistry, be wholly reduced to chrono-geography? The companion question is, of course: Is mind emergent from events? Can the science of mind, as it appears in psychology, be wholly reduced to chrono-geography?

Russell says that if the answer to either is negative, there are emergent properties. Following Broad's *Mind and its Place in Nature*, Russell characterizes an emergent property as a property of a structure that cannot be wholly explained in terms of the properties of the parts that constitute the structure. Appealing to Sir Eddington's *Mathematical Theory of Relativity*, which interprets Einstein's theory of relativity as making matter consist of a "material-energy tensor," Russell suggests the answer to the first question is negative. Thus matter is not emergent from the series of events (transient particulars) which constitute it. Put starkly, there is no matter (i.e. there are no perfectly rigid bodies persisting through time that traditional materialists advocated). Moreover, there are no emergent properties in chemistry because its laws reduce to those of physics. Russell does not address the question of whether biology reduces to chemistry. Modern molecular biology today strongly suggests such a reduction is inevitable. If so, Russell would say that there are no emergent properties in biology. But in the case of psychology, Russell is quite explicit in embracing emergence. The science of psychology does not reduce to biology because certain irreducibly psychological properties emerge from a series of transient particulars which constitute minds. Russell writes:

> Chrono-geography is concerned only with the abstract mathematical properties of events, and cannot conceivably, unless it is radically transformed, prove that there are visual events, or auditory events, or events of any of the kinds we know by perception. In this sense, psychology is certainly emergent from chrono-geography and also from physics, and it is hard to see how it can ever cease to be so. The reason for this is that our knowledge of data contains features of a qualitative sort, which cannot be deduced from the merely mathematical features of the space-time events inferred from the data, and yet these abstract mathematical features are all that we can legitimately infer. The above argument decides also that mind must be emergent from matter, if it is a material structure. No amount of physics can ever tell us all that we do in fact know about our own percepts.
>
> (*OP*, p. 284)

Transient particulars, series of which constitute minds, do not have qualitative features intrinsic to them. Nonetheless, Russell holds that qualia emerge from such series.

Russell's argument for emergence is difficult. It grows out of his rejection of behaviorism's adamant contempt for introspective awareness. The argument is akin to the "knowledge argument" made popular by Frank Jackson.[13] Russell explains:

> Do we know events in us which would not be included in an absolutely complete knowledge of physics? I mean by a complete

> knowledge of physics a knowledge not only of physical laws, but also of what we may call geography, i.e., the distribution of energy throughout space-time. If the question is put in this way, I think it is quite clear that we do know things not included in physics. A blind man could know the whole of physics, but he could not know what things look like to people who can see, nor what is the difference between red and blue as seen. He could know all about wavelengths, but people knew the difference between red and blue as seen before they knew anything about wave-lengths. The person who knows physics and can see knows that a certain wave-length will give him a sensation of red, but his knowledge is not part of physics.
>
> (*OP*, p. 174)

Russell embraces introspective "knowledge." But the behaviorist sympathies of Russell's neutral monism led him to define "knowledge" as an ability of an organism to successfully engage the world. He writes that

> ... if we wish to give a definition of "knowing," we ought to define it as a manner of reacting to the environment, not as involving something (a "state of mind") which only the person who has knowledge can observe.[14]

A person who knows all of physics but has never experienced anything red gains, upon the experiencing of something red, a new ability of color discrimination which does not appeal to the physics of wavelengths. The nature of such an ability of discrimination, however, is itself a physical process in a brain and is thus completely understood as such by the person independently of acquiring the ability. Interestingly, the conception of knowing as an ability is commonly employed to reject the knowledge argument. This makes Russell's knowledge argument, if it is intelligible, much stronger than Jackson's argument.

Is it intelligible? Russell's conception of introspection is quite different from that of Descartes. Consider the following amusing juxtaposition of the Cartesian position that one only reliably knows—indeed, incorrigibly knows—the qualitative features of one's own states of mind and Watson's behaviorist thesis that knowledge of rats in mazes is the more reliable. Russell writes:

> Dr. Watson, like Descartes, is skeptical of many things which others accept without question; and like Descartes, he believes that there are some things so certain that they can be safely used as the basis of a startling philosophy. But the things which Dr. Watson regards as certain are just those which Descartes regarded as doubtful, and the thing which Dr. Watson most vehemently rejects is just what Descartes regarded as absolutely unquestionable. Dr. Watson maintains that there is no such thing as thinking. No doubt he believes in his own existence, but not because he thinks he can think. The things that strike him as absolutely indubitable are rats in mazes, time-measurements, physiological facts about glands and muscles, and so on. What are we to think when two able men hold such opposite views? The natural inference would be that *everything* is doubtful. This may be true, but there are degrees of doubtfulness, and we should like to know which of these two philosophers, if either, is right as to the region of minimum doubtfulness.
>
> (OP, p. 162)

Russell does not embrace Descartes's methodological solipsism: doubt everything that can be doubted to find a foundation for empirical knowledge. Russell accepts, provisionally, what we take ourselves to know since everything—everything contingent—is doubtful in some degree. Observe as well that Russell rejects Descartes's views on introspection in a way every bit as unsettling as Dennett's diatribe against qualia. Descartes demands that one cannot doubt the qualitative states of one's own mind. The qualitative experience normally produced by scalding hot water running on my hand is known immediately to me. Dennett might point out that I might well change my mind and describe the sensation as having been cold when I later realize that the water's temperature was 0 degrees Celsius. But Descartes would reply that the known regularity of low temperatures producing cold sensations and high temperatures producing heat sensations in no way impugns the fact that my original sensation was that of heat. No volume of scientifically well-established regular correlations between physical states of the body and sensation types can ever trump my own introspective awareness. It was, in fact, respect for the inviolability of that awareness that led to the scientific correlations—according to Descartes. But we see that Russell is with Dennett in this matter.

Russell does not think of introspection in a Cartesian way. The four-dimensionalism of Russell's neutral monism seems to get in the way of what it would normally mean to know the qualitative nature of an experience. No quale (the singular of "qualia") is ever an object to a transient subject, for qualia never occur in transient particulars. In Russell's view, qualia emerge from the series of brain states which constitute introspective awareness. The crux of the issue, therefore, turns on whether Russell can successfully recover introspection. He does it by a thesis that, at first, seems wholly jarring and unintelligible: Introspective knowledge is knowledge of one's own brain!

Russell's thesis provoked a storm of outrage—mostly, however, by its having been misunderstood. In his paper, for the Schilpp *festschrift* on Russell, Ernest Nagel bridled, not realizing the thesis is couched in four-dimensionalist neutral monism. It is worth quoting Russell's reply at length:

> Mr. Nagel says: "I know that I have never seen any portion of my brain, and that I have seen many physical objects." He goes on to explain that he is using "see" in its customary sense. It may be that my theory of matter is quite absurd, but at any rate it is not the theory that Mr. Nagel is refuting. I do not think that my visual

percepts are a "portion" of my brain; "portion" is a material concept. Briefly, omitting niceties and qualifications, my view is this: A piece of matter is a system of events; if the piece of matter is to be as small as possible, these events must all overlap, or be "compresent." Every event occupies a finite amount of space-time, i.e., overlaps with events which do not overlap with each other. Certain collections of events are "points" or perhaps minimum volumes, since the existence of collections generating points is uncertain. Causal laws enable us to arrange points (or minimum volumes) in a four-dimensional order. Therefore, when the causal relations of an event are known, its position in space-time follows tautologically. The causal and temporal connections of percepts with events in afferent and efferent nerves give percepts a position in the brain of the perceiver. Observe that a "portion" of a brain is a set of points (or minimum volumes); an event may be a member of certain points (or minimum volumes) that are members of the brain, and is then said to be "in" the brain, but it is not "part" of the brain. It is a member of a member of the brain.[15]

The causal correlations grounded in light interactions between events characterize the fineness of the overlapping. They may not be fine enough to construct stages which are "points," but rather only yield "minimum volumes," as Russell puts it. But in any case, it is the stages of the processes of neural activity that are "in" the brain, though not a "portion" of the brain (since a portion of a material continuant is itself a material continuant). Russell goes on:

> The inferences by which physicists pass from percepts to physical objects (which we are assuming valid) only enable us to know certain facts about the structure of the physical world as ordered by means of causal relations, compresence, and contiguity. Beyond certain very abstract mathematical properties, physics can tell us nothing about the character of the physical world. But there is one part of the physical world which we know otherwise than through physics, namely that part in which our thoughts and feelings are

situated. These thoughts and feelings, therefore, are members of the atoms (or minimum material constituents) of our brains. This theory may seem fantastic, but in any case, it is not the theory that Mr. Nagel refutes.[16]

The thesis is not fantastic when stated in terms of four-dimensionalism.

The thesis is fantastic, however, when put in terms of "seeing" and "knowing." Nagel is right to object to Russell's putting things in that way. Russell says:

> Let us suppose that a physiologist is observing a living brain—no longer an impossible supposition, as it would have been formerly. It is natural to suppose that what the physiologist sees is in the brain he is observing. But if we are speaking of physical space, what the physiologist sees is in his own brain. It is in no sense in the brain that he is observing, though it is in the percept of that brain, which occupies part of the physiologist's perceptual space. Causal continuity makes the matter perfectly evident; light-waves travel from the brain that is being observed to the eye of the physiologist, at which they only arrive after an interval of time, which is finite though short. The physiologist sees what he is observing only after the light-waves have reached his eye; therefore the event which constitutes his seeing comes at the end of a series of events which travel from the observed brain into the brain of the physiologist. We cannot, without a preposterous kind of discontinuity, suppose that the physiologist's percept, which comes at the end of this series, is anywhere but in the physiologist's head.
>
> (*OP*, p. 140)

Nagel is concerned that Russell's four-dimensionalism mandates a change in what it is to "see" something. Seeing is a process through time, not at a time. The stages of neural activities in the physiologist's brain are not properly described as cases of "seeing." It is rather a series of them that constitutes seeing. Russell writes figuratively to make his point dramatic. He is interested in recovering, against Watson, a form of introspection (i.e. self-observation). Thus he presents his position as if Watson, in looking at rats in mazes, is actually observing his own brain. In this way, Russell can say, against Watson, that subjectivity arises in spite of behaviorism's admirable efforts to introduce objectivity into psychology. Russell explains:

> But I shall be asked, what do you know about what is happening in the brain? Surely nothing. Not so, I reply. I know what is happening in the brain exactly what naïve realism thinks it knows about what is happening in the outside world.
>
> (*OP*, p. 132)

What Russell means to say is that knowledge consists of series of one's own brain stages—some of which are brain stages connected causally in series to stages which constitute matter (and so provide an organism's ability to successfully engage the world) and others of which are brain stages not so connected. Introspective knowledge is constituted by a series of physical transient stages of one's own brain. Qualia emerge from these series. Accordingly, naïve realism's colors, pitches, smells, tastes, and textures are emergent properties of series of brain states constituting introspection. They are not, as the naïve realist hoped, properties of matter. Nonetheless, they may be said to form the "hard" (i.e. more likely reliable) data from which our knowledge of matter must begin. In this, Descartes was correct and Watson mistaken.

The battle cry of behaviorism, Russell reminds us, is "death to images," "death to introspection" (*OP*, p. 176). Russell accepts images and introspection. But he is not a methodological solipsist and does not have a Cartesian view of introspection. Descartes was not correct that introspection is a special form of knowing different in kind from so-called knowledge that is physical. Introspective knowledge is not fundamentally different in kind from ordinary knowledge of external objects. Russell writes:

> There is thus something subjective and private about what we take to be external perception, but this is concealed by precarious extensions into the physical world. I think introspection, on the contrary, involves precarious extensions into the mental world; shorn of these, it is not very different from external perceptions shorn of its extensions.
>
> (OP, p. 11)

The behaviorist demands external perception, hoping to find objectivity. But in fact, Russell says, the behaviorist cannot secure a difference in kind between those series of his brain processes caused by events outside of his body and those caused independently and internally by his brain and sensory organs. In all cases, knowledge consists in series of his brain states. But the behaviorist's introspective knowledge is more immediate and less doubtful than his other knowledge. Introspective processes, in Russell's view, are at the foundation of all knowledge. All knowledge consists in inferences which essentially involve having been engaged in introspective, emergently qualitative knowledge constituted by physical transient particulars which make up one's own brain states.

Thus, Russell's neutral monism offers a strange twist on Jackson's knowledge argument. Suppose a person has complete knowledge of physics (the laws of material continuants persisting in time). Thus the person has complete knowledge of what happens neurologically when the states constituting "knowing what it is like to experience something red" occur. But there is no sub-series among the series stages that constitute such a person that constitute "knowing what it is like to experience red." The brain process of "knowing what it is like" has not occurred in the person. Thus physical knowledge can be complete and yet, essentially, exclude "knowing what it is like."

THE PROBLEM OF INDEXICALS

Russell's first evaluation of neutral monism in "On the Nature of Acquaintance" (1913) found worries that prevented him from adopting it. In the end, however, he did not find his worries very telling against the theory—except one: the problem of indexicals. The use of words such as "this," "now," "I," and "here" seem to involve selective mental acts of a mind or self which makes one object, one subject and one time, intimate, near and immediate, as no other object or subject or time can be to that subject at that time. Obviously, since Russell converted to neutral monism, it is important to see how he came to find this problem not insurmountable.

According to a four-dimensionalist form of neutral monism, the self is a series of stages. Russell raised the problem of indexicals because the content of a mental state of an object's being present is naturally expressed (in the first person) by saying "this." Now if there is no self, what is psychologically involved at a stage of a mind cannot be an acquaintance with self, but rather would be expressed as an acquaintance with a subject (leaving it open as to whether the subject in one stage is or is not identical with the subject occurring in another stage). Thus Russell says that in acquaintance with "this" there is a stage of the form

$$S'\text{-}P\text{-}(S\text{-}A\text{-}O)$$

of subject S' standing in a relation P of being present to a complex $S\text{-}A\text{-}O$ of a subject S being acquainted with object O. Russell writes that

> [w]hen such an experience occurs, we may say that we have an instance of "self-consciousness," or "experience of a present experience." But it is to be observed that there is no good reason why the two subjects S and S' should be numerically the same: the one "self" or "mind" which embraces both may be a construction, and need not so far as the logical necessities of our problem are concerned, involve the identity of the two subjects.[17]

Russell then hastens to add that it must be possible to pick out an experience as present without perceiving the above fact of presence, else we would be "embarked on a infinite regress." He writes that "... the subject concerned in the presence to 'me' must be defined by means of presence."[18] The main point is that when an object is in one's present experience, one is acquainted with it immediately, without the necessity of any further reflection upon the experience. The object is known to one without any further reflection as to its properties or relations.

Russell's thesis is that explicit reflection is not needed for an object to be present to acquaintance. He holds that presentness to a subject (not a mind) is important for understanding the indexical "this," which he says does not in any way describe the object to which it applies—though it applies to different objects on different occasions of its use. The indexical names at the moment at which the mind selects an object present to it. In this way, Russell explains, we speak of the subject of attention of a given subject at a given moment. The object described is the object which that subject at that moment will call "this." But, Russell goes on

> ... it would be an error to suppose that "this" means "the object to which I am now referring". "This" is a proper name ... "This" is not waiting to be defined by the property of being given, but is given; first it is actually given, and then reflection shows that it is "that which is given."[19]

Russell takes "this" to be the fundamental indexical. Other indexicals, "emphatic particulars," as Russell then called them, are defined in terms of "this." Russell defines "I" as "the subject attending to this" and "now" as "the time at which I am attending to this."

Russell's concern in "On the Nature of Acquaintance" with accommodating indexicals into neutral monism turns on his account of the "this-ness" which occurs at a stage.

His worry was that only a selective act of attention—something that only a mind does through time—could explain the "this" which occurs in a presentation at a stage. In *Analysis of Mind* Russell hopes to address this problem as a behaviorist. The selective act of a mind (persisting through time) is not required if, instead of selection, one imagines the verbal utterance "this is" produced causally in response to a stimulus. Russell writes:

> A verbal reaction to a stimulus may be immediate or delayed. When it is immediate, the afferent current runs into the brain and continues along an efferent nerve until it affects the appropriate muscles and produces a sentence beginning "this is." When it is delayed, the afferent impulse goes into some kind of reservoir, and only produces an efferent impulse in response to some new stimulus. The efferent impulse, in this case, is not exactly what it was in the previous case, and produces a slightly different sentence, namely one beginning "that was."
>
> (*IMT*, p. 112)

Russell hopes to ease his readers into accepting this account with the illustration of a machine which, when a red light falls upon it, "... sets in operation a mechanism which causes it first to say 'this is red,' and then after various internal processes have been completed, 'that was red.'"[20] But this illustration is no help at all if we consider the "this" of something's being present as a form of awareness, a consciousness. Russell's example shows clearly that consciousness is not part of the story. Machines, so far as have been developed even today, do not say anything; noises come out of them. Minds construct machines so that noises come out of them that they like—noises that they interpret and use for their purposes. A causal relation of the sort Russell invokes cannot hope to do justice to a conscious state of the form "this being present." But we decided that Russell's neutral monism is of the form B1. Consciousness (insofar as it involves the notion of qualia occurring at a stage) has dropped out of the story entirely.

The matter of reducing all indexicals to one fundamental indexical (i.e. "this") is taken up more fully in *Inquiry Into Meaning and Truth* (1940). Russell writes:

> All egocentric particulars can be defined in terms of "this." Thus: "I"

means "The biography to which this belongs"; "here" means "The place of "this"; "now" means "The time of this"; and so on. We may therefore confine our inquiry to "this." It does not seem equally feasible to take some other egocentric word as fundamental, and define "this" in terms of it. Perhaps, if we gave a name to "I-now," as opposed to "I-then," this name could replace "this"; but no word of common speech seems capable of replacing it.

(*IMT*, p. 108)

In Inquiry, Russell explains why he believes that neutral monism, according to which a conscious mind is a fiction constructed as a series of events, can accommodate the indexical "I." He writes:

The word "I," since it applies to something that persists through a certain period of time, is to be derived from "I-now" as that series of events which is related to "I-now" by certain causal relations. . . . The connection between "I-now" and "this" is obviously very close. "I-now" denotes a set of occurrences, namely all those that are happening to me at the moment. "This" denotes some one of these occurrences.

(*IMT*, p. 114)

Reichenbach's token-reflexive theory of indexicals was unpublished at the time Russell wrote Inquiry. But Russell offered a footnote to Reichenbach, noting that ". . . I don't think there is any inconsistency between his theory and mine, which complete each other."[21] It must be understood, however, that Reichenbach's theory has nothing to do with neutral monism. Reichenbach is discussing the use of indexicals by persons (i.e. minds) in communication.

On Reichenbach's view, every token of a given token reflexive word will refer to a different physical token, namely itself. All token reflexive words can be defined in terms of "this token." For example, "I" means "the person who utters this token" and "now" means "the time at which this token is uttered."[22] Like Russell's theory, Reichenbach's theory can reduce all indexicals to "this."

But the two are discussing different issues entirely. Reichenbach is discussing the use of indexicals in acts of communication. This use relies on shared conventions that minds contrive to make communication possible. Successful communication with pure indexical words such as "I" and "now" and demonstratives such as "here," "this," and "that" (which typically involve gesturing with one's body) require that a speaker understand something of the attitudes, beliefs, and perspectives of his or her audience. If minds are series of events, then so also is communication with the indexical "this." Russell would surely accept this consequence. Thus, it is quite a different notion of "this" that Russell is addressing. Russell is considering a theory which can explain how a stage of a mind can involve "being presented by this." Neither consciousness nor anything like phenomenal awareness plays a role in his account.

What then was Russell's opinion of the Cartesian "I think, therefore I am," which seemed for centuries to be at the foundation for modern philosophy, whether empiricist or rationalist? Russell writes: "It would be difficult to pack so large a number of errors into so few words."[23] Cartesians should bridle at so facile a dismissal. Russell wrongly takes Descartes's point to turn essentially on errors—one of which is to take "I am" to be the ungrammatical "I exist" which makes existence into a property. Russell makes his point comically:

> For it is obvious that, if you think of all the things there are in the world, they cannot be divided into two classes—namely, those that exist, and those that do not. Non-existence, in fact, is a very rare property. Everyone knows the story of the two German pessimistic philosophers of whom one exclaimed: "How much happier were it never to have been born." To which the other replied with a sigh: "True! But how few are those that achieve this happy lot."
>
> (*PfM*, p. 147)

But Descartes's point—that the presence of self-reflective awareness, when it occurs, is undoubtable—can be made without taking existence as a property. Moreover, his point does not even turn on the use of "I," which, it seems to me, is required only for communication with others. Self-reflexive awareness is not something which can be constituted at a stage by a relation between a transient *subject* and a transient object. For at a stage, there is no awareness at all, no phenomenal qualia, and no consciousness. It seems that Russell's original instincts were correct that neutral monism flounders on the problem of the subject, the problem of the conscious presentness of this.

IMAGES AND SENSATIONS CONSTITUTE MINDS

Russell's analysis of mind is intent on showing that minds can be constituted by series of images and sensations. Images are very important for series of them account for memories, dreams, hallucinations, and emotions—much of the life of the mind. Recall that in Russell's four-dimensionalist neutral monism the process of light reflecting from the surface of an object impinging on the sense organs and causing neural activity in the brain and nervous system is partitioned into stages. Sensations are the physical stages of the process that are neurological activities in the brain, nervous system, and sense organs. Certain neural activities in the brain and sense organs are grouped by causal laws into series in such a way that we speak of them as "caused" by material objects external to the mind. Others, however, belong in series which are grouped by mnemic laws, and as such we say that they are caused "internally." Stages of such neural activities grouped into series by mnemic laws are "images."

To account for emotions, Russell is attracted to the controversial James-Lange theory. James states the view as follows:

> Our natural way of thinking about these coarser emotions (e.g. "grief, fear, rage, love") is that the mental perception of some fact excites the mental affection called the emotion, and that this latter state of mind gives rise to the bodily expression. My theory, on the

contrary, is that *the bodily changes follow directly the perception of the exciting fact, and that our feeling of the same changes as they occur IS the emotion.*[24]

On James's view, it seems, we feel sorry because we cry! Whoever embraces this view, it seems to me, has lost sight of the phenomenal character of an emotion entirely. Of course, there are objections from the standpoint of physiology. Sometimes we cry when we feel glad and different affectations of the viscera may accompany dissimilar emotions. But the physiological data are not conclusive on either side. If James is right, an emotion may be regarded as involving a confused perception of the viscera concerned in its causation. Competing physiological data suggests that an emotion involves a confused perception of its external stimulus. In either case, Russell concludes that "the ingredients of an emotion are only sensations and images and bodily movements succeeding each other according to a certain pattern" (AMi, p. 284). Thus only images and sensations are needed in accounting for them.

Concerning dreams and hallucinations, it is natural, following Hume, to think that images can be distinguished from sensations because they are faint, less vivid, and by the absence of their compelling us to believe they are caused by material objects outside our own bodies. Ultimately, however, Russell rejects these criteria for distinguishing them. Russell writes:

> To begin with: we do not always know whether what we are experiencing is a sensation or an image. The things we see in dreams when our eyes are shut must count as images, yet while we are dreaming they seem like sensations. Hallucinations often begin as persistent images, and only gradually acquire that influence over belief that makes the patient regard them as sensations. When we are listening for a faint sound—the striking of a distant clock, or a horse's hoofs on the road—we think we hear it many times before we really do, because expectation brings us the image, and we mistake it for sensation. The distinction between

> images and sensations is, therefore, by no means always obvious to inspection.
>
> (*AMi*, p. 145)

Of course a representative realist puts the point by saying that dreams and hallucinations can be qualitatively phenomenally indistinguishable from sense-experiences caused by material objects outside the body. The phenomenal indistinguishability between a dream or a hallucinatory state and a sensation lies at the root of thinking that images, especially visual images, are "copies" of sensations "as regards the simple qualities that enter into them." Russell reminds us that it is generally believed that we can neither imagine a color that we have never seen, nor a sound that we have never heard. Images often resemble antecedent sensations. That is why images are regarded as "images of" this or that. Russell notes the importance of this for memory, but he expresses doubts as to whether a theory that images are copies of sensations is adequate to the data.[25] Russell does not characterize the distinction between images and sensations by appeal to any phenomenal features for, as we have seen, the phenomenal has dropped out of his neutral monism.

Russell concludes that the only universally applicable criterion to distinguish images and sensations is the fact that their causes and effects are different. Of course, the implication is that it is only by appeal to the different sorts of series in which they occur that they can be distinguished. An image is a stage of a series of neural states which is not also a constituent of another series which constitutes material continuants persisting in time outside of our bodies.

Russell explains:

> However, this may be, the practically effective distinction between sensations and images, the stimulation of nerves carrying an effect into the brain, usually from the surface of the body, plays an essential part. And this accounts for the fact that images and sensations cannot always be distinguished by their intrinsic nature. Images also differ from sensations as regards their effects.

Sensations, as a rule, have both physical and mental effects. As you watch the train you meant to catch leaving the station, there are both the successive positions of the train (physical effects) and the successive waves of fury and disappointment (mental effects). Images, on the contrary, though they may produce bodily movement, do so according to mnemic laws, not according to the laws of physics. All their effects, of whatever nature, follow mnemic laws. But this difference is less suitable for definition than the difference as to causes.

(*AMi*, p. 151)

In this respect, Russell's neutral monism offers an aid to behavioristic psychology. It shows how to embrace images without reintroducing features of consciousness anathema to Watson's behaviorism. Watson was intent on excising visual imagery from the science of psychology since he thought that accepting images runs a grave danger of reintroducing into psychology qualitative, unmeasurable features of consciousness awareness. Russell is no friend of the qualitative in his acceptance of images as distinct from sensations. But his appeal to differences in causes and effects distinguishes neural states that may be called "images" as opposed to "sensations," and thus rehabilitates the notion. In an amusing passage chiding Watson, Russell writes:

Professor Watson says: "I should throw out imagery altogether and attempt to show that all natural thought goes on in terms of sensori-motor processes in the larynx." This view, seems to me flatly to contradict experience. If you try to persuade any uneducated person that she cannot call up a visual picture of a friend sitting in a chair, but can only use words describing what such an occurrence would be like, she will conclude that you are mad. (This statement is based upon experiment.) Galton, as everyone knows, investigated visual imagery, and found that education tends to kill it; the Fellows of the Royal Society turned out to have much less of it than their wives. I see no reason to doubt his conclusion that the habit of

Mind and Matter

> abstract pursuits makes learned men much inferior to the average in power of visualizing, and much more exclusively occupied with words in their "thinking." And Professor Watson is a very learned man.
>
> (*AMi*, p. 154)

There is nothing more distracting from the obvious than being caught up in a theory, and Watson was certainly caught up in a theory when he attempted to replace imagistic thinking by micro motor movements in the larynx. Nonetheless, Russell is more sympathetic with the view than he lets on. We see this when he writes that "[o]ur power of acting with reference to what is sensibly absent is largely due to this [copying] characteristic of images, although, as education advances, images tend to be more and more replaced by words."[26]

Images play a central role in memory. It is here that Russell becomes most worried about Hume's principle that images are copies. The sensation that an image is supposed to copy is past when the image exists, and thus it can only be known by memory. And a past sensation can only be known by memory by means of present images. But of course, one can have a "memory-belief" which depicts an event that never transpired. In a passage that is now famous, Russell notes that ". . . there is no logical impossibility in the hypothesis that the world sprang into existence five minutes ago, exactly as it then was, with a population that 'remembered' a wholly unreal past."[27] Obviously, an image cannot copy something that never existed. If we are to maintain that images are copies of sensations, it must be based on something more than the occurrence of images from which our beliefs are formed. Of course, images without beliefs do not constitute memory and, Russell points out, associations and habits are even less sufficient. Russell concludes that behaviorists encounter insuperable difficulties in their attempt to explain memory. "The behaviourist," he writes, "who attempts to make psychology a record of behaviour, has to trust his memory in making the record."[28] Memory-images can be explained by association and habit, but memory-beliefs which confer on memory-images the conception that the image points to something that occurred in the past, cannot. A memory-belief is expressed by "this occurred," but Russell hastens to point out that "this" is used vaguely in such a belief since its reference is not literally to the existing image, but to a past sensation which is to be what it copies.[29] But it is needed for his account; moreover, the past tense of "occurred" is explained by Russell as merely a "feeling of familiarity."

NEUTRAL MONISM AND TRUTH

In the *Analysis of Mind*, Russell explicitly rejects Franz Brentano's famous thesis that the feature essential to what is mental—as opposed to physical—is intentionality. Mental "objects" are about other objects. Russell writes that "Until very lately I believed, as he [Brentano] did that mental phenomena have essential reference to objects, except possibly in the case of pleasure and pain. Now I no longer believe this, even in the case of knowledge" (*AMi*, p. 18)." The problem of representation is particularly acute if one adopts neutral monism. As a series of stages, a mind is not a whole that can have properties which are not products of the overall pattern of the ordering of its stages. Yet the notion of representation (and misrepresentation) seems to require an appeal to the needs, purposes, and capacities to learn of the mind. No "thing" is a representation in virtue of features intrinsic to it. So, it would seem, no stage can be a representation! There is a popular example due to Hilary Putnam that illustrates the point:

> An ant is crawling on a patch of sand. As it crawls, it traces a line in the sand. By pure chance the line that it traces curves and re-crosses itself in such a way that it ends up looking like a recognizable caricature of Winston Churchill. Has the ant traced a picture of Winston Churchill, a picture that depicts Winston

Churchill? . . . If lines in the sand, noises, etc., cannot "in themselves" represent anything, then how is it that thought forms can "in themselves" represent anything? . . . What is important to realize is that what goes for physical pictures also goes for mental images, and for mental representations in general; mental representations no more have a necessary connection with what they represent than physical representations do. The contrary assumption is a survival of magical thinking.[30]

Putnam goes on to say that

[e]ven a large and complex system of representations, both verbal and visual, still does not have an intrinsic, built-in, magical connection with what it represents—a connection independent of how it was caused and what the dispositions of the speaker or thinker are. And this is true whether the system of representations . . . is physically realized—the words are written or spoken, and the pictures are physical pictures—or only realized in the mind. Thought words and mental pictures do not intrinsically represent what they are about.[31]

A thing can be said to be a representation for an organism only insofar as the organism uses it to realize its purposes.

Putnam is correct that something's being a representation is tied essentially to the sorts of causal relations it has—causal relations which, it would seem, involve a mind's activities in nature. Neutral monism seems to make matters even more puzzling, for a mind is a series of stages, none of which, if Putnam is correct, is intrinsically a representation. It is not enough to simply say, on behalf of neutral monism, that, whatever constitutes the causal process through time of an organism's representing its environment, one can always chop up the process into a fleeting series of stages. The nature of representation is particularly mysterious at the level of the mind; it is at the center of the problem of naturalizing the mind.

Seen in this way, it is not clear that neutral monism is playing a significant role in addressing the mind-body problem where representation is concerned. The work is being done by naturalism and behaviorism. Russell agrees that it is a mind or self which knows, not a stage of a mind which knows. Dewey, deferring to the evolution of behavior patterns in animals, would say that a mind "knows" in virtue of the series of its belief states being in proper attunement (i.e. "equilibrium") with states of the world. But which states of the world are the appropriate ones and what counts as attunement? In evolution little more can be said about this attunement than that it is produced by the survival of an organism long enough to reproduce. As we shall see, Russell hopes to preserve more of the traditional meanings of "representation" and "knowledge" in his account. Nonetheless he writes:

> We may regard knowledge, from a behaviourist standpoint, as exhibited in a certain kind of response to the environment. This response must have some characteristics which it shares with those of scientific instruments, but must have others that are peculiar to knowledge. . . . We may regard a human being as an instrument, which makes various responses to various stimuli. If we observe these responses from the outside, we shall regard them as showing knowledge when they display two characteristics, *accuracy* and *appropriateness*.
>
> (*AMi*, p. 254)

Viewing a person "from the outside" means that we eschew appeals to beliefs, desires, wants, and the like. Russell explains that accuracy is not enough for knowledge. He writes:

> A thermometer which went down for warm weather and up for cold might be just as accurate as the usual kind; and a person who always believes falsely is just as sensitive an instrument as a person who always believes truly. The observable and practical difference between them would be that the one who always believed falsely would quickly come to a bad end. This illustrates once more that

accuracy of response to a stimulus does not alone show knowledge, but must be reinforced by appropriateness, i.e., suitability for realizing one's purposes.

(AMi, p. 261)

Anticipating concerns in Fred Dretske's "Misrepresentation" (1986), Russell notes that accuracy of response is possessed equally by machines such as thermometers as well as pigeons, but he adds that the key is appropriateness, which requires appeal to needs and purposes of an organism. "We do not say the machine knows the answer," Russell writes, "because it has no purpose..."[32]

Dretske reminds us that some anaerobic marine bacteria have organs which enable them to orient and swim to oxygen-depleted environments on the sea floor. In what respect can these organs be said to represent oxygen-depleted areas? Appeal to the needs and purposes of the bacteria to be free from oxygen is not enough to assure representation. Evolutionary selection works equally well if the organ of the bacterium orients to the magnetic north rather than to oxygen depletion. The bacterium will survive and reproduce as long as the ocean floor is in the direction of magnetic north. Dretske's reply is that the bacterium does not represent, and so does not misrepresent. Only those organisms that can learn and adapt to changes in the environment may be said to represent. I think Russell's response is the same. Consider the following passage concerning what it is for an organism to "know" something. Russell writes:

> We may say generally that an object whether animate or inanimate, is "sensitive" to a certain feature of the environment if it behaves differently accordingly to the presence or absence of that feature. Thus, iron is sensitive to anything magnetic. But sensitiveness does not constitute knowledge, and knowledge of a fact which is not sensible is not sensitiveness to that fact, as we have seen in distinguishing the fact known from the sensation. As soon as we

> pass beyond the simple case of question and answer, the definition of knowledge by means of behaviour demands the consideration of purpose. A carrier pigeon flies home, and so we say it "knows" the way. But if it merely flew to some place at random, we should not say that it "knew" the way to that place, any more than a stone rolling down hill knows the way to the valley. On the features which distinguish knowledge from accuracy of response in general, not much can be said from a behaviourist point of view without referring to purpose.
>
> (AMi, p. 260)

A Cartesian would revile at talk of iron being "sensitive" to a magnet. It is at best figurative speech. Iron moves in the presence of a magnet, but so also does a stone move in rolling downhill. Neither is "sensitive" to anything. Newtonians rejected the Cartesian demand to use only mechanical tools of explanation, but they too would revile at this use of "sensitive"—unless, of course, one can write a quantitative law and corroborate experimentally this new relation of "being sensitive to." That sort of quantitative law can be done for the electromagnetic currents, expansion of mercury in a thermometer, and the firing potential of a neuron in the retina. But this has precious little to do with the notion of "sensation" in the ordinary use of the word, the notion that refers to a mind's conscious qualitative experiences. Be this as it may, the important point in the passage is that in Russell's view, that notion of something having "knowledge" presupposes that the thing has purposes which can be fulfilled by learning an appropriate response to an ever changing environment.

But how then is a naturalist to define the notion of purpose? If an organism is just a complex system of chemicals responding to physical laws, then purpose seems difficult to recover. Surely a plant has no purpose in undergoing photosynthesis any more than a rock has a purpose in rolling down a hill. Many, if not most, animals might then be viewed similarly; at least simple animals such as insects and small vertebrates can be viewed this way. Russell could say that the plant's turning its leaves to the sun is an appropriate response to the stimulus because in so doing the plant continues to live. But life is not a notion that has any particular status in Russell's philosophy. He writes that

> ... the distinction between what is living and what is dead is not absolute. There are viruses concerning which specialists cannot make up their minds whether to call them living or dead, and the principle of the conditioned reflex, though characteristic of what is living, finds some exemplification in other spheres. For example, if you unroll a roll of paper, it will role itself up again as soon as it can. But in spite of such cases, we may take the conditioned reflex as characteristic of life, especially in its higher forms, and above all as characteristic of human intelligence.
>
> (*PfM*, p. 154)

Perhaps, however, it is by appeal to complex capacities for learning that the notion of purpose can finally be excised from naturalism. An animal that can learn to respond to environmental changes may be said to have a self-defined purpose in the sense that by learning new responses it changes, as it were, its own programming.

We are beginning to see that the four-dimensionalism of neutral monism has little role to play in the recovery of ordinary notions of representation and knowledge. Naturalism is propping up neutral monism, addressing the mind/matter problem, not the other way around. Naturalism (in an unstable alliance with certain behaviorist ideas) is the centerpiece of Russell's neutral monism. The neutral monism comes in fundamentally to disabuse readers of their ordinary belief in the existence of mind and matter (as continuants persisting in time). Seeing both as series of stages which are physical allows us to transcend what appears to be an unbridgeable chasm between mental and material. But the heart of the theory is naturalism, which is doing all the work.

There is, however, something of an exception in the case of Russell's attempt to recover the notions of truth and falsehood. The neutral monism of James and Dewey is a form of naturalism about the mind, and they each recognized the problem of recovering traditional notions of representation, belief, and truth within it. James's pragmatism abandoned the notion of truth altogether, hoping to replace it by the notion of workability or success. Dewey's naturalism led him to a form of pragmatism which abandoned representation and truth in favor of the notion of attunement or a state of equilibrium of an organism with its environment. Indeed, Dewey was, at times, even willing to take his naturalism to the extreme position that the organism/environment distinction should be transcended! Perhaps an example will illustrate how he arrived at such an untoward philosophical thesis.

Consider a bee colony. One may marvel at the complex relationship between the colony and the flowers from which the bees extract the pollen so central to their survival. How do the bees find the flowers? Is there something within each individual bee that represents the flower and directs its quest? Can we attribute true beliefs to a bee concerning flowers? Dewey's homage to evolution is radical; we are to consider a system of chemicals composing what we call flowers and bees. It is the system of chemicals that has reached a state of equilibrium (i.e. stability) by a process of evolution. Our questions concerning representational states in the bee, belief, and truth are confused. The bee does not exist as an organism in nature that is properly separable from the flower. We confusedly consider it as if it were a separate organism, and it is this that generates our problem of understanding its little mind and the problem of representation. The bees and the flowers evolved together as a system of chemicals, not separately as independent organisms which need to get matched up.

Russell's neutral monism, no less than Dewey's, embraces naturalism, but he does not embrace Dewey's abandonment of traditional notions of representation, belief, and truth. Indeed, Russell lampooned the Peirce/James's pragmatist notion of truth as workability and Dewey's notion of equilibrium. Russell writes:

> Why does Peirce think that there is an "ideal limit towards which endless investigation would tend to bring scientific belief"? Does it contain any element of prophesy, or is it a merely hypothetical statement of what would happen if men of science grew continually cleverer? Whether the theory of relativity will be believed twenty years hence depends mainly on whether Germany wins the next war. Whether it should be believed by people cleverer than we are we cannot tell without being cleverer than we are.[33]

The pragmatist seems at a loss to explain "the long run" and what is "workable" without appealing parochially to the interests and goals of some particular favored group. Dewey hoped that appeal to evolution and the success of a theory in engaging the world solves the problem. Russell has a naturalist account of knowing as an ability of an organism to successfully engage its environment, but he cannot bring himself to supplant the ordinary definition of "truth" by a notion of the success of a theory. In Russell's view, Dewey's naturalism runs together the epistemic matter of knowing and the ontological matter of truth. The Aristotelian and Ptolemaic conception of the earth at rest enabled for centuries a successful engagement with the world, but in the fifteenth century it was no longer successful. Ptolemaic epicycles posed serious difficulties for navigation by the stars on the treacherous oceans. The lucrative economy of sea trade demanded new navigational tools and favored Copernicus's simple system with the sun at the center. But this change in success is irrelevant to whether the earth is at the center of the cosmos. Russell takes the example of the sentence "Caesar was assassinated." Caesar's assassination was produced by a single event that happened long ago; nothing that has happened since (e.g. the use of this statement to successfully pass exams in school, the writing of lucrative history books, etc.) or what will happen in the future (e.g.

cross-checking history books and manuscripts) can affect its truth or falsehood. Russell writes:

> The broad issue may be stated as follows: Whether we accept or reject the words "true" and "false," we are all agreed that assertions can be divided into two kinds, sheep and goats. Dr. Dewey holds that a sheep may become a goat, and vice versa, but admits the dichotomy at any given moment: The sheep have "warranted assertibility" and the goats have not. Dr. Dewey holds that the division is to be defined by the *effects* of assertions, while I hold, at least as regards empirical assertions, that it is to be defined by their *causes*. An empirical assertion which can be known to be true has percepts, or a percept, among its proximate or remote causes. But this only applies to knowledge: so far as the *definition* of truth is concerned, causation is only relevant in conferring meaning upon words.[34]

Evolution has no end or goal, and those temporarily favored by selective pressures now may well not be fit enough to survive selective environmental pressures at a later time. We do not need the notions of representation, belief, and truth if we are trying to explain by the process of natural selection that animals living today have become and continue to be suited to their environment. The tools of evolutionary theory (i.e. natural selection) seem too weak to support the recovery of the ordinary notions.

In the *Analysis of Mind* Russell endeavors to sketch a way to recover the orthodox correspondence theory of truth that a belief (at least in the simplest case) is true when it corresponds to a fact. His first problem is to recover the notion of belief. Without a mind persisting in time, this is far from straightforward. What is it about a series of sensations and images that makes them constitute a mind believing that something is the case? Now following behaviorism, one might think to define a belief as a disposition which has a certain sort of causal efficacy, which Russell calls "voluntary movements," distinct from reflex. The behaviorist, of course, is careful to exclude consciousness or will in the characterization of "voluntary movements." They are rather those "vital movements which are distinguished from reflex movements as involving the higher nervous centers." Russell finds the behaviorist definition promising but ultimately inadequate since some beliefs seem not to be dispositions toward behavior.[35]

Russell's positive theory is that there are at least three kinds of belief: memory-belief, expectation-belief, and bare assent. Each, he says, is constituted by a feeling which is a complex of sensations attached to the content believed.[36] Russell's account is very sketchy and in want of improvement. In the case of expectation-belief, Russell considers the non-verbal image-belief that it will rain. He writes:

> We have here two interrelated elements, namely the content and the expectation. The content consists of images of (say) the visual appearance of rain, the feeling of wetness, the patter of drops, interrelated, roughly, as the sensations should be if it were raining. Thus the content is a complex fact composed of images. Exactly the same content may enter into the memory "it was raining" or the assent "rain occurs." The difference of these cases from each other and from expectation does not lie in the content. The difference lies in the nature of the belief-feeling. I, personally, do not profess to be able to analyse the sensations constituting respectively memory, expectation and assent; but I am not prepared to say that they cannot be analysed. There may be other belief-feelings, for example in disjunction and implication; also a disbelief-feeling.
>
> (*AMi*, p. 250)

Russell's task is daunting. Consider how difficult it is to accommodate such complicated (and yet wholly commonplace) beliefs as: Everything iron is such that if it is raining then it will rust unless it is painted. One might have supposed that the problem is with the content of the belief. The syntactic compositionality of the words seems to reflect the semantic compositionality of a complex belief content. Russell's approach suggests, to the contrary, that there are several contents composed of images (e.g. "it is iron," "it is raining," "it will rust," "it is painted"), and these are put together by belief feelings of different sorts. There is the assent-feeling, the if-then-feeling, the not-feeling (or perhaps dissent or disbelief feeling), the everything-is-such-that-feeling, and the expectation-feeling since future tense is involved. Russell's view seems hopeless. But it is not preposterous. The computer age was just dawning in 1921. Using modern computational theories of mind, one could make sense of Russell's different belief-feelings in terms of computational states, where logical operations (i.e. Boolean operations) are implemented by binary electric circuits.

The difference between Russell's recovery of the notions of belief and representation and Dewey's elimination of these notions parallels, in an interesting way, the modern dispute between recursive (Turing and von Neumann) models of computation and connectionist (distributed or non-representational) models. If neural states implement recursive transitions over structural features of units (i.e. representations) which can be stored and retrieved, then we have a modern analog of Russell's idea. Interestingly, one of the currently popular metaphors used in understanding memory in a way that departs from a recursive storage-retrieval model is Russell's own suggestion that memory is an activation pattern which has been induced into the brain in a way akin to the way water flowing over a plain produces troughs which over time deepen to form rivers.[37] The connectivity of neurons in the brain is staggering even at birth, and by a process of reinforcement and atrophy certain pathways become rigidified. It is not an all or none affair. Certain features of cognition may be performed in a non-representational way; others (e.g. deductive reasoning, applied statistics, and other forms of reflective applications of inductive reasoning) may well require representations implemented by neural activity.

Memory-beliefs consist of images, and the contents of these images are called "image propositions." In contrast, some belief contents are images which have become associated with utterances in words. Image-propositions antedate word-propositions since they do not require learning the associations which constituted mastery of a natural language. Russell hopes to accommodate, in the fashion of behaviorism, the "meaning of words" by appealing to associations between images and sound patterns given when one learns a language. At long last Russell arrives at the following:

> The purely formal definition of truth and falsehood offers little difficulty. What is required is a formal expression of the fact that a proposition is true when it points to its objective, and false when it points away from its objective. In very simple cases we can give a very simple account of this: we can say that true propositions actually resemble their objectives in a way in which false propositions do not. But for this purpose it is necessary to revert to image-propositions instead of word propositions. . . . In this case the correspondence which constitutes truth is very simple.
> (AMi, p. 273)

Thus in the simple case, the content of a true memory-belief (i.e. a structured event) can have parts caused in such a way that its structure is isomorphic to the structure of the event causing it; and if it is, Russell speaks of it as "corresponding" to that event. An image-proposition, it must be noted, cannot be the content of an image of something's being absent (AMi, p. 276). There are no such images. The absence of something cannot cause a sensation. The notion of correspondence for such simple cases of image-propositions is not very interesting, however. One wants an account of the complicated notion of correspondence for word-propositions.

Recall that the recursive theory of truth and falsehood of Principia (together with the attempted refinements in Problems and the unfinished book Theory of Knowledge) offered a detailed account of the different notions of correspondence. The foundation of the recursive theory was Russell's multiple-relation theory of belief and the theory of definite descriptions. The notion that a given sentence is true was to be analyzed by forming a definite description of the structure of the would-be corresponding fact and asserting its existence. If there is no such fact, the sentence is false. Hence "falsehood," in the simple cases, is defined as the absence of a corresponding fact. But Russell came to hold this theory fails and that universals have only a predicable nature and so cannot occur as one of the relata in a belief fact or stand in a simple two-placed relation of acquaintance between a mind and a universal. Russell was left with the problem that there is no way to use definite descriptions to describe the would-be corresponding facts. Russell remarks that in his 1914 lectures at Harvard he was inclined to accept negative facts in his ontology, in spite of its "nearly producing a riot." In his 1919 paper "On Propositions: What They Are And How They Mean" he discusses his inclination for negative facts as follows:

> There might be an attempt to substitute for a negative fact the mere absence of a fact. If A loves B, it may be said, that is a good substantial fact; while if A does not love B, that merely expresses the absence of a fact composed of A and *loving* and B, and by no means involves the actual existence of a negative fact. But the absence of a fact is itself a negative fact; it is the fact that there is not such a fact as A loving B. Thus, we cannot escape from negative facts in this way.[38]

Russell himself had tried to escape from negative facts in just this way. His own multiple-relation theory maintained that the sentence "A loves B" is false when there is no corresponding fact. Now converted to neutral monism, the problem of correspondence is acute. Unfortunately, Russell never succeeded in rendering an account.

Russell's argument for negative facts seems to me unconvincing. To say "The absence of a fact is itself a fact" uses the word "fact" in two distinct ways. On the recursive theory of truth, a fact is a complex composed of a relation relating certain entities. It may well be a fact that there does not exist a given complex composed (in the right order) of A and B and the relation *loving*. But that is simply to say that the sentence "There is no fact consisting of A being related by 'loves' to B" is true. This is a complex sentence involving quantification and negation. What makes it true, according to the recursive theory, is not any single fact. Do absences have causal powers? We often speak this way; the absence of a person acting in our lives seems to cause emptiness and loneliness. It is a very interesting question, however, whether in a physical process the absence of something plays a role. For example, all too readily we speak as if the absence of water causes the cell membranes in a plant to break. But surely it is the presence of unequal pressure on either sides of the cell membrane that causes it to break. The presence of water, among the many other functions it serves for plants, keeps the pressure equal. The concept of negation or of absence seems, however, to be ineliminable.

Russell's failure to do justice to belief and truth is the Achilles' heel of his neutral monism. One striking consequence of neutral monism is the extensionality of belief. Perhaps Russell's best efforts to show that this consequence is not absurd are in the second edition of *Principia*, where he attempted to sketch a theory according to which contexts of belief are extensional. The steps were largely retraced in *Inquiry into Meaning and Truth*.

STRUCTURAL REALISM

Russell's neutral monism is a theory which eliminates traditional matter and mind in favor of series (i.e. relations) of transient particulars, some of which realize laws of relativistic physics and some of which realize mnemic laws of (behaviorist) psychology. A given series persists through a temporal interval in virtue of having some sub-series of its transient particulars occur at times in that interval. In Russell's view, some transient particular may occur in both series. Transient particulars are physical events, but they are neutral with respect to what sort of series they may be part of. This is a four-dimensionalist theory of persistence (i.e. sameness through change). It rejects methodological solipsism. Russell is giving a theory of how we know from the perspective of what we know (i.e. physics and psychology).

It must be understood, however, that in Russell's view what we know in science is the structure of the world, not the intrinsic properties of the objects (if any) that compose it. The success and progress of science is explained by our improved accounts of its structure. Much of nineteenth-century science was predicated on a wave model of the physical world. Various subtle fluids were assumed to account for heat transfer (caloric fluid), combustion (phlogiston), the nature and propagation of light (luminiferous aether), and so on. These scientific theories were very successful at accounting for a vast field of phenomena and proved very useful for predicting and explaining the world and controlling nature. But from the perspective of twentieth-century physics they got the objects quite wrong. There is no caloric, no phlogiston, and no luminiferous aether. The success of these early wave theories is best explained, however, not by some sociological account that divorces science from being made true by the world. It is best explained by the fact that they did get something approximately right: the structure.

In Russell's view, the new science of relativity and especially the new quantum mechanics reveal that nothing can be known about the nature of material simples. Russell writes that "Whatever we infer from perception it is only structure that we can validly infer; and structure is what can be expressed by mathematical logic" (*AMa*, p. 254). He goes on to say that "The only legitimate attitude about the physical world seems to be one of complete agnosticism as regards all but its mathematical properties" (*AMa*, p. 270).

A curious episode occurred when Russell's structural realism was criticized by a Cambridge mathematician, M. H. A. Newman, who published a little piece in 1928 suggesting that if Russell's structural realism is correct, it trivializes physics.[39] The exchange between the two, later revealed in Russell's *Autobiography*, went largely unnoticed. Russell wrote a gracious letter to Newman, agreeing in part with his criticism:

> Dear Newman:
> Many thanks for sending me the off-print of your article about me in Mind. I read it with great interest and some dismay. You make it entirely obvious that my statements to the effect that nothing is known about the physical world except its structure are either false or trivial, and I am somewhat ashamed at not having noticed the point for myself.
>
> (*A*, vol. II, p. 176)

We must not exaggerate Russell's chagrin.[40] He goes on in the letter to explain that a more refined statement of his position is viable. In fact, Russell never gave up his structural realism.

The general mathematical theory of order-types of structure is a theory of well-ordering relations over a field. (A relation is a linear ordering if it orders the members of the field so that, for any two, one is before the other. It is well-ordered if also any non-empty subset of them has a first in the ordering.) A given structure is thus defined by Russell as the collection of well-ordering relations which are isomorphic to one another and which structure the field in question. If a field is infinite (like the natural numbers), many different non-isomorphic relations can well order the field. There is, for example, the structure given by the relation < which gives the natural ordering of the natural numbers. But there are others that are not isomorophic with <. For instance, there is a well-ordering relation that puts all the natural numbers besides 2 and then the number 2. If, on the other hand, the field is finite, then the cardinal number of objects in the field is sufficient to fix the structure. For example, if there are exactly two objects a and b in the field, then the well-ordering relation R may be simply the thesis that aRb. Any other well-ordering relation over that field will be isomorphic to it. For instance eSd is isomorphic in structure. A one-to-one function f can be found such that $fa = e$ and $fb = d$ and is such that:

aRb if and only if $fa\ S\ fb$.

The number of objects (i.e. the cardinality) in the field is all that matters. Now if the number of objects of the world relevant to a given empirical theory in question is finite, then any structural realist theory for that field seems to be isomorphic to any other which has the same cardinal number in its field. The finite cardinality of the field by itself determines structure type that is realizable. This would, therefore, make the physical theory (as a theory of structure) in that field uninteresting—it speaks, ultimately, only about cardinality.

Of course, if the field of the relation embraces infinitely many objects, then cardinality is not sufficient to determine the kind of structure in question. But Russell's kind letter of reply did not wish to put too much emphasis on this point.[41] Instead, Russell explains that he spoke too emphatically; there is a bit more known about the world in a given field of physics than the structure type. He writes:

> I had always assumed spacio-temporal continuity with the world of percepts, that is to say, I had assumed that there might be co-punctuality between percepts and non-percepts, and even that one could pass by a finite number of steps from one event to another compresent with it, from one end of the universe to the other. And copunctuality I regarded as a relation which might exist among percepts and is itself perceptible.
>
> (*A*, vol. II, p. 260)

Russell is suggesting that he had assumed that it can be known that the structure of a given percept (a stage in a mind) must be isomorphic to the structure of the event that causes it. Thus, strictly speaking, something more than merely the mathematical structure type is known.[42]

Whatever may be said about the strengths and weaknesses of Russell's analysis of mind, it is a truly admirable work of philosophy. So also is Russell's analysis of matter. We have already had occasion to discuss the analysis of matter in connection with Russell's many emendations to *Our Knowledge of the External World*. The issues were taken over, of course, in *Analysis of Matter*, where a technical interpretation of Einstein's theory of relativity is given and a four-dimensionalist theory of material continuants is attempted. We need not suffer over the complicated details. Russell agrees with Eddington's four-dimensionalist interpretation of relativity which, he thinks, helps in understanding the strange new theory where time and space are not invariant under different reference frames. This is a structuralist theory, and it also comes to the aid of the problem of understanding the objects of the odd new quantum theory with its indeterminacies and non-localities of the "particles" composing the atom. Russell explains:

> The physical world, both through the theory of relativity and through the most recent doctrines as to the structure of the atom, has become very different from the world of everyday life and also from that of scientific materialism of the eighteenth-century variety. No philosophy can ignore the revolutionary changes in our physical ideas that the men of science have found necessary; indeed, it may be said that all traditional philosophies have to be discarded, and we have to start afresh with as little respect as possible for the systems of the past. . . . Until 1925, theories of the structure of the atom were based upon the old conception of matter as indestructible substance, although this was already regarded as no more than a convenience. Now, owing chiefly to two German physicists, Heisenberg and Schrodinger, the last vestiges of the old solid atom have melted away, and matter has become as ghostly as anything in a spiritual séance.
>
> (*OP*, p. 97)

The aim of the new quantum theory, Russell goes on:

> . . . is to confine the theory to what is empirically verifiable, namely radiations; as to what there is where the radiations come from, we

cannot tell, and it is scientifically unnecessary to speculate. The theory requires modifications in our conception of space, of a sort not yet quite clear. It also has the consequence that we cannot identify an electron at one time with an electron at another, if in the interval, the atom has radiated energy. The electron ceases altogether to have the properties of a "thing" as conceived by common sense; it is merely a region from which energy may radiate.

(*OP*, p. 106)

Thus the new theories in physics, both from the quantum mechanics of the 1920s and from Einstein's theory of relativity (special 1905; and general 1915), have demolished the theory of matter of the science and philosophy that preceded it. The following is quite wonderful:

The main point for the philosopher in the modern theory is the disappearance of matter as a "thing." It has been replaced by emanations from a locality—the sort of influences that characterize haunted rooms in ghost stories.... the theory of relativity leads to a similar destruction of the solidity of matter, by a different line of argument. All sorts of events happen in the physical world, but tables and chairs, the sun and the moon, and even our daily bread, have become pale abstractions, mere laws exhibited in the successions of events which radiate from certain regions.

(*OP*, p. 106)

Russell saw, as did Eddington, that a four-dimensional neutral monism, with space-time events as the fundamental "stuff," suggests a way to best understand the new physics and bridge the gap between mind and matter.

Neutral monism cautiously accepts the new relativity and quantum sciences of physics and (with some reservation) the new science of behaviorism in psychology and thereby offers promise for the formulation of a naturalized theory of perception: a theory showing how knowledge of the strange new physics is, itself, a process of transient particulars (i.e. space-time events) which can come about in the world. The explanation of the process does not require, as traditional philosophical epistemology concluded, an appeal to primitive intentional powers of mind such as aboutness (i.e. intentionality), consciousness, and will.

Unfortunately, Russell's project has been seen though the colored lenses of philosophers who, inspired by his work, tried to resurrect some atheistic form of the phenomenalistic "immaterialism" of Berkeley.[43] C. I. Lewis's Mind and the World Order (1929) identified matter as "bundles" of mental particulars with intrinsic phenomenal character. The verificationist and empiricist reductive project that Carnap endeavored to carry out in his work Der Logische Aufbau der Welt (1928) aimed to provide operational definitions rendering empirical (observational) significance conditions for theoretical terms of the sciences, including a rehabilitated psychology. In this way Carnap hoped to show that the sciences exclude metaphysics. Carnap's Aufbau and his 1932 paper "The Elimination of Metaphysics Through Logical Analysis of Language,"[44] employed the newly uncovered logical tools of Whitehead and Russell's Principia Mathematica to analyze the concepts of the sciences, showing their precise inferential relationships to observation. Each sentence involving theoretical terms gets its empirical significance in virtue of its inferential (logical) connections to terms referring only to observations or, in its extreme form, to sentences asserting the occurrence of a sense-experience. The "verification theory of meaning," as it came to be called, held that the meaning of a theoretical assertion is given by the evidentiary conditions that would establish (in principle) its empirical confirmation or disconfirmation in observation. In Carnap's early view, speculative metaphysical theories (e.g. the existence of Aristotelian entelechies, life, vital forces, purposes, God, the soul, and the like) are empirically meaningless. They fail to have proper evidentiary relationships to observation.

Carnap's *Aufbau* revealed the formidable difficulties inherent in radical empiricism, which assumes that there is a conceptual or inferential reduction of each theoretical statement to a group of observation (or sensory) statements which confirms or disconfirms it. Duhem's work, later adopted by Quine, sealed its fate.[45] Examination of the scientific practice of the verification (confirmation or disconfirmation) of a hypothesis revealed that only in the context of a large body of theory does a given hypothesis confront the tribunal of observational evidence. Hence, the empirical meaning of a given theoretical term of a hypothesis can neither be adequately characterized in terms of potential observational evidence alone, nor can it be specified for the hypothesis taken in isolation. The empirical meaning of a statement in a scientific research program is reflected in the totality of its deductive relationships to all other statements in theories within that program. This is an important discovery concerning the nature of Newton's scientific method. It undermines Carnap's program, but it does not impact Russell's program.

We saw that Russell was not a methodological solipsist building knowledge of matter out of the hard data available to a given mind. Russell's neutral monism gives a theory of mind and matter and a theory of perception (i.e. knowing) from a vantage point outside of any given mind. Russell accepts other minds and their private spaces as well as transient particulars that are not sensations (since they occur in no mind). It is from this "view from nowhere" that Russell concluded that the data about matter that is available to any given mind is data constituted by brain states. This is the hard data accepted by methodological solipsism in epistemology. Russell admits, as he had in *Our Knowledge*, that there is an alternative theory which in its construction of matter adheres only to the hard data. Berkeley's "immaterialism" is viable, though untoward. Russell explains:

> It would be possible, without altering the detail of previous discussions ... to give a different turn to the argument, and make matter a structure composed of mental units. I am not quite sure

that this is the wrong view. It arises not unnaturally from the argument as to data . . . We saw that all data are mental events in the narrowest and strictest sense, since they are percepts. Consequently all verification of causal laws consists in the occurrence of expected percepts. Consequently, any inference beyond percepts (actual or possible) is incapable of being empirically tested. We shall therefore be prudent if we regard the non-mental events of physics as merely auxiliary concepts, not assumed to have any reality, but only introduced to simplify the laws of percepts. Thus matter will be a construction built out of percepts, and our metaphysics will be essentially that of Berkeley.

(*OP*, p. 290)

But this is really not the metaphysics of Berkeley. It does not accept minds as continuant and does not, or so we concluded, accept that mental states have phenomenal character intrinsically. Most importantly, it does not accept Berkeley's postulation of the existence of God to assure that our experiences will have the permanence, passivity, and coherence that would be expected for them if there were material objects causally responsible for them. Russell, once quoted[46] an amusing limerick written by Ronald Knox (1888–1957) to help students remember Berkeley.

> There once was a man who said, "God
> Must think it exceedingly odd
> If he finds that this tree
> Continues to be
> When there's no one about in the Quad."

Reply

> Dir Sir:
> Your astonishment's odd:
> I am always about in the Quad.
> And that's why this tree
> Will continue to be,

> Since observed by
> Yours faithfully,
> God

Russell is well aware of what happens if God is removed from Berkeley's metaphysics. "If there are no non-mental events," Russell observes,

> causal laws will be very odd; for example, a hidden Dictaphone may record a conversation although it did not exist at the time, since no one was perceiving it. But although this seems odd, it is not logically impossible. And it must be conceded that it enables us to interpret physics with a smaller amount of dubious inductive and analogical inferences than is required if we admit non-mental events.
>
> (*OP*, p. 290)

The benefit in one quarter is a significant loss in another. "I cannot bring myself to accept it," Russell goes on, "though I am not sure that my reasons for disliking it are any better than Dr. Johnson's." Johnson hoped to refute Berkeley by simply kicking a rock. We do not kick mental states, after all. But of course this is no refutation since, as Berkeley would have it, kicking is a series of mental states. Russell puts the point in terms of the new physics: "If he had known that his foot never touched the stone, and that both were only complicated systems of wave-motions, he might have been less satisfied with his refutation" (OP, p. 279).

FURTHER READING

Tom Burke, *Dewey's New Logic: A Reply to Russell* (Chicago: University of Chicago Press, 1994).

E. A. Burtt, *The Metaphysical Foundations of Modern Science* (Atlantic Highlands, NJ: Humanities Press, 1952).

William Demopoulos and Michael Friedman, "The Concept of Structure in *The Analysis of Matter*," in C. Wade Savage and C. Anthony Anderson, eds., *Rereading Russell* (Minneapolis: University of Minnesota Press, 1989), pp. 183–199.

Ronald Jaeger, *The Development of Bertrand Russell's Philosophy* (London: George Allen & Unwin, 1972).

Peter Ludlow, Yujin Nagasawa, and Daniel Stoljar, eds., *There's Something About Mary: Essays on Phenomenal Consciousness and Frank Jackson's Knowledge Argument* (Cambridge, MA: MIT Press, 2004).

Ahmed Mafizuddin, *Bertrand Russell's Neutral Monism* (New Delhi: Mittal Publications, 1989).

Samuel Meyer, ed., *Russell and Dewey: An Exchange* (New York: Philosophical Library, 1985).

Francesco Orilia, *Tropes, Universals and the Philosophy of Mind* (Paris: Ontos Verlag, 2008).

Robert Tully, "Russell's Neutral Monism," in Nicholas Griffin, ed., *The Cambridge Companion to Russell* (Cambridge: Cambridge University Press, 2003), pp. 332–370.

Richard Westfall, *The Construction of Modern Science* (Cambridge: Cambridge University Press, 1977).

Seven

Principia's Second Edition

> One point in regard to which improvement is obviously desirable is in the axiom of reducibility *12.1.11
> *Introduction to the Second Edition* (1925)

In 1911 a young Austrian, Ludwig Wittgenstein, who had been studying at Manchester in preparation for a career in aeronautical engineering, took a passionate interest in the foundations of mathematics. With characteristic British humor, Russell reports that

> ... for a whole term I could not make up my mind whether he was a man of genius or merely an eccentric. At the end of his first term at Cambridge he came to me and said: "Will you please tell me whether I am a complete idiot or not?" I replied: "My dear fellow, I don't know. Why are you asking me?" He said: "Because, if I am a complete idiot, I shall become an aeronaut; but if not, I shall become a philosopher."[1]

It is difficult to believe that either thought that engineering can be performed by idiots. But in any case, Russell soon came to recognize Wittgenstein's potential and took him under his wing. In time, he came to believe Wittgenstein was an eccentric savant who, between mania and depression, may well make the next great advance in mathematical logic.

The portraits of Wittgenstein given to us by Russell tell a colorful and engaging story, which, over the years, has been greatly expanded into a legend of a genius who shook the world of philosophy. Of course, Russell's life and philosophical achievements are no less the substance of genius and legend. Russell and Wittgenstein both left voluminous work notes and letters and they knew a great many people, statesmen, poets, academicians, lovers, and friends who themselves wrote memoirs. The wealth of material naturally lends itself to a variety of interpretations. The two have become popular subjects for philosophers, biographers, and even filmmakers.[2]

Russell regarded Wittgenstein as a protégé and did much to establish a career for him. He secured the publication of Wittgenstein's oracular and unorthodox *Tractatus Logico-Philosophicus*. He presided over the *Viva* which accepted the *Tractatus* as a dissertation for Wittgenstein's degree (1929). He was instrumental in Wittgenstein's Fellowship at Trinity College (1930) and in evaluating his *Philosophische Bermerkungen* on behalf of his research funding. Russell describes Wittgenstein as "... perhaps the most perfect example I have ever known of genius as traditionally conceived, passionate, profound, intense, and dominating. He had a kind of purity which I have never known equaled except by G. E. Moore."[3] A good story must, however, have an antagonist, and the legends have produced one, presenting Wittgenstein as both temperamentally and philosophically opposed to Russell, with Wittgenstein earnest, inspired, and emotional and Russell methodical, rational, and detached. Their relationship was certainly complicated.

There are many episodes that serve as Rorschach inkblots for interpretations of Russell and Wittgenstein. It is all too easy to be seduced by them into presenting disparaging portraits of the two. Russell wrote that "[Wittgenstein's later work] ... remains to me completely unintelligible. Its positive doctrines seem to me trivial and its negative doctrines unfounded."[4] Wittgenstein got in a few barbs at Russell's popular writings, reportedly calling Russell's *Conquest of Happiness* "vomitive" and his *What I Believe?* "harmful."[5] Drury recounts him saying that

> Russell's books should be bound in two colours: those dealing with mathematical logic in red, and all students of philosophy should read them; those dealing with ethics and politics in blue, and no one should be allowed to read them.[6]

Neither philosopher, it seems, could resist hyperbole. But the truth is that the two were allies.

To evaluate some of Wittgensein's Tractarian ideas, *Principia*'s 1925 second edition offers a new introduction and three new appendices A, B, and C. Appendix A offers a system of deduction without free variables adequate to quantification theory. It is the first of its kind. (Quine's system did not appear until 1940.) It marks Russell's first steps toward logical purity, so that the formal theory of logic does not embrace any existential theorems concerning individuals of lowest type. Appendix B investigates a revision of *Prinicpia*'s language and Wittgenstein's idea that a more thorough extensionality would enable one to abandon the strong comprehension principle of Reducibility in favor of the weaker comprehension principles consistent with the view that logic consists of tautologies. Appendix C appeals tacitly to neutral monism's elimination of the mind to reconceptualize notions of belief and thought that are extensional.

The new introduction and appendixes of the second edition were written by Russell alone. Russell attempted to include Whitehead in working on the second edition. But Whitehead, who found Wittgenstein's personality intolerable, declined. Later he resoundingly disowned the new introduction, publishing a note in *Mind* that Russell alone was responsible for it.[7] After the publication of the second edition, Whitehead sketched his own ideas for revisions to *Principia* and published them as "Indication, Classes, Numbers, Validation."[8] Likely, he felt that Russell had gone too far in using their book to advance research on Wittgenstein's ideas. The new introduction and appendices of *Principia*'s second edition contain Russell's exploration of Wittgenstein's ideas. To understand them, we have to understand something of the historical development of Russell's influence on Wittgenstein. What follows is a crash course.

RUSSELL'S APPRENTICE

Wittgenstein's work for his degree in philosophy involved reworking the first parts of *Principia* concerning the propositional calculus. Wittgenstein's dear friend David Pinsent wrote the following entry in his diary (August 1913): "It is probable that the first volume of *Principia* will have to be re-written, and Wittgenstein may write himself the first eleven chapters. That is a splendid triumph for him!"[9] Eleven "chapters" of *Principia* takes us through section *12, which completes the foundations the system of logic. Wittgenstein's original focus, however, was not to provide a lofty new foundation for logic. His focus was the more modest project of reducing propositional logic to one truth-functional connective.

In 1913 Russell had received a paper from Sheffer demonstrating that one sign, now written as "$p \downarrow q$," is adequate to express all truth-functions expressible by the signs of *Principia*. The dagger has the truth-conditions of $\sim(p \vee q)$. The dual is the Sheffer stroke p/q which has the truth condition $\sim(p \& q)$. The expressive adequacy of *Principia*, as well as the stroke and dagger to express all truth-functions awaited the work of Post in 1920. But Sheffer's paper captivated the mind of Wittgenstein. Russell read a paper to the Cambridge Moral Sciences Club in April 1912 entitled "On Matter." On the back page of a later draft of the paper entitled "On Matter— The Problem Stated," there are jottings in Russell's hand and Wittgenstein's hand which reveal that they were discussing Sheffer's work.[10] The Sheffer dagger operation appears in Wittgenstein's *Notes on Logic*, which was composed during a self-imposed isolation in Norway to "solve *all* the problems of logic." In a letter to Russell from Norway (30 October 1913) Wittgenstein proclaims to have found such a reduction: "One of the consequences of my new ideas will—I think—be that the whole of Logic follows from one Pp only!"[11] Wittgenstein never found the reduction. Jean Nicod found it in 1916. Nicod demonstrated that only one axiom, together with the rule of uniform substitution and one other inference rule governing Sheffer's stroke, suffices to generate *Principia*'s sentential calculus.[12] Nicod died tragically in 1924 of tuberculosis. In the 1925 introduction to the second edition of *Principia*, Russell recommended that Sheffer "rewrite" the *Principia* in accordance with the new methods.[13]

Wittgenstein's isolation in Norway did not solve the task at hand of finding a reduction of propositional logic to rules governing the Sheffer dagger, but it did produce something Wittgenstein thought to be a breakthrough toward a lofty new foundation for logic and arithmetic. Caught up in the insanity that led to the First World War, the breakthrough would have to wait. Wittgenstein insisted in enlisting with Austria, his homeland. War intervened, and Russell lost contact with him until June of 1919. When Russell finally did get news, he found that Wittgenstein had managed to write a book while in the Austrian army. With the war at an end, Wittgenstein wrote a letter to Russell from an Italian prison camp in Cassino. In it, he announced that he had reached solutions:

> I've written a book called *Logisch-philosophische Abhandlung* containing all my work of the past 6 years. I believe I've solved all our problems finally... This may sound arrogant, but I can't help believing it.... But it upsets all our theory of truth, of classes of numbers and all the rest...[14]

The letter makes it clear that Wittgenstein took his book, the title of which was later changed to *Tractatus Logico-Philosophicus*, to be addressing "our" problems (i.e. problems shared with Russell).

Recall that as early as 1901 Russell wrote that time-honored antinomies long used to motivate philosophical systems were falling to the new rigor in mathematical logic. Russell wrote:

> In the whole philosophy of mathematics, which used to be at least as full of doubt as any other part of philosophy, order and certainty

have replaced the confusion and hesitation which formerly reigned. Philosophers, of course, have not yet discovered this fact, and continue to write on such subjects in the old way. . . . many of the topics which used to be placed among the great mysteries—for example, the natures of infinity, of continuity, of space, time and motion—are not no longer in any degree open to doubt or discussion.

(*MM*, p. 63)

New breakthroughs came with Dedekind on irrationals, Cantor on continuity, and Weierstrass on limits. But it was Russell's own constructions eliminating non-logical metaphysical ontological assumptions and building notions of existence, class, and truth into structured variables that ushered in the philosophy of Logical Atomism. A vast array of philosophical puzzles in the philosophy of mathematics, matter, mind, space, time, and motion could now, in principle, be (dis)solved.

Russell's method is to solve philosophical problems by eliminating certain questionable ontological commitments and building structure into variables. That is, the admissible range of a variable is internally limited by its significance conditions and not said by statements of the language of the formal theory. The idea that limits are not restrictions, but are given by the structure of the variables captivated Wittgenstein. In the *Tractatus* we find the following:

> When something falls under a formal concept as one of its objects, this cannot be expressed by means of a proposition. Instead it is shown in the very sign for this object. (A name shows that it signifies an object, a sign for a number that it signifies a number, etc.) The expression for a formal property is a feature of certain symbols. So the sign for the characteristics of a formal concept is a distinctive feature of all symbols whose meanings fall under the concept. . . . So the expression for a formal concept is a propositional variable in which this distinctive feature alone is constant.
>
> [*TLP* 4.126]

> Thus, the variable name "*x*" is the proper sign of the pseudo-concept *object*. Whenever the word "object" ("thing," "entity," etc.) is rightly used, it is expressed in logical symbolism by the variable name. . . . The same holds for the words "complex," "fact," "function," "number," etc. They all signify formal concepts and are presented in logical symbolism by variables . . . .
>
> [*TLP* 4.1271]

Russell's idea of building structure into variables is part of his notion that formal concepts are properly shown by structured variables.

Wittgenstein's expression of this idea in the *Tractatus* is somewhat hidden. It is easy to miss the significance in the following passage: "My fundamental idea is that the 'logical constants' are not representatives" (TLP 4.0312). The passage surely does not simply mean that the logical particles ~, v and & etc., are not signs representing logical relations. That was clearly Russell's idea, and it already occurs in *Principia*. Wittgenstein's conception of the logical constants includes much more than the statement connectives of predicate logic.[15] He held that words like "complex," "fact," "function," "number," etc. all signify formal concepts, and are represented in conceptual notation by variables. The notion of a formal concept here means to cover any expression that involves logical (or semantic) content. Wittgenstein wrote:

> (I introduce the expression in order to exhibit the source of the confusion between formal concepts and concepts proper, which pervades the whole of traditional logic.) When something falls under a formal concept as one of its objects, this cannot be expressed by means of a proposition. Instead it is shown in the very sign of this object . . . Formal concepts cannot, in fact, be represented by means of a function, as concepts proper can.
>
> (*TLP* 4.126)

Wittgenstein uses "logical constant" synonymously with his use of the expressions "formal concept" and "internal property (relation)." That is, the logical constants include all and only notions with logico-semantic content. Among such notions, Wittgenstein included identity, universal, particular, name, fact, necessity, possibility, and all semantic notion such as truth, reference, belief, representation, content, and the like.

Wittgenstein's fundamental idea is identical with his more famous doctrine of showing. In a letter to Russell of 1919 Wittgenstein responded to some questions Russell had raised about the *Tractatus*. He writes:

> Now I'm afraid you haven't really got hold of my main contention, to which the whole business of logical propositions is only corollary. The main point is the theory of what can be expressed (*gesagt*) by propositions—i.e., by language (and, what comes to the same, what can be thought) and what cannot be expressed by propositions, but only shown (*gezeigt*); which, I believe, is the cardinal problem of philosophy.[16]

In Wittgenstein's view, all (and only) logical (and semantic) notions are to be shown by the syntax of structured variables in an ideal language for science. The problems of philosophy arise when such notions are taken to be genuine properties (or relations) governing a realm of strange new philosophical objects (e.g. classes, numbers, properties, selves/souls, and the like).

Wittgenstein agrees with the fundamental doctrine of Russell's Logical Atomism that the only necessity is logical necessity (TLP 6.375). Any purportedly necessary metaphysical connection that is non-logical requires a logical analysis that separates the logico-semantic components of the concepts involved from the empirical (material) components. But the *Tractatus* goes much further. Wittgenstein held that belief contexts and non-extensional contexts generally call for much deeper reconstructions than Russell had hitherto found. The promise of the program of Logical Atomism can only be fulfilled when all logical properties are eliminated in favor of structured variables which show logical necessity. Wittgenstein held that Russell's analyses had not gone far enough. Russell's multiple-relation theory of belief, at the foundation of *Principia*'s recursive semantic definition of "truth," presupposed the legitimacy of notions such as universal, fact, and logical form. Such notions become primitives governed by informative axioms of a science of logic. According to the *Tractatus*, there is no science of logic.

In his introduction to the *Tractatus*, Russell was quick to point out that, inspiring as it is, the work seems to be self-refuting. Its own austere demands threaten to destroy its own theses and constructions. Wittgenstein was disappointed. He had asked Russell to write an introduction to help in the book's chances for publication. The work could not find a publisher without Russell's introduction. While sympathetic, the Introduction calls attention to this fundamental tension. Wittgenstein's reply was that Russell had failed to see the central point of the work: the austere demand that all logical and semantic notions must disappear into structured variables. Far from a problem for the *Tractatus*, it is supposed to be its triumph. The work closes with this: "Whereof one cannot speak, thereof one must be silent" (TLP, 7). The extreme form of analysis Wittgenstein seeks, where all logico-semantic concepts are pseudo-concepts, leaves one employing the structures of the ideal framework with complete silence observed when it comes to their explanation and justification. Any attempt at justification of the new framework would use logical or semantic notions as if they were legitimate and thus be self-refuting.

But it is hard to acquiesce in the advice to "be silent." Wittgenstein offers the following consolation:

> My propositions serve as elucidations [*erläutern*] in the following way: anyone who understands me eventually recognizes them as nonsensical [*unsinnig*], when he has used them—as steps—to climb up beyond them. (He must, so to speak, throw away the ladder after he has climbed up.) He must transcend these propositions, and then he will see the world alright.
>
> (*TLP* 6.54)

But again it is hard to feel consoled by the notion that one can, having climbed a ladder and standing on its last rung, kick away the ladder. Perhaps, Russell mused in his Introduction, there is some escape from Wittgenstein's conclusion that ultimately one must be silent—perhaps a "... loophole through a hierarchy of languages." Carnap was also unsatisfied with Wittgenstein's supposed silence:

> ... he [Wittgenstein] seems to me to be inconsistent in what he does. He tells us that one cannot make philosophical statements, and that whereof one cannot speak, thereof one must be silent; and then instead of keeping silent, he writes a whole philosophical book.[17]

Ramsey nicely sums up the situation with a quip: "But what we can't say we can't say, and we can't whistle it either."[18] Wittgenstein's extreme doctrine of showing is either self-refuting or reduces philosophy to the pronuncations of an oracle.

Central to the *Tractatus* is that there can be no science of logical analysis—a science of Logical Atomism. Indeed, all notions of a would-be science of logic and deduction are illicit. Logic must, if Wittgenstein's fundamental idea is correct, be decidable. Wittgenstein accepted this consequence. He thought he had found a decision procedure for logic: a notation such that all and only logical equivalents have one and the same expression. Translation into the notation is a decision procedure for logical truth since in such a notation the very expression's structure will show whether it is a tautology, a contingent statement, or a contradiction.

An early attempt at finding such a notation for the propositional calculus is embedded in the following story told by Russell of the odd events of Wittgenstein first meeting the Whiteheads:

> Whitehead described to me the first time that Wittgenstein came to see him. He was shown into the drawing room during afternoon tea. He appeared scarcely aware of the presence of Mrs. Whitehead, but

marched up and down the room for some time in silence, and at last said explosively: "A proposition has two poles. It is *apb*." Whitehead, in telling me, said: "I naturally asked what are *a* and *b*, but I found I had said the wrong thing. '*a* and *b* are indefinable,' Wittgenstein answered in voice of thunder."[19]

Wittgenstein hoped to convince Russell that the *ab*-Notation's decision procedure (or some such procedure) can, in principle, be extended from the propositional calculus to quantification theory.[20] Section *9 of *Principia* was his inspiration. It offered an approach to quantification theory which showed that any instance of an axiom (i.e. schema) of quantification theory can be arrived at by generalizations on tautologies. The inference rules are derivable as well. Excitedly, Wittgenstein wrote to Russell:

> Of course the rule I have given applies first of all only for what you call elementary propositions. But it is easy to see that it must also apply to all others. For consider two Pps in the theory of apparent variables *9.1 and *9.11. Put then instead of φx, $(\exists y).\varphi y. y = x$ and it becomes obvious that the special cases of these two Pps like those of all the previous ones become tautologous if you apply the *ab*-Notation. The *ab*-Notation for Identity is not yet clear enough to show this clearly but it is obvious that such a Notation can be made up. I can sum up by saying that a logical proposition is one of the special cases of which are either tautologous—and then the proposition is true—or self-contradictory (as I shall call it) and then it is false. And the ab-Notation simply shows directly which of these two it is (if any).[21]

Wittgenstein erroneously concluded that logic consists of tautologies and generalizations of tautologous forms. This energized Wittgenstein's intuitions about the nature of logic, but it turned out that his intuitions were wrong. Logic is not "tautologous" in his sense of being decidable.

Propositional diagrams used by John Venn in the 1880s are an excellent example of the kind of notation that Wittgenstein sought when it comes to representing propositional (i.e. quantifier-free) statements. Expressed by Venn diagrams, all and only logically equivalent propositions have one and the same expression. The reason is that the Venn diagram expresses only the truth-conditions (i.e. the structure) of the proposition. Wittgenstein parallels Venn's result, writing truth conditions with:

$(\gamma_1, \ldots \gamma_{2n})(p_1, \ldots, p_n)$

This approach adopts a convention of ordering the sequence of rows of truth-conditions on the right-hand side of a truth-table. We can see the parallel to Venn's propositional diagrams by simply numbering the rows. Consider the proposition $p \supset (q \supset r)$. Wittgenstein's technique simply lists the truth-conditions in the column for the statement:

$(t, t, t, t, f, t, t, t)(p, q, r)$

	p	q	r	$p \supset (q \supset r)$	$(p \& q) \supset r$
1	t	t	t	t	t
2	f	t	t	t	t
3	t	f	t	t	t
4	f	f	t	t	t
5	t	t	f	f	f
6	f	t	f	t	t
7	t	f	f	t	t
8	f	f	f	t	t

The truth-table uses t and f to depict truth conditions. Venn's diagrams use a spatial notion, so that the truth of p is the area inside of the circle tagged p and falsehood of p is the area outside of it.

Returning to our example, Venn's technique shades areas to depict truth-conditions, while the Venn diagram shades all and only those areas that get an f in its truth-table. Venn simply shades area 5. The

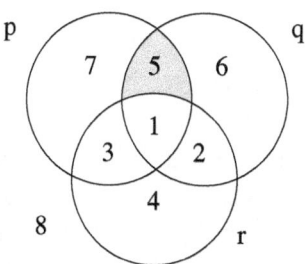

Venn diagrammatic approach makes it clear why this system of representation depicts all and only logical equivalents in one and the same way. For example, the proposition (p & q) ⊃ r has the same representation. In Wittgenstein's view, the appearance of logic having a content to be studied as if a science is due simply to a poor system of representation which uses logical particles such as v, &, ⊃, ~, ≡, and the like. Venn did not draw this conclusion, but he certainly beat Wittgenstein to the representational system.

In his *Tractatus* Wittgenstein thought he had found a notation that applies not only to propositional logic, but to quantification theory with identity. Wittgenstein hoped to treat universal quantifiers in terms of potentially infinite conjunctions and existential quantifiers as potentially infinite disjunctions. Consider the simple case of expressing ~(∀x)Fx in the same way as the logically equivalent (∃x)~Fx. If there are exactly n-many objects, the statement ~(∀x)Fx is equivalent to this:

~(Fx$_1$ &, ..., &, Fx$_n$).

Similarly, over exactly n-many objects, (∃x)~Fx is equivalent to this:

~Fx$_1$ v, ..., v, ~Fx$_n$.

Both then have the general form

$$(f_1, t_2, \ldots t_{2n})(Fx_1, \ldots, Fx_n)$$

where each x_i is read as picking out a distinct object. But Wittgenstein realized that expressing by means of truth-conditions cannot work for the expression of quantifiers. The trouble is that we do not know how many objects there are, and in some cases an increase in the number of objects changes the positions of the ts and fs in a given $(\gamma_1, \ldots \gamma_{2n})(p_1, \ldots, p_n)$. Thus the schematic expression for a given statement will fail to be adequate.

Wittgenstein's solution was his N-operator notation. Unfortunately, his discussion of the N-operator is baffling, and many erroneously associate it with Sheffer's dagger. It was discovered independently by George Spencer Brown and published in his book *Laws of Form* (1971). In Russell's blurb for the book, he writes: "In this book, G. Spencer Brown has succeeded in doing what, in mathematics, is very rare indeed, he has revealed a new calculus, of great power and simplicity ..."[22] The book is as obscure as the *Tractatus*, but it is unfortunate that Russell did not notice that Brown's "primary algebra" is akin to the algebra of Wittgenstein's N-operator. Because of Brown's formal work, we can finally understand Wittgenstein. Once we put a propositional formula in the notion of the dagger, we can readily see how to use N-operator notation to make a picture of its truth conditions. We replace each negation sign and each dagger with an N. But the rules governing the N-operator rules transcend what is going on with the dagger notation. We can then use rules governing calculations by the N-operator to determine whether or not a formula is a tautology. All and only tautologies have their truth-conditions pictured by

$$NN(\ldots N\xi, \ldots \ldots \xi, \ldots)$$

where the order of appearance of $N\xi, \ldots \ldots \xi, \ldots$ does not matter. Wittgenstein assumed the rules of transformation were obvious; Brown tries to state them. To glimpse the way it works, consider the following:

$p \supset (q \supset p)$
$\sim(\sim p \downarrow \sim(\sim q \downarrow p)$ by translation to Sheffer dagger notation
NN[Np, NN[Nq, p]] by translation to Wittgenstein's N operator notation
NN[Np, Nq, p] by the rule of dropping embedded double Ns.

Thus we have calculated that $p. \supset. q \supset p$ is a tautology. In this way, calculation by means of the N-operator notation forms a decision procedure for tautologyhood. In Wittgenstein's view, propositional logic is a practice of calculating equations using the N-operator.

Quantificational formulas restricted to an arbitrarily large number of objects can be expressed in the schematic N-operator notation. But the schematic feature of the N-operator notation gets in the way of applying the rules of the N-operator. The rules require that the number of propositions (and thus the number of objects) be fixed at a finite number. This is precisely what fails to happen since quantification theory allows there to be infinitely many objects. In the 1930s Church showed that there is no procedure for determining whether or not a given formula is a logical truth of quantification theory. The result spoils Wittgenstein's idea that logic is not a science with a body of truths about a subject matter. There is a science of logic after all.

Wittgenstein had hoped to find a notation which renders one and the same expression for all and only logical truths of quantification theory with identity. One might think a natural plan for making true identity statements into generalized tautologies would be to simply follow *Principia* and define the identity as follows:

$x = y =\text{df} (\forall \varphi)(\varphi x \equiv \varphi y)$

Wittgenstein maintained that this approach is inadequate for his purposes. The nominalistic semantics of *Principia* interprets predicate variables φ, of lowest order/type, in terms of formulas that can contain logical signs and quantifiers binding individual variables—formulas which have logical relations. In virtue of the nominalistic semantics, these predicate variables are not genuine. The logical independence of universals inhering in facts was a consequence of Principia's nominalistic semantics since its recursive theory of truth and falsehood makes the facts that are truth-makers logically independent. Wittgenstein saw this and extended the thesis. The only genuine properties (i.e. "material properties") he accepts are those that are logically independent. Genuine properties F and G are such that it is always logically possible for any object to exemplify both. Thus, sharing all properties is not sufficient for identity. Accordingly, one cannot construe true identity statements as tautologies by defining identity in terms of sharing all properties.

Writing to Russell from Norway in 1913, he says that

> ... identity is the very Devil and *immensely important*; very much more so than I thought ... I have all sorts of ideas for a solution of the problem but could not yet arrive at anything definite. However, I don't lose courage and go on thinking.[23]

In his *Tractatus* the identity sign is abandoned as illicit. The expression $(\forall x)(x = x)$ is thereby excluded from logical notation. Wittgenstein reads a quantifier in the scope of another as having a range that excludes the other. Unfortunately, since he thought a science of deduction is illicit, he never set out a formal theory of deduction for exclusive quantifiers. It turns out that in a formal deductive system one must syntactically mark exclusivity in a more rigorous way than simply by quantifier scope. We can do this by superscripting variables. Thus one can write

$$(\exists x)(\psi x \,\&\, (\forall z^x) \sim \psi z)$$

to say that something is ψ and everything else (other than x) is not ψ. The elimination of identity introduces many complications into logic, and it might at first seem to undermine Russell's theory of definite descriptions (since that theory used the identity sign). But Wittgenstein assured Russell in a letter that "... your theory of descriptions is *quite undoubtedly* right, even if the individual primitive signs in it are quite different from what you believe."[24]

At first, the elimination of identity seemed to Wittgenstein to have an exciting consequence for *Principia* (TLP 5.535). It would show, by the mere fact that the language of logic has infinitely many distinct variables, that there are infinitely many logical simples, and it would thereby avoid *Principia*'s troubles with assuring there are infinitely many natural numbers. Recall from our Chapter Two that the statement of the infinity of natural numbers is this:

$$(\forall \mathbf{m})(N_\varphi[\mathbf{m}_x \varphi x] \supset (\forall \psi)(\mathbf{m}_x \psi x \supset (\exists x) \sim \psi x)).$$

This says that every natural number m is such that for all ψ if there are exactly m-many ψs, then something is not a ψ. (In other words, no natural number numbers everything.) No general proof of infinity is forthcoming in the logic of exclusive quantifiers. But exclusive quantifiers nonetheless enable a proof of every instance of the infinity statement. Consider the following:

$$N_\varphi[\mathbf{0}_x \varphi x] \supset (\forall \psi)(\mathbf{0}_x \psi x \supset (\exists y) \sim \psi y).$$

This says that if 0 is a natural number then every ψ is such that if there are exactly zero many ψs then there is something that is not ψ. The antecedent is true. Next, replace $\mathbf{0}_x \psi x$ with the equivalent expression $(\forall x) \sim \psi x$ and we arrive at:

$$(\forall \psi)((\forall y) \sim \psi y \supset (\exists y) \sim \psi y).$$

This is a theorem of classic logic and of Wittgenstein's logic of exclusive quantifiers. It says that for all ψ, if everything is not ψ then something is not ψ. Similar results happen for the other natural numbers. Consider the following:

$$N_\varphi[\mathbf{1}_x \varphi x] \supset (\forall \psi)(\mathbf{1}_x \psi x \supset (\exists y) \sim \psi y).$$

The antecedent is true. Replace $\mathbf{1}_x \psi x$ by the equivalent $(\exists x)(\psi x \,\&\, (\forall z^x) \sim \psi z)$ and we arrive at:

$(\forall \psi) ((\exists x)(\psi x \,\&\, (\forall z^x) \sim\!\psi z) \supset (\exists y) \sim\!\psi y).$

This is also a theorem of exclusive quantifiers. In the theory of exclusive quantifiers, the assertion

$(\exists x)(\psi x \,\&\, (\forall z^x) \sim\!\psi z).$

of ψs being exemplified by exactly one thing logically entails that there is more than exactly one thing.[25]

This technique for helping to avoid *Principia*'s difficulties over infinity initially attracted Wittgenstein. The advance made by the adoption of exclusive quantifiers in avoiding an infinity axiom was, however, a net loss. Wittgenstein came to think that his elimination of identity as a relation undermines the applicability of the notion of counting in terms of relations of one-to-one correspondence. No material properties or relations are sufficient to establish the needed one-to-one correspondence relations.

With identity abandoned, a new logical foundation for natural numbers must be found. Wittgenstein concluded that *Principia* must be done "afresh." Ramsey put matters as follows: "W[ittgenstein] and I think it is wrong to suppose with Russell that mathematics is more complicated formal logic (tautologies); and I am trying to make definite the vague ideas we have of what it does consist of."[26] Wittgenstein's Tractarian approach construes arithmetic as "equations," not tautologies. "Numbers are exponents of operations" (TLP 6.021). In this way, mathematics is a method of logic (TLP 6.235). In Wittgenstein's form of logicism, both arithmetic and logic have a common origin in recursive calculations of operations. Russell tended to ignore Wittgenstein's view that arithmetic involved equations rather than tautologies. He could not bring himself to accept Wittgenstein's abandonment of identity. When Russell's friend, mathematician G. H. Hardy, read a paper at the Moral Sciences Club in Cambridge in 1940, he attributed to Wittgenstein the view that mathematics consists of tautologies. Reportedly, Wittgenstein attended and denied having ever held the view, pointing to himself and saying in an incredulous tone of voice "Who I?"[27]

It soon became clear that the fundamental axiom of Principia's ^{CP}logic, its so-called "axiom of reducibility" *12.1n, is not validated by the official nominalistic semantics that Whitehead and Russell offered in the first edition. The order indices on predicate variables are philosophically explained in terms of the recursively defined orders of truth and falsehood. This validates comprehension principles far weaker than Reducibility. The recursive truth-definition grounds only comprehension schema for the theory of predicative order/types. Predicative comprehension principles are acceptable to Wittgenstein. They are consistent with his view that logic is not a genuine science; it consists of generalized tautologies.

Russell came to agree that the nominalistic semantics does not validate his comprehension axiom *12.1n. From the perspective of that semantics and the official ontology of Principia, the axiom is unjustified. Russell had worries even in Principia, and he expressed a hope that *12.1n might be removed from the foundations of mathematics. He wrote:

> That the axiom of reducibility is self-evident is a proposition which can hardly be maintained. . . . In the case of the axiom of reducibility, the inductive evidence in its favour is very strong, since the reasoning which it permits and the results to which it leads are all such as appear valid. But although it seems improbable that the axiom should turn out to be false, it is by no means improbable that it should be found to be deducible from some other more fundamental and more evident axiom.[28]

In Introduction to Mathematical Philosophy (1919) he goes so far as to say that given its dependence upon Reducibility, Principia's theory of classes is "not finally satisfactory" and is "less complete" than the theory of descriptions.[29] It was Russell himself who inspired his enthusiastic student Wittgenstein to search for a replacement.

RUSSELL AND RAMSEY ON THE ORACLE

The *Tractatus* offers only programmatic and intuitive gestures toward constructions which supposedly dissolve the problems of philosophy. Reflecting on his work in *My Philosophical Development*, Russell says that "... he himself [Wittgenstein], as usual, is oracular and emits his opinion as if it were a Czar's ukase, but humbler folk can hardly content themselves with this procedure."[30] "The philosopher must drag beliefs into the light of day," Russell once wrote," and see whether they still survive. Often it will be found that they die on exposure."[31] It was left to Russell in the 1925 second edition of *Principia* and Ramsey in "The Foundations of Mathematics"(1925) and "Mathematical Logic" (1926) to develop and assess the viability of some of Wittgenstein's ideas for rectifying *Principia*.

In Appendix C of *Principia*'s second edition, Russell offers a reconstruction of belief and assertion to investigate Wittgenstein's thesis that all contexts are extensional and truth-functional. His concluding assessment of Wittgenstein's thesis of extensionality is this:

> It is not necessary to lay any stress upon the above analysis of belief, which may be completely mistaken. All that is intended is to show that "A believes p" may very well not be a function of p, in the sense in which p occurs as a truth-function.[32]

When he returned to the issue in *An Inquiry into Meaning and Truth* (1940), Russell rejected Carnap's (quasi-behaviorist) proposal that belief is a relation (i.e. disposition) of a person to assent to an expression. But he reaffirmed that his analysis in the second edition of *Principia* had shown that contexts of propositional attitudes such as belief cannot be used to form a telling argument against extensionality.[33] In *My Philosophical Development* (1956) he writes: "I have examined the problem at length in *An Inquiry into Meaning and Truth* (pages 267ff), but the conclusion at which I arrived is somewhat hesitant" (MPD, p. 118).

In contrast, Russell's evaluation of Wittgenstein's ideas for avoiding Reducibility in Appendix B and the new introduction were largely negative. Russell writes:

> .... We are not prepared to assert that this theory is definitely right, but it has seemed worthwhile to work out its consequences in the following pages. It appears that everything in Vol. 1 remains true (though often new proofs are required); the theory of inductive cardinals and ordinals survives; but it seems that the theory of infinite Dedekind and well-ordered series largely collapses, so that irrationals and real numbers can no longer be adequately dealt with. Also Cantor's proof that $2^n > n$ breaks down unless n is finite.
> (PM, xiv)

When technically worked out, the Tractarian ideas destroy too much that is important. Wittgenstein never seems to have seen Russell's notes for the second edition. Ramsey, however, read Russell's notes in 1923 and discussed them with him.[34] In Ramsey's 1926 paper "Mathematical Logic," Russell's technique in the second edition for recovering a proof of mathematical induction without the Reducibility Axiom is described as "ingenious." Nonetheless, subsequent readers often misunderstand the constructions of the second edition because of a confusion between the original system and the radically different system, $Principia^W$, that Russell formulated to evaluate Wittgenstein's ideas. Indeed, it is still common today to find interpretations that mischaracterize Russell as having abandoned the system of the first edition in favor of that of the second edition!

John Myhill was so perplexed by the syntax of the $Principia^W$ that he could only imagine it to be a jumble of "slipshod notions."[35] The syntax allows the expression

$$^a\varphi^{((o))}\, (^b\psi^{(o)})$$

to be well-formed even when the order index b is larger than that of a. This is a radical departure from $Principia^I$, which requires that there can be only predicative predicate variables and formulas such as:

$$^2\varphi^{((o))} \, (^1\psi^{(o)}).$$

It is no less radical a departure from Principia^C which requires that a be greater than b. Gödel seems to have understood that there were changes in the formal syntax of the new system. Indeed, in working through Russell's proofs, he found a flaw in a proof at *89.16 that played a central role in rectifying mathematical induction without Reducibility.[36] The flaw can be fixed.[37] Interestingly, and quite unbeknownst to Russell, Principia^W yields a proof of the following:

$$(\forall \, ^n\psi^{(o)})(\exists \, ^1\varphi^{(o)})(\forall x^o)(^1\varphi^{(o)}(x^o) \equiv \, ^n\psi^{(o)}(x^o)).$$

This theorem is not Reducibility *12.1n. As we noted, the syntax of Principia^W is quite different from that of the original system. Moreover, Reducibility *12.1n is a theorem schema, and, in the grammar of Principia^L it cannot be otherwise. Nonetheless, because of this theorem, the system Principia^W remains of interest.

The Tractatus suggests that Reducibility would not be needed in a system in which there has been a complete dissolution of all non-extensional contexts. Neither logic nor mathematics are sciences producing bodies of truths about a subject matter. Mathematical notions such as "... is a number" are pseudo-properties in just the same way as are logical notions such as "... exists." Tautologies say nothing, but their structure mirrors the structure of the world (TLP 6.13). In the same way, "... every proposition of mathematics must go without saying" (TLP 6.2341). Wittgenstein's ideas captivated a new genius at Cambridge: Frank Plumpton Ramsey.

Ramsey's review of the second edition of Principia is rather unenthusiastic in spite of his kindly remarks of Russell's genius. Ramsey wrote:

> The principal of mathematical methods which appear to require the Axiom of Reducibility are mathematical induction and Dedekindian section, the essential foundations of arithmetic and analysis respectively. Mr. Russell has succeeded in dispensing with the axiom in the first case, but holds out no hope for a similar success

in the second. Dedekindian section is thus left as an essential unsound method, as has often been emphasized by Weyl, and ordinary analysis crumbles to dust. That these are its consequences is the second defect in the theory of *Principia Mathematica*, and, to my mind, an absolutely conclusive proof that there is something wrong. For as I can neither accept the Axiom of Reducibility nor reject analysis, I cannot believe in a theory which permits me with no third possibility.[38]

In Ramsey's view, Russell's second edition works out Wittgenstein's ideas in an unsatisfactory way. Mathematical induction is saved, but analysis is lost. Ramsey could not accept Russell's negative assessment of Wittgenstein's ideas. He hoped that some other interpretation of the oracle might be successful.

Ramsey has become famous for separating the paradoxes (i.e. contradictions) into two groups: logical and semantic. Semantic paradoxes essentially involve semantic notions concerning "reference," "naming," or "truth." He regarded these paradoxes, unlike paradoxes of attributes and classes, as not relevant to logicism.[39] This traditional interpretation is mistaken. In fact, it was Russell himself in 1906 that first set out a formal theory which separated the paradoxes.[40] The Russell paradox of classes, Burali-Forti's paradox of ordinals, and Cantor's Paradox of the Greatest Cardinal are all solved by Russell's substitutional theory of propositional structure—a theory which is type free, but which emulates an ontology of simple types of attributes. Russell dismisses the semantic paradoxes of definability and nameability, such as Berry's paradox of the nameability of the least integer not nameable in less than nineteen syllables. He dismisses them on grounds that they are based on confused notions of nameability and definability. Ramsey's 1926 paper "Mathematical Logic" suggests that he understood well enough that Russell had advocated a nominalistic semantics which does not validate *Principia*'s Reducibility axiom *12.1n. Ramsey is not advocating the view that there is a science of logic with impredicative comprehension axioms for an ontology of simple types of attributes. Like Russell, Ramsey intends a nominalistic semantics for *Principia*'s predicate variables. But unlike Russell, Ramsey thinks he has found a nominalistic semantics that at once justifies axiom *12.1n and is consistent with Wittgenstein's view that logic is not a science and consists of tautologies.

Ramsey's ideas developed out of his reading of Russell's work notes for the second edition. In his introduction to the second edition Russell investigates and rejects the idea of developing infinite conjunctions and disjunctions.[41] In contrast, Ramsey writes:

> In this lies the great advantage of my method over that of *Principia Mathematica*. In *Principia* the range of φ is that of functions which can be elementarily expressed, and since $(\forall \varphi).f(\varphi!\hat{y}, x)$ cannot be so expressed it cannot be a value of φ!; but I define the values of φ not by how they can be expressed, but by what sort of senses their values have, or rather, by how the facts their values assert are related to their arguments. I thus include function which could not even be expressed by us at all, let alone elementarily, but only by a being with an infinite syllogistic system. And any function formed by generalization being actually predicative, there is no longer any need for an Axiom of Reducibility.[42]

In his paper "Mathematical Logic" Ramsey ties the idea to Wittgenstein's conception of quantification. He writes:

> On Wittgenstein's theory a general proposition is equivalent to a conjunction of its instances, so that the kind of fact asserted by a general proposition is not essentially different from that asserted by a conjunction of atomic propositions. But the symbol for a general proposition means its meaning in a way different from that in which a symbol for an elementary proposition means it. . . . Hence the orders of propositions will be characteristics not of what is meant, which is alone relevant in mathematics, but of the symbols used to mean it. . . . Applying this *mutatis mutandis* to propositional

functions, we find that the typical [order] distinctions between functions with the same arguments apply not to what is meant, but to the relation of meaning between symbol and object signified. Hence they can be neglected in mathematics.[43]

Reducibility is not semantically justified in the original nominalistic semantics Russell gave for Principia (1910). Ramsey's new plan is to semantically interpret the predicate variables of Principia by appeal to functional assignments (i.e. "propositional functions in extension"), some of which take objects to infinitely long formulas. Thus by developing Wittgenstein's theory of general and existential propositions, Ramsey says that we can "get rid of the Axiom of Reducibility."[44] What Ramsey means is that in his new infinitary nominalistic semantics, *12.1n is semantically justified.

In *My Philosophical Development* Russell recalls his delight in Ramsey's work. Ramsey suggests a way one might preserve the structure of a simple (impredicative) type theory, leaving ramification aside. Russell had labored for years to preserve the structure of simple types. During the era of the substitutional theory he was explicit about the separation of logical paradoxes (e.g. classes, attributes, and Burali-Forti), which require reformulation of logical first principles, and semantic paradoxes (e.g. Berry, Richard and Koenig Dixon), which are dismissed as based on confused notions of nameable and definable. But the substitutional theory floundered due to a unique logical paradox of propositional structure. Principia's nominalistic semantics was the successor. The nominalistic semantics for predicate variables—which realizes Russell's thesis that only the individual variables of Principia are genuine—requires recursive definitions of "truth" and "falsehood." The recursive definitions of "truth" and "falsehood," however, bring ramification (i.e. the validity of only predicative instances of *12.1n) with them. Ramsey offers a way out. Russell expresses his sincere hope that Ramsey's theory may be right (MPD, p. 126).

Ramsey's infinitary nominalistic semantics also plays a central role in his treatment of identity. In a letter of 1923 to his mother, Ramsey wrote that he had reported his knowledge of Russell's work notes for the second edition of *Principia* to Wittgenstein. He put the response vividly:

> He [Wittgenstein] is, I can see, a little annoyed that Russell is doing a new edit[ion] of *Principia* because he thought he had shown Russell that it was so wrong that a new edition would be futile. It must be done altogether afresh.[45]

Wittgenstein regarded the elimination of identity to be a central achievement of the *Tractatus*. It was precisely because of the elimination of identity that he maintained that logicism must reconceptualize arithmetic truths in terms of equations rather than tautologies. The rejection of identity would thoroughly alter the constructions of first edition of *Principia*. Ramsey corroborates this interpretation in his letter to Wittgenstein:

> *I went to see Russell a few weeks ago*, and am reading the manuscript of the new stuff he is putting into the *Principia*. *You are right that it is of no importance*; all that it really *amounts to is a clever proof of mathematical induction without using the axiom of reducibility*. There is no fundamental changes; identity is just as it used to be.[46]

The same criticism of Russell appears in Ramsey's review of the second edition for *Nature*.[47]

Russell admitted that for a time he accepted Wittgenstein views on identity, but he soon came to the conclusion that it made mathematical logic impossible and that Wittgenstein's criticism is invalid.[48] Though Ramsey's initial letters are in sympathy with Wittgenstein on identity, it was not long until he too had a change of heart. Ramsey's diary entry of February 1924 reports that in his meeting with Russell to discuss the second edition Russell was ". . . rather good against W's [Wittgenstein's] identity . . ." In his 1925 work "The Foundations of Mathematics" he wrote that he had spent a lot of time developing Wittgenstein's construal of identity and the theory of mathematics as equations, but he found it to be "faced with insuperable difficulties."[49] Identity must be recovered in some way.

Ramsey's semantics introduces propositional function in extension, which enables *Principia*'s definition of identity to remain intact. For example, Ramsey's semantics for *Principia*'s predicate variables $\varphi^{(o)}$ exploits the function f_e from individuals to formulas of a language L_1 that contains at most bound individual variables. Consider the following instance of *Principia*'s definition of identity for lowest type:

$$x^o = y^o =\text{df } (\forall \varphi^{(o)})(\varphi^{(o)}(x^o) \equiv \varphi^{(o)}(y^o)).$$

On Ramsey's view, this is to be semantically interpreted so that it comes out true if and only if for every extensional function f_e and all individuals x and y (*in the domain*), there are formulas A and B of L_1 such that $f_e(x) = A$ and $f_e(y) = B$ and "$A \equiv B$" is true. Under Ramsey's semantics, if the formula assigned to the variable x is the same as the formula assigned to y, then we get the tautology "$A \equiv A$." On the other hand, if the individual x is not y, then there is certainly a function f_e and some formula B of L_1 such that $f_e(x) = B$ and $f_e(y) = \sim B$. Hence we get the contradiction "$B \equiv \sim B$." Accordingly, the semantics makes $(\forall \varphi^{(o)})(\varphi^{(o)}(x^o) \equiv \varphi^{(t)}(y^o))$ come out either as a tautology or a contradiction. Next Ramsey explains that his semantics makes:

> "There is at least 1 individual"
> "There are at least 2 individuals"
> "There are at least n individuals"
> "There are at least $\aleph_0$ individuals"
> "There are at least $\aleph_1$ individuals."

and so on, either tautologies or contradictions.[50] The series starts out tautologous, and somewhere it becomes contradictory. Ramsey concludes that his semantics offers a compromise between Russell and Wittgenstein on identity.

Ramsey's infinitary nominalistic semantics endeavors to find a compromise between Wittgenstein's thesis that logic consists of tautologies and Russell's logicism. The formal grammar and the constructions of Principia remain intact. But, Ramsey explains,

> by using these variables [functions in extension] we obtain the system of *Principia Mathematica*, simplified by the omission of the Axiom of Reducibility, and a few corresponding alterations. Formally it is almost unaltered; but its meaning has been considerably changed.[51]

Ramsey rejects Wittgenstein's thesis that arithmetic consists of equations, not tautologies. The notations of Principia remain unaltered, though the semantics has changed their meanings. Principia would not have to be "done afresh" after all.

Russell's evaluation of Tractarian ideas in Principia's second edition fails to vindicate the oracle. Not surprisingly, Russell's assessment did not please Wittgenstein. He regarded the elimination of identity to be perhaps the greatest of the achievements in the *Tractatus*. It is ignored in the second edition of Principia. This explains Wittgenstein's cold reaction to Russell's development of his views. In light of their early support, how disappointing it must have been for Wittgenstein to find both Russell and Ramsey abandoning him.[52]

FURTHER READING

Nino Cocchiarella, *Logical Studies in Early Analytic Philosophy* (Columbus: Ohio State University Press, 1987).

Pasquale Frascolla, *Wittgenstein's Philosophy of Mathematics* (London: Routledge, 1994).

James Griffin, *Wittgenstein's Logical Atomism* (Seattle: University of Washington Press, 1969).

Brian McGuinness, *Wittgenstein: A Life* (Berkeley, CA: University of California Press, 1988).

Frank P. Ramsey, *The Foundations of Mathematics and other Logical Essays* (New York: Harcourt, Brace and Co., 1931).

G. H. Von Wright, *Wittgenstein* (Oxford: Basil Blackwell, 1982).

Eight

Probable Knowledge

> In this sense, it must be admitted, empiricism as a theory of knowledge has proved inadequate, though less so than any other previous theory of knowledge. Indeed, such inadequacies as we have seemed to find in empiricism have been discovered by strict adherence to a doctrine by which empiricist philosophy has been inspired: that all human knowledge is uncertain, inexact, and partial. To this doctrine we have not found any limitation whatever.
>
> *Human Knowledge* (1948)

Trinity College Cambridge awarded Russell a five-year lectureship in 1944. It resulted in his last major work, *Human Knowledge: Its Scope and Limits*. During the first six months, Russell says he ". . . enjoyed the feeling of peacefulness in spite of V1's and V2's."[1] Naturalized epistemology is still in full force, though the book comes to conclude, after carefully examining the different accounts of probability, that ". . . scientific inference requires, for its validity, principles which experience cannot render even probable."[2] This result, Russell says, effectively undermines the viability of empiricism in its pure form—though by cobbling it together with naturalism, Russell hopes to soften the sting. Naturalism shows that the traditional (methodologically solipsistic) conception of knowledge should be replaced by something that ". . . has its roots more deeply embedded in unverbalized animal behavior than most philosophers have been willing to admit" (HK, p. xv). The traditional epistemologist would ask whether we know the postulates of scientific inference. Russell's reply is that this is not so definite a question as it seems:

> The answer must be: in one sense, yes, in another sense, no; but in the sense in which "no" is the right answer we know nothing whatsoever, and "knowledge" in this sense is a delusive vision. The perplexities of philosophers are due, in large measure, to their unwillingness to awaken from this blissful dream.[3]

LOGIC IS *NOT* PART OF PHILOSOPHY?

Human Knowledge opens in a rather odd way. Russell writes in the preface:

> I think it is unfortunate that during the last hundred and sixty years or so philosophy has come to be regarded as almost as technical as mathematics. Logic, it must be admitted, is technical in the same way as mathematics is, but logic, I maintain, is not part of philosophy.[4]

In *Our Knowledge of the External World* (1914), logic is the "essence of philosophy" and the very foundation of the philosophy of Logical Atomism and its new scientific approaches to epistemology, mind, and matter. What happened?

As Russell's endeavors to dissolve the paradoxes plaguing logicism became ever more extensive, he found himself retreating further and further from the mystical splendor generated by the Pythagorean (or better, Platonistic) conception that logic and pure mathematics are founded upon the residents of (Plato's) heaven. Looking back over the many years of his long life, Russell wrote: "My philosophical development, since the early years of the present century, may be broadly described as a gradual retreat from Pythagoras" (MPD, p. 208). The retreat traces Russell's gradual and cautious steps toward a scientific philosophy of naturalism, the home in which he finds himself in *Human Knowledge*. In *My Philosophical Development* (1959), Russell wrote:

> The solution of the contradiction... seemed to be only possible by adopting theories which might be true but were not beautiful. I felt about the contradictions much as an earnest Catholic must feel about wicked Popes. And the splendid certainty which I had always hoped to find in mathematics was lost in a bewildering maze.[5]

Russell goes on to describe himself as reluctantly submitting to truths which were to him repugnant—in particular, the view that logic and mathematics consist of tautologies. Russell recalls the role of Wittgenstein in this:

> Wittgenstein maintains that logic consists wholly of tautologies. I think he is right in this, although I did not think so until I read what he had to say on the subject.
>
> Mathematics has ceased to seem to me non-human in its subject matter. I have come to believe, though very reluctantly, that it consists of tautologies. I fear that, to a mind of sufficient intellectual power, the whole of mathematics would appear trivial, as trivial as the statement that a four-footed animal is an animal.... I cannot any longer find any mystical satisfaction in the contemplation of mathematical truth.[6]
>
> (*MPD*, pp. 119, 212)

But we have seen that Wittgenstein meant something very different than Russell when he spoke of logic consisting of tautologies; he meant that logic is decidable.

One can find Russell advocating the view that logical truths are tautologies in *The Analysis of Matter* and in his introduction to the second edition of *The Principles of Mathematics* (1937). But at the same time, in the latter work and in *Inquiry into Meaning and Truth*, Carnap's conventionalist approach to logic is rejected. Carnap imagines two logical languages, one of which admits the multiplicative axiom and the axiom of infinity as "analytic," while the other does not. In Russell's view, Carnap makes analyticity "arbitrary" (i.e. pragmatic) and to be settled by choice of a formal linguistic calculus. Russell explains:

> I cannot myself regard such a matter as one to be decided by our arbitrary choice. It seems to me that these axioms either do, or do not, have the characteristic of formal truth which characterizes logic, and that in the former event every logic must include them.
>
> (*PoM*, p. xii)

Russell rejected Carnap's account of "analyticity" and the thesis that logical truth (i.e. logical necessity) is "linguistic" in the sense of being conventional (i.e. the adoption of grammatical rules governing the non-descriptive particles of a given language form). It is, therefore, unfortunate that Russell describes the view that logic consists of tautologies as a doctrine that logic and mathematics are "linguistic." He writes:

> Logical constants must be treated as part of the language, not as part of what the language speaks about. In this way, logic becomes much more linguistic than I believed it to be at the time when I wrote the *Principles*.[7]

In Principia Russell rejected his early view that logical constants stand for relations. His early ontology of propositions was abandoned. Modern logic agrees, but has no patience for a conception of logic as linguistic. It is therefore misleading to characterize Russell's mature view as a thesis that logic is linguistic.

Russell's retreat from Pythagoras is a retreat from the postulation of logical entities. Faced with the paradoxes plaguing logicism, Russell had come to hold that the formulas of mathematical languages are to be re-conceptualized and recovered in formulas of the proper formal language for logic—formulas which, by means of Russell's logical constructions, eschew Platonic (Pythagorean) ontological commitments to mathematical objects such as numbers, classes, relations-in-extension, and functions. Russell's desire to build the structure of orders of propositions into a nopropositions recursive theory of truth led him to reject his early conviction that the logical particles are signs for logical relations between propositions. In *Principia*, the logical connectives are statement connectives flanked by statements to form statements. The logical particles do not stand for relations between propositions and (though there may be general facts and negative facts) no facts that are truth-makers contain ontological counterparts of the tilde, the conditional, the generality sign, etc. Logical truth or "truth in virtue of logical form" turns on the structures that are rendered by the logical particles. Now the logical particles, Russell tells us, are "concerned with syntax." In this respect, he speaks of his having written an "epitaph on Pythagoras." As he puts it: ". . . the propositions of logic and mathematics are linguistic," and they ". . . are concerned with syntax"; and ". . . all the propositions of mathematics and logic are assertions as to the correct use of a certain small number of words."[8] But the correct use of the logical particles of the language for logic is not, in Russell's estimation, determined by our having adopted certain linguistic rules in using the language. Russell rejected Carnap's conventionalist position that there are different formal systems for logic with different logical particles. As we saw in *My Philosophical Development*, Russell described the evolution of his thinking on mathematical logic as a "retreat from Pythagoras," for he came to believe "logic and mathematics are linguistic" and "tautologous." But this is quite different from the homophonic forms of the thesis advocated by Carnap and by interpreters of Wittgenstein's later philosophical ideas.

Instead of characterizing Russell's mature view as making logic and mathematics "linguistic," we should speak of Russell coming to accept a naturalism in the philosophy of mind. Russell made several efforts toward re-constructions of "belief," "truth," "knowledge," "perception," "matter," and "mind." His neutral monism led him to a naturalized epistemology, and this, in turn, led him to a new appreciation for Hume's empiricism. He was pushed to a psychological conception of knowing as an activity. Inference is a habit built out of stimulus-response patterns governed by the Law of Effect.[9] In *Outline of Philosophy* Russell writes:

> To "understand" even the simplest formula in algebra, say $(x+y)^2 = x^2 + 2xy + y^2$ is to be able to react to two sets of symbols in virtue of the form which they express, and to perceive that form is the same in both cases. This is a very elaborate business, and it is no wonder that boys and girls find algebra a bugbear. But there is no novelty in principle after the first elementary perceptions of form. And perception of form consists merely in reacting alike to two stimuli which are alike in form but very different in other respects.[10]

Knowledge of mathematics is thus acquired a posteriori by a form of pattern matching and reflection. There may yet be an a priori component: the recognition of logical relations between patterns or structures. But it is clear that its role has significantly diminished in Russell's later writings. Russell, it seems, embraces the naturalization of knowledge of logic and mathematics.

Dewey was also advocating a naturalized evolutionary epistemology and theory of logic which developed from his pragmatism. On Dewey's view, the traditional notion of an organism's representation of the world as being true or false is to be abandoned in favor of notions of organism-environment states of equilibrium or disharmony ("inquiry") with accompanying degrees of "success."[11] Recovering the traditional notion of truth within naturalism proved to be quite important to Russell, and it was the focus of some stormy exchanges with Dewey. In writing *Human Knowledge*, Russell's retreat from Pythagoras was complete. Russell's program of Logical Atomism began in moderation, with logic and knowledge of logic exempted from analysis. By the 1940s Russell's Logical Atomism had reached the position that knowledge of logic must itself succumb. Knowledge of logic (and so also mathematics) no longer occupies a lofty place in epistemology or metaphysics.

PROBABILITY AND INDUCTION

Russell distinguishes three main sorts of probability: the mathematical theory, the Keynesian theory of degrees of credibility, and the Mises-Reichenbach frequency theory. Keynes's notion of probability involves assigning a degree of credence in reasoning in situations of uncertainty. In contrast, the mathematical theory makes probability a relation between two propositions (i.e. statements), p and h. Russell sets out Broad's axioms for the mathematical theory as follows:

$Axiom_1$ For any p and h, There is a unique value $\frac{p}{h}$.

$Axiom_2$ The value $\frac{p}{h}$ is such that $0 \leq \frac{p}{h} \leq 1$, in the rationals or in the reals.

$Axiom_3$ If $h \supset p$ then $\frac{p}{h} = 1$.

$Axiom_4$ If $h \supset \sim p$ then $\frac{p}{h} = 0$.

$Axiom_5$ $\frac{p \& q}{h} = \frac{p}{h} \times \frac{q}{p \& h}$ and $\frac{p \& q}{h} = \frac{q}{h} \times \frac{p}{q \& h}$.

$Axiom_6$ $\frac{p \vee q}{h} = \frac{p}{h} + \frac{q}{h} - \frac{p \& q}{h}$.

(HK, p. 345)

These postulates may be interpreted in different ways. One interpretation yields the usual system of mathematical probability, the postulates of which are more familiar.

The mathematical theory tells us that if the sample space has exactly n-many independent outcomes, then we may define the probability of any one of them occurring to be $\frac{1}{n}$. The mathematical theory has it that if a sample space S has n many independent outcomes and m of them have a certain characteristic, the probability that an unspecified member of S has the characteristic is $\frac{m}{n}$. For example, if a dice is six-sided, and tossing it has exactly six independent equally likely outcomes, then the probability of rolling a 6 on one toss is $\frac{1}{6}$. The following more usual "probability postulates" are provable in logic without appeal to sets. Where S is the sample space, we have:

(1) If $A \subseteq S$ then $\text{Prob}(A) = \frac{\#A}{\#S}$ and $0 \leq \frac{\#A}{\#S} \leq 1$

(2) If $A = S$ then $\text{Prob}(A) = 1$

(3) If $A \subseteq S$ and $B \subseteq S$ and $A \cap B = \emptyset$ then

$\text{Prob}(A \cup B) = \text{Prob}(A) + \text{Prob}(B)$.

These are obvious given the mathematical definition of probability. One can then prove:

If $A \subseteq S$ then $\text{Prob}(S \cap Ă) = 1 - \text{Prob}(A)$

Just let B in (3) be $S \cap Ă$ and since the antecedent clauses hold, we get $\text{Prob}(A \cup (S \cap Ă)) = \text{Prob}(A) + \text{Prob}(S \cap Ă)$. Since we know that $\text{Prob}(A \cup (S \cap Ă)) = 1$ the theorem is immediate. One can also prove:

If $A \subseteq S$ and $B \subseteq S$ then $\text{Prob}(A \cup B) = \text{Prob}(A) + \text{Prob}(B) - \text{Prob}(A \cap B)$

This is intuitively clear (see figure overleaf). Since, $A \cap (B \cap Ă) = \emptyset$ (3) yields $\text{Prob}(A \cup (B \cap Ă)) = \text{Prob}(A) + \text{Prob}(B \cap Ă)$ and since $A \cup (B \cap Ă) = A \cup B$, $\text{Prob}(A \cup B) = \text{Prob}(A) + \text{Prob}(B \cap Ă)$. Next notice that $(A \cap B) \cap (B \cap Ă) = \emptyset$. Hence (3) yields

$\text{Prob}((A \cap B) \cup (B \cap Ă)) = \text{Prob}(A \cap B) + \text{Prob}(B \cap Ă)$.

Probable Knowledge

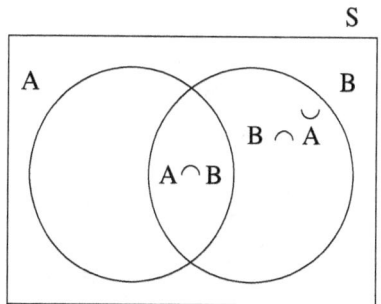

Since $(A \cap B) \cup (B \cap \breve{A}) = B$, this yields $\text{Prob}(B) = \text{Prob}(A \cap B) + \text{Prob}(B \cap \breve{A})$. A little algebra yields $\text{Prob}(B) - \text{Prob}(A \cap B) = \text{Prob}(B \cap \breve{A})$. The theorem follows by putting these two together.

A notion of conditional probability is then defined. Where $B \neq \emptyset$, one defines the conditional probability of A given B as follows:

$$\text{Prob}(A/B) =_{df} \frac{\text{Prob}(B \cap A)}{\text{Prob}(B)}.$$

Once again, the definition is obvious. From this, Bayes's famous theorem is immediate:

$$\text{Prob}(B/A) = \frac{\text{Prob}(A/B) \times \text{Prob}(B)}{\text{Prob}(A)}.$$

The proof is simple:

$$\text{Prob}(A/B) =_{df} \frac{\text{Prob}(B \cap A)}{\text{Prob}(B)}$$

$$\text{Prob}(A/B) \times \text{Prob}(B) = \text{Prob}(B \cap A)$$

$$\text{Prob}(B/A) =_{df} \frac{\text{Prob}(A \cap B)}{\text{Prob}(A)}$$

$$\text{Prob}(A \cap B) = \text{Prob}(B \cap A)$$

$$\text{Prob}(B/A) =_{df} \frac{\text{Prob}(B \cap A)}{\text{Prob}(A)}$$

$$\text{Prob}(B/A) \times \text{Prob}(A) = \text{Prob}(B \cap A)$$
$$\text{Prob}(B/A) \times \text{Prob}(A) = \text{Prob}(A/B) \times \text{Prob}(B)$$
$$\text{Prob}(B/A) = \frac{\text{Prob}(A/B) \times \text{Prob}(B)}{\text{Prob}(A)}.$$

This is all from the definitions with very little algebra.

Returning to Russell's statement of Broad's postulates, we can now see that they may be interpreted so as to coincide with the mathematical notion of probability. This interpretation reads as $\frac{p}{h}$ as Prob(P/H), where P is the group of outcomes that make the statement p true and H is the group of outcomes that make the statement h true. That is:

$$\frac{p}{h} = \frac{\text{Prob}(P \cap H)}{\text{Prob}(H)}$$
$$\frac{p \,\&\, q}{h} = \text{Prob}((P \cap Q)/H) = \frac{\text{Prob}(P \cap Q \cap H)}{\text{Prob}(H)}$$
$$\frac{p \vee q}{h} = \text{Prob}((P \cup Q)/H) = \frac{\text{Prob}(P \cup Q \cup H)}{\text{Prob}(H)}.$$

Of course, if h is the number of outcomes in the sample space itself, we have:

$$\frac{p}{h} = \frac{\text{Prob}(P \cap S)}{\text{Prob}(S)} = \frac{\#P}{\#S}.$$

For example, a Venn diagram of outcomes makes clear Broad's Axiom 3 (see figure overleaf). The shading represents "if h then p." All regions in H are in P. We can readily see that $\frac{p}{h} = 1$. That is, $\frac{\text{Prob}(P \cap H)}{\text{Prob}(H)} = \frac{6}{6} = 1$. Obviously it will not matter what numbers are in the regions.

Probable Knowledge 379

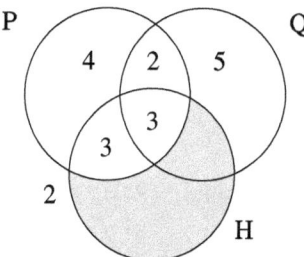

Similarly, a Venn diagram makes clear Broad's Axiom 3.

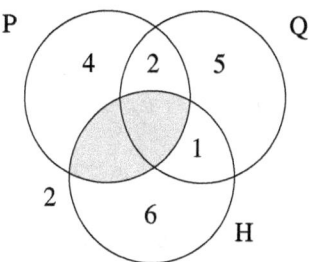

In this case we have "If h then not p" and this shades the area which is the intersection of H and P. Our Venn diagram now quite clearly shows that $\frac{p}{h} = 0$. That is, $\frac{\text{Prob}(P \cap H)}{\text{Prob}(H)} = \frac{0}{7} = 0$. These cases are more or less straightforward. Indeed, the other axioms fall into place on this interpretation as well. A Venn diagram of outcomes makes clear Broad's Axiom 5.

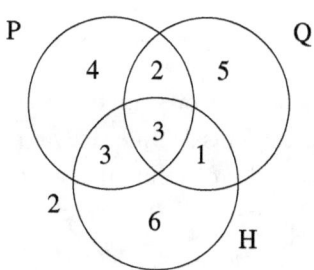

Recalling the translation is one of conditional probability, our interpretation will transform Broad's axiom $\frac{p \& q}{h} = \frac{p}{h} \times \frac{q}{p \& h}$ into a statement about conditional probabilities. The axiom becomes

$$\text{Prob}((P \cap Q)/H) = \text{Prob}(P/H) \times \text{Prob}(Q/(P \cap H)).$$

That is: $\frac{3}{13} = \frac{6}{13} \times \frac{3}{6}$. And similarly, the figure above makes clear Broad's Axom 6 which is written as $\frac{p \vee q}{h} = \frac{p}{h} + \frac{q}{h} - \frac{p \& q}{h}$. The present interpretation renders

$$\text{Prob}((P \cup Q)/H) = \text{Prob}(P/H) + \text{Prob}(Q/H) - \text{Prob}(P \cap Q)/H).$$

That is: $\frac{7}{13} = \frac{6}{13} + \frac{4}{13} - \frac{3}{13}$. Under this interpretation, the purely mathematical (statistical) theory of probability enjoys the status of being logically necessary (as with all of mathematics) on Russell's view. This is entirely as it should be if probability is to be understood as a purely mathematical theory.

It is important to note that assignments of initial probabilities in cases of very limited information rely on applications of a principle of indifference. The principle states that two possible occurrences are equally probable if there is no reason to suppose one will happen rather than the other. This raises difficulties. As in the case of tossing a coin, we certainly do not want to say that the probability of a random object being red is $\frac{1}{2}$ because every object is either red or not red. The classification of something as non-red does not properly cut nature at its joints. With exactly n-many distinct colors possible, the mathematical probability that a random object is non-red should intuitively be $\frac{n-1}{n}$.

In cases where infinity is involved, serious difficulties arise. We feel confident, given the consecutive ordering of the natural numbers, that the probability of randomly choosing an odd natural number is $\frac{1}{2}$. But this confidence is not because the cardinal number of evens is the same as the cardinal number of odds. Indeed, as Russell points out, the cardinal number of primes is the same as the cardinal number of odds, but we would be very unwise to think that the probability is $\frac{1}{2}$ of randomly choosing a prime (HK, p. 367). In the case of the primes, the gap between the primes increases ever more widely. Thus, as we progress consecutively in the usual ordering of the natural numbers, the frequency of a prime appearing gets smaller without end. Unlike the primes, we say that "half of the natural numbers are odd." But what this means is that in consecutive ordering of the natural numbers every other natural number is odd. It is because of this ordering that we are intuitively inclined to say the probability of hitting an even number is $\frac{1}{2}$. We must also be careful about thinking in terms of a midpoint in an infinite series. The existence of a midpoint 0 in the integers is certainly not enough to suggest that the probability of randomly choosing a negative integer is $\frac{1}{2}$. Once again, such a probability would only be justified by reordering the integers so that every other is positive.[12]

Salmon[13] offers a curious Bertrand-style[14] paradox concerning the application of a principle of indifference. Suppose a car transverses a mile at a uniform speed inclusively between 60 seconds and 120 seconds. We have no further information. What then is the probability that the time it took the car to transverse the mile is between 60 seconds and 90 seconds? To arrive at an answer, we might think to impose a median time of this interval. The median of a finite group of outcomes is the number such that the cardinal number of outcomes less than it is the same as the cardinal number greater than it.[15] For instance, if the outcomes are 1, 3, 5, 7, 11 the median is 5. But the imposition of a median will not make good sense if the interval is infinite and dense (such as the rationals), for then every number is a median since there will be the same number of rationals that are less than it as there are greater than it. Hence, imposing a median requires that the outcomes are not dense. If our temporal interval from 60 seconds to 120 seconds contains only finitely many temporal units, say n-many, then the median is 90 seconds. Hence, if we apply the principle of indifference and assume that each of the n-many temporal units (of equal duration) has the same probability of $\frac{1}{n}$, then the probability is $\frac{\left(\frac{n}{2}\right)}{n}$ that the time it takes the car to transverse the mile is between 60 seconds and 90 seconds. That is, it is $\frac{1}{2}$. Observe, however, that this restricts the possible speeds at which the car may travel and indeed the speeds will not be equally spaced from one another. For example, if the finite number of units of time are the natural numbers t such that $60 \leq t \leq 120$, then the speeds that the car can travel are restricted to $\frac{1 \text{ mile}}{t \text{ seconds}}$. The car travels at only some speeds between $\frac{1 \text{ mile}}{60 \text{ seconds}}$ (60 mph) and $\frac{1 \text{ mile}}{120 \text{ seconds}}$ (30 mph). It cannot travel at the speed 31mph for this is $\frac{1 \text{ mile}}{\frac{3600}{31} \text{ seconds}}$ and $\frac{3600}{31}$ is not a natural number. Due to the restriction on the possible speeds, the median of the allowable speeds is $\frac{1 \text{ mile}}{90 \text{ seconds}}$ (40 mph).

$$\frac{1}{60} \quad 60 \qquad 120 \quad \frac{1}{120}$$

$$\frac{1}{61} \quad 61 \qquad 119 \quad \frac{1}{119}$$

$$\vdots \qquad \vdots$$

$$\frac{1}{89} \quad 89 \qquad 91 \quad \frac{1}{91}$$

$$90$$

$$\frac{1}{90}$$

Thus, the probability that the car traveled at a speed between 60 mph and 40 mph is $\frac{1}{2}$. That might seem to be a paradox. But it is not paradoxical once we recall that the number of possible speeds has been restricted by imposing a median in the time interval. Observe, however, that instead of a median in the time interval, we thought to impose a median in the speed interval. If there are finitely many possible speeds (say, m-many) at equal intervals from one another between $\frac{1 \text{ mile}}{60 \text{ seconds}}$ (60 mph) and $\frac{1 \text{ mile}}{120 \text{ seconds}}$ (30 mph), the median is $\frac{1 \text{ mile}}{80 \text{ seconds}}$ (45 mph). By the principle of indifference, each speed unit has the same probability of $\frac{1}{m}$. So the probability that the car will travel at a speed between 60 mph and 45mph is $\frac{\left(\frac{m}{2}\right)}{m}$. That is, it is $\frac{1}{2}$. But now the allowable time increments for the car have been restricted. Salmon concludes that application of the principle of indifference is unprincipled. It yields incompatible probability assessments.[16] But the proper lesson is that the interval is dense and, since there is no way to exact a satisfactory median, there is no way to apply indifference to the case.

Paradoxes belonging in the domain of the pure mathematics of the infinite are solved by thinking correctly about infinite series. It is not these paradoxes, but the questions surrounding the application to the world that cause trouble for the viability of the mathematical theory of probability. The mathematical notion says absolutely nothing about probability as applied to outcomes of actual physical events. Consider, for example, an actual throw of a physical dice. To apply even the most simple of these probability results requires making a vast number of empirical, and in some cases very reasonably doubtful, assumptions about the given situation. Do the cutouts etched on its surfaces to represent numbers unbalance its center of gravity? Is its shape really cubical? Are the molecular bonds on one side of it less stable than on the other so that it does not deform unevenly when it impacts a surface? Do the surfaces of its faces have different topographies so that it is not more likely to land on one face than another? And how can these assumptions be plausibly made for dice in general, even if they apply to some few specific dice?

Hans Reichenbach was very interested in the relationship between the purely mathematical notion of probability and the question of the probability of a physical outcome occurring in a consecutive series of physical events. In tossing a coin the probability is $\frac{1}{2}$ of it being heads, but he is well aware that this is not simply a mathematical notion of probability. "It is an empirical fact," Russell explains, and

> it does not follow from the fact that in tossing a coin there are only two possibilities, heads and tails. If it did, we could infer that the chance of a stranger being called Ebenezer Wilkes Smith is a half, since there are only two alternatives, that he is so called or that he isn't.

(*HK*, p. 370)

According to Reichenbach, the probability of getting heads

in tossing a coin is $\frac{1}{2}$ because the frequency of heads, the proportion

$$\frac{\text{number of heads}}{\text{number of total tosses so far}}$$

in consecutive repeated physical tosses of the coin will get nearer and nearer to $\frac{1}{2}$ as the number of tosses increases. Since probability is measured in terms of a ratio, and since this notion has no meaning when the numerator and denominator are infinite, Russell reminds us that Reichenbach's notion employs limits of ordered consecutive series (HK, pp. 357, 370). If, for example, we repeatedly toss a coin, then at any given finite number of total tosses the proportion of heads will sometimes be more than half the total, sometimes less. Thus the portion of n tosses that were heads oscillates about the limit $\frac{1}{2}$.

In *Human Knowledge*, Russell was concerned with evaluating Reichenbach's view that the frequency theory of probability has an important bearing on the problem of induction. The problem of justifying induction owes its most famous formulation to David Hume (1711–1776), a Scottish philosopher whose empiricism and skepticism spread like a firestorm. Inductive inference is central to all empirical knowledge. But little more than conditioned responses and habits of expectation seem to lie behind the eagerness with which an association of cases of As and Bs lead us to conclude that the next A we see will be a B or that all As are Bs.

Which inductive arguments are justified? If just one A is found with a B it seems a hasty inductive generalization to conclude that all As are Bs. But an increase in the cases found does not assure an improved induction. What empirical conditions play a role in assessing inductive arguments?

Unlike deductive validity, induction seems not to be about structure. Two structurally similar enumerative inductive arguments may be evaluated quite differently. Suppose n-many As (emeralds) are observed to be B (green). We inductively conclude that all As are B. This seems a reasonably good induction. But notice that the premises of this induction imply that n-many As (emeralds) are grue, where "grue" means either observed on or before 2010 and green or observed after 2010 and blue. Yet we dislike the conclusion that all emeralds are grue. It commits us to holding that after 2010, all observed emeralds are blue. This is Goodman's so-called "new riddle of induction." There is something more to a good induction than structure. We must somehow perform our inductions on genuine properties of the world, not contrived notions such as "grue" that do not "cut nature at its joints." But which of our concepts characterize genuine properties? This matter cannot be decided from the armchair by appealing to complexity or simplicity of the expressions for the properties in question. Many scientific, well-established properties are only expressible quantitatively and by means of complex expressions involving disjunctions, quantifiers and other logical particles. It is far from clear how we are find the joints, except by a circular appeal to inductive arguments.

Hume thinks it impossible to offer an argument justifying induction. Suppose we find an argument for a set of criteria for selecting only the good inductive arguments. Hume observes that our argument would either be deductive or inductive. If one offers an inductive argument for a way of choosing good inductive arguments, we are in a vicious circle. On the other hand, if we offer a deductive argument, the premises cannot themselves be inductively justified, else we are in a regress. Hence, any empirical premises in the argument must be about the past or the present. But no deductive argument which does not contain premises about the future can have a conclusion that has import for the future. Inductive arguments do contain conclusions that have import for the future. How can Hume's dilemma be avoided? One might think to add a new premise to a deductive argument for induction asserting that nature is uniform: "The future will be like the past." The premise is rather vague especially in its use of likeness since by different criteria of similarity most any two events are alike. In any case, this new empirical premise could only be accepted as a conclusion from an inductive argument because it makes claims about the future. Accordingly, no deductive argument could justify a choice of good inductive inferences.

Reichenbach offered a theory of "scientific induction" based on the frequency notion of probability. He held that his frequency theory is able to find the uniformities of nature, if any theory can. Reichenbach hopes, thereby, to give a deductive argument justifying scientific induction. He argues that if any theory shows which are the good inductive arguments, scientific inductive logic does. If there is a uniformity in nature associating As with Bs, then the frequency has a limit and so scientific induction by enumeration will eventually find the limit. If, on the other hand, there is no uniformity in nature connecting As and Bs, then the frequency has no limit and no method whatsoever of induction can ascertain it. There is no way to know, outside of applying inductive methods, whether a physical consecutive sequence of events of Bs occurring when As occur converges to a limit. But Reichenbach explains, if any approach can find that there is a limit, then scientific induction can find it.

Russell's main worry about Reichenbach's defense of scientific induction is that it depends on the existence of frequencies (i.e. probabilities) that are hypothetical and forever unascertainable (HK, p. 372). The frequencies in physical outcomes are idealized recurring event types (e.g. tossings of a coin) projected toward infinity. Russell wonders how are we to decide if it is likely (i.e. probable) that there are such frequencies. The only way would be by employing induction and proclaiming that it shows this or that to be the probability there are such frequencies. Russell remained unconvinced of Reichenbach's view. In his book *The Rise of Scientific Philosophy*—a book very sympathetic to Russell's own scientific naturalism—Reichenbach complained that his ideas on induction had not been understood.[17] Unfortunately, a debate between them on these issues never materialized.

In his *Treatise on Probability*, Keynes made an extensive investigation of the viability of providing a justification of induction by appeal to the purely mathematical (statistical) theory of probability. One of Russell's purposes in *Human Knowledge* was to reveal that induction cannot be derived from the mathematical theory of probability. He sets forth "postulates of scientific inference" to make clear the empirical assumptions that have to be fulfilled in order that a high probability can be conferred on the conclusions of the right sort of inductive arguments. Keynes investigated the following question:

> Given a number of instances of A's which are B's and no known contrary instances, in what circumstances does the probability of the generalization "All A's are B's" approach certainty as a *limit* when the number of A's that are B's is continually increased?

Keynes says that the circumstances are these: (1) before we know any instances of As and Bs the sentence "All A are B" should have a finite degree of credibility[18] relative to all the rest of what we take ourselves to know; (2) the probability of our observing only favorable instances, if our statement is false, should tend to zero as a limit when the number of inferences is sufficiently increased. Russell sets forth "postulates of scientific inference" that he says are necessary (but not sufficient) conditions for (1). Russell's purpose in *Human Knowledge* is to make clear that fulfillment of these empirical assumptions is necessary in order that a high mathematical probability can be conferred on the conclusions of certain inductive arguments.

Russell's postulates of scientific inference concerning matter are five in number and very illuminating if one looks retrospectively at his constructions of matter both in *Our Knowledge* and *The Analysis of Mind*. The postulates are these:

(1) The postulate of quasi-permanence (assuring that a material continuant persists through change).
(2) The postulate of separable causal lines (assuring that material objects which produce certain (e.g. acoustical) events may also produce other events (e.g. electromagnetic).
(3) The postulate of spatio-temporal continuity in causal lines (denying action at a distance).
(4) The postulate of structure (assuring that there is a coherent structural similarity underlying related events that may not be qualitatively similar).
(5) The postulate of analogy (assuring the existence of other minds, other perspectives from which we construct matter as a series of events).

The postulates form the basis of the kind of coherence which gives rise to the increased mathematical probability involved in inductive inference. Russell says that they replace the more traditional notion which underlies a justification of inductive inference, namely the postulate of the uniformity of nature.

The central argument of *Human Knowledge* is, however, a dilemma. One must either adopt an extremely skeptical methodological solipsism or reject in part empiricism. Russell writes:

> I think this argument proves that we have to choose between two alternatives. Either we must accept skeptical solipsism in its most rigorous form, or we must admit that we know, independently of experience, some principle or principles by means of which it is possible to infer events from other events, at least with probability. If we adopt the first alternative, we must reject far more than solipsism is ordinarily thought to reject; we cannot know of the existence of our own past or future, or have any ground for expectation as to our own future, if it occurs. If we adopt the second alternative, we must partially reject empiricism; we must admit that we have knowledge as to certain general features of the course of nature . . .
>
> (*HK*, p. 179)

Russell explains further this strict solipsism as follows:

> The solipsist, therefore, if he is to attain the logical safety of which he is in search, will be confined to what I call "solipsism of the moment." He will say not only "I do not know whether the physical world exists or whether there are minds other than my own," but he will have to go further and say, "I don't know whether I had a past or shall have a future, for these things are just as doubtful as the existence of other people or of the physical world." No solipsist has ever gone so far as this, and therefore every solipsist has been inconsistent in accepting inferences about himself which have no better warrant than inferences about other people and things.
>
> (*MPD*, p. 181)

Russell is unequivocal in his rejection of the solipsistic alternative. His concessions to Hume are many in *Human Knowledge*, but they do not derive from the methodological solipsism of traditional empiricism. They result from his naturalism. It is important to not lose sight of this.

One can, of course, hope to reject solipsism without rejecting methodological solipsism in epistemology. But Russell's target is the frivolity of those empiricist philosophers who demand epistemology be methodologically solipsistic and then cannot bring themselves to adhere to the austere requirements of such a view. Russell writes:

> As against solipsism it is to be said, in the first place, that it is psychologically impossible to believe, and is rejected in fact even by those who mean to accept it. I once received a letter from an eminent logician, Mrs. Christine Ladd Franklin, saying that she was a solipsist, and was surprised that there were no others. Coming from a logician, this surprise surprised me. The fact that I cannot believe something does not prove that this is false, but it does prove that I am insincere and frivolous if I pretend to believe it. Cartesian doubt has value as a means of articulating our knowledge and

showing what depends on what, but if carried too far it becomes a mere technical game in which philosophy loses seriousness.

(*HK*, p. 180)

In *Human Knowledge* Russell is rejecting empiricist methodological solipsism in epistemology.

Surprisingly, Russell's dilemma has gone unnoticed. Perhaps a main reason is his comments on naïve realism. In his *Inquiry into Meaning and Truth* he says that

> we all start from naïve realism, i.e., the doctrine that things are as they seem. . . . The observer, when he seems to himself to be observing a stone, is really, if physics is to be believed, observing the effects of the stone upon himself. . . . Naïve realism leads to physics and physics, if true, shows naïve realism is false. Therefore, naïve realism, if true, is false; therefore it is false.
>
> (*IMT*, p. 15)

These comments have made it appear that Russell demands a retreat from naïve realism to the hard data accepted by the methodological solipsist. In *Human Knowledge* Russell extends his comment about naïve realism:

> Historically, physicists started from naïve realism, that is to say, from the belief that external objects are exactly as they seem. On the basis of this assumption, they developed a theory which made matter something quite unlike what we perceive. Thus their conclusion contradicted their premise, though no one except a few philosophers noticed this. We therefore have to decide whether, if physics is true, the hypothesis of naïve realism can be so modified that there shall be a valid inference from percepts to physics. In a word: If physics is true, is it possible that it should be known?
>
> (*HK*, p. 197)

Once again, many interpretations have given into the temptation that Russell is arguing for a methodological solipsism. We are to consider the conjunction p & q & r . . . of all would-be (naïve) empirical knowledge about the mind independent world. Call this conjunction P. Next we recall the following logical law:

If P implies not P, then not P.

Thus, if we can show that P implies not P, then we may conclude that not P, and that naïve realism is false. This argument, however, does not establish methodological solipsism. Russell maintained in *Human Knowledge* that empirical knowledge in one quarter is required to cast doubt on empirical knowledge in another. Suppose we find that P implies not P, then we know that the propositions that compose P are inconsistent. But the inconsistency merely shows that one or other among p, q, r., etc. of our conjunction constituting P is false. This does not cast any doubt whatsoever on any particular piece of empirical knowledge. Indeed, it is logically impossible to arrive at an empirical claim without asserting any empirical premises.[19]

Russell concludes *Human Knowledge* with the position that empiricism has serious limitations. Probable inference has now won the day over all other forms of knowing, including introspection and grasp of logic and mathematics. Reflecting on the work, Russell writes:

> I came to the conclusion that, although scientific inference needs indemonstrable extra-logical principles, induction is not one of them. It has a part to play, but not as a premise. . . . Another conclusion which was forced upon me was that not only science, but a great deal that no one sincerely doubts to be knowledge, is impossible if we only know what can be experienced and verified. I felt that too much emphasis had been laid on experience, and that, therefore, empiricism as a philosophy must be subjected to important limitations.[20]
>
> (*MPD*, p. 191)

It takes a good deal of empirical knowledge to provide an adequate theory of perception answering the question of how we have empirical knowledge of physical continuants, especially if the laws of physics are correctly characterized by the quantum and relativistic physicists current in Russell's day. Russell has not abandoned Logical Atomism and neutral monism in *Human Knowledge*. As before, he advocates a scientific approach to epistemology. The investigation of how we know about matter (i.e. continuants in time) is to be given by appeal to our knowledge of physics, chemistry, evolutionary biology, and psychology. It is these scientific fields that explain how we can come to know the new physics. In Russell's view, such an explanation is viable because, in the new physical sciences, we need to know only about structure.

ON THE NOTION OF CAUSE

The battle cry of his Logical Atomism is the thesis that the only necessity is logical necessity. The evolution of Russell's work—his retreat from Pythagoras—can be understood as an attempt to realize this. Logical necessity is fundamentally an issue of structure, not an issue of the inner essence of an object. Where A is a statement whose only free variables are $x_1, \ldots x_k$ and involving no bound predicate variables and no individual constants (names), Russell construes [ ]A (i.e. It is logically necessary that A) in terms of the truth of

$$(\forall \varphi_1) \ldots (\forall \varphi_n) (\forall x_1) \ldots (\forall x_k)(A^*)$$

where A^* replaces all the predicate letters $F_1, \ldots, F_n$ in A with predicate variables $\varphi_1, \ldots, \varphi_n$. What then of causal necessity?

Human Knowledge repeats Russell's early thesis in "On the Notion of Cause" that "causal necessity," so central to traditional philosophy and especially prominent in the Kant transcendental attempt to provide a foundation for Newtonian science, plays no interesting role in science.

This seems to place Russell within the camp of those holding the regularity theory of causation. The regularity theory, of course, owes its origins to Hume. From observed regularities of the past, we form inductive generalizations. That is, we are habituated to a pattern and thus develop expectations in accordance with habit. The main problem for a regularity theory is how to distinguish genuine scientific causal laws from accidentally true general relationships which do not warrant the title "laws" of nature. Both genuine laws of nature and accidentally true general statements have the form:

> Every event type e_1 which occurs is such that there is a temporal interval t after which an event of type e_2 will occur.

But a genuine law supports counterfactuals of the form "if e_1 were to happen then e_2 would happen after a finite interval." Counterfactuals can ground the distinction, however, only if they embody a form of necessity that is not logical. Russell's program does not embrace any such necessity.

Russell wants to deny that science has any sympathy for the philosophical idea that "Every event has a cause." Galileo was able to find a function between time and distance for bodies falling in a vacuum (so the shape of the object and the pressure of the air on it does not play a role in the equation). Thus he has:

> Every event type of releasing a body from rest in the proximity to the earth in a vacuum is such that there is a temporal interval t^2 after which follows the event type of its having travelled distance $\frac{1}{2} at^2$.

For Galileo, the sun, moon, distant stars, the shape of the earth at the release site, and the like were not mentioned in the statement of the event type e_1. As Newton came to see, however, all of these play a role, and they will show up in more refined observations. Galileo's event type e_1 never has an instance in the actual world because there are myriad other components in play and constantly changing. Newton's universal law of gravitation offers a new, more precise statement of the sort of event type needed. Differential equations can be found which hold for every particle in the system of particles (with mass) which are such that they compute, given the configuration and velocities of the system at one time, the configuration and velocities that will occur after a temporal interval. But even this was insufficient when observations became more refined. Einstein's even more complicated system of tensors is needed to account for the more refined observations involved in, for example, the perihelion of the orbit of Mercury. In Russell's view, we cannot, therefore, speak of individual causes and each of their effects. All the relevant objects play a role. We single out, among all these inputs to the function, ones that are significant for our purposes (at a given time) and speak as though only these are relevant to those outcomes of the function in which we take an interest. But physics is one thing and satisfying our goals and interests is quite another.

The closest thing to a "law of causality" that Russell can find and which is applicable to the actual practice of empirical science is this:

> There is a constant relation between the state of the universe at any instant and the rate of change in the rate at which any part of the universe is changing at that instant, and this relation is many-one [functional], i.e., such that the rate of change in the rate of change is determinate when the state of the universe is given.[21]

Russell goes on to say that "If the 'law of causality' is to be something actually discoverable in the practice of science, the above proposition has a better right to the name than any 'law of causality' to be found in the books of philosophers."[22] Most importantly, he hastens to add that in this form the law of causality is not knowable a priori (as Kant thought), makes no difference as to past and future, is not such that outcomes are compelled (since one can, given the outcome state, every bit as well deterministic which of various inputs to the function would yield this outcome state), and presupposes that nature is uniform.

The uniformity of nature, Russell explains, is the thesis that there are laws of nature. The notion of a law of nature is the notion of something permanent, something that always describes the transitions of the states of the universe in a given field. But once again in disagreement with Kant, Russell maintains that adopting the thesis of the uniformity of nature is not a precondition for the possibility of empirical science. Science can accept that some functions, which accurately characterize transitions, will have to be altered. The gravitational "constant" G, for example, in Newton's law of gravitation might change over time. Russell puts it amusingly:

> In the National Almanac for 1915 it will assume that the law of gravitation will remain true up to the end of that year; but it will make no assumption as to 1916 until it comes to the next volume of the Almanac.[23]

Of course, if the universe comes to an end, then theoretically there will be a function (and thus a law of nature in Russell's sense) that completely describes its transition states in all fields, from physics and chemistry to biology and economics. But whether the functions that characterize its transitions in a given field are permanent or changing, science (and induction) is powerless to say.

Science methodologically chooses simple functions. This has a great benefit since if a function hitherto correct begins to diverge from observations, the simplest formula in it that remains is often selected as the point of departure for finding a new more accurate function. Russell thus suggests that we might formulate the principle of the uniformity of nature as the requirement that no scientific law (i.e. transition function among event types) be formulated in such a way that mentions any particular time (though it may mention lapses of time).

Russell's considerations interestingly impact the intelligibility of the traditional philosophical problem of free will which became acute with Kant's philosophical reaction to the successes of

Newtonian science. According to Russell, science does not presuppose uniformity (i.e. the permanence of all the laws of nature) and does not, therefore, suppose that our will is determined by initial conditions which were imputs to functions (i.e. laws of nature) present long ago, well before humans. Russell wants to disabuse us of the belief that "... causes compel their effects, or that nature forces obedience to its laws as governments do." Russell explains that

> these are mere anthropomorphic superstitions, due to assimilation of causes with volitions and of natural laws with human edicts. We feel that our will is not compelled, but that only means that it is not other than we choose it to be. It is one of the demerits of the tradition theory of causality that it has created an artificial opposition between determinism and the freedom of which we are introspectively conscious.[24]

In some ways, Russell is advocating what has come to be called "compatibilism," that our bodily motions are free when the functions that have them as outputs involve our volitions. If these volitions, ultimately, are characterized by functions (i.e. laws of nature) with inputs long ago, well before we evolved, then so be it. It in no way makes them compelled.

FURTHER READING

R. M. Sainsbury, "On Induction and Russell's Postulates," in C. Wade Savage and C. Anthony Anderson, eds., *Rereading Russell* (Minneapolis: Minnesota Studies in the Philosophy of Science, 1989), pp. 200–219.

Erik Götlind, *Bertrand Russell's Theories of Causation* (Uppsala, Almquist & Wiksells Boktryckeri AB, 1912).

Nine

Icarus

> Icarus, having been taught to fly by his father Daedalus, was destroyed by his rashness. I fear that the same fate may overtake the populations whom modern men of science have taught to fly.
>
> *Icarus or the Future of Science*

Russell's views on ethics evolved significantly during his long life. It is not incidental to the evolution of his ideas that he witnessed some of the most horrific episodes of human history, including nine million civilian deaths in the First World War, almost forty-two million civilian deaths in the Second World War, with the Nazis' extermination of over six million Jewish people, Stalin's extermination of fifteen million (a conservative estimate), the Soviet military dominance of Eastern Europe, and the world on the brink of a thermonuclear holocaust during the Cuban Missile Crisis. He began as an objectivist, agreeing with Moore that one can intuit the good. Next he became a Spinozist, for whom ethics lies in the elimination of self-interest and the contemplation of God (as nature). Soon he became a consequentialist, hoping to find scientific principles that could harmonize and control the conflicts of desires and values that threaten the extinction of mankind.

A LIBERAL DECALOGUE

Perhaps it is best to begin with Russell's ten commandments—something he thought should replace those which, historical storytelling relates, originated from a discussion between Moses and God. Russell writes[1] that the Ten Commandments or "Liberal Decalogue" that, as a teacher, I should wish to promulgate, might be set forth as follows:

(1) Do not feel absolutely certain of anything.
(2) Do not think it worthwhile to proceed by concealing evidence, for the evidence is sure to come to light.
(3) Never try to discourage thinking, for you are sure to succeed.
(4) When you meet with opposition, even if it should be from your husband or your children, endeavor to overcome it by argument and not by authority, for a victory dependent upon authority is unreal and illusory.
(5) Have no respect for the authority of others, for there are always contrary authorities to be found.
(6) Do not use power to suppress opinions you think pernicious, for if you do the opinions will suppress you.
(7) Do not fear to be eccentric in opinion, for every opinion now accepted was once eccentric.
(8) Find more pleasure in intelligent dissent than in passive agreement, for, if you value intelligence as you should, the former implies a deeper agreement than the latter.
(9) Be scrupulously truthful, even if the truth is inconvenient, for it is more inconvenient when you try to conceal it.
(10) Do not feel envious of the happiness of those who live in a fool's paradise, for only a fool will think that it is happiness.

The trouble with Moses's commandments is that they are either wholly unethical or require the finesses of the greatest among ethicists and theologians to decipher. What is proscribed in the commandment "Thou shall not kill?" Is killing in self-defense permitted? What of killing chimpanzees or other animals? What is proscribed in the commandment "Thou shall not steal?" Is stealing permitted when necessary to save the life of a child? In order to decide, we must already know a lot about how to think about ethical matters. The commandment is therefore worthless. Matters become worse still. What is proscribed by the commandments "Thou shalt keep the Lord's day holy" and "Thou shalt have no gods before me?" Does this require that there be a world government, a state religion exacting penalties for not worshiping God in accordance with the state's requirements? If it does, then it is surely not an ethical commandment. The penalty, according to the Bible, for disobeying the commandment "Thou shalt keep the Lord's day holy," is stoning to death! And we see only too well in the European religious wars, inquisitions, Crusades, and so on the danger of enforcing the commandment "Thou shalt have no gods before me." Perhaps a skilled theologian can finesse such commandments. But to all appearances it is merely the product of a primitive culture engaged in an effort to preserve the power structure of the ruling elite. In Russell's view, it should be an embarrassment to an enlightened culture that such confusions about ethics decorate its legal institutions. They belong in a museum.

Mere commandments, whether they come from Moses or Russell, do nothing for the foundation of ethics. Russell would be the first to agree. If there is a God in the usual sense (i.e. all powerful, all knowing, and all good), then this God knows analytic ethics. If Moses proclaimed himself to have spoken to God and been given commandments which are right merely because God commands them, we can readily discern that Moses is lying. No God who knows any ethics holds that an action is right merely because He commands it. The foundation of ethics, if there is any foundation, cannot lie in mere deference to the commandments of any being, even God. To be sure, if a person is ideally justified in believing that God (an all good, all knowing being) is advising him, that person does well to take the advice. But this holds because the person is ideally justified in his belief that God is advising him. His belief that God is advising him cannot even be marginally justified without employing an independent ethical theory to evaluate the advice. If the command to Abraham is to kill his dear son Isaac, and if Abraham's best ethical assessments show that this is wrong, then he will not be properly justified in thinking the command came from God. We will decide if a command is, indeed, the command of an all-good being by evaluating its ethical status. Indeed, there is a curious test God can give us to see whether we are ethical. He merely needs to command us to do something. If we do it merely because we believe He commands it, we fail the test.

The commitment to rationally evaluate whether an action is ethical trumps all attempts to base ethics on a belief in commandments from God. But what are the dictates of reason when the pros and cons are at evidential stalemate? William James once maintained that, in the absence of evidence for or against a position, reason allows "tender mindedness" and does not demand inaction. He writes:

> Our passional nature not only lawfully may, but must, decide an option between propositions, whenever it is a genuine option that cannot by its nature be decided on intellectual grounds; for to say, under such circumstances "Do not decide, but leave the question open" is itself a passional decision, just like deciding yes or no, and is attended with the same risk of losing the truth . . .[2]

W. K. Clifford, a contemporary of James, dissented strongly: "It is wrong *always and for anyone* to believe anything on insufficient evidence."[3] Clifford's attitude reflects Russell's scientific-minded philosophy. Religion is dangerous when it prohibits debate or restricts it to apologetics for dogmatism. Its dogmatisms thereby become the tools for manipulating the many by the few in power. In *An Outline of Intellectual Rubbish* (1943) Russell wrote: "There is no nonsense so arrant that it cannot be made the creed of the vast majority by adequate governmental action" (OIR, p. 104). Russell was tireless in pointing out the political and psychological dangers of religious dogmatism and the atrocities committed in its name. In his little book *Religion and Science* Russell was like Voltaire, ever ready to lampoon religion as the enemy of common sense and reason.

Russell reminds us that between 1450 and 1550 one hundred thousand witches were tortured and put to death. The torture and murder of witches persisted in some degree even into the eighteenth century. When people of reason had the fortitude to argue that plagues, sickness, tempests, hailstorms, thunder, and lightning were not caused by the machinations of women, that their confessions were due to their desire to escape tortures of the rack, they too were accused of being corrupted by Satan, and subsequently tortured and murdered. Voltaire wrote that "anyone who has the power to make you believe absurdities has the power to make you commit injustices." Russell offers the following conclusion:

> The harm that theology has done is not to create cruel impulses, but to give them the sanction of what professes to be a lofty ethic, and to confer apparently sacred character upon practices which have come down from more ignorant and barbarous ages.
>
> (*RaS*, p. 106)

After lambasting theological proclamations that endeavored to prevent the mitigation of human suffering by the use of anaesthetics, Russell goes on to warn that ". . . the intervention of theology in medical questions is not at an end; opinions on such subjects as birth control, and the legal permission of abortion in certain cases, are still influenced by Bible texts and ecclesiastical decrees" (*RaS*, p. 106). He goes on:

> The consequent improvement in health and increase of longevity is one of the most remarkable and admirable characteristics of our age. Even if science had done nothing else for human happiness, it would deserve our gratitude on this account. Those who believe in the utility of theological creeds would have difficulty in pointing to any comparable advantage that they have conferred upon the human race.
>
> (*RaS*, p. 109)

Yet even in the context of Russell's very harsh criticisms of religion, the book presents a sensitivity that contemporary endeavors on the same subject lack.[4] Russell writes:

> I cannot admit any method of arriving at truth except that of science, but in the realm of the emotions I do not deny the value of the experiences which have given rise to religion. Through the association with false beliefs, they have led to much evil as well as good; freed from this association, it may be hoped that the good alone will remain.
>
> (*RaS*, p. 189)

Russell hoped that awareness of the history of religious ignorance and intolerance might break the hold religion has on the minds of future generations.

Religion perpetuates itself by the indoctrination of children, thus only a religion-free public education can break the cycle. In truth, many religious world views have collapsed in the presence of a scientific secular world view—not so much because their doctrines have been empirically disconfirmed, since one can often insulate the dogmas from any possibility of disconfirmation, but because whatever explanatory merits they may once have had have been replaced by art and science. They have gone the way of Greek mythology and the gods of the harvest and home. They no longer offer comfort in the face of hardship and death; their rituals are empty. There is no need or intellectual burden on science to refute them. The burden is on them to offer something explanatory in light of a scientific world view. To illustrate this point, Russell once told a story of a teapot. He writes:

> If I were to suggest that between Earth and Mars there is a china teapot revolving about the sun in an elliptical orbit, nobody would be able to disprove my assertion provided I were careful to add that the teapot is too small to be revealed even by our most powerful telescopes. But if it were to go on to say that, since my assertion cannot be disproved, it is an intolerable presumption on the part of

human reason to doubt it, I should rightly be thought to be talking nonsense. If, however, the existence of such a teapot were affirmed in ancient books, taught as the sacred truth every Sunday, and instilled into the minds of children at school, hesitation to believe in its existence would become a mark of eccentricity and entitle the doubter to the attentions of the psychiatrist in an enlightened age of the Inquisitor in an earlier time.[5]

Russell's celestial teapot was designed to show that an atheist (or agnostic) does not have the burden of disproving the existence of this or that man's belief in god(s). Russell's teapot analogy is still used today.[6]

Russell rejects James's doctrine of "tender mindedness." But there is more to James than first appearances might suggest. The scientific evaluation of a theory is far from a simple process. Scientists do not abandon a comprehensive theory over an anomaly in a given experiment. For one thing, the experiment itself might be flawed or the anomaly might be relegated to the physiology or psychology. Consider the famous moon illusion that the harvest moon appears larger at the horizon than high in the sky. Is this a problem in physical optics, psychology, or neurology? We often live with anomalies, preferring one view of the world over another for its metaphysical merits in spite of the anomaly. But eventually, when enough significant anomalies (empirical and metaphysical) accumulate, there is a breach, and the world view collapses. This is what happened to Aristotelianism, the Cartesian mechanical science, Newtonian physics, and so on. For example, it was rational to adhere to Copernicus's thesis that the earth revolves about the sun in spite of the negative outcomes of experiments designed to test it.[7] A moving earth posed serious problems for terrestrial physics which were not solved for many generations, and Newton's gravitation attraction "at a distance"—a serious metaphysical anomaly—was a challenge well into the twentieth century for even the greatest of minds to accept. The accumulation of evidence is a difficult matter, and rival world views may be on a par with respect to the overall balance of their significant empirical and metaphysical anomalies. Thus, it is not always irrational to continue working within a theory that faces anomalies.

How then is a scientific ethics possible? Is normativity compatible with a modern scientific conception of the world? We shall see that Russell came to hold a consequentialist ethical theory and hoped to found a science of ethics. But Russell's road to this position, as to most all of his positions, is long and winding.

When he was influenced by Moore's *Principia Ethica* (1902), Russell held that the concept of good is innate in humans and that we know a priori certain general truths about the kinds of things that are good. For instance, we know a priori that we ought to act so as to promote good and prevent what is not good. This view persists in Russell's thinking as late as *Problems* (1912). Russell maintains that some ethical propositions such as "One ought to do what is good" are known a priori. But this reflects more the meaning he assigned to "ought" and "good" than it does a kinship with Moore. Russell explains that he abandoned Moore's view when he read Santayana's book *Winds of Doctrine*. It is not clear what, precisely, was in Santayana's book that influenced Russell. One thing is clear: Theism has no bearing whatsoever on the question of whether there are objective ethical truths. In fact, we have seen that any theism which invokes a divine command theory is quite antithetical to ethics. The same is true for intuitionism. One person's intuitions of the good are another's horrors, and as fundamental intuitions they epistemically warrant no respect at all from others.

The mere fact that different cultures disagree about what are proper social practices, that social norms are often taught by the indoctrination of children, and that some cultures accept odious practices (e.g. infanticide, ownership of women and children, caste systems preventing equal access to education, child labor, etc.) are not good reasons for thinking that ethical laws are not every bit as objective as are the laws of physics. There is, however, a problem of understanding how a scientific world view can accommodate the property of being good and the relation of obligation. Moreover, even when this problem is solved, there remains the problem of finding principles which balance what is good.

The scientific world view apparently leaves a gap between good and obligation. This gap is a favorite theme for a new form of the Divine Command Theory. The new theory offers a pessimistic induction based on the long history of failure when it comes to finding a theory that forges a logical connection between what is good and what is obligatory. On this view, it is time to admit defeat. Obligation has its foundation in power alone! Only the power of an absolute sovereign can motivate action and thereby provide the foundation for obligation. Thus, on the new divine command theory, God's commandments have nothing to do with what is good or ethical; they have everything to do with what is obligatory. The theory then offers the consolation that if God exists, the two coincide. God is all good and all knowing, as well as the all-powerful sovereign. Russell certainly resists this pessimistic induction. It is an obligation to do only what is good, no matter what is commanded by an all powerful being. This intuition is certainly lost if we give into pessimism and abandon man's analytical quest to discover a logical connection between the two.

The first problem, that of accommodating the property of being good within a scientific world view, is easier than the second. There are two main approaches. The scientific world view must accommodate consciousness somehow. And good is logically tied to consciousness. Only conscious creatures can be harmed or benefited; it is only in its effects on them that something can be or fail to be good. The objectivity of what is good is apparent in the fact that conscious creatures may fail to recognize what is good for (i.e. benefits or harms) them. The other approach also makes good logically connected with consciousness. Only conscious creatures can value things (i.e. consider something to be good in some measure). On either of these views, the property "good" is compatible with a scientific world view. Russell came to adopt the latter view. To solve the problem of finding a balance (i.e. harmony) of goods (i.e. things valued), we shall see that Russell adopted a form of consequentialism.

SUB SPECIE AETERNITATIS

In 1912, Russell published a paper entitled "The Essence of Religion," a piece excerpted from a failed book project called *Prisons*, which Russell wrote in 1911 while his affair with Ottoline Morrell was new. Russell wrote:

> Religion consists in union with the universe. Formerly, union was achieved by assimilating the universe to our own conception of the Good . . . we must find a mode of union which asks nothing of the world, and depends solely upon ourselves . . . The moralist divides the world into good and bad . . .
>
> But besides this dualistic attitude, there is another, wholly compatible with it, but monistic: an attitude which ignores the differences between the good and the bad, and loves all alike. This is the essence of religion; but because it has not been clearly distinguished from the moralist's attitude, it has been supposed, wrongly, to require the belief that the world is good . . . Every such demand [that the world shall conform to our standards] is an endeavour to impose Self upon the world . . . The essence of religion is the union with the universe achieved by subordination of the demands of Self . . . This subordination is not complete if it depends upon a belief that the universe satisfies some at least of the demands of Self . . .[8]

At this time, Russell was a Spinozist. The same ideas emerge in Russell's discussion of "true philosophic contemplation" in *Outline of Philosophy*. Russell wrote:

> By thus making a barrier between subject and object, such personal and private things become a prison to the intellect. The

free intellect will see as God might see, without a *here* and *now*, without the hopes and fears, without the trammels of customary beliefs and traditional prejudices, calmly, dispassionately, in the sole and exclusive desire of knowledge—knowledge as impersonal, as purely contemplative, as it is possible for man to obtain.[9]

Self-interest and subjectivity are a "prison," in Russell's view, because they shut out the possibility of impersonal contemplation of the world—a Spinozistic "intellectual love of God" interpreted as an attitude produced by viewing the world "*sub species aeternitatis.*"[10] According to the paper "The Essence of Religion," the "infinite self" is universal and impartial, and peace comes to this self through harmony or agreement with the whole by means of its experience of "wisdom." Russell approvingly calls this "mysticism," though he warns that it is misguided to interpret it as a "perception of new objects." It is, instead,

> a different way of regarding the same objects, a contemplation more impersonal, more vast, more filled with love than the fragmentary, disquiet consideration we give to things when we view them as a means to help or hinder our own purposes.[11]

Russell maintains that constructing a metaphysics tailored to the values of humans is a fundamental source of error in both religious thinking and in philosophy. This position is set out nicely in Russell's "On Scientific Method in Philosophy":

> The ethical element which has been prominent in many of the most famous systems of philosophy is, in my opinion, one of the most serious obstacles to the victory of scientific method in the investigation of philosophical questions. Human ethical notions, as Chuang Yzu perceived, are essentially anthropocentric, and involve, when used in metaphysics, an attempt, however veiled, to legislate for the universe on the basis of the present desires of men. In this way, they interfere with that receptivity to fact which is the essence of the scientific attitude towards the world.[12]

Russell contrasts this self-interested approach with his new philosophy of Logical Atomism—a philosophy which takes a global and non-self-interested perspective. In Russell's view, logical analysis has cleared away centuries of metaphysical muddles that were introduced because of an emotional attachment to a particular ethical view. It is emotional detachment that Russell finds praiseworthy in the mysticism of Spinoza. In "Mysticism and Logic" Russell wrote:

> Good and bad, and even the higher good that mysticism finds everywhere, are the reflections of our own emotions on other things, not part of the substance of things as they are in themselves. And therefore an impartial contemplation, freed from all preoccupation with Self, will not judge things good or bad, although it is very easily combined with that feeling of universal love which leads the mystic to say that the whole world is good.[13]

Russell demanded a scientific (i.e. analytic) approach to philosophical problems—an approach which embraces atheism and abandons spiritual, emotional, and religious perspectives. Nonetheless, he grappled to find some analogue of the mystical that might accrue to the scientific and intellectual contemplation of the world. What this analog might be is explored early on in Russell's "A Free Man's Worship" (1903), and it was a recurring focus of discussion during Russell's relationship with Lady Ottoline. Eventually Russell settled on a new meaning for "the mystical" and illustrated it by Spinoza's intellectual contemplation of the universe *sub specie aeternitatis*.

Russell confessed to Ottoline that Wittgenstein "detested" his paper "The Essence of Religion." In Wittgenstein's view he "... had been a traitor to the gospel of exactness and wantonly used words vaguely; also that such things are too intimate to print."[14] Russell would surely agree that Leopardi had put the ideas better in his poems *L'Infinito* and *La Ginestra o Fiori del Deserto*. He quotes *L'Infinito* in full in his book *The Impact of Science on Society* (1952), prefacing it by writing: "This point of view is well expressed in a little poem by Leopardi and expresses, more nearly than any other known to me, my own feelings about the universe and human passions." Here are a few of its lines translated by R. C. Trevelyan (1941):

> Dear to me always was this lonely hill,
> And this hedge that excludes so large a part
> Of the ultimate horizon from my view.
> But as I sit and gaze, my thought conceives
> Interminable vastness of space
> Beyond it, and unearthly silences,
> And profoundest calm; whereat my heart almost
> Becomes dismayed. And as I hear the wind
> Rustling though these branches, I find myself
> Comparing with this sound that infinite silence:
> And then I call to mind eternity,
> And the ages that are dead, and this that now
> Is living, and the noise of it. And so
> In this immensity my thought sinks drowned:
> And sweet it seems to shipwreck in this sea.[15]

Russell and Ottoline were fond of reading Leopardi together while working on *Prisons*.[16] Wittgenstein's remarks do not show that he disagreed with Russell's ideas.[17] They reflect his objection to Russell having expressed them analytically. In fact, it is the very same Spinozistic ideas that appear in Wittgenstein's famous *Tractatus* (1921) and his earlier 1914–1916 *Notebooks*. Wittgenstein wrote that "the good life is the world seen *sub specie aeternitatis*.... The thing seen *sub specie aeternitatis* is the thing seen together with the whole of logical space."[18] Wittgenstein goes on to say that: "In order to live happily I must be in agreement with the world. And that is what 'being happy' means."[19] In Wittgenstein's view, one's internal harmony is shown by steadfastly refusing to say anything prescriptive.

A SCIENCE OF ETHICS

Russell managed to preserve most of his Spinozism during the First World War. Intellectual distance, as practiced by Spinoza, is surely consistent with action against evil, especially when the evil has its source in stupidity and ignorance. It was, in his view, a war produced by greed, in which no nation could claim a high ground. Nonetheless, Wittgenstein enlisted for his homeland, Austria, joining an artillery at Cracow. Russell's pacifism eventually strained his relations with the Whiteheads. This was especially difficult because the war took Whitehead's dear son Eric. Russell's Spinozism certainly did not make him indifferent to the horrors of the war. He actively spoke against it. In 1916 he was dismissed from Trinity College, following his conviction under the Defence of the Realm Act. He took responsibility for comments of an anti-war leaflet objecting to the severe prison sentence of two years hard labor decreed to the conscientious objector Ernest Everett. The leaflet, unbeknownst to Russell, had been circulated without his name on it by the No Conscription Fellowship. Russell was merely fined. But on principle, he refused to pay and this landed him six months in Brixton prison in 1918.

The events of the war produced a change in Russell that brought him to a new discussion of ethics. Russell wrote two little books which are each gems: *Icarus* (1924) and *What I Believe* (1925). Wittgenstein's comment that *What I Believe* is "harmful" is baffling; I imagine he reacted negatively to Russell's comment that "[E]ven more harmful than theological superstition is the superstition of nationalism, of duty to one's own State and to no other."[20] It is an inspiring little book which expresses Russell's hopes after the war for a better world. Its companion is the gloomy and prophetic *Icarus*, in which Russell expresses his fears that the new science will continue to be used to destroy civilization. In *Icarus*, Russell's enthusiasm for rational democratic ideals led him to entertain that nothing short of a world government could prevent new wars ever more horrible to come. He was as relieved as anyone that America's involvement ended the long, senseless, and bloody war of attrition. He ends the book with the following:

> ... at present all that gives men power to indulge their collective passions is bad. That is why science threatens to cause the destruction of our civilization. The only solid hope seems to lie in the possibility of a world-wide domination by one group, say the United States, leading to the gradual formation of an orderly economic and political world-government. But perhaps, in view of the sterility of the Roman Empire, the collapse of our civilization would in the end be preferable to this alternative.
>
> (*I*, p. 63)

Woodrow Wilson, the American president at the time, established the League of Nations, something significantly more modest than a world government and significantly more ineffectual at preventing the coming holocaust of the Second World War.

In *What I Believe* Russell reveals that he holds no hope that reason legislates only those desires worthy of having and destroys others. In opposition to Kant, and in deference to Hume, he thinks that reason enables only a calculation of how, practically, to realize the satisfaction of desires already given. Russell accepts the brute fact that different people may desire different things for themselves. Anything whatsoever, in principle, can be desired by some deranged person—"deranged," that is, from the perspective of another. Russell accepts this. He hopes, however, that reason can find principles for balancing the desires a person finds within himself or herself and find principles for balancing the desires of different people and nations. Thus he finds himself with a consequentialist ethics.[21] Russell's version of consequentialism seems to have the following form: An action is ethical if no other action that can be performed in the situation yields consequences that are a better balance of all desires of all the individuals, cultures, nations, etc. involved.[22] Ethics is therefore a science of calculating probable outcomes with respect to balancing overall desires. What distinguishes ethics from science is, therefore, not any special kind of intuitive knowledge of a strange property goodness. The knowledge required in ethics is exactly like the knowledge in science. What is special to the field of ethics is that there is desire.

Russell explains that this consequentialist orientation toward a science of ethics is embodied in his conception of the good life. He writes that: "The good life is one inspired by love and guided by knowledge." The logical content of the thesis, he explains, is that

> in a community where men live in this way, more desires will be satisfied than one where there is less love or less knowledge. I do not mean that such a life is "virtuous" or that its opposite is "sinful," for these are conceptions which seem to me to have no scientific justification.[23]

A scientific ethics balances desire, and "[o]utside human desires there is no moral standard."[24]

Russell's emphasis on knowledge is very important to his perspective, for without knowledge, good intentions, kindliness, and love can lead to serious harm. Russell recalls that in medieval times, when a pestilence was ravaging a country, holy men advised the population to congregate in churches and pray for salvation. Their ignorance spread the infection to the unsuspecting supplicants. Physicians ignorant that blood circulates, thought the blood is normally absorbed in the extremities except in cases of disease in which poisons build up. Bloodletting to release "plethora" was a common practice among well-intentioned physicians following Galenic medicine. The more severe the disease, the more blood would be removed and, of course, in most all cases this was the very thing that prevented the patient from fighting the disease.

There are many forms of ignorance, and a very important one Russell was tireless in combating is due to blind adherence to a religious metaphysics. Russell's views in ethics were a favorite topic for criticism by moralists who largely attend not to evaluating his consequentialist calculations as to what best balances desires, but to his campaign for social reformation in education, marriage, and family. In reading Russell it must be recalled that he lived in a time when the churches had a hold on social and legal institutions. Reforms were sorely needed, and Russell did not hesitate to engage in hyperbole to make his point heard. "Boys and girls," he writes,

> should be taught that nothing can justify sexual intercourse unless there is mutual inclination. This is contrary to the Church, which holds that, provided the parties are married and the man desires another child, sexual intercourse is justified however great may be the reluctance of the wife.
>
> (B, p. 48)

No doubt the Church thought it an obligation of a wife to bear children for her husband, but it certainly did not sanction rape. Russell is right, however, to call attention to the fact that, given the property-model of marriage and children adopted in the religions, the very conception of rape within marriage is barely intelligible. The notion that woman are not dependents, but autonomous, rational beings with rights to direct their own futures, reproductive or otherwise, itself proved to be an elusive concept to articulate within religious institutions. Similar points apply to the evils of slavery, which, for centuries, the Church seemed incapable of noticing. Once again the religious doctrines served the economic power structures of the day, which felt familiar and natural to those wielding the power. Russell wrote:

> It might be objected that it is right to hate those who do harm. I do not think so. If you hate them, it is only too likely that you will become equally harmful; and it is very unlikely that you will induce them to abandon their evil ways. Hatred of evil is itself a kind of bondage to evil. The way out is through understanding, not through

hate. I am not advocating non-resistance. But I am saying that resistance, if it is to be effective in preventing the spread of evil, should be combined with the greatest degree of understanding and the smallest degree of force that is compatible with the survival of the good things that we wish to preserve.

(*PfM*, p. 176)

Russell's message remains important in these days where passenger airplanes are used as bombs and preemptive invasions are supposed to protect the world from "evil."

Russell offers remarkable insights in these two little books. In *Icarus* he tells a wonderful parable of a secret scientific community of physiologists hoping to bring about the new millennium by kidnapping all the leaders of the nations and injecting into their blood a substance which produces in them optimal rationality and benevolence toward their fellow creatures. "But alas," writes Russell,

the physiologists would first have to administer the love-philtre to themselves. And so we come back to the old dilemma: only kindliness can save the world, and even if we knew how to produce kindliness we should not do so unless we were already kindly.[25]

The dilemma is worse than Russell thinks, for it would certainly not be kindliness/love guided by knowledge (i.e. a respect for intellectual autonomy and sovereignty) to kidnap people and subject them to a drug that produces in them one's own parochial conception of what constitutes kindliness. Russell privileges kindliness over knowledge, even suggesting that "[t]he late War afforded an example of knowledge without love."[26] This is the wrong emphasis. It is knowledge that produces genuine kindliness and love and not, as Russell suggests, kindliness that ". . . leads intelligent people to knowledge."

In the end, however, Russell had the correct insight and he offers an important lesson that is still valid today. He observed that it is a persisting confusion to think that the latest war is the "war to end all war" by destroying the evil individuals, tyrants, capitalists, Germans, etc. who are allegedly the cause of cruelty and misery. Russell realized that this is a shallow diagnosis of the causes of suffering in the world. Revolutions are sometimes necessary, Russell admits,

> ... but they are not short cuts to the millennium. There is no short cut to the good life, whether individual, or social. To build up the good life, we must build up intelligence, self-control, and sympathy. This is a quantitative matter, a matter of gradual improvement, of early training, of educational experiment. The gradual improvement that is possible, and the methods by which it may be achieved, are a matter for future science.[27]

FURTHER READING

Robert Adams, "A Modified Divine Command Theory of Ethical Wrongness," in Gene Outka and John P. Reeder, eds., *Religion and Morality: A Collection of Essays* (New York: Doubleday, 1973). Reprinted in *The Virtue of Faith and Other Essays in Philosophical Theology* (New York: Cambridge University Press, 1987).

Kenneth Blackwell, *Russell's Spinozistic Ethics* (London: Allen & Unwin, 1985).

Charles Pigden, ed., *Russell on Ethics: Selections from the writings of Bertrand Russell* (London: Routledge, 1999).

—— "Bertrand Russell: Moral Philosopher or Unphilosophical Moralist?," in Nicholas Griffin, ed., *The Cambridge Companion to Bertrand Russell* (Cambridge: Cambridge University Press, 2003), pp. 475–506.

Michael K. Potter, *Bertrand Russell's Ethics* (London: Continuum Press, 2006).

Alan Ryan, *Russell: A Political Life* (Oxford: Oxford University Press, 1993).

Al Seckel, ed., *Bertrand Russell on God and Religion* (Buffalo, NY: Prometheus Books, 1986).

Glossary

Analytic Truth Hume: A sentence that is true in virtue of relations between ideas that are not merely associations forged by experience; Kant: An instance of identity a = a or categorical sentence which is such that the meaning of its predicate term is contained in the meaning of its subject term. For example, "All bachelors are unmarried"; Frege: A sentence that is true in virtue of $^{\varphi}$Logic alone. For example, "there is an attribute φ such that for all objects x, φx if and only if x = x"; Russell: A sentence true in virtue of logical structure alone; a fully general truth about structure in the language of logic; Carnap: A sentence that is true in virtue of the meaning of the logical words in it alone. For example, "All unmarried men are unmarried"; Wittgenstein: A sentence that is tautologous.

A Priori Truth A truth that is knowable without any empirical investigation. Contrasted with "a posteriori truth," a truth known by means of an empirical investigation.

Behaviorism The thesis that a genuine (Newtonian empirical) science of psychology is only viable if notions of consciousness, introspection, will, soul, and the like are banished. Only the notions of stimulus, operant, and behavioral response (i.e. bodily motions as outcomes of the stimulus) are admissible in a scientific psychology.

Cartesianism The mechanical philosophy of René Descartes (1596–1650). All causal explanations of material (i.e. extended) substances are to be given in terms of the mathematical (i.e.

quantitative) mechanical laws governing the motions of a number of impacting rigid bodies with different shapes and sizes. Descartes accepted a dualism of mental and material substance and accepted that there is causal interaction between mind and body (i.e. matter). Unlike his followers, he did not embrace material indivisible rigid simples (i.e. atoms). But he held that it is innocuous to speak in terms of rigid body impacts rather than what is strictly more accurate: compression waves in a extended fluid substance. The material has only properties such as shape, size, motion, and number.

Class Given any condition, there is an object (i.e. class) whose members are all and only those entities that meet the condition. For example, if the condition is being a bird, there is the class of all and only birds. If the condition is being a class, there is the class of all and only classes. If the condition is self-identity, there is a universal class of all entities. (See also Set.)

Comprehension Axiom Classes: An axiom (schema) of the form $(\exists y)(\forall x)(x \in y \equiv Ax)$ that asserts the existence of a class y all and only of whose members x meet a given condition A. Attributes: An axiom (schema) of the form $(\exists \varphi)(\forall x_1), \ldots, (\forall x_n)(\varphi(x_1, \ldots, x_n) \equiv A$, that asserts the existence of an n-placed attribute/relation that entities $x_1, \ldots, x_n$ have if and only if they satisfy the condition A.

Consequentialism A theory in ethics which defines "right" action as that action which is such that no other action that can be performed in the circumstance has consequences on everyone affected with higher utility. Forms of consequentialism differ in how they define "utility." A hedonistic form, advanced by Jeremy Bentham (1748–1832) and modified by John S. Mill (1806–1873), defines "utility" in terms of the sum of pleasure (assigned a positive quantitative/qualitative measure) and pain (assigned a negative quantitative/qualitative measure). Other forms may choose friendship, autonomy, love, justice, etc. among the set of parameters to be balanced. Russell's definition takes as utility the desires, whatever they may be, of the people affected.

Deductive Argument An argument in which premises are given with the intent to provide a guarantee of the conclusion.

Determinism The thesis that every event, except the first (if there is such), is the inevitable outcome of temporally preceding events or conditions.

Empiricism The theory that all synthetic knowledge is obtained by inductive inference from the data of sense-experiences.

Extensional Context *Sentential*: A sentence C in which a subordinate sentence A occurs which does not change in truth (or falsehood) when we replace one or more occurrences of A with a sentence B which holds if and only if A holds. For example, let C be "either A or D," let A be "Africa is a continent" and B be "Borneo is tropical." *Predicate*: A sentence C in which a predicate expression φ occurs which is such that it does not change in truth (or falsehood) when we replace one or more occurrences of φ with a predicate ψ which is such that $(\forall x_1), \ldots, (\forall x_n)(\varphi(x_1, \ldots, x_n) \equiv \psi(x_1, \ldots, x_n))$. For example, let C be "everything is φ," let φ be the predicate of being a creature with a heart, and let ψ be the predicate of being a creature with a kidney.

If-Thenism Arithmetic and geometry do not require special inference rules (as Kant thought). The only inference rules needed to derive theorems of arithmetic and geometry from the axioms of these fields are the inference rules of logic.

Inductive Argument An argument in which premises are given with the intent to provide reasons which make the conclusion highly probable. An enumerative induction has the form:

A_1 is a B
A_2 is a B
. . .

A_n is a B
Therefore, All As are Bs.

Intensional Context *Propositional*: A sentence C in which a proposition term p occurs and which changes in truth (or falsehood) when we replace one or more occurrences of p with a proposition term q which holds if and only if p holds. For example, let C be "p = p" and let p be "the cat's being on the mat," and let q be "the cat's being on the earth." Replacement yields "the cat's being on the mat = the cat's being on the earth" and so we went from a truth to a falsehood. *Predicate*: A sentence C in which φ occurs which is such that it does change in truth (or falsehood) when we replace one or more occurrences of φ with a predicate ψ which is such that $(\forall x_1), \ldots, (\forall x_n)(\varphi(x_1, \ldots, x_n) \equiv \psi(x_1, \ldots, x_n))$. For example, let C be "φ = φ" and let φ be the property self-identity, and let ψ be the property of being not self-identical. Replacement yields "the property of being a creature with a heart = the property of being a creature with a kidney" and so we went from a truth to a falsehood.

Logicism *Frege*: Arithmetic truth is logical truth. *Russell*: Mathematical truth is logical truth; mathematical necessity is logical necessity. Logicism does not entail the thesis that logic is consistently axiomatizable and that all arithmetic/mathematical truths are derivable as theorems from the axioms.

Matter *Cartesian atomist*: An extended mind-independent substance or rigid body persisting through time whose only properties are shape, size, motion, and number. *Lockean*: A mind-independent substance whose fundamental properties are shape, size, motion, and number and which is knowable only as a cause of sensory experiences. *Berkelian*: A structure of mental sensory states (actual and possible) made coherent, permanent, and independent of any given mind by the will of God. Also known as "Berkelian Phenomenalism." *Phenomenalist*: A structure of mental sensory states (actual) which are coherent. *Russellian*: A coherent series of stages (transient particulars) stretched out in a temporal order and constituted by causal laws of physics. Also known as "four-dimensionalism."

Methodological Solipsism The Cartesian thesis that epistemology must begin from a foundation which is discovered by methodologically rejecting all beliefs except those that are undoubtable. Given it is possible, at any given moment that I am dreaming, ordinary beliefs about the world cannot be foundational. Strict adherence rejects beliefs about mathematics and logic and beliefs about the past and memory beliefs.

Naïve Realism A theory of perception which accepts mind/body dualism and two-way causal interaction. It holds that matter causes mental representations that resemble it both in sensations of shape, size, motion, number and sensations of color, taste, smell, pitch, and texture.

Naturalized Epistemology The thesis that the sciences of physics, chemistry, evolutionary biology, and psychology are to be used in framing a theory of how the brains and nervous systems of humans and animals have developed causal connections to the world that enable their remarkable behaviors.

Occam's Razor A principle of parsimony named after William of Occam (1290–1349) which states that "entities are not to be multiplied beyond necessity." Explanations with fewer hypothesized entities and processes are to be preferred.

One-to-One Correspondence Between As and Bs The existence of a one-to-one function where for each a that satisfies A there is some b that satisfies B such that afb, and for each b that satisfies B there is an a that satisfies A such that afb.

Ontological Argument A deductive proof from the concept (i.e. essence) of God (i.e. a perfect being) to the existence of God. The most famous version was advanced by St. Anselm (1033–1109).

Pragmatism A philosophical theory originating with C. S. Peirce (1839–1914) and William James (1842–1910), according to which the empirical import of a sentence lies in its practical implications for action. The theory holds that a statement is true if it facilitates actions which successfully engage the environment in an idealized limit of human endeavors.

Rationalism The theory that some truths are known a priori but are about the world and not about the meanings of words. Some examples are: $2 + 3 = 5$, every event is caused, rectilinear inertia, and every equilateral triangle is equiangular.

Reductive Elimination Theory A theory which endeavors to (broadly) recover laws of an earlier successful theory without preserving or identifying its objects with any objects of the new theory. For example, there is no caloric, no phlogiston, no luminiferous aether, no Newtonian gravitational force, and no Newtonian mass, but the laws of the earlier theories set out a structure that is preserved in the new theory.

Reductive Identity Theory A theory which endeavors to show that a process or object characterized in one way is identical to a process or object characterized in another way. For instance, the field of genetics predates modern molecular biology and introduced the notion of a gene as a fixed unit of heredity in a living organism. In molecular biology, a gene may be identified as a segment of deoxyribonucleic acid (DNA). Another example is the notion of valence, which concerns the potential for atoms to bond together into molecules. In the atomic theory of the 1920s valence is identified as the number of pairs of electrons which any given atom shares with the adjacent atoms and is called the "covalence" of that atom. Modern quantum theory hopes to preserve the concept in yet a different way.

Representative Realism A theory of perception which accepts mind/body dualism and two-way causal interaction. It holds that matter causes mental representations that resemble it only in respect to shape, size, motion, and number.

Set Sometimes used synonymously with "class." Often used to refer to the objects assured by a theory originating with Ernest Zermelo in 1908 according to which union, pairing, and power-set axioms are given as well as an axiom of separation that says that if we are first given one set, then we are assured that there is another set which is its subset and whose members meet any given condition.

Solipsism The thesis that I (i.e. my mind) alone exists.

Stipulative Definition A definition which announces that a term or phrase is to be used in a certain way. It contrasts with a lexical definition which reports on how a given term or phrase happens to be used by speakers of the linguistic community in question.

Synthetic Truth A non-analytic truth.

Teleological Explanation An explanation of an object or a process by appealing to the purposes, goals, or balance of a larger system in which it plays a central part. Its paradigmatic use is in biological explanations of living organisms. For example, the heart's shape is explained by appeal to the purpose it plays in pumping oxygen and nutrients to the cells to keep an organism alive. Plant growth is explained by appeal to the role plants play in removing carbon dioxide and replenishing oxygen for aerobic organisms and in the food chain which sustains life on earth.

Transcendental Aesthetic Kant's theory that the necessity of geometric truth lies in a spatial scaffolding imposed on sense-experience by the structure of consciousness. A mind, human or otherwise, can only experience spatially in a Euclidean three-dimensional way. Similarly, Kant held that the necessity of arithmetic lies in a sequential scaffolding imposed on sense-experience by the structure of consciousness. A mind, human or otherwise, can only experience things in a temporal consecutive series. The series of natural numbers is grounded in our awareness of this temporal scaffolding.

Truth *Coherence*: A belief is true if it coheres with a system of beliefs better than its negation does. "Coherence" is usually defined in terms of logical relationships and requires reference to the maximally consistent system of beliefs of a possible ideally rational being. *Correspondence*: A belief is true when it corresponds to a (the) fact(s). This theory uses the expression "fact" to mean a part of the world that is independent of any particular mind. *Pragmatist*: A belief is true if it enables the organism (and its descendents) to successfully engage the environments encountered throughout history.

Verificationism The thesis that the empirical meaning of a theoretical statement about the world lies in its implications for experimental tests with observational outcomes. The theory supposes that there is a fundamental difference in kind between what is theoretical and what is observable. Theoretical statements hypothesizing the existence of metaphysical entities (e.g. God, vital forces, natural places, and Aristotelian entelechies) or processes are empirically meaningless because they have no test implications for observation.

Zeno (490 BCE–?) A sophist from Elea, known only though Plato's *Parmenides*, who invented and collected paradoxes designed to show that motion and change are unreal.

Notes

ONE LIFE AND WORK

1 Bertrand Russell, "My Mental Development," in Philosophy of Bertrand Russell, ed., Paul Schilpp (Chicago: Northwestern University Press, 1944), p. 12.
2 See Tractatus 6.36111. Ludwig Wittgenstein, Tractatus Logico-Philosophicus (London: Routledge & Kegan Paul, 1921), p. 141.
3 Hertz's models came to be of central interest to Wittgenstein.
4 This is a letter from Frege to Russell from June 1902. It can be found in Gottfried Gabriel, et al., eds., Gottlob Frege Philosophical and Mathematical Correspondence (Chicago: The University of Chicago Press, 1980), pp. 131–132.
5 Russell reports that Frege responded in a letter that "Die Arithmetik ist ins Schwanken geraten."
6 Ronald Clark, The Life of Bertrand Russell (New York: Alfred A. Knopf Inc., 1979, p. 111).
7 See Gottlob Frege, Philosophical and Mathematical Correspondence, Brian McGuinness et al., eds. (University of Chicago Press, 1980), p. 159.
8 Russell's doctrine was a development of Frege's way out applied to properties rather than classes. See Gregory Landini, "Russell to Frege 24 May 1903: 'I believe I have discovered that classes are entirely superfluous,'" Russell 12 (1992), pp. 160–185.
9 See Ramsey, "Philosophy" in R. B. Braithwaite and Frank Plumpton Ramsey, eds., The Foundations of Mathematics and Other Essays (New York: Harcourt, Brace and Co., 1931), pp. 263–269.
10 See A, vol. I, p. 112. By "free love" Russell seems to mean protected sex of lovers outside of marriage, but certainly not open marriage.
11 See Caroline Moorehead, Russell: A Life (New York: Viking Press, 1993), p. 94.
12 Bertrand Russell, The ABC of Relativity (New York: Harper & Brothers, 1925), p. 167.
13 I have called it Russell's "p_o/a_o Paradox." See Gregory Landini, Russell's Hidden Substitutional Theory (Oxford: Oxford University Press, 1998).

426 Notes

14 See Anne-Françoise Schmid, ed., *Bertrand Russell: Correspondence sur la Philosophie, la Logique et la Politique avec Louis Couturat 1897–1913* (Paris: édition Kimé, volumes I, II, 2001).
15 It will be discussed in detail in Chapter Three. Readers may skip Chapter Three without missing Russell's conception of philosophy as science.
16 We will have occasion to discuss this further in Chapter Three.
17 The complement of the empty set is the universal set. The union of any set and its complement is the universal set.
18 Beauty is in the eye of the beholder.
19 See Quine, "Ontological Relativity" in *Ontological Relativity and Other Essays* (New York: Columbia University Press, 1969), p. 43.
20 Bertrand Russell, *The Selected Letters of Bertrand Russell: The Public Years: 1914–1920*, ed. Nicholas Griffin (New York: Routledge, 2001), p. 225.
21 For a detailed explanation of this see B, p. 20.
22 See P. A. Schilpp, *John Dewey* (Le Salle, IL: Northwestern University Press, 1939).
23 See Avrum Stroll, *Twentieth Century Analytic Philosophy* (New York: Columbia University Press, 2000), p. 252.
24 Caroline Moorehead, *Bertrand Russell: A Life* (New York: Viking, 1992), p. 458.
25 Bertrand Russell, "Man's Peril" in *Portraits From Memory* (New York: Simon & Schuster, 1956), pp. 223–238. Read on the BBC 23 December 1954. The quote is used in the *Russell-Einstein Manifesto* issued in London on 9 July 1955.
26 There is an interesting connection here to the assignation of President Kennedy. There is evidence that the US was planning a further attack on Cuba in violation of the agreement and with the involvement of Lee Harvey Oswald. Oswald turned traitor and murdered the President.
27 Quoted from Caroline Moorehead, *Bertrand Russell: A Life* (New York: Viking, 2002), p. 548.

TWO MATHEMATICS AND THE METAPHYSICIANS

1 Ray Monk, *Russell* (New York: Routledge, 1999), p. 50.
2 Plato held the doctrine of *anamnesis*, according to which we have knowledge of mathematics due to the fact that before the soul is incarnate it resides in the world of perfect Forms: ethical, biological, and mathematical.
3 Irene Pepperberg, "Talking with Alex: Logic and Speech in Parrots," *Scientific American Presents: Exploring Intelligence*, vol. 9 (no. 4), Winter (1998).
4 A set theoretical formulation of this is:

$$x +_c y =_{df} \acute{u} \, (\exists F)(\exists G)(x = \acute{A}(\acute{z} \, Fz) \,.\&.\, y = \acute{A}(\acute{z} \, Gz) :\&: (\forall x)(Fx \supset {\sim} Gx) \,.\&.\, u \approx \acute{z} \, (Fz \vee Gz)).$$

5 In *Principia*, we find a clever analysis that provides the needed generality. To see the technique, put:

$$+x\left(\frac{p}{q}\right)+y =_{df} (\exists a)(\exists b)(a(+x)^q b \ \& \ a(+y)^p b)$$

The notion $aR^{n+1} b$ says that there are $z_1, \ldots z_n$ such that:

$aR z_1 \ \& \ z_1 R z_2 \ \&, \ldots, \& \ z_n R b$

It follows that:

$$x\left(\frac{p}{q}\right)y \equiv_{x\,y} (+x)\left(\frac{p}{q}\right)(+y)$$

For example, $3\left(\frac{1}{2}\right)6$ if and only if for some a and b

$a(+3)^2 b \ \& \ a(+6)^1 b$

Now we also have:

$$\frac{x}{y}\left(\frac{\left(\frac{a}{b}\right)}{\left(\frac{c}{d}\right)}\right)\frac{z}{w} \equiv_{x\,y\,z\,w} \left(+\frac{x}{y}\right)\left(\frac{a \times d}{b \times c}\right)\left(+\frac{z}{w}\right)$$

For example, $\left(+\frac{1}{2}\right)\left(\frac{4}{6}\right)\left(+\frac{3}{4}\right)$ if and only if for some a and b

$a\left(+\frac{1}{2}\right)^6 b \ \& \ a\left(+\frac{3}{4}\right)^4 b$

Thus, Whitehead and Russell are able to provide one definition to handle all the cases. *Principia* has

$$R\left(\frac{p}{q}\right)S =_{df} (\exists a)(\exists b)(aR^q b \ \& \ aR^p b)$$

The general technique originates with Euclid.

6 Observe that $\left(\frac{p}{q}\right)_{x/y} \equiv_{x\,y} \frac{p}{q} = \frac{x}{y}$

7 More exactly, we define the notion of a square root for Reals as follows:

$(\sqrt{\xi})_{r,s} =_{df} (\exists \delta)(\text{Real}_{p\,q} \{\delta_{p/q}\} \ \& \ \delta_{r/z} \ .\&. \ (\delta_{p/q} \times_{pq} \delta_{p/q})_{u/v} \equiv_{u\,v} \xi_{u/v})$

$$(\sqrt{2})_{p/q} \equiv_{p\,q} \frac{p^2}{q^2} < \frac{2}{1}$$

8 See Bertrand Russell, MPD, p. 93.
9 Bertrand Russell, IMP, p. 60.
10 A relation that is transitive, antisymmetric, and connected linearly orders its field.

> R is transitive = df $(\forall x)(\forall y)(\forall z)(xRy \& yRz .\supset. xRz)$.
> R is antisymmetric = df $(\forall x)(\forall y)(xRy \& yRx .\supset. x = y)$.
> R is connected = df $(\forall x)(\forall y)(xRy \lor yRx)$.

11 We will have occasion to discuss such "semantic" pseudo-paradoxes in Chapter Three.
12 Bertrand Russell, IMP, p. 92.
13 Cantor struggled with this for years. It is now known that it is independent of the axioms of Zermelo-Frankel set theory.
14 Hugh MacColl, "Symbolic Reasoning," Mind 14 (1905), pp. 74–81. Reprinted in ed., Douglas Lackey, *Essays In Analysis By Bertrand Russell* (London: Allen & Unwin, 1973), pp. 308–316.
15 Eugen Müller, *Abriss der Algebra der Logik*; Reprinted in Ernst Schröder, *Algebra der Logik*, vol. III (New York: Chelsea Publishing Co., 1966), p. 708.
16 Charles Sanders Peirce, "Description of a Notation for the Logic of Relatives," *Memoirs of the American Academy*, 9 (1870), pp. 317–378.
17 Jean Van Heijenoort, "Logic as Calculus and Logic as Language," Synthese vol. 17 (no. 1), (1967), pp. 324–330
18 The role correlation plays in Frege's account of numbers as objects was first noted by Cocchiarella, who drew attention to what he calls Frege's "double correlation thesis." See Nino Cocchiarella, "Frege, Russell and Logicism: A Logical Reconstruction" in L. Haaparanta and J. Hintikka, eds., *Frege Synthesized* (Dordrecht: Reidel, 1986).
19 See Gregory Landini, "Frege's Cardinals as Concept-Correlates," Erkenntnis 65 (2006), pp. 207–243.
20 Actually, Principia's *120.03 is stated with typical ambiguity. I have expanded some definitions and made the intended type clear to avoid unnecessary complications.
21 George Boolos, "The Advantages of Honest Toil Over Theft," in Richard Jeffery, ed., *Logic, Logic, and Logic* (Cambridge, MA: Harvard University Press, 1998), pp. 225–274.
22 Beatrice Webb, *Living Philosophers: A series of Intimate Credos* (Forum Publishing, 1930), pp. 295–305.

23 Bertrand Russell, "The Philosophy of Logical Analysis" (Chapter 31) of HWP, p. 829.
24 More exactly, it is a relation on real numbers.
25 Frege discusses several in his *Grundlagen*.

THREE *PRINCIPIA MATHEMATICA*

1 Hans Magnus Enzensberger, *The Number Devil* (New York: Metropolitan Books, 1998), p. 232.
2 Philip Jourdain, *The Philosophy of Mr. Bertrand Russell* (London: Allen & Unwin. Ltd., 1918), p. 77.
3 Bertrand Russell, "Mathematical Logic as Based on the Theory of Types," *American Journal of Mathematics*, vol. 30 (no. 3) (July 1908), pp. 222–262.
4 See Gregory Landini, *Russell's Hidden Substitutional Theory* (Oxford: Oxford University Press, 1998), p. 260.
5 The sign $\forall$ seems to have originated with Gerhard Gentzen in the mid-1930s.
6 We shall not, however, alter quotations from *Principia*.
7 William Hatcher. *The Logical Foundations of Mathematics* (Oxford: Pergamon Press, 1982), p. 106.
8 Individual variables are also predicative because their order is the order of their simple-type symbol, namely 0.
9 It has no complex predicate terms formed by circumflexing variables in formulas. See Gregory Landini, *Russell's Hidden Substitutional Theory* (Oxford: Oxford University Press, 1998), p. 265.
10 This inference rule is not explicitly stated in *Principia* but is implied in the omission of *9.xx and *9.yy. See Gregory Landini, *Russell's Hidden Substitutional Theory* (Oxford: Oxford University Press, 1998).
11 This is not to say that logic itself consists of generalized tautologies, not at least in standard second-order calculi count as capturing logic. The comprehension principle of standard second-order logic is not a generalized tautology. Ramsey seems to recognize this in exempting *Principia*'s Axiom of Reducibility.
12 See Gregory Landini, "Quantification Theory in *9 of *Principia Mathematica*," *History and Philosophy of Logic* vol. 21 (no. 1) (2000), pp. 57–78.
13 Available online. http://www.britannica.com/nobelprize/article-9064464
14 I count *Principia*'s individual variables as predicative in a trivial sense.
15 A. J. Ayer, "Bertrand Russell as a Philosopher" in *The Meaning of Life* (New York: Macmillan, 1990), p. 152.
16 A. N. Whitehead and B. Russell, *Principia Mathematica to *56* (Cambridge: Cambridge University Press, 1964), p. 174.

430 Notes

17 This device is used in Hughes and Cresswell, *Introduction to Modal Logic* (New York: Routledge, 1996), p. 325.
18 We are omitting issues concerning predicativity. Thus we have removed the sign ! from *Principia*'s definition of the identity sign.
19 See W. V. O. Quine, *Set Theory and Its Logic* (Cambridge, MA: Harvard University Press, 1980), p. 259.
20 Bertrand Russell, *Autobiography 1872–1914*, vol. 1 (Boston: Little Brown and Co., 1967), p. 79.
21 Bertrand Russell, *Introduction to Mathematical Philosophy* (London: Allen & Unwin, 1953), p. 182.
22 Op. cit., pp. 130, 133.
23 We have added the scope marker (*Principia* to *56, p. 80) and dropped the issue of predicativity since ramification is not relevant to the present discussion. Moreover, circumflex notation is removed to avoid controversies surrounding the interpretation of predicate variables in *Principia*.
24 I have added the scope marker. As with *20.01, the scope marker must be part of the definition *20.08. Its omission is an oversight.
25 Whitehead and Russell explicitly draw the analogy. See *Principia* to *56, p. 81.
26 See Warren Goldfarb, "Russell's Reasons for Ramification," in C. Wade Savage and C. Anthony Anderson, eds., *Rereading Russell: Essays on Bertrand Russell's Metaphysics and Epistemology* (Minnesota: Studies in Philosophy XI, 1989), pp. 24–40.
27 Bertrand Russell, "On The Notion of Cause," in *Mysticism and Logic and Other Essays* (London: Longmans, Green and Co., 1921), pp. 180–208.
28 Ibid.
29 A. N. Whitehead and Bertrand Russell, *Principia Mathematica to *56* (Cambridge: Cambridge University Press, 1964), p. 44.
30 *Principia Mathematica to *56*, p. 48.
31 Bertrand Russell, "On the Nature of Truth," *Proceedings of the Aristotelian Society* 7 (1907), pp. 28–49.
32 Instead of "statements" we shall speak of "wffs" (well-formed formulas of the formal language of *Principia*).
33 We shall discuss the multiple-relation theory of truth in Chapter Five.
34 *Principia Mathematica to *56*, p. 42.
35 *Principia Mathematica to *56*, p. 46.
36 Whitehead and Russell, PM, vol. 1, p. 162.
37 Alonzo Church, "A Note on the Entscheidungsproblem," *Journal of Symbolic Logic*, vol. 1 (no. 1), (1936), pp. 40–41.
38 In a standard theory, predicate variables can occur only in predicate positions.

Thus the theory is consistent and Russell's paradox of attributes cannot arise within it.
39 More exactly, the matrices p/a emulate an ontology of attributes.
40 Alternatively, f(x, y, b, q) = {x/y;b! q}. This occurs in Russell's letter to Hawtrey. See Chapter One.
41 See Gregory Landini, *Russell's Hidden Substitutional Theory* (Oxford: Oxford University Press, 1998), p. 119.
42 Quoted from InS, p. 197.
43 InS, p. 213.
44 Bertrand Russell, "Les Paradoxes de la Logistique," *Revue de Métaphysique dt de Morale* vol. 14 (no. 5), (September 1906), pp. 627–650. The English manuscript is: "On 'Insolubilia' and Their Solution by Symbolic Logic," in ed., Douglas Lackey, *Essays in Analysis By Bertrand Russell* (London: Allen & Unwin, 1973), p. 206.
45 Quoted from Michael Holroyd, *Lytton Strachey* (London: Heinemann, 1967), p. 290.
46 I think that I have found a way to avoid this and thereby save the theory of InS. See Landini 2004. "Logicism's 'Insolubilia' and Their Solution by Russell's Substitutional Theory" in Godehard Link, ed., *One-Hundred Years of Russell's Paradox* (Berlin: De Gruyter, 2004), pp. 373–399.
47 Cocchiarella (1980) was first to notice this, pointing out that the theory of *Principia Mathematica* is quite different and rejects an ontology of propositions all together.
48 Unfortunately, one still finds expositions of *Principia* which say that ramification was produced by Russell's desire to solve semantic paradoxes, and some even go so far as to include the Grelling. This paradox concerns the semantic property of being heterological. A predicate expression is heterological if and only if it designates a property that it does not exemplify. For example, "is tall" is not tall. Hence ". . . is tall" is heterological. But ". . . is short" is short. Hence "is short" is not heterological. But what of ". . . is heterological"? It is heterological if and only if it is not heterological. Russell never addressed this paradox, in spite of its discovery in 1908, well in time for inclusion in *Principia*. It is easy to see why. During the era of substitution, Russell would readily dismiss it along with the other semantic paradoxes as it essentially employs a confused notion of designation. The Russell of *Principia* would dismiss it as well. It cannot be expressed in the language of *Principia* because it conflicts with the nominalistic interpretation of the type indices of the work. That is, an expression $D^{(o,\,(o))}(c^o, \varphi^{(o)})$ is interpreted by the nominalistic semantics in such a way that the predicate $\varphi^{(o)}$ occurs in a predicate position in formulas that are instances of

the form. But if it is to stand for an expression designating a property, this is impossible.

FOUR THE PHILOSOPHY OF LOGICAL ATOMISM

1. Bertrand Russell, *The Art of Philosophizing* (New York: Philosophical Library, 1968) p. 7.
2. David Pears, *The False Prison*, vol. 1 (Oxford: Oxford University Press, 1987), p. 25.
3. David Pears, *The False Prison*, vol. 1, p. 63.
4. Bertrand Russell, "On Scientific Method in Philosophy," in *Mysticism and Logic* (Oxford: Barnes & Noble, 1976), p.84.
5. Op. cit.
6. Bertrand Russell, "Logical Atomism," in ed., Robert Marsh, *Bertrand Russell: Logic and Knowledge: Essays 1901–1950* (London: Allen & Unwin, 1977), p. 326.
7. Russell Bertrand, *Our Knowledge of the External World* (London: Allen & Unwin, 1969), p. 7.
8. R. M. Sainsbury, *Paradoxes* (Cambridge: Cambridge University Press, 2009), p. 1.
9. Thanks to Francesco Orilia and Ben Hassman for discussions of this.
10. By similar definition, any repeating decimal expresses a ratio. For instance:

$$.\overline{123} = df \lim_{n \to \infty} \sum \frac{123}{10^{3(n+1)}}$$

This is the ratio $\frac{123}{999}$.

11. Bertrand Russell, "Mathematics and the Metaphysicians" (printed with the title "Recent Work in the Philosophy of Mathematics"), *The International Monthly* vol. 4 (1901), pp. 83–101. Reprinted in *Mysticism and Logic and Other Essays* (Burlington, VT: Barnes & Noble, 1976), pp. 59–74.
12. Ibid.
13. Op cit., p. 833.
14. Bertrand Russell, "Logical Atomism," in ed., Robert Marsh, *Logic and Knowledge: Essays 1901–1950* (London: Allen & Unwin, 1977), p. 326.
15. Op. cit., pp. 264, 287.
16. Op. cit., p. 296.
17. Bertrand Russell, "Mathematics and the Metaphysicians," in *Mysticism and Logic* (Totawa, NJ: Barnes and Noble, 1976), p. 63.
18. This example is from Richard Montague.
19. The phrase has been attributed to Russell, but its origin is unclear.

20 Bertrand Russell, *The Art of Philosophizing* (New York: Philosophical Library, 1968), p. 1.
21 W. V. O. Quine, "On What There Is," in *From a Logical Point of View* (Cambridge, MA: Harvard University Press, 1964), pp. 1–19.
22 W. V. O. Quine, "On What There Is," p. 15.
23 Including Russell himself in *The Principles of Mathematics*.
24 Plato: *The Collected Papers*, ed., Edith Hamilton and Huntington Cairns (New York: Pantheon Books, 1961), p. 894.
25 Frank Plumpton Ramsey, "Philosophy" in R. B. Braithwaite, ed., *The Foundations of Mathematics and other logical essays* (New York: Harcourt, Brace and Co., 1931), p. 263.fn.
26 See OD, p. 116. Quine, wondering about non-existent possible fat men in his doorway, alluded to this problem in his 1948 paper "On What There Is."
27 More exactly, he discovered that any consistent recursively axiomatizable theory of arithmetic, in which every recursive function is expressible, is negation incomplete.
28 This example is from Gareth Evans, "The Causal Theory of Names," *Aristotelian Society: Supplementary Volume 47* (1973), pp. 187–208.
29 See Nevia Dolcini, "Indexicals and Perception," *Rivista di Filosofia del Linguaggio 2* (2010), pp. 19–41.
30 Russell writes that "... the thought in the mind of a person using a proper name correctly can generally only be expressed explicitly if we replace the proper name by a description" (PP, p. 54). But it quickly becomes clear that Russell means finding the "thought" in the sense of finding precise truth-conditions, whether or not they are known to the speaker.
31 See Graham Priest, "How the Particular Quantifier Became Existentially Loaded Behind our Backs," in *The Soochow Journal of Philosophical Studies: Special Issue*, ed., Chienkuo Mi (Taipei: Soochow University, 2007), p. 199.
32 Bertrand Russell, "The Philosophy of Logical Atomism," p. 233.
33 Gottlob Frege's *Foundations of Arithmetic*, J. L. Austin, trans. (Evanston, IL: Northwestern University Press, 1980), p. 65.
34 See "On Denoting," p. 109.
35 See Bertrand Russell, "A Debate on the Existence of God," in ed., Al Seckel, *Bertrand Russell on God and Religion* (Buffalo, NY: Prometheus Books, 1986), pp. 123–146.
36 We can ask "Why $(\exists\varphi)(\exists x)\varphi(x)$?" (i.e. "Why is some property is exemplified by some individual?"). But this is not the question one meant to ask. The denial of $(\exists\varphi)(\exists x)\varphi(x)$ is $(\forall\varphi)(\forall x)\sim\varphi(x)$. But this yields $(\forall x)(p\ \&\ \sim p\ .\&.\ \psi x)$, which in *Principia* is equivalent to the contradiction $p\ \&\ \sim p\ .\&.\ (\forall x)\psi x$.

434 **Notes**

37 Rene Descartes, "Meditation V," in John Cottingham et al., eds., *The Philosophical Writings of Descartes* (Cambridge: University Press, 1984), p. 46.
38 Bertrand Russell, "The Existential Import of Propositions," in ed., Douglas Lackey, *Essays in Analysis By Bertrand Russell* (London: Allen & Unwin, 1973), p. 98.
39 Thanks to Richard Fumerton for this point.
40 Bertrand Russell, Review of A. Meinong's *Ueber die Stellung der Gegenstandstheorie im System der Wissenschaften*, Mind, n.s. 16: 436–39. Reprinted in *Essays In Analysis By Bertrand Russell*, ed., Douglas Lackey (London: Allen & Unwin, 1973), pp. 89–93.
41 The term a must be free for x in C and replace all free occurrences of x in the formula C.
42 The variable must be free for the variable x and replace all free occurrence of the variable x in the formula C.
43 Compare Leonard Linsky, *Oblique Contexts* (Chicago: University of Chicago Press, 1983).
44 Nino B. Cocchiarella, "The Primary and Secondary Semantics of Logical Necessity," *Journal of Philosophical Logic* vol. 4 (no. 1), (1975), pp. 13–27.

FIVE SCIENTIFIC EPISTEMOLOGY

1 When the newspaper *Boston Transcript* reported at length on his Lowell Lectures, they were called "Scientific Method in Philosophy." Perhaps Open Court thought that using the same title would be good for marketing in the United States. (Thanks to Kenneth Blackwell for this point.)
2 Bertrand Russell, "On the Relation of Sense-Data to Physics," in *Mysticism and Logic* (Totowa, NJ: Barnes & Noble, 1976), p. 110.
3 Letter to Russell 19 September 1910. Quoted from Ronald Clark, *The Life of Bertrand Russell* (New York: Knopf, 1979), p. 148.
4 *La Ginestra* was among the favorites of Russell.
5 There were attempts, however, to build up a form of logicism from this conception of logic as quantification theory.
6 Plato, *The Meno*, in ed., Edith Hamilton, *Plato: Collected Dialogues* (New York: Pantheon Books, 1961, p. 367).
7 The law of large numbers describes the long-term stability of the mean of a random variable. Given a random variable with a finite expected value, if its values are repeatedly sampled, as the number of these observations increases, their mean will tend to approach and stay close to the expected value. The law has many important applications, but in application the muddy streets can upset the usefulness of the mathematical/logical truth. The law only applies (as the name indicates) when a large number of observations are considered.

There is no principle that a small number of observations will converge to the expected value.

8 The central limit theorem states that the re-averaged sum of a sufficiently large number of identically distributed independent random variables each with finite mean and variance will be approximately normally distributed.

9 See TK, pp. 22, 31.

10 See Theodore Sider, *Four-Dimensionalism* (Oxford: Oxford University Press, 2001).

11 Bertrand Russell, "On Order in Time," reprinted in ed., Robert Marsh, *Logic and Knowledge: Essays 1901–1950* (London: Allen & Unwin, 1977), p. 352.

12 Edmond Gettier, "Is Justified True Belief Knowledge?" *Analysis* vol. 21 (no. 6), (1963), pp. 121–123.

13 See Thomas Harman, "Selections from Thought," in George Pappas and Marshall Swain, eds., *Essays on Knowledge and Justification* (Ithaca, NY: Cornell University Press, 1978), p. 213.

14 See Timothy and Lydia McGrew, *Internalism and Epistemology* (New York: Routledge, 2007).

15 It is far from obvious that such facts are composed of the same constituents since the psychological states and dispositions involved in *a* loving *b*, may well be (when *a* is not *b*) necessarily quite different from those involved in *b* loving *a*.

16 Unfortunately, confusion on this point is prevalent. It is found, for example, in Herbert Hockberg, "Propositions, Truth and Belief: The Wittgenstein–Russell Debate," *Theoria* 66 (2000), pp. 3–40. See also Thomas Ricketts, "Wittgenstein Against Frege and Russell," in Erich Reck, ed., *From Frege to Wittgenstein: Perspectives on Early Analytic Philosophy* (Oxford: Oxford University Press, 2002), pp. 217–251.

17 Hockberg claims that my account assumes that Russell took correspondence as a primitive relation. See Herbert Hochberg, "Propositions, Truth and Belief: The Wittgenstein–Russell Debate," *Theoria* 66 (2000), pp. 3–40. See also Herbert Hochberg, "Propositions, Truth and Belief: The Wittgenstein–Russell Debate," *Theoria* 66 (2000), pp. 3–40. I do not take correspondence to be a primitive relation. The multiple-relation theory is the basis of recursive definitions of "truth" and "falsehood." In the base case of the recursion, the correspondence (truth) conditions of a belief-complex are defined as the existence of a fact consisting of certain constituents of that complex.

18 The expression seems due to Nicholas Griffin. See his "Russell on the Nature of Logic," *Synthese* vol. 45 (no. 1), (1980): pp. 117–188. See also, Nicholas Griffin, "Russell's Multiple-Relation Theory of Judgment," *Philosophical Studies* vol. 47 (no. 2), (1985), pp. 213–247.

Notes

19 G. F. Stout, "The Object of Thought and Real Being," *Proceedings of the Aristotelian Society* 11 (1911), pp. 187–208.
20 Bertrand Russell, "On the Nature of Truth and Falsehood," Chapter VII of his *Philosophical Essays* (London: Longmans, 1910), p. 158.
21 Op. cit., p. 86.
22 Bertrand Russell, P, p. 128.
23 Bertrand Russell, TK, pp. 122ff.
24 Giaretta claims that my account of the multiple-relation theory assumes that Russell excludes type* differences. This is not correct. See Pierdaniele Giaretta, "Analysis and Logical Form in Russell: The 1913 Paradigm," *Dialectica* vol. 51 (no. 4), (1997), pp. 273–293.
25 Op. cit., p. 122.
26 Op. cit., p. 101.
27 Bertrand Russell, TK, p. 147.
28 For a dissenting opinion see Herbert Hochberg, "Propositions, Truth and Belief: The Wittgenstein–Russell Debate," *Theoria* 66 (2000), pp. 3–40.
29 Bertrand Russell, *Theory of Knowledge*, p. 97.
30 Ibid., p. 100.
31 Op cit., p. 132.
32 Bertrand Russell, PLA, p. 211.
33 Richard McDonough, *The Argument of the Tractatus* (Albany, NY: SUNY Press, 1986), p. 19.
34 Bertrand Russell, LA, pp. 183, 234.
35 Russell, Bertrand. PLA, p. 211.
36 Op. cit., pp. 196, 197, 211.
37 Bertrand Russell, MPD, p. 135.
38 Nicholas Griffin, ed., *The Selected Letters of Bertrand Russell* (Boston: Houghton Mifflin Co., 1892), p. 459.
39 Op. cit., p. 226.
40 Russell, Bertrand, PLA, p. 225.
41 Ibid.
42 In Davidson's theory, the sentence "Galileo believed that the earth moves" captures "The earth moves and Galileo believed that." Here both "moves" and "believes" are acting assertorically as verbs. See Donald Davidson, "On Saying That," *Synthese* vol. 19 (no. 2), (1968–1969), pp. 130–146.
43 Ludwig Wittgenstein, *Letters to Russell, Keynes and Moore* (Ithaca, NY: Cornell University Press, 1974), p. 24. Letter R13, dated 22 July 1913.
44 G. H von Wright, ed., *Ludwig Wittgenstein: Letters to C. K. Ogden* (Oxford: Basil Blackwell, 1983), p. 84.

45 The doctrine that universals are capable of a twofold occurrence was unchanged from Russell's 1903 *Principles of Mathematics* through 1914.
46 Ibid., p., 68.
47 Bertrand Russell, "On Denoting," [EA], p. 119.
48 Bertrand Russell, "Knowledge by Acquaintance and Knowledge by Description, in *Mysticism and Logic* (Totowa, NJ: Barnes & Noble, 1976), p. 159. Bertrand Russell, P, p. 58.
49 Op. cit., p. 205.
50 Bertrand Russell, "The Philosophy of Logical Atomism," pp. 205, 225–226.
51 *MPD*, p. 101.
52 Ibid.
53 See *OP*, pp. 67, 129, 172. Russell did not fully embrace behaviorism, however.
54 Robert Tully "Three Studies of Russell's Neutral Monism," *Russell* vol. 13 (no. 2), (1993), pp. 7, 35.
55 See *OP*, p. 248; *History of Western Philosophy*, pp. 812, 833; "Logical Atomism," p. 342
56 His Basic Law V.
57 See Gottlob Frege, *The Basic Laws of Arithmetic: Exposition of the System*, trans. by Montgomery Furth (Berkeley: University of California Press, 1964), p. 127.

SIX MIND AND MATTER

1 Of course, in Spinoza's view, this substance is God.
2 Thomas Nagel, "What Is it Like to be a Bat?" *Philosophical Review* vol. 83 (no. 4), (1974), pp. 435–450.
3 William James, "Does Consciousness Exist?" *Journal of Philosophy, Psychology, and Scientific Methods* vol. 1 (no. 18), (1904), pp. 477–491.
4 Bertrand Russell, Letter to the editor published in *The Journal of Philosophy, Psychology and Scientific Methods* 12 (1915), pp. 391–392. Reprinted in [CP8], p. 87.
5 Op. cit.
6 This is the title of a paper Russell wrote in 1913 in preparation for his 1914 lectures at Harvard University.
7 See Edna Heidbreder, *Seven Psychologies* (New York: D. Appleton-Century, 1933).
8 *Bertrand Russell*, *A*, vol. I. p. 53.
9 John Searle, *The Mystery of Consciousness* (New York: New York Times Review Books), p. 5.
10 Op. cit., p. 14.
11 *AM*, p. 144.
12 Daniel Dennett, "Quining Qualia" in William Lycan, ed., *Mind and Cognition: A Reader* (Oxford: Basil Blackwell, 1990), pp. 519–547.

13 Frank Jackson, "Epiphenomenal Qualia", *Philosophical Quarterly*, vol. 32 (no. 127), (1982), pp. 127–136.
14 OP, p. 17.
15 See Russell's reply to Nagel in Paul Arthur Schilpp, ed., *The Philosophy of Bertrand Russell* (Chicago: Northwestern University Press, 1944), p. 705.
16 Russell's reply to Nagel in Paul Arthur Schilpp, ed., *The Philosophy of Bertrand Russell* (Chicago: Northwestern University Press, 1944), p. 706.
17 "On the Nature of Acquaintaince," in ed., Robert Marsh, *Logic and Knowledge: Essays 1901–1950* (London: Allen & Unwin, 1977), p. 166.
18 Russell, "On the Nature of Acquaintance," p. 166.
19 Op. cit., p. 168.
20 Op. cit., p. 111.
21 Op. cit., p. 115.
22 Hans Reichenbach, *Elements of Symbolic Logic* (New York: The Free Press, 1947).
23 PfM, p. 147.
24 William, James, *Psychology*, vol. II (New York: Henry Holt & Co., 1899), p. 449.
25 See AM, p. 155.
26 AM, p.156.
27 AM, p. 159.
28 AM, p. 160.
29 AM, p. 184.
30 Hilary Putnam, *Reason, Truth and History* (London: Cambridge University Press, 1980), p. 1.
31 Ibid., p. 5.
32 Op. cit., pp. 259, 261.
33 Bertrand Russell, "Dewey's New Logic," in Paul Arthur Schilpp, ed., *The Philosophy of John Dewey* (Chicago: Open Court, 1951), p. 146.
34 Quoted from Sameul Meyer, *Dewey and Russell: An Exchange* (New York: Philosophical Library, 1985), p. 62.
35 AM, p. 247.
36 AM, p. 250.
37 Gerald Edelman and Giulio Tononi, *A Universe of Consciousness* (New York: Basic Books, 2000).
38 Bertrand Russell, "On Propositions: What They Are And How They Mean," in ed., R.C. Marsh, *Bertrand Russell: Essays 1901–1950* (Allen & Unwin, 1977), p. 288.
39 M. H. A. Newman, "Mr. Russell's Causal Theory of Perception," *Mind* vol. 5 (no. 146) (1928), pp. 137–148.
40 An overestimation is found in Ray Monk, *Bertrand Russell: The Ghost of Madness 1921–1970* (New York: The Free Press, 2000), pp. 72, 244.

41 In Russell's letter, "finite" is supposed to be "infinite," or so I think.
42 This issue has been wrongly associated with an argument due to Putnam against the intelligibility of metaphysical realism. Putnam uses that result, not known until the 1930s and well after Newman wrote, that every consistent first order theory has an infinite model (i.e. an interpretation of its predicate letters over a domain that makes the axioms of the theory true).
43 It is atheistic in the sense that it removes Berkeley's appeal to the existence of God to solve the problems of the perceiver independence of matter.
44 Rudolf Carnap, "The Elimination of Metaphysics Through Logical Analysis of Language," in Alfred Ayer, ed., *Logical Positivism* (Glencoe, IL: Macmillan, 1959), pp. 60–81.
45 A major difficulty, pointed out by Duhem, is that a theoretical statement can be submitted to an empirical observational test only when it is taken together with a host of auxiliary theoretical statements pertaining to the testing conditions. Another difficulty is that a rigid distinction between "observable" and "theoretical" is difficult to sustain, even when observations are characterized as immediate sense-experiences. Even first-person sensory reports can be corrupted by theoretical assumptions.
46 Quoted from Russell, HWP, p. 648. It is not certain who wrote the reply. Russell himself has been suggested as the author.

SEVEN *PRINCIPIA*'s SECOND EDITION

1 Bertrand Russell, *Portraits from Memory* (New York: Simon & Schuster, 1959), p. 23.
2 For example, *Tom and Viv* (directed by Brian Gilbert, 1994). See also, *Wittgenstein* (directed by Derek Jarman, 1993).
3 Bertrand Russell, *A*, vol. II, p. 137.
4 Bertrand Russell, MPD, p. 217.
5 See Ray Monk, *Wittgenstein: The Duty of a Genius* (New York: The Free Press, 1990), p. 294.
6 M. O'Connor Drury, "Some Notes on Conversations with Wittgenstein" and "Conversations with Wittgenstein," in *Ludwig Wittgenstein: Personal Recollections*, ed. Rush Rhees (Totowa, NJ: Rowman and Littlefield, 1981), p. 127.
7 Whitehead had little patience for Wittgenstein's aphorisms. See Victor Lowe, *Alfred North Whitehead: The Man and his Work* vol. II (Baltimore: The Johns Hopkins Press, 1990), pp. 273–278.
8 A. N. Whitehead, "Indication, Classes, Numbers, Validation," in *Essays in Science and Philosophy by Alfred North Whitehead* (New York: Philosophical Library, 1948) pp. 227–240.

9 Quoted from Brian McGuinness, *Wittgenstein: A Life* (London: Duckworth, 1988), p. 180.
10 See Brian McGuinness, *Wittgenstein: A Life* (London: Duckworth, 1988), p. 160.
11 Ludwig Wittgenstein, Extracts from Letters to Russell 1912–1920, in ed., G. H. von Wright and G. E. M. Anscombe, *Notebooks 1914–1916* (Chicago: University of Chicago Press, 1979), pp. 123, 126.
12 Jean Nicod, "A Reduction in the Number of the Primitive Propositions of Logic," *Proceedings of the Cambridge Philosophical Society* vol. 19 (no. 1), (1917), pp. 32–41. The paper was read before the Society 30 October 1916.
13 Bertrand Russell, PM, p. xv.
14 Bertrand Russell, A, vol. II, p. 162.
15 McGuinness notices this. He argues that Wittgenstein's original notion of a logical constant was "... anything that had been supposed to be a logical object." See Brian McGuinness, "The *Grundgedanke* of the *Tractatus*," in G. Vesey, ed., *Understanding Wittgenstein* (London: Macmillan, 1974).
16 *Letters*, 19 August 1919.
17 Rudolf Carnap, *Philosophy and Logical Syntax* (London: Kegan Paul, 1935).
18 Frank Ramsey, "General Propositions and Causality," in *The Foundations of Mathematics*, ed., R. B. Braithwaite (London: Harcourt, Brace and Co., 1931), p. 238.
19 Bertrand Russell, A, vol. II, p. 139.
20 Op. cit., p. 126.
21 Op. cit., p. 126.
22 See Russell, A, vol. III, p. 238. The quoted comments are found on the book's dust jacket.
23 Ludwig Wittgenstein, *Notebooks 1914–1916*, p. 123.
24 Letter of Nov. 1913 in *Notebooks 1914–1916*, second edition by G. H. von Wright & G. E. M. Anscombe (Chicago: Blackwell, 1979), p. 129. Wittgenstein objected to Russell's use of the identity sign in his theory of definite descriptions.
25 For an account of Wittgenstein's exclusive quantifiers see Gregory Landini, *Wittgenstein's Apprenticeship with Russell* (Cambridge: Cambridge University Press, 2007). For an interpretation that does not assure infinity see Kai Wehmeier, "Wittgenstein's Predicate Logic," *Notre Dame Journal of Formal Logic* vol. 45 (no. 1), (2004), pp. 1–11.
26 Frank Ramsey, Letter to Moore of 6 February 1924. Reprinted in Josef Rothhaupt, ed., *Farbthemen in Wittgensteins Gesamtnachlass: philologisch-philosophische Untersuchungen im Längschnitt und Querschnitten*, Monografien Philosophie, 273 (Weinheim: Beltz, 1966.), p. 46.
27 See Mays Wolfe, "Recollections of Wittgenstein," in K. T. Fann, ed., *Ludwig*

Wittgentein: The Man and His Philosophy (Ewing, NJ: University of California Press, 1967), p. 82.
28 *Principia Mathematica to* *56, p. 60.
29 Bertrand Russell, IMP, p. 183.
30 Bertrand Russell, MPD, p. 88. Not surprisingly, the passages from the 1940 *Inquiry* echo Russell's ideas in Appendix C of the second edition of *Principia*.
31 Op. cit., p. 5.
32 Op. cit., p. 404.
33 Bertrand Russell, IMT, p. 273.
34 Russell's *A*, vol. II, pp. 245, 249 makes it clear that Nicod was also aware the plans for a second edition. In a letter, he asked Russell to include the result that *Principia*'s *1.4 p v q .⊃. q v p can be proved from *1.2, *1.3, *1.5, *1.6 if *1.3 is altered to q . ⊃. q v p. This result was in his paper "A Reduction in the Number of Primitive Propositions of Logic," *Proceedings of the Cambridge Philosophical Society*, vol. 19 (no. 1), (1917): pp. 32–41. Russell did not mention this, but instead included Nicod's result reducing the propositional calculus to one axiom (i.e. schema) and one inference rule. Nicod died of tuberculosis in February of 1924.
35 John Myhill, "The Undefinability of the Set of Natural Numbers in the Ramified *Principia*," in George Nakhnikian, ed., *Bertrand Russell's Philosophy* (New York: Harper & Row, 1974), pp. 19–27.
36 Kurt Gödel, "Russell's Mathematical Logic," in Paul Arthur Schilpp, ed., *The Philosophy of Bertrand Russell* (Evanston, IL: Northwestern Univeristy, 1944), pp. 125–153.
37 See Gregory Landini, "The Definability of the Natural Numbers in the 1925 *Principia Mathematica*," *Journal of Philosophical Logic* vol. 25 (no. 6), (1996): pp. 597–615.
38 Frank Ramsey, "The Foundations of Mathematics," in R. B. Braithwaite, ed., *The Foundations of Mathematics and Other Essays by Frank Plumpton Ramsey* (London: Harcourt, Brace and Co., 1931), p. 29.
39 Ramsey, op. cit., p. 77.
40 Bertrand Russell, "On 'Insolubilia' and Their Solution by Symbolic Logic," in ed., Douglas Lackey, *Essays In Analysis By Bertrand Russell* (London: George Allen & Unwin, 1973), pp. 190–214. The view is even more salient in Russell's manuscript "On the Substitutional Theory of Classes and Relations," in ed., Douglas Lackey, *Essays In Analysis By Bertrand Russell* (London: George Allen & Unwin, 1973), pp. 165–189.
41 In spite of this, Potter maintains that Russell's second edition embraced infinite

conjunctions and disjunctions. See Michael Potter, *Reason's Nearest Kin* (Oxford: Oxford University Press, 2000), p. 204

42 Op. cit., p. 42.
43 Ramsey, "Mathematical Logic," in R. B. Braithwaite, ed., *The Foundations of Mathematics and Other Essays by Frank Plumpton Ramsey* (London: Harcourt, Brace and Co., 1926), p. 77.
44 Op. cit., p. 79.
45 Ramsey, Frank. Letter to Wittgenstein of 20 September 1923, in eds., G. H. von Wright, *Ludwig Wittgenstein: Letters to C. K. Ogden* (Oxford: Basil Blackwell, 1973), p. 78.
46 Ramsey, Frank. Letter to Russell of 20 February 1924, in eds., G. H. von Wright *Ludwig Wittgenstein: Letters to C. K. Ogden* (Oxford: Basil Blackwell, 1973), p. 84.
47 Ramsey, Frank. "Review of the Second-Edition of *Principia Mathematica*," *Nature* vol. 116 (no. 2908), (1925), pp. 127–128.
48 See Bertrand Russell, MPD, p. 115. Russell endorses Wittgenstein against identity in OKEW, p. 212. A footnote to "unpublished work of Wittgenstein" in the first edition was altered in subsequent editions to reference the *Tractatus*.
49 Frank Ramsey, "The Foundations of Mathematics," in ed., R. B. Braithwaite, *The Foundations of Mathematics and Other Essays by Frank Plumpton Ramsey* (London: Harcourt, Brace & Co., 1931), p. 17.
50 Marion erroneously characterizes Ramsey as holding that these are all tautologies. See Matthieu Marion, *Wittgenstein, Finitism and the Foundations of Mathematics* (Oxford: Clarendon Press, 1998), p. 69.
51 Frank Ramsey, op. cit., p. 56.
52 See Frank Plumpton Ramsey, *Notes on Philosophy, Probability and Mathematics*, ed., Maria Carla Galavotti (Naples: Bibliopolis, 1991) pp. 336–346.

EIGHT PROBABLE KNOWLEDGE

1 MPD, p. 190.
2 HK, p. xv.
3 HK, p. xvi.
4 HK, p. v.
5 Bertrand Russell, MPD, p. 212.
6 Bertrand Russell, MPD, pp. 119, 212.
7 Bertrand Russell, PoM, p. xi.
8 Bertrand Russell, "Is Mathematics Purely Linguistic?" in ed., Douglas Lackey, *Essays In Analysis By Bertrand Russell* (London: Allen & Unwin, 1973), p. 306.
9 Bertrand Russell, OP, p. 27.
10 Bertrand Russell, OP (New York: W.W. Norton & Co. Inc., 1927), p. 86.

11 See Tom Burke, *Dewey's New Logic: A Reply to Russell* (Chicago, University of Chicago Press, 1994).
12 The function that orders integers one-to-one with natural numbers so that every other one is negative $(0, -1, +1, -2, \text{etc.})$ is this:

$$f m = \begin{cases} (-1)^m \left(\dfrac{m}{2}\right), & \text{if } m \text{ is even} \\ (-1)^m \left(\dfrac{m+1}{2}\right), & \text{if } m \text{ is odd} \end{cases}$$

13 Wesley C. Salmon, "Inductive Inference," in Baruch Brody, ed., *Readings in the Philosophy of Science* (Prentice Hall, 1970), pp. 597–671.
14 Joseph Bertrand, *Calculi des probabilités* (Paris: Gauthier-Villars, 1887).
15 If there are an even number of outcomes, then the median is computed by sorting and then taking the average of the two middle outcomes.
16 Special thanks to Jeremy Shipley for discussion of Bertrand style paradoxes.
17 Hans Reichenbach, *The Rise of Scientific Philosophy* (Berkeley: University of California Press, 1951), p. 247.
18 I Agree with Ayer that Russell intended "degree of credibility" here and not mathematical probability. See A. J. Ayer, *Russell* (New York: Viking Press, 1972), p. 99.
19 Thanks to Gregory Jesson for a reminder of this.
20 See HK, p. 507.
21 Bertrand Russell, "On the Notion of Cause," *Proceedings of the Aristotelian Society*, (May 13 1912–1913), p. 142.
22 Op. cit., p. 142.
23 Op. cit., p. 143.
24 Op. cit., p. 150.

NINE   ICARUS

1 Bertrand Russell, "A Liberal Decalogue," *A*, vol. III, pp. 71–72.
2 William James, *The Will to Believe and other Essays in Popular Philosophy* (New York: Longmans Green and Co., 1907).
3 W. K. Clifford, *Lectures and Essays* (London: Macmillan, 1879).
4 See for instance, Richard Dawkins, *The God Delusion* (Boston: Houghton Mifflin Harcourt, 2006) and Christopher Hitchens, *God is Not Great* (New York & Boston: Twelve Books, 2007).
5 Bertrand Russell, "Is There a God?" commissioned in 1952 by *Illustrated* magazine but never published.

6 Richard Dawkins used it in his book *A Devil's Chaplain* (2003).
7 For instance, there was the problem of the absence of stellar parallax. A distant star, at different times of the year, should be in different places in the sky. It was solved by optics, when more refined techniques for grinding lenses became possible and Newton invented the reflecting telescope.
8 Russell Bertrand, "Prisons I" (Morrell Papers, University of Texas at Austin). Quoted from Ken Blackwell, *The Spinozistic Ethics of Bertrand Russell* (London: Allen & Unwin, 1985), p. 111.
9 Bertrand Russell, P, p. 160.
10 Ken Blackwell, *Russell's Spinozistic Ethics* (London: Allen & Unwin, 1985), p. 160f.
11 Bertrand Russell, "The Essence of Religion," *Hibbert Journal*, II (October 1912), pp. 46–63. Reprinted in CP vol. 12, eds., Richard Rempel, Andrew Brink and Margaret Moran (London: Allen & Unwin, 1985), pp. 110–122.
12 Bertrand Russell, "On Scientific Method in Philosophy," Herbert Spencer Lecture (Oxford: Oxford University Press, 1914). Reprinted in *Mysticism and Logic* (Oxford: Barnes & Noble, 1976), p. 82
13 Bertrand Russell, "Mysticism and Logic" in *Mysticism and Logic* (Totowa, NJ: Barnes & Noble, 1976), p. 27.
14 Nicholas Griffin, *The Selected Letters of Bertrand Russell* (Boston: Houghton Mifflin Company, 1992), p. 437.
15 Giacomo Leopardi, *I Canti di Giacomo Leopardi Nelle Traduzioni Inglesi*, ed., G. Singh (Recanati: Centro Nazionale di Studi Leopardiana, 1990), p. 163.
16 Russell and Ottoline were fond of reading Leopardi together while working on Prisons. See ed., Robert Gathorne-Hardy, *Ottoline: The Early Memoirs* (London: Faber and Faber) p. 226. Russell quotes from La Ginestra in *Power: A New Social Analysis* (New York: W. W. Norton & Co., 1938), p. 33. He quotes L'Infinito in full in his book *The Impact of Science on Society* (London: Allen & Unwin 1952), p. 98, prefacing it by writing: "This point of view is well expressed in a little poem by Leopardi and expresses, more nearly than any other known to me, my own feeling about the universe and human passions."
17 Ray Monk, *Bertrand Russell: The Spirit of Solitude* (New York: The Free Press 1996), p. 280.
18 Ludwig Wittgenstein, *Notebooks 1914–1916*, ed. by G. H. von Wright, and G. E. M. Anscombe (Chicago: University of Chicago Press, 1979), p. 77. See also TLP 6.45.
19 Op. cit., p. 75.
20 B, p. 51.
21 B, p. 29.
22 See especially, B, p. 33.

23 B, p. 34.
24 B, p. 32.
25 I, p. 62.
26 B, p. 21.
27 B, p. 64.

Bibliography

WORKS BY RUSSELL

(ABC) *The ABC of Relativity*, revised edition (London: Routledge, 1997). Original edition (New York: Harper & Brothers, 1925).
(AofP) *The Art of Philosophizing And Other Essays* (New York: Philosophical Library, 1968).
(AMa) *The Analysis of Matter* (London: Kegan Paul, 1927).
(AMi) *The Analysis of Mind* (London: Allen & Unwin, 1921).
(A) *The Autobiography of Bertrand Russell*, vol. I 1872–1914 (Boston: Little, Brown & Co., 1968); vol II 1914–1944 (Boston: Little, Brown & Co., 1968); vol. III 1944–1969 (New York: Simon & Schuster, 1969).
The Collected Papers of Bertrand Russell, vol. 4, *Foundations of Logic: 1903–1905*, ed. by Alsdair Urquhard (London: Routledge, 1994).
The Collected Papers of Bertrand Russell, vol. 6, *Logic and Philosophy Papers: 1901–1913*, ed. by John G. Slater (London: Routledge, 1992).
(TK) *The Collected Papers of Bertrand Russell*, vol. 7, *Theory of Knowledge: The 1913 Manuscript*, ed. by Elizabeth Ramsden Eames in collaboration with Kenneth Blackwell (London: George Allen & Unwin, 1984).
The Collected Papers of Bertrand Russell, vol. 8, *The Philosophy of Logical Atomism and Other Essays 1914–1919*, ed. by John G. Slater (London: George Allen & Unwin, 1986).
The Collected Papers of Bertrand Russell, vol. 9, *Essays on Language, Mind and Matter: 1919–1926*, ed. by John G. Slater (London: Unwin Hyman, 1988).
(CH) *The Conquest of Happiness* (London: Allen & Unwin, 1930).
Essays In Analysis By Bertrand Russell, ed. by Douglas Lackey (London: Allen & Unwin 1973).
(FT) *Free Thought and Official Propaganda* (New York: B. W. Huebsch, 1922).
(HWP) *A History of Western Philosophy* (New York: Simon and Schuster, 1945).
(HK) *Human Knowledge: Its Scope and Limits* (New York: Simon & Schuster, 1948).
(I) *Icarus or The Future of Science* (New York: E.P. Dutton & Company, 1924).
The Impact of Science on Society (London: Allen & Unwin 1952).

(IPI) "In Praise of Idleness," *Harper's Magazine* (October 1932), pp. 552–559. Reprinted in *In Praise of Idleness and Other Essays* (New York: Routledge, 2000), pp. 11–25.

(IMP) *Introduction to Mathematical Philosophy* (London: Allen & Unwin, 1919, 1953).

(IMT) *An Inquiry into Meaning and Truth* (London: Allen & Unwin, 1940, 1966).

"Knowledge by Acquaintance and Knowledge be Description," in *Mysticism and Logic*, pp. 152–168. First published in the *Proceedings of the Aristotelian Society* 1910–1911, pp. 108–128. Reprinted in *Collected Papers*, vol. 6, pp. 147–161.

"Letter of 13 August 1919," *Russell* 10 (no. 2), 1990, pp. 101–124.

"Letter to the editor of the Athenaeum," in *Collected Papers*, vol. 8, p. 87. First published in *The Journal of Philosophy, Psychology and Scientific Methods* vol. 12 (1915), pp. 391–392.

(LA) "Logical Atomism," in ed., Robert Marsh, *Logic and Knowledge: Essays 1901–1950* (London: Allen & Unwin, 1977), pp. 323–343. First published in *Contempory British Philosophy: Personal Statements* (London: Allen & Unwin, 1924), pp. 356–383. Reprinted in *Collected Papers*, vol. 9, pp. 160–180.

(LK) *Logic and Knowledge: Essays 1901–1950*, ed., by Robert Marsh (London: Allen & Unwin, 1977).

(ML) "Mathematical Logic as Based on the Theory of Types," in *Logic and Knowledge: Essays 1901–1950*, pp. 59–102. First published in *The American Journal of Mathematics* 30 (1908), pp. 222–262.

(MM) "Mathematics and the Metaphysicians," in *Mysticism and Logic* (Totowa, NJ: Barnes and Noble, 1976), pp. 59–74.

(MMD) "My Mental Development" in ed., Paul Arthur Shilpp, *The Philosophy of Bertrand Russell* (Evanston, IL: Northwestern University Press, 1944), pp. 3–20.

(MPD) *My Philosophical Development* (New York: Simon & Schuster, 1959).

(MyL) *Mysticism and Logic and Other Essays* (Totowa, NJ: Barnes & Noble Books, 1917, 1976).

"Necessity and Possibility," in *Collected Papers*, vol. 4, pp. 507–520.

(NEP) *Nightmares of Eminent Persons and Other Stories* (New York: Simon & Schuster, 1954).

(OD) "On Denoting," in *Essays in Analysis*, pp. 103–119. First published in *Mind* 14 (1905), pp.479–493.

"On Fundamentals," *Collected Papers*, vol. 4, pp. 359–413.

(InS) "On 'Insolubila' and Their Solution By Symbolic Logic," in *Essays in Analysis*, pp. 190–214. First published as "Les Paradoxes de la Logique," *Revue de Métaphysique et de Morale*, vol. 14 (no. 5), (1906) pp. 627–650.

"On The Logic of Relations," in *Logic and Knowledge: Essays 1901–1950*, pp. 3–38. First published as "Sur la logique des relations," *Rivista di Mathematica*, vol. vii, (1901), pp. 115–148.

"On the Nature of Acquaintance," *Logic and Knowledge: Essays 1901–1950*, pp. 127–174.

"On the Nature of Truth," *Proceedings of the Aristotelian Society* vol. 7 (1907), pp. 28–49.

"On Propositions: What they Are and How they Mean," in *Logic and Knowledge: Essays 1901–1950*, pp. 283–320. First published in the *Aristotelian Society Supplementary Volume* 2 (1919), pp. 1–43. Reprinted in *Collected Papers*, vol. 8, pp. 276–306.

"On the Relation of Mathematics to Logic," in *Essays in Analysis*, pp. 260–271. First published as "Sur la Relation des Mathématiques B la Logistique," in *Revue de Métaphysique et de Morale* vol. 13, (1905) pp. 906–917.

"On the Relations of Universals and Particulars," in *Logic and Knowledge: Essays 1901–1950*, pp. 103–124.

(OIR) *An Outline of Intellectual Rubbish* (Girard, KS: Haldeman-Julius Publications, 1943).

(ORSP) "On the Relation of Sense-Data to Physics," in *Mysticism and Logic*, pp. 108–131. First published in *Scientia* vol. 4, 1914. Reprinted in *Collected Papers*, vol. 8, pp. 3–26.

"On Scientific Method in Philosophy", in *Mysticism and Logic*, pp. 78–93. First given as the Herbert Spencer Lecture (Oxford: Oxford University Press, 1914). Reprinted in *Collected Papers*, vol. 8, pp. 55–73.

(TN) "On Some Difficulties in the Theory of Transfinite Numbers and Order Types," in *Essays in Analysis*, pp. 135–164. First published in *Proceedings of the London Mathematical Society* 4 (March 1906), pp. 29–53.

(STCR) "On the Substitutional Theory of Classes and Relations," in *Essays in Analysis*, pp. 165–189. Manuscript received by the London Mathematical Society on 24 April 1905.

(OT) "On the theory of Transfinite Numbers and Order Types," *Proceedings of the London Mathematical Society*, 4, series 2 (1905), pp. 29–53. Reprinted in *Essays in Analysis*, pp. 135–164.

(OKEW) *Our Knowledge of the External World*, second edition, with new preface and revisions (London: Allen & Unwin, 1929). First published in London by Open Court, 1914. Second edition with revisions (London: Allen & Unwin, 1926).

(OP) *Outline of Philosophy* (New York: W.W. Norton & Co. Inc., 1927).

"Philosophy in the Twentieth-Century," *The Dial* vol. 77 (October 1924), pp. 271–290. Reprinted in *Collected Papers*, vol. 9, pp. 450–466.

(PLA) "The Philosophy of Logical Atomism" in *Logic and Knowledge: Essays 1901–1950*, pp. 175–281. First published in *The Monist* 28 (1918), pp. 495–527; 29 (January, April, July 1919), pp. 32–63, 190–222; 345–380. Reprinted in *Collected Papers*, vol. 8, pp. 155–244.

(PfM) *Portraits From Memory* (New York: Simon & Schuster, 1956).
(Pr) *Power: A New Social Analysis* (New York: W. W. Norton & Co., 1938).
(PTB) *The Practice and Theory of Bolshevism* (London: Allen & Unwin, 1920).
(PM) *Principia Mathematica* (coauthored by A. N Whitehead), second edition (Cambridge: Cambridge University Press, 1925, 1962); First edition, Cambridge, vol. 1 (1910), vol. 2 (1911), vol. 3 (1913).
(PM to *56) *Principia Mathematica to *56* (Cambridge: Cambridge University Press, 1964).
(PoM) *The Principles of Mathematics*, second edition (New York: W.W. Norton & Co., 1937, 1964). First edition (London: Allen & Unwin, 1903).
(PSR) *Principles of Social Reconstruction* (London: Allen & Unwin, 1917).
(P) *The Problems of Philosophy* (London: Oxford University Press, 1912).
(PIC) *The Prospects of Industrial Civilization* (London: Allen & Unwin, 1923).
(RaS) *Religion and Science* (London: Oxford University Press, 1935).
(Letters) *The Selected Letters of Bertrand Russell: vol. I, Private Years 1884–1914*, ed. by Nicholas Griffin (Boston: Houghton Mifflin Co., 1992).
The Selected Letters of Bertrand Russell: vol. II The Public Years 1914–1970, ed. by Nicholas Griffin (Boston: Routledge, 2001).
"Truth-Functions and Meaning-Functions" (1923) in *Collected Papers*, vol. 9, pp. 156–159.
(B) *What I believe* (New York: E. P. Dutton & Company, 1925).
"What is Meant by 'A believes p'?" (1923) in *Collected Papers*, Vol. 9, p. 159.

BOOKS AND ARTICLES

Abscombe, G. E. M. *An Introduction to Wittgenstein's Tractatus*, second edition (New York: Harper and Row, 1959).

Anellis, Irving. "The Genesis of the Truth-Table Device," *Russell* vol. 24 (no. 1), (2004), pp. 55–70.

Ayer, A. J. "Bertrand Russell as a Philosopher," in *The Meaning of Life* (New York: Macmillan, 1990).

Bostock, David. *Logic and Arithmetic: Natural Numbers* (London: Oxford University Press, 1974).

Black, Max. "The Identity of Indiscernibles," *Mind* vol. 6 (no. 1), (1952), pp. 153–164.

Blackwell, Kenneth. "The Early Wittgenstein and the Middle Russell," in Irving Block, ed., *Perspectives on the Philosophy of Wittgenstein* (Cambridge, MA: MIT Press, 1981).

——— *The Spinozistic Ethics of Bertrand Russell* (London: Allen and Unwin, 1985).

Brown, George Spencer. *Laws of Form* (New York: The Julian Press, 1967).

Bibliography

Burke, Tom. *Dewey's New Logic: A Reply to Russell* (Chicago: University of Chicago Press, 1994).

Burtt, E. A. *The Metaphysical Foundations of Modern Science* (Atlantic Highlands, NJ: Humanitites Press, 1952).

Carnap, Rudolf. *Philosophy and Logical Syntax* (London: Kegan Paul, 1935).

—— *Meaning and Necessity*, second edition (Chicago: University of Chicago Press, 1947, 1956).

—— "The Elimination of Metaphysics through Logical Analysis of Language," in Alfred Ayer, ed., *Logical Positivism* (Glencoe, IL: Macmillan, 1959), pp. 60–81.

Church, Alonzo. "A Note on the *Entscheidungsproblem*," *Journal of Symbolic Logic* vol. 1 (no. 1), (1936), pp. 40–41.

Clark, Ronald. *The Life of Bertrand Russell* (New York: Knopf, 1976).

Cocchiarella, Nino. "On the Primary and Secondary Semantics of Logical Necessity," *Journal of Philosophical Logic* vol. 4 (no. 1), (1975), pp. 13–27.

—— "Philosophical Perspectives on Quantification in Tense and Modal Logic," in D. Gabbay and F. Guenthner, eds., *Handbook of Philosophical Logic*, vol. 2., (Dordrecht: D. Reidel, 1983), pp. 309–353.

—— "The Development of the Theory of Logical Types and the Notion of a Logical Subject in Russell's Early Philosophy," *Synthese* vol. 45 (1980), pp. 71–115. Reprinted in *Logical Studies in Early Analytic Philosophy* (Columbus: Ohio State University Press, 1987), pp. 19–63.

—— "Logical Atomism and Modal Logic," in *Logical Studies in Early Analytic Philosophy* (Columbus: Ohio State University Press, 1987), pp. 222–243.

—— "Logical Atomism, Nominalism and Modal Logic," *Philosophia, Philosophical Quarterly of Israel* vol. 4 (no. 1), (1974), pp. 41–44. Reprinted in *Logical Studies in Early Analytic Philosophy* (Columbus, OH: Ohio State University Press, 1987), pp. 244–284.

—— *Logical Studies in Early Analytic Philosophy* (Columbus, OH: Ohio State University Press, 1987).

—— "Russell's Theory of Logical Types and the Atomistic Hierarchy of Sentences," in C. Wade Savage and C. A. Anderson, eds., *Rereading Russell* (Minneapolis: University of Minnesota Press, 1989), pp. 41–62. Reprinted in Nino Cocchiarella, *Logical Studies in Early Analytic Philosophy* (Columbus: Ohio State University Press), pp. 193–221.

—— "Logical Necessity Based on Carnap's Criterion of Adequacy," *Korean Journal of Logic* vol. 5 no. 2 (2002) pp. 1–21

—— *Formal Ontology and Conceptual Realism* (Dordrecht: Springer, 2007).

Coffa, Alberto. *The Semantic Tradition from Kant to Carnap: To the Vienna Station* (Cambridge: Cambridge University Press, 1991).

Bibliography

Copi, Irving. *The Theory of Logical Types* (London: Routledge and Kegan Paul, 1971).

Demopoulos, William and Friedman, Michael. "The Concept of Structure in the Analysis of Matter," in C. Wade Savage and C. Anthony Anderson, eds., *Rereading Russell* (Minneapolis: Minnesota Studies in the Philosophy of Science, 1989), pp. 183–199.

Dolcini, Nevia. "Indexicals and Perception," *Rivista de Filosofia del Linguaggio* 2 (2010), pp. 19–41.

—— *Le parole e i sensi: Una teoria degli indicali basata sulla percezione* (Macerata: eum, 2009).

Enzensberger, Hans Magnus, *The Number Devil: A Mathematical Adventure* (New York: Metropolitan Books, 1998).

Fogelin, Robert. *Wittgenstein* (London: Routledge and Kegan Paul, 1976).

Frascolla, Pasquale. *Wittgenstein's Philosophy of Mathematics* (London: Routledge, 1994).

—— "The Tractarian System of Arithmetic," *Synthese* vol. 112 (no. 3), (1997), pp. 353–378.

—— "The Early Wittgenstein's Logicism: Rejoinder to M. Wrigley," *Acta Analytica* 21 (1998), pp. 133–137.

—— *The Tractatus Logico-Philosophicus of Wittgenstein* (Rome: Carocci, 2003).

Frege, Gottlob. *Grundgesetze der Arithmetik*, Vol. I (Jena, 1893), vol. II (Jena 1903) (Reprinted by Darmstadt Hildesheim: Georg Olms Verlag, 1962).

—— *The Basic Laws of Arithmetic: Exposition of the System*, translated with an editor's introduction by Montgomery Furth (Berkeley: University of California Press, 1964).

—— "On Concept and Object," in eds., Peter Geach and Max, Black, *Translations from the Philosophical Writings of Gottlob Frege* (Oxford: Basil Blackwell, 1977), pp. 21–41. First published as *Über Begriff und Gegenstand*" in *Vierteljarsschrift fṃr wissenschaftliche Philosophie*, vol. XIV 1892, pp. 192–205.

—— "On Sense and Reference," in eds., Peter Geach and Max, Black, *Translations from the Philosophical Writings of Gottlob Frege* (Oxford: Basil Blackwell, 1977), pp. 56–78. First published as "*Über Sinn und Bedeutung*" in *Zeitschfirt fṃr Philosophie und philosophische Kritik*, 1892, pp. 25–50.

—— *The Foundations of Arithmetic*, translated by J. L. Austin (Evanston, IL: Northwestern University Press, 1980). First published as *Die Grundlagen der Arithmetik: eine Logisch-Mathematische Untersuchung Über den Begriff der Zahl* (Breslau: W. Koebner, 1884).

—— *Philosophical and Mathematical Correspondence*, edited by Gottfried Gabriel, Hans Hermes, Friedrich Kambartel, Christian Thiel, and Albert Verrart and abridged from the German edition by Brian McGuinness and translated by Hans Kaal (Chicago: University Press, 1980).

Götlind, Erik. *Bertrand Russell's Theories of Causation* (Uppsala: Almquist & Wiksells Boktryckeri AB, 1912).
(GG) Grattan-Guinness, Ivor. *Dear Russell-Dear Jourdain* (London: Duckworth, 1977).
―― *In Search for Mathematical Roots 1870–1940: Logic, Set Theories and the Foundations of Mathematics from Cantor Through Russell to Gödel* (Princeton, NJ: Princeton University Press, 2001).
Grayling, A. C. *Wittgenstein: A Very Short Introduction* (Oxford: Oxford University Press, 1988).
Griffin, James. *Wittgenstein's Logical Atomism* (Oxford: Oxford University Press, 1964). (Pagination is to the paperback edition (Seattle: University of Washington Press, 1969).
Griffin, Nicholas. *Russell's Idealist Apprenticeship* (Oxford: Clarendon Press, 1991).
―― ed., *The Cambridge Companion to Bertrand Russell* (Cambridge: Cambridge University Press, 2003).
Hacker, P. M. S. *Wittgenstein's Place in Twentieth-Century Philosophy* (Oxford: Blackwell, 1996).
Hatcher, William. *The Logical Foundations of Mathematics* (Oxford: Pergamon Press, 1982).
Hylton, Peter. *Russell, Idealism and the Emergence of Analytic Philosophy* (Oxford: Oxford University Press, 1990).
Kuhn, Thomas. *The Structure of Scientific Revolutions* (Chicago: University of Chicago Press, 1962).
Landini, Gregory. *Russell's Hidden Substitutional Theory* (Oxford: Oxford University Press, 1998).
―― "Russell's Separation of the Logical and Semantic Paradoxes," in Philippe de Rouilhan, ed., *Russell en héritage* (Revue Internationale Philosophie 3, 2004), pp. 257–294.
―― "Frege's Cardinals as Concept Correlates," *Erkenntnis* 65 (2006), pp. 207–243.
―― *Wittgenstein's Apprenticeship With Russell* (Cambridge: Cambridge University Press, 2007).
―― "The Number of Numbers," *Philosophia Mathematica*, forthcoming.
Laudan, Larry. *Progress and its Problems* (Berkeley: University of California Press, 1977).
Lowe, Victor. *Alfred North Whitehead: The Man and his Work* (Baltimore: The Johns Hopkins Press, 1990).
Marion, Mathieu. *Wittgenstein, Finitism, and the Foundations of Mathematics* (Oxford: Clarendon Press, 1998).
McGuinness, Brian. *Approaches to Wittgenstein: Collected Papers of Brian McGuinness* (London: Routledge, 2002).

––––– *Wittgenstein: A Life* (Berkeley: University of California Press, 1988).
Monk, Ray. *Ludwig Wittgenstein: The Duty of Genius* (New York: Free Press, 1990).
––––– *Bertrand Russell: The Spirit of Solitude 1872–1921* (New York: Routledge, 1999).
––––– *Bertrand Russell: The Ghost of Madness 1921–1970* (New York: The Free Press, 2001).
Muller, Eugen. *Abriss der Algebra der Logik*; Reprinted in E. Schröder, *Algebra der Logik*, vol. III (New York: Chelsea Publishing Co., 1966).
Orilia, Francesco. *Predication, Analysis and Reference* (Bologna: CLUEB, 1999).
––––– *Ulisse, il quadrate rotondo e l'attuale re di Francia* (Pisa: Edizion Ets, 2002).
––––– *Singular Reference: A Descriptivist Perspective* (Dordrecht, Netherlands: Springer, 2010).
Orilia, Francesco and Gozzano, Simone. *Tropes, Universals and the Philosophy of Mind: Essays at the Boundary of Ontology and Philosophical Psychology* (Frankfurt: Ontos Verlag, 2008).
Parsons, Terence. "Essentialism and Quantified Modal Logic," *Philosophical Review* vol. 78 (1969), pp. 35–52.
Pears, David. *The False Prison*, vol. 1 (Oxford: Oxford University Press, 1987).
Pinsent, David. *A Portrait of Wittgenstein as a Young Man*, ed., by G.H von Wright (Oxford: Blackwell, 1990).
Potter, Michael. *Reason's Nearest Kin* (Oxford: Oxford University Press, 2000).
Quine, W. V. O. "Carnap's Views on Ontology," in *The Ways of Paradox and Other Essays by W.V. O. Quine* (Cambridge, MA: Harvard University Press, 1976), pp. 203–211.
––––– *Set Theory and Its Logic* (Cambridge, MA: Harvard University Press, 1980).
Ramsey, Frank. "Review of the Second-Edition of *Principia Mathematica*," *Nature* vol. 116 (no. 2908), (1925): pp. 127–128.
––––– "Mathematical Logic," in ed., R. B. Braithwaite, *The Foundations of Mathematics and Other Essays by Frank Plumpton Ramsey* (London: Harcourt, Brace and Co. 1926), pp. 62–81.
––––– "Facts and Propositions," in ed., R. B. Braithwaite, *The Foundations of Mathematics and Other Essays by F. P. Ramsey* (London: Harcourt Brace & Co., 1931).
––––– "The Foundations of Mathematics," in ed., R. B. Braithwaite, *The Foundations of Mathematics and Other Essays by Frank Plumpton Ramsey* (London: Harcourt, Brace and Co., 1931), pp. 1–61. First published in the *Proceedings of the London Mathematical Society*, 25 (1925), pp. 338–384.
––––– "Philosophy," in ed., R. B. Braithwaite, *The Foundations of Mathematics* (New York: Harcourt, Brace and Co., 1931).
––––– Letter to Moore of 6 February 1924. Reprinted in ed., Josef Rothhaupt, *Farbthemen in Wittgensteins Gesamtnachlass: philologisch-philosophische Untersuchungen im Längsschnitt und Querschnitten*, Monografien Philosophie, 273 (Weinheim: Beltz, 1966).

——— Frank Plumpton Ramsey: *Notes on Philosophy, Probability and Mathematics,* ed., Maria Carla Galavotti (Naploi: Bibliopolis, 1991).

Rouilhan, Philippe de (1996). *Russell et le cercle des paradoxes* (Paris: Presses Universitaries de France), p. 275.

Ryan, Allan. *Bertrand Russell: A Political Life* (New York: Hill and Wang, 1988).

Sackur, Jerome, *Formes et faits* (Paris: Librairie Philosohique J. Vrin, 2005).

Salmon, Wesley C. *Zeno's Paradoxes* (New York: Bobbs-Merrill Co., 1977).

Savage, C. Wade and Anderson, C. A. *Rereading Russell* (Minneapolis: University of Minnesota Press, 1989).

Schilpp, Paul A. *The Philosophy of Bertrand Russell,* vol. 1 (Evanston, IL: Harper Torchbooks, 1963).

Schmid, Anne-Françoise. ed., with commentary, *Bertrand Russell: Correspondence sur la Philosophie, la Logique et la Politique avec Louis Couturat 1897–1913* (Paris: édition Kimé, volume I, II, 2001).

Schröder, Ernst. *Algebra der Logik,* vol. III (New York: Chelsea Publishing Co., 1966).

Shosky, John. "Russell's Use of Truth-Tables," *Russell* vol. 17 (no. 1), (1997), pp. 11–26.

Van Heijenoort, Jean. "Logic as Calculus and Logic as Language," *Synthese* vol. 17 (no. 1), (1967), pp. 324–330.

Von Wright, G. E. *Wittgenstein* (Oxford: Blackwell, 1982).

Wahl, Russell. "Impossible Propositions and the Forms of Objects in Wittgenstein's *Tractatus,*" *The Philosophical Quarterly* vol. 44 (1995), pp. 190–198.

Westfall, Richard. *The Construction of Modern Science* (Cambridge: Cambridge University Press, 1977).

Whitehead, A. N. *An Introduction to Mathematics* (London: Williams and Norgate, 1911).

——— "Indication, Classes, Number, Validation," *Mind* vol. 43 (no. 171), (1934), pp. 281–297. Reprinted in *Essays in Science and Philosophy by Alfred North Whitehead* (New York: Philosophical Library, 1948), pp. 227–240.

Wittgenstetin, Ludwig. *Notebooks 1914–1916,* ed., G. H. von Wright and G. E. M. Anscombe, translated by G. E. M. Anscombe (Oxford: Blackwell, 1961).

——— "Notes Dictated to G. E. Moore in Norway," in Appendix II of *Notebooks.*

——— "Notes On Logic," *Journal of Philosophy* (1957); reprinted as Appendix I of *Notebooks.*

——— (TLP) *Tractatus Logico-Philosophicus,* German text with English translation translated by D. F. Pears and B. McGuinness (London: Routledge, 1961) First published in *Annnalen der Naturphilosophie,* 1921. German text English translation by C. K. Ogden (London, 1922).

Wolfe, Mays. "Recollections of Wittgenstein," in K. T. Fann, ed., *Ludwig Wittgentein: The Man and His Philosophy* (Ewing, NJ: University of California Press, 1967).

Index

a posteriori truths 213, 374, 417
a priori truths 223, 225–6, 405, 417
ABC of Atoms, The 23
ABC of Relativity, The 23, 177, 290–1
abstract general facts 265–8
abstraction 4–5
accuracy 319–20
'Achilles and the Tortoise' paradox 172–5
acquaintance 229–30, 240, 242, 268; and logic 273–9
addition 43–4, 52–3, 62, 103; infinite cardinals 70; motion modeled as consecutive addition 172–5; of ratios 59–60; real numbers 63–4; repeated and multiplication 53–4
alephs 77; aleph naught 70, 93
albebraic approach to logic 80–4, 85–6
algebraic law of cancellation 169
Amberly, Viscount 1
American Civil Liberties Union 30
analogy, postulate of 389
Analysis of Matter, The 24, 178, 334
Analysis of Mind, The 22, 282–3, 294–5, 314–16, 319–21, 325–6
analytic geometry 100–3
analytic truths 222–5, 417
analyticity 371–2
anamnesis 225–6, 229, 426

anomalies 404–5
Anselm, St 200, 202–4, 421
anti-conscription campaign 21
appropriateness 319–20
Aristotelian essentialism 214
Aristotelian logic 79–80
Aristotelian science 79, 284, 286–7
Aristotelian Venn diagrams 81–2
Aristotle 79
arithmetic, status of 222–5, 226–7
assent 326–7
associations of ideas 222–3
Atlantic Peace Foundation 40
atomism 163, 165–6; Logical *see* Logical Atomism
attributes (propositional functions) 120–1, 124, 125–6, 364–5; levels of 86–9; numbers as 94–5; paradox of 9, 124–5, 136–61
Authority and the Individual 35
Ayer, A.J. 28, 116

Banach, S. 72
Barnes, A.C. 30–1
Barnes Foundation 30
barometric pressure 287
Barry, G. 26
Bayes's theorem 377–8
BBC 35, 38

Index

Beacon Hill school 23
behaviorism 275, 283, 287–8, 293, 305–6, 335, 417; and visual imagery 315–16
belief 343, 360; neutral monism and truth 325–30; belief-complexes 256–64; belief paradox 208–11
Beltrami, E. 228
Bentham, J. 418
Berkeley, G. 236, 237–8, 337–9
Berlin Airlift 36
Bertrand Russell Peace Foundation 40
biblical commandments 398–9, 399–401, 406
Black, Dora (later Russell) 20–1, 22, 23, 25–6
bloodletting 413
Bloomsbury Group 20
Bolshevism 22
Bolyai, J. 227
Boole, G. 79, 83
Boolean algebra 80–2
Boolean Venn diagrams 80–1
Boolos, G. 97, 98
Bradley, F.H. 3, 254
brain 302–6
Brentano, F. 205, 317
British Government 35
Broad's probability postulates 375–6, 378–80
Brown, G.S. 354
Bukken Bruse seaplane accident 36

Cantor, G. 4, 6–7, 46, 67, 69, 106, 152, 346; continuity 175–6; power-class theorem 145–6, 152
cardinal numbers 5, 46–55, 56, 91–2, 167; infinite 70–2
Carnap, R. 336–7, 350, 371–2

Cartesianism 284–6, 288–9, 417–18
Castro, F. 39–40
categorical forms 79–83, 223–4
cause 393–7; mnemic causation 294–5
China 22–3
choice, axiom of 71–2
chrono-geography 298, 299
Church, A. 108, 112–15, 134, 160, 355
circles 100–1
City College of New York 29–30
classes 418; paradox of 6–9, 93–5, 136–61; *see also* no-classes theory
Clifford, W.K. 401
Cocchiarella, N.B. 217
coherence 242–3, 423
coin-tossing 384–5
communication 180–1; use of indexicals 310–11; using proper names 191–4
compatibilism 397
complex numbers 66–7
complex questions 186
comprehension axioms: for attributes 86, 87–8, 359, 418; for classes 118–19, 134–5, 418
conditional probability 377, 379
conditioning 288
connectionist models of memory 327
Conquest of Happiness, The 25
consciousness 282, 292–3, 309, 406
consequentialism 398, 407, 412–16, 418
constructions, substitution for inferences 166–7, 177–8
continuity 175–6
continuum hypothesis 77
contraposition 80–1
Copernican revolution 214, 284

Copernicus, N. 79, 289, 324, 404
copies, images as 316
Copleston, F. 35, 199–200
correlation 90–3; axiom of 276–7
correspondence theory of truth and falsehood 129–34, 155, 251–72, 325–30, 365, 423
counting 46–8, 52
Couturat, L. 15, 153
credibility, degrees of 375, 388
Cuban Missile Crisis 39–40, 398

dagger notation 344–5, 354–5
decalogue 398–407
decidability of logic 350–6
Dedekind, J.W.R. 4, 55–6, 72, 175, 346; Dedekind cuts 63; Dedekind gap 56
deduction 85, 343
deductive arguments 386–7, 419
definability, paradox of 136, 155–6, 363
definite descriptions, theory of 9, 130, 141–3, 145, 257–8, 328–9; Logical Atomism 184–206; logical mirage 206–17; no-classes theory 116–24
Dennett, D. 297–8
denoting concepts 142–5
denseness of rational numbers 62, 67, 172
derivative knowledge 240–1
Descartes, R. 233–4, 289, 305, 311–12, 417–18; introspection 301–2; methodological doubt 219, 239–40; ontological argument 200–2; substance dualism 284–6
description, knowledge by 241
determinism 419
'Determinism and Physics' 26

Dewey, J. 28–9, 30, 323–4, 325, 374
dice-throwing 384
dismissal, philosophy by 34
divine command theory 399–401, 405; new form of 406
division by zero, paradox of 169–70
dogmatism 13–15, 401
doubt, methodological 219, 239–40
dream argument 240
dreams 313–14
Dretske, F. 320
Duhem, P. 337
Dulles, J.F. 39

Eddington, A. 283, 289, 291, 334
egocentric particulars 309–10
Ehrenfels, C. von 205
Einstein, A. 17, 30, 31, 39, 289; theory of relativity 283–4, 290, 395
Einstein-Russell manifesto 39
Eisenhower, D.D. 39
ellipses 100–1
emergence 298–302
emotions 312–13
empiricism 289–91, 369, 419; probability and induction 389–93; and rationalism 222–43
empty class 80, 82, 90
epistemology 218–79; acquaintance and logic 273–9; Our Knowledge of the External World 244–51; Problems of Philosophy 221–43; Theory of Knowledge 251–72
equilibrium 29, 323–4, 374
Essay on the Foundations of Geometry 3
'Essence of Religion, The' 20, 407–10
essentialism, Aristotelian 214

ethics 232, 398–416; Russell's ten commandments 398–407; science of 411–16; Spinozism 20, 398, 407–10, 411
Euclidean geometry 99–102, 226
Everett case 21, 411
evolution 323–5
exclusive quantifiers 357–8
existence 185–6, 198–200, 311–12; of God 200–4, 338–9
expectation-belief 326–7
extensional contexts 135, 343, 360, 419; no-classes theory as a recovery of 115–24
extensionality principles 89

facts 254–7; abstract general 265–8; negative 267, 329–30
falsehood, recursive definition of truth and 129–34, 155, 251–72, 325–30, 365, 423
feelings 326–7
Finch, Edith (later Russell) 37, 38
finite cardinals 55
finite ordinals 74–5
First World War 13, 21, 345, 398, 411–12, 415
formal concepts 346–8
four-dimensionalism 220, 248–9, 280, 282, 291–2, 304
Franklin, C.L. 32, 390
Free Thought and Official Propaganda 24
free will 396–7
Freedom and Organization 26
Frege, G. 5, 7–8, 71–2, 124–5, 198, 276–7; belief paradox 208–9; logic 79, 84–7; numbers as objects 90–3; numeric quantification 48, 49, 51, 54–5

frequency theory of probability 384–5, 387–8
fundamental indexical 308–10

Galileo 67, 183, 394
Galton, F. 315–16
general facts, abstract 265–8
general propositions 139; *see also* no-general propositions theory
general relativity 19, 283–4
generalized tautologies 85, 110–11, 134–5, 359
geometry 2, 3, 99–103; hyperbolic 227–9; status of arithmetic and 222–5, 226–7
George VI, King 36
German Social Democracy 3
Gettier, E. 251
God: commandments from 398–9, 399–401, 406; existence of 200–4, 338–9
Gödel, K. 31, 362
Goodman's new riddle of induction 386
gravitation, law of 286, 394, 396, 404
'Gray's Elegy' argument 143–5

hallucinations 313–14
happiness 24–5
Hardy, G.H. 358
Harvey, W. 285–6
hatred of evil 414–15
heart 285–6
Hegel, G.W.F. 2–3, 100, 188–9
heliocentric theory 79, 183, 324
heterological paradox of being 431–2
hierarchy of levels of attributes 86–9
History of Western Philosophy, A 29, 31, 176, 201

Home University Library 221
Human Knowledge: Its Scope and Limits 31–2, 231, 369–97; logic is not part of philosophy 370–5; on the notion of cause 393–7; probability and induction 375–93
Hume, D. 5, 222, 313, 316, 385, 386–7, 393
hyperbolic geometry 227–9

Icarus 24, 398, 411–12, 415
identity 355–8, 366–7; elimination of 356–8, 366, 368; of ratios 58–9, 61; universal law of 206–17
If-thenism 97–8, 420
ignorance 413
image-propositions 327–8
images 294–5, 312–17
immaterialism 336–9
implication 138
impredicative characterization 105–6, 152–3, 156
'In Praise of Idleness' 26
indexicals, problem of 306–12
indifference, principle of 380–3
individual variables 107, 109, 112, 126–7, 136, 161, 272
induction 230–1, 375–93
inductive arguments 385–7, 419
inference 80–1, 109–10, 374; postulates of scientific inference 369–70, 388–9, 392; substitution of construction for 166–7, 177–8
infinite cardinals 70–2
infinite ordinals 75–7
infinity 67–77; of natural numbers 95–103, 357–8; paradoxes and 172–6; probability 380–4
infinity axiom 96–7

innate ideas, doctrine of 225–6
Inquiry into Meaning and Truth, An 28, 29, 309–10, 360
instantaneous velocity 249–50
intensional context 120, 419–20
intentionality 317; directedness of 204–6
international atomic development agency 36
International War Crimes Tribunal 40
Introduction to Mathematical Philosophy 21, 125–6
introspection 299–306
intuitionism 405
intuitive knowledge 241
irrational numbers 55–6, 62–3, 66–7, 167; irrational real numbers 65
isomorphism 72–3; partial 259

Jackson, F. 299
James, W. 282, 323, 401, 404, 421
James-Lange theory 312–13
Johnson, S. 339
Jourdain, P. 106
justification 251–2

Kant, I. 6, 78, 97, 218, 223, 396; space and time 226–7, 228–9
Kennedy, J.F. 40, 426
Kepler, J. 79
Kerry, B. 125
Keynes, J.M. 20, 231, 375, 388
Khrushchev, N. 39, 40
kindliness 415
Klein model 228
knowledge 41, 242–3; definition 251–2; epistemology *see* epistemology; *Human Knowledge* *see* *Human Knowledge: Its Scope and Limits*;

representation and 319–21; scientific ethics and 413, 415; sources 240–1
knowledge argument 299–302, 306
Kripke, S. 191, 213

language: linguistic nature of logic 371–3; ordinary and technical 180–3
laws of nature 395–6
League of Nations 412
learning 322
Leibniz, G.W. 3, 200–2
Leopardi, G. 20, 27, 221, 409–10
levels of attributes 86–9
Lewis, C.I. 336
Liar paradoxes 139–40, 154, 155
liberal decalogue 398–407
light 281
limit, Weierstrass's notion of 249–50
lines 101–2; paradox of dividing a line in half 170–1
Linsky, B. 120
Lobachevsky, N. 227
Locke, J. 236–7
logic: acquaintance and 273–9; not part of philosophy 370–5; Wittgenstein and decidability of 350–6
logic of relations 4–5, 44, 78, 83–90
Logical Atomism 24, 162–217, 218, 273, 275–6, 346, 348, 374, 393, 409; definite descriptions 184–206; logical mirage 206–17; paradoxes 168–84
logical constants 347–8, 372
logical forms 196–9; of complexes 261–3; ontological nature of 264–8
logical mirage 206–17

logical necessity 5–6, 99–103, 162, 184, 214–17, 348, 393
logical paradoxes 136–61, 277–9, 363, 365
logicism 78–90, 97–8, 224, 420
love 41, 415

MacColl, H. 82
Mach, E. 289–90, 291, 293
marriage 25, 413–14
materialism 283
'Mathematical Logic as Based on the Theory of Types' 15, 16, 158–60
mathematical theory of probability 375–80, 384–5
'Mathematician's Nightmare, The' 44–5
matter 178–9, 232–4, 237–8, 244–51, 420; mind and 280–340
McTaggart, J.M.E. 3, 4, 179
mechanical atomism 289
median 381–3, 444
medicine 402
Meinong, A. 204–5
memory 241, 316–17, 327; memory-belief 326–8
methodological doubt 219, 239–40
methodological solipsism 219–20, 239–40, 420; and induction 389–92
Mill, J.S. 1, 418
mind 233–4, 237–8; constituted by images and sensations 312–17; and matter 280–340
mirage, logical 206–17
mitigating axioms 15–16, 155, 158
mnemic causation 294–5
monism 99, 407; neutral see neutral monism

Moore, G.E. 3, 405
Morrell, O. 19–20, 31, 221, 253, 409, 410
Morrell, P. 19
Moses's commandments 398–9, 399–401, 406
motion 173–4, 289–91
multiple-relation theory 129–34, 253–72, 328–9, 349
multiplication 53–4; infinite cardinals 70–2; of ratios 59–60; real numbers 63–4
multiplicative axiom (axiom of choice) 71–2
Murray, G. 221
My Philosophical Development 39, 125, 218, 219–20, 269, 273–4, 360, 370–1, 373
Myhill, J. 361
mysticism 408, 409

N-operator notation 354–5
Nagel, E. 302, 304
Nagel, T. 281
naïve principle 206
naïve realism 32, 391–2, 421
nameability, paradox of 136, 154, 155–6, 363
narrow direction problem 258–60, 263–4
natural numbers 54–5, 65, 66–7, 73; equations without solutions 56–7, 60; infinity of 95–103, 357–8; natural real numbers 65; number of 95–103; as objects 90–5; one-to-one correspondence with rationals 67–8; probability, infinity and 380–1
naturalism 322–3, 370, 390

naturalized epistemology 24, 221, 369, 373–5, 421
nature: laws of 395–6; uniformity postulate 387, 389, 395–7
necessity 162, 211–17; geometric 99–103; logical 5–6, 99–103, 162, 184, 214–17, 348, 393
negative facts 267, 329–30
neutral monism 22, 24, 164–5, 275–6, 280–340; abandonment of multiple-relation theory 269–72; and truth 317–30
New York City College 29–30
Newman, M.H.A. 331–2
Newton, I. 289, 290, 394–5
Newtonian science 214, 229, 286–7
Nicod, J. 344–5, 441–2
Nightmares of Eminent Persons 37
no-attributes of attributes theory 146
no-classes theory 9–11, 16–17, 18–19, 94–5, 115–24, 146–7, 150–1, 155
No-Conscription Fellowship (NCF) 21
no-general propositions theory 15, 155, 156–8
no-relations in extension theory 123–4
nominalistic semantics 124–35, 355–6, 363–8
non-Euclidean geometries 227–9
non-permutative complexes 260, 262–3
non-predicative variables 108, 112, 113–15
Notes on Logic 344
nuclear proliferation 36–7, 37–9
nuclear testing 39
Number Devil, The 43–4, 105
numbers 43–77; cardinal 5, 46–55, 70–2, 91, 167; irrational 55–6, 62–3, 65, 66–7, 167; natural

see natural numbers; number of 95–103; ordinal 72–3, 74–7; rational *see* rational numbers; real 63–7, 73, 152–3; and truth conditions 197–9

objectivism 398, 405–7
objects: natural numbers as 90–5; of thought 185–6, 195
obligation 406
Occam's razor 421
omega 75
'On Denoting' 9, 168, 186, 200, 205, 210, 274
On Education 24
'On the Existential Import of Propositions' 201
'On 'Insolubilia' and Their Solution by Symbolic Logic' 153–4, 156–8
'On the Logic of Relations' 4
On Marriage and Morals 25
'On Matter' 344
'On the Nature of Acquaintance' 282, 306–8
'On the Nature of Truth and Falsehood' 258
'On the Notion of Cause' 126, 393
'On Order in Time' 26, 250
'On Propositions' 329
'On Scientific Method in Philosophy' 408
'On the Substitutional Theory of Classes and Relations' 150–1
'On the theory of Transfinite Numbers and Order Types' 146–7
one-to-one correspondence 46–50, 67–9, 91, 93, 96, 103, 421
ontological argument 2, 200–4, 421
ontological self-reference 139–40

ontology 164, 180–1, 183–5; of logic 162–3, 184
operant conditioning 288
order component of the order/type indices 108, 129–34
order/type indices 107, 108, 128–34
orders of propositions 16, 158–60
ordinal numbers 72–7
ordinary language 180–1, 182
Oswald, L.H. 426
other minds 247–8
Our Knowledge of the External World 19, 218–19, 220, 244–51, 253, 296, 370
Outline of Intellectual Rubbish, An 401
Outline of Philosophy 24, 178, 280, 298

p0/a0 paradox of propositions 15–16, 147–52, 155, 156–7
paradoxes 6–9, 277–8; logical 135–61, 277–9, 363, 365; Logical Atomism 168–84; mathematics of the infinite 381–4; of propositions 145–6, 147–52, 155; semantic 136, 363, 365; *see also under individual paradoxes*
partial isomorphism 259
particulars 240, 260
Pascal, B. 33, 287
Pauli, W. 31
Pavlov, I. 288
Peano, G. 4, 85
Pears, D. 163–4
Peirce, C.S. 83–4, 324, 421
permutative complexes 260, 262–3
pestilence 413
phenomenal states 291–2, 293–4
phenomenalism 219, 237, 289–92
Philosophy of Leibniz, The 3

'Philosophy of Logical Atomism, The' 24
physical continuants 232–4, 238; *see also* matter
physical correlations 171–2
physical length 176–7
Piaget, J. 52
Pinsent, D. 344
pity 41
place value 49
Plato 45, 185–6, 225, 251, 426
Poincaré, H. 15, 106, 127, 152, 153, 154, 156; disk model 228; half-plane model 228
points 170–1, 244
Portraits from Memory 38
position relations 259–63, 264
Power: A New Social Analysis 27–8
power-class theorem 145–6, 152
Practice and Theory of Bolshevism, The 22
pragmatism 28–9, 323–4, 421
Prantl, C. 78–9
predicate category 79–82
predicate variables 84, 107, 109, 112, 161, 272; nominalistic semantics 124, 126–35
predicative comprehension principle 135
predicative variables 108, 114
presence 307–8
primary scope 189–90
Principia Mathematica 12–13, 15, 16–17, 19, 34, 44, 105–61, 253, 278, 279, 373; Church's interpretation 112–15; evolution from *Principles of Mathematics* 135–61; interpretation faithful to authors' intent 107–12; no-classes theory 115–24; nominalistic semantics 124–35;

number of numbers 97–9; quantification theory 85, 109–11, 134–5, 155, 157; Second Edition 341–68
Principles of Mathematics, The 5–6, 9–10, 43
probability 230–1, 375–93
probable opinion 242–3
Problem of China, The 22
Problems of Philosophy, The 20, 219, 221–43, 251, 252
proper names 191–4, 199
properties, paradox of 9
propositional calculus 350–6
propositional functions *see* attributes
propositional liar 157
propositions 274; paradoxes of 15–16, 139–40, 145–6, 147–52, 155, 156–7; Russell's concept 137–9, 253–5; substitutional theory of propositional structure 9–11, 15–16, 120, 137–61, 363, 365
Prospects of Industrial Civilization, The 40
pseudo-concepts 271–2, 349
pseudo-paradoxes 73
pseudosphere 228
psychology 287–8, 299; behaviorism *see* behaviorism
Ptolemaic system 79, 324
Ptolemy 289
purpose 321–2
Putnam, H. 317–18
Pythagoras 370

qualia 292, 297–302, 305
quantification: analysis of the variables of 136–43; and number 49–52; ontology and 185
quantification theory 84–6, 276; logic that transcends 86–90; *Principia*

Mathematica 85, 109–11, 134–5, 155, 157; Wittgenstein 351–4
quantum theory 177, 334–5
quasi-permance, postulate of 389
Quine, W.V.O. 24, 119, 164, 184, 185, 211–12

radical empiricism 337
ramification 16, 158–60, 365; ramified theory of types 111–12
ramified type symbols (r-type symbols) 112–15
Ramsey, F.P. 134–5, 272, 360, 361, 362–8
rape 414
rational numbers 56–62, 66–7, 73; arithmetic sum of a series 173–5; denseness of 62, 67, 172; one-to-one correlation with natural numbers 67–8; rational real numbers 65
rationalism 421; and empiricism 222–43
ratios 169–70; construction of rationals as 56–62; identity of 58–9, 61; lack of one-to-one correspondence with natural numbers 69
real numbers 63–7, 73; well-ordering of 152–3
reason, and ethics 401
recursive models of memory 327
recursive theory of truth and falsehood 129–34, 155, 251–72, 325–30, 365, 423
reducibility, axiom of 16, 159–60, 278, 359, 362–3, 364–5
reductive elimination theory 177–9, 331, 422

reductive identity theory 116, 178–9, 422
reflexive conditioning 288
regularity theory of causation 393–4
Reichenbach, H. 310, 384–5, 387–8
relations of ideas 222–3
relativity 176–7, 180, 289–91, 334–5; general 19, 283–4; special 19, 229
religion: and ethics 398–404, 407–10, 413–15; *see also* God
Religion and Science 26, 401–3
representation 317–21
representative realism 234–7, 421–2
revolutions 416
Riemann, B. 227–8
Roman numerals 49
Russell, Alys Pearsall (née Smith) 3, 11–12
Russell, Bertrand 1–42; anti-conscription campaign 21; appeal for nuclear test ban 39; Barnes and his Foundation 30–1; BBC 35, 38; birth 1; Brixton prison 21, 411; Bryn Mawr college 31; Chicago University 28; children 20, 23, 26, 29, 37; City College of New York 29–30; collaboration with Alfred Whitehead 4, 12–13, 244, 343; Cuban Missile Crisis 39–40; death 41; debate with Dewey 28–9, 325; debt problems 26; despair at trends in philosophy 32–3; discovery of a new paradox 6–9; dismissal from Trinity College, Cambridge 21, 411; early life 1–2; Einstein-Russell manifesto 39; elected to the Royal Society 5; and Evelyn Whitehead 13; Everett affair 21, 411; First World War 21, 411; Harvard University 30;

Honorary Fellowship of the British Academy 35; importance of Russell's contribution to philosophy 34–5; inheritance of earldom 26; International War Crimes Tribunal 40; logic of relations 4–5; Logical Atomism 24; marriage to Alys 3, 11–12; marriage to Dora 20–1, 22, 23, 25–6; marriage to Edith 37, 38; marriage to Patricia 26, 28, 31, 37; mistrust of American power 37; no-classes theory 16–17, 18; Nobel Prize for Literature 36; nuclear proliferation 36–7, 37–9; Order of Merit 36; and Ottoline Morrell 19–20, 31, 221, 253, 409, 410; Oxford University 28; parliamentary candidate 13–14; passions governing 40–1; Peace Foundations 40; physics 23; popular essays and books 26–8; premature reports of his death 22–3; Princeton University 31; propositional structure 15–16; relationship with Wittgenstein 33–4, 341–3; Research Fellow at Cambridge University 3; return to Trinity College, Cambridge 31; seaplane accident 35–6; student at Cambridge University 2–3; theory of definite descriptions 9–11; Trinity College, Cambridge and the fellowship for life 35; University of California, Los Angeles (UCLA) 28, 29, 30; Vietnam War 40; views on marriage 25, 413–14; visit to China 22–3; visit to Russia 22; work for the British Government 35–6; *see also under names of publications*
Russell, Conrad 26, 37

Russell, Dora (née Black) 20–1, 22, 23, 25–6
Russell, Edith (née Finch) 37, 38
Russell, Frank 1, 2, 26
Russell, John (grandfather) 1
Russell, John (son) 23, 29
Russell, Kate 23, 29
Russell, Patricia (née Spence) 26, 28, 31, 37
Russia *see* Soviet Union

Salmon, W.C. 381–3
sameness of structure 72–3
Santayana, G. 405
Sartre, J.-P. 40
Satan in the Suburbs 37
Schröder, E. 82, 83–4
scientific epistemology *see* epistemology
scientific ethics 411–16
scientific induction 387–8
scientific world view 403–7
scope 118, 188–93, 202, 203–4, 216; markers 117–18, 122
Searle, J. 292–3
Second World War 36, 398
secondary scope 190, 192
seeing 304–5
self-consciousness 307
self-evidence 241–2, 243, 278
self-interest 221–2, 407–9
self-reference, ontological 139–40
self-reflective awareness 311–12
semantic paradoxes 136, 363, 365
sensations 293–7; minds constituted by images and 312–17
sense-data 164, 220–1, 232–9, 234, 241, 244–7, 275, 295–7

sensibilia (unperceived sense data) 245–7
sensitiveness 320–1
separable causal lines, postulate of 389
separation, axiom of 18
series of ratios 68–9
set theory 17–19, 422
sets *see* classes
sexual relationships 414
Sheffer, I.M. 344–5
showing, doctrine of 348, 350
signed (positive and negative) numbers 62, 66
simple type theory 88–9, 107–8, 135–6, 140–2, 365
Skinner, B.F. 288
slavery 414
slingshot 207–8
Smith, Alys Pearsall (later Russell) 3, 11–12
social reformation, campaign for 413–15
Socratic method 225
solipsism 31, 219, 233, 389–90, 422; methodological *see* methodological solipsism
Soviet Union 35, 36–7, 39–40
space 176–7, 226–9, 246
Spalding, D.A. 1
spatio-temporal continuity, postulate of 389
special relativity 19, 229
Spence, Patricia (later Russell) 26
Spinoza, B. 20, 221, 280–1
Spinozism 20, 398, 407–10, 411
spirituality, scientific 20
Spivak, L. 34–5
square root of 2 56, 65–6

stages 293–4; brain stages 303–6; self a series of 307; transient particulars 296–7, 299, 330
Stevenson, A. 37
stipulative definition 422–3
Stout, G.F. 258
Strachey, L. 20, 154
structural realism 24, 330–9
structure 78, 95; building structure into variables 346–7; postulate of scientific inference 389; substitutional theory of propositional structure 9–11, 15–16, 120, 137–61, 363, 365; theory of order-types of 332–3
subject category 79–82
subjectivity 294–5
substance dualism 284–6
substance monism 280–1
substitutional theory of propositional structure 9–11, 15–16, 120, 137–61, 363, 365
symmetrical complexes 260
synthetic truths 224, 225, 422

Tarski, A. 72, 126, 155
tautologies 82–3, 354–6, 358, 371–2; generalized 85, 110–11, 134–5, 359
teapot analogy 403–4
technical language 180–3
teleological explanation 320–2, 423
temperature 181–2
ten commandments: biblical 398–9, 399–401, 406; Russell's 398–407
tender mindedness 401, 404
Theory of Knowledge 251–72
this (fundamental indexical) 308–10
time 176–7, 226–9, 248–51

token-reflexive theory of indexicals 310–11
Tolstoy, L. 33
transcendental aesthetic 226–7, 423
transient particulars 296–7, 299, 330
triangles 99–100, 101–2; meeting of perpendicular lines from sides 231–2
Trinity College, Cambridge University: dismissal of Russell 21, 411; Russell declines to be reinstated 22; Russell as Research Fellow 3; Russell returns to 31; Russell as student 2–3; Russell's fellowship for life 35
truth 423; neutral monism and 317–30; recursive theory of truth and falsehood 129–34, 155, 251–72, 325–30, 365, 423
truth-conditions 352–4; finding 186–90; structural representation 195–9, 215–16
truth-tables 83, 352
Tully, R. 276
type component of the order/type indices 107, 128–9
type theory 10–11, 16–17, 18–19, 121–4; of 1906 150–1; simple type theory 88–9, 107–8, 135–6, 140–2, 365
types* distinctions 260–3

uniformity of nature postulate 387, 389, 395–7
United Nations 36
United States of America (USA) 37, 39–40, 411–12
universal class/set 7, 18, 426
universal law of identity 206–17

universals 240, 254, 260–1, 271–2; theory of acquaintance with 229–30
University of California, Los Angeles (UCLA) 28, 29, 30
unperceived sense-data 245–7
unrestricted variable, doctrine of the 136
unsymmetrical complexes 260
Urban VIII, Pope 183

valence 422
Van Heijenoort, J. 85, 86
velocity, instantaneous 249–50
Venn diagrams 80–2, 351–3, 378–80
verificationism 290–1, 423–4; verificationist theory of empirical meaning 236–7, 336–7
Vesuvius, Mount 27
vicious circle principle (VPC) 106, 127, 153, 155
Vietnam War 40
Voltaire 401–2
voluntary movements 325–6

warranted assertibility (workability) 28–9, 323–5
Watson, J.B. 287, 301, 315–16
wave theories 331
Webb, B. 31, 98
Weierstrass, K. 4, 174–5, 179, 249–50, 346
Weiss, P. 31
well-ordering relations 73, 75–7, 332–3
What I Believe 24, 411, 412–16
Which Way to Peace? 26
Whitehead, A.N. 2, 4, 8, 12–13, 30, 244, 343, 350–1, 411
Whitehead, Eric 13, 411

Whitehead, Evelyn 13, 411
Wilson, W. 412
Wimbledon byelection of 1907 13–14
witches, torture and murder of 402
Wittgenstein, L. 32–4, 134–5, 341–68, 371, 411; development of Russell's influence on 344–59; relationship with Russell 33–4, 341–3; and Russell's abandonment of multiple-relation theory 269–72; and Russell's views on ethics 409–10; *Tractatus Logico-Philosophicus* 33, 342, 345, 346–50, 356, 360, 362, 366, 368; viability of Wittgenstein's ideas for rectifying *Principia Mathematica* 360–8
women's suffrage 13–14
word propositions 328
Words and Facts 28
workability (warranted assertibility) 28–9, 323–5
world government 412

Zeno of Elea 172–5, 179, 424
Zermelo-Frankel (ZF) set theory 17–19, 120, 422
zero 90–1; concept 48–9; paradox of division by 169–70

eBooks – at www.eBookstore.tandf.co.uk

A library at your fingertips!

eBooks are electronic versions of printed books. You can store them on your PC/laptop or browse them online.

They have advantages for anyone needing rapid access to a wide variety of published, copyright information.

eBooks can help your research by enabling you to bookmark chapters, annotate text and use instant searches to find specific words or phrases. Several eBook files would fit on even a small laptop or PDA.

NEW: Save money by eSubscribing: cheap, online access to any eBook for as long as you need it.

Annual subscription packages

We now offer special low-cost bulk subscriptions to packages of eBooks in certain subject areas. These are available to libraries or to individuals.

For more information please contact webmaster.ebooks@tandf.co.uk

We're continually developing the eBook concept, so keep up to date by visiting the website.

www.eBookstore.tandf.co.uk

For Product Safety Concerns and Information please contact our EU representative GPSR@taylorandfrancis.com
Taylor & Francis Verlag GmbH, Kaufingerstraße 24, 80331 München, Germany

www.ingramcontent.com/pod-product-compliance
Lightning Source LLC
Chambersburg PA
CBHW071221230426
43668CB00011B/1259